D1250003

BEHAVIOR RESEARCH
AND TECHNOLOGY IN
HIGHER EDUCATION

Conference on Behavior Research and technology in Higher Education, Georgia State University, 1973.

BEHAVIOR RESEARCH AND TECHNOLOGY IN HIGHER EDUCATION

WITHDRAWN

Edited by

JAMES M. JOHNSTON
Georgia State University

CHARLES C THOMAS • PUBLISHER
Springfield • Illinois • U.S.A.

Published and Distributed Throughout the World by

CHARLES C THOMAS • PUBLISHER

Bannerstone House

301–327 East Lawrence Avenue, Springfield, Illinois, U.S.A.

This book is protected by copyright. No part of it
may be reproduced in any manner without written
permission from the publisher.

© *1975, by* CHARLES C THOMAS • PUBLISHER

ISBN 0-398-03315-3

Library of Congress Catalog Card Number: 74-13261

With THOMAS BOOKS *careful attention is given to all details of manu-
facturing and design. It is the Publisher's desire to present books that are
satisfactory as to their physical qualities and artistic possibilities and
appropriate for their particular use.* THOMAS BOOKS *will be true to those
laws of quality that assure a good name and good will.*

Library of Congress Cataloging in Publication Data

Conference on Behavior Research and Technology in
Higher Education, Georgia State University, 1973.
Behavior research and technology in higher education.

Bibliography: p.
1. College teaching—Congresses. 2. Individualized
instruction—Congresses. I. Johnston, James M., ed.

II. Title.
LB2301.C6366 1973   378.1′79′4   74–13261
ISBN 0–398–03315–3

Printed in the United States of America

CC-11

290508

LB
2301
C 6366
1973

DEDICATION

This volume is dedicated to the thousands of students whose cooperation with their teachers in these research programs made possible the continuing investigation of more effective and enjoyable college teaching.

PERSONNEL FOR THE 1973 CONFERENCE ON BEHAVIOR RESEARCH AND TECHNOLOGY IN HIGHER EDUCATION

CHAIRMAN

JAMES M. JOHNSTON
Georgia State University

CO-CHAIRMEN

JAMES S. MCMICHAEL
C. W. Post College

JACK L. MICHAEL
Western Michigan University

GEORGE SEMB
University of Kansas

J. GILMORE SHERMAN
Georgetown University

CONFERENCE ASSISTANTS

DAVID BARKMEIER

STEPHEN GARBER

KATHLEEN KELLY

GEORGE W. O'NEILL

DANIEL PAULK

JEAN A. RASHEED

WILLIAM M. WALTERS
Georgia State University

CONFERENCE COORDINATOR

SHARON GREENE
Division of Public Service
Georgia State University

CONFERENCE SECRETARY

DIANE KISTNER

INTRODUCTION

Audiotutorial instruction, computer-assisted instruction, compe-
tency- or mastery-based instruction, contingency contracting, con-
tingency-managed instruction, individualized instruction, Keller plan,
minicourses, modularized instruction, programmed instruction, per-
sonalized system of instruction, precision teaching, self-paced instruc-
tion, etc.

In recent years, an impressive list of terms has worked its way into the vocabularies of teachers, researchers, and administrators in higher education: audiotutorial instruction, computer-assisted instruction, competency- or mastery-based instruction, contingency contracting, contingency-managed instruction, individualized instruction, Keller plan, minicourses, modularized, programmed instruction, personalized system of instruction, precision teaching, self-paced instruction, etc.

By now at least a few of these terms are familiar to almost every college teacher. Most are generic terms representing only a general philosophy, while others such as PSI and AT refer to an instruction method with specific procedural details. The oldest of these approaches to instruction in higher education, programmed instruction, is barely twenty years old, and all derive directly or indirectly from the general influence of behavioral psychology on education and the direct application of principles of behavior to the college academic environment. In fact, a close inspection of the referents of these terms forces the observation that they share far more similarities than they exhibit differences. On strength of a common lineage and their procedural similarities, a good case can be made for viewing these methods as a single overall approach to college and university-level instruction.

The Personalized System of Instruction is characterized by five basic features: 1) The students progress through the course with relatively more choice about their pace than in more traditional courses. 2) The students are permitted to move on to new material only after mastering all prior material. 3) Lectures are used for demonstration and motivation rather than for dissemination of information. 4) There is considerable stress placed upon the written verbal performance of the student in teacher-student communications. 5) Undergraduate students who have already completed the course are used as proctors for repeated testing, immediate feedback, and tutoring on an individual basis.

As many of the papers in this volume will show, each of these features are often varied in their application depending on the circumstances of each course. The point in these variations at which the method should no longer be called PSI is arbitrary and probably not important.

With this background, the First National Conference on Behavior Research and Technology in Higher Education was held October 25–27, 1973 at Georgia State University in Atlanta. The 1973 Conference was primarily, although not solely, concerned with PSI. It was the result of a year's planning and discussion among leaders in this field who felt that a number of major purposes could be served by such a meeting. These may be summarized with the goal of bringing researchers and teachers together from across the country to present and to hear about the latest research and applications in this rapidly developing approach to teaching in order to facilitate research, develop technology, and consider the future directions of this entire field.

All of the accepted papers which comprise this volume constitute only a quarter of the total number of manuscripts which were submitted for review from across North America. They were selected on the basis of a variety of criteria including general content, methodological quality, and the balance of the overall program. This last dimension was particularly important in order to present papers concerned with many different facets of these kinds of instructional methods. Thus a program was selected that presented research on a variety of components of these teaching tactics and that described applications of this approach to different kinds of courses. Although these papers are only a small portion of the existing literature, this volume thus represents a statement of the current status of this particular teaching methodology.

ACKNOWLEDGMENTS

This volume is the result of the considerable efforts of those listed on the previous page as well as many others. The review and revision process which these papers underwent involved the conference co-chairmen and assistants, as well as the authors themselves. A major contribution to the entire endeavor has been the skill and devotion of Diane Kistner from the first review to the final typing.

All during this process the support of the Department of Psychology has been a critical supplement to the partial funding of the conference and the proceedings preparation by the Urban Life Center at Georgia State University. The advice and assistance of Dr. Clyde Faulkner has been particularly important at many points in successfully bringing plans to fruition.

J.M.J.

CONTENTS

Page

Section I

NEW APPLICATIONS

Section II

EXPERIMENTAL COMPARISONS

Section VIII
SOME GENERAL PROPOSALS

BEHAVIOR RESEARCH
AND TECHNOLOGY IN
HIGHER EDUCATION

SECTION I

NEW APPLICATIONS

THE FOUR PAPERS IN THIS SECTION are examples of the application of individualized teaching methods to new settings, content areas, and problems. "The Use of Personalized Instruction in a University Field-Work Course" describes the application of a system of contingencies to teach a practicum-type of course in an off-campus setting. The second paper, "Expansion of PSI in Engineering: A Progress Report," is a brief description of a major attempt to apply PSI widely to the curricula of a college of engineering. The content area dealt with in the next paper, "Behavioral Analysis of Women's Roles," is quite different from engineering, and is notable because the course material is scattered widely among various books and articles, rather than being available in a single textbook. The final paper, "The Use of Concept Programming" to Teach Behavioral Concepts to University Students," is an excellent development of a program to teach students to generalize textbook content to real world situations.

THE USE OF PERSONALIZED INSTRUCTION IN A UNIVERSITY FIELD-WORK COURSE

STEPHEN B. FAWCETT
L. KEITH MILLER

STUDENT DEMANDS for socially relevant university courses have once again pointed up the importance of the applied component in educational programs. Applied training often takes the form of field-work courses in appropriate community settings (Lowy, Bloksberg, and Walberg, 1971). In the disciplines of sociology and social work, students are sometimes placed with community groups—such as local volunteer drug information centers and neighborhood service centers—where much of the activity takes place outside of the agency. Field experience in these settings may consist largely of street work in the surrounding neighborhood. The occurrence of street activities such as home visits in the neighborhood-at-large makes the direct monitoring of these activities very difficult.

This study is based upon a thesis submitted by the senior author to the Department of Human Development, University of Kansas in partial fulfillment of the requirements for the Master of Arts degree. Thanks to Drs. Donald M. Baer, Donald Green, Donald Bushell, and Bill L. Hopkins for their valuable advice and assistance. Reprints may be obtained from Stephen F. Fawcett, Department of Human Development, University of Kansas, Lawrence, Kansas.

The college professor interested in implementing a field-work program is faced with the problems of tailoring the student's educational experiences for the particular community placement and of making the student accountable for his or her performance in this nonuniversity setting (Matson, 1967). The first consideration—that of specifying student work activities—would presumably require a first-hand knowledge of the operations of a number of community groups, a requirement not often feasible for a professor with other teaching responsibilities. Literature on community intervention strategies suggests the importance of the inclusion of the community group in the specification of activities of volunteers in these neighborhood settings (Warren, 1963). This suggest a possible course operation in which the members of the placement setting identify the community service behaviors to be performed by field-work students.

A second problem confronting the field-work instructor—that of providing an account of student performance in the nonuniversity setting—necessitates the development of a feasible on-site evaluation system. The Keller model of classroom instruction illustrates an effective method of monitoring the academic behavior of university students by means of student proctors (Keller, 1968). One aspect of this procedure calls for students to act as independent observers in the scoring of the academic behavior of other students. This suggests the possibility of a student-staffed system for recording work activities in the field placement setting.

Underlying all considerations of field-work course operation is the problem of maintaining the community service activities of students in the particular setting. Reinforcement techniques have been applied to the problem of maintaining student academic performance in a number of university classroom settings (McMichael and Corey, 1969) ; Sheppard and MacDermott, 1970; Born, Gledhill, and Davis, 1972; Alba and Pennypacker, 1972; Whitehurst, 1972; Weaver and Miller, 1973; Semb, Hopkins, and Hursh, in press). This suggests the potential effectiveness of a point system backed up by a grade contingency in the maintenance of community service behaviors.

The present study demonstrates a practical procedure for

the operation of a field-work course in the neighborhood-at-large, incorporating community specification of student work activities as recorded by a student-staffed monitoring system. The study also examines the effect of reinforcement on the community service behavior of college field-work students placed in a neighborhood service.

METHOD

Subjects and Setting

Five males and five females enrolled in a field-work course at the University of Kansas served as subjects. The students (sophomores, juniors, and seniors) were placed with a neighborhood self-help group. Their majors included Social Welfare, Architecture, and Human Development. All of the students expressed a strong verbal interest in community work.

The placement and base of operations for the students' community work was an old, two-story dwelling located in a low-income area of East Lawrence, Kansas. This center, known as Penn (Pennsylvania) House, functions as a neighborhood service center staffed by low-income and minority group residents of the community. Activities and services provided by Penn House include peer-counseling, crisis intervention services, a non-profit neighborhood food cooperative, and knitting and sewing classes.

Recording Procedure

The community service behaviors specified for individual work sessions were similar to those necessary for the maintenance and operation of any neighborhood service center (Ohlin, 1969). Table 1-I lists some of the community service behaviors provided by the subjects during the experiment. Each week Penn House members specified a number of work activities which were written on a Work List. This Work List was then posted by a member of Penn House for the next student work session.

Five community work sessions (totaling fifteen hours) were scheduled each week at Penn House during specified times. Students attending any work session chosen from among the Work

TABLE 1-I

Community Service Behaviors

A. Canvassing:
    1. Conducting a community survey to determine needed services
    2. Providing door-to-door information in the neighborhood on Penn House services
    3. Follow-up visit to families requesting services
    4. Collecting emergency food
    5. Distributing announcements in the neighborhood

B. Services:
    1. Organizing a knitting class
    2. Teaching a weekly knitting class
    3. Teaching a weekly sewing class
    4. Organizing and operating a neighborhood concert
    5. Making home visits to elderly and shut-in neighbors
    6. Delivering groceries to shut-in neighbors
    7. Cleaning the yard for shut-in neighbors
    8. Providing transportation to pick up Food Stamps

C. Miscellaneous:
    1. Researching and compiling neighbors' names and addresses from the City Directory
    2. Sewing aprons for Penn House sewing project
    3. Working of Penn House Newsletter

List activities and then signed in and out on a Sign-up Sheet with a Work Coordinator or student proctor. The proctor functioned as supervisor and independent observer, recording the time-in and time-out as well as the location and nature of each work activity for all subjects. The proctors were two males and two females (all undergraduate students) and a male teaching assistant-experimenter.

A community service behavior was recorded as occurring if the subject was present at the specified location and engaged in the particular activity, the latter criterion according to casual commonsense observations. Total time spent working was defined as that period lasting from when the subject signed-in at Penn House for a particular work activity until he or she returned from that activity to sign-out at Penn House.

Reliability checks were taken by an independent observer in each experimental condition by spot-checking for the presence or absence of the worker at the specified location. This was done for 48 percent of the total number of sign-ins for work sessions. The percentage of agreement between the Sign-up Sheet entries and these observations of worker activity was 100 percent in all conditions. This figure was obtained by multiplying one-hundred times the number of agreements divided by the number of agreements plus disagreements.

Point System

During the treatment conditions, students earned points for community service behaviors. Points were earned contingently at the rate of twelve points per hour of work activity. For example, during these conditions, zero hours of work resulted in a zero point consequence and eight and one-half hours of work resulted in a hundred point consequence. In the nontreatment phases, points were given noncontingently; students received one-hundred points at the beginning of each week regardless of their subsequent work output for that week. For example, during these conditions, zero hours and eight and one-half hours of work resulted in the same point consequence of one-hundred points.

Points earned in the course were exchangable for a grade at the end of the semester. Students were instructed that they should earn one-hundred points per week during each of fourteen weeks, for a total of 1400 points. (They could earn more than one-hundred points per week during the contingent points conditions.) Students were informed that grades would be determined by the percentage earned of the 1400 point total— i.e. 90 percent or more would earn a grade of A, 80 percent to 89 percent would earn a grade of B, and so on. Feedback was provided for all students just prior to the first work session of each week. This consisted of making information about current weekly point totals available to students upon request.

Experimental Conditions

The effect of contingent points on the maintenance of community service behaviors was analyzed by a reversal design. The number of hours of work activities was recorded during all four conditions: baseline, contingent points, reversal, and contingent points.

BASELINE. During baseline and all subsequent conditions, subjects were informed that they were expected to do ten hours of community work each week. No point consequence was made contingent upon work activity for this period. During baseline, one-hundred points were awarded each student on the first day of each work week.

CONTINGENT POINTS. In this phase, twelve points were made contingent upon each hour of community service behavior. The contingent point condition was explained at a weekly class meeting following the four weeks of baseline condition.

REVERSAL CONDITION. After four weeks in the contingent point phase, the baseline condition was reinstated with respect to community service behavior.

CONITNGENT POINTS. Finally, two weeks later, points were again made contingent upon community service behavior.

RESULTS

Figure 1-1 presents the mean number of work hours per student in each work session. The "X's" represent the weekly average number of hours per student in work sessions. Solid lines connect these weekly average points. The mean number of hours per student decreased from a mean of 0.9 during the first ten sessions to a level of about 0.3 hours per session over the last ten sessions of baselines. The mean number of hours for all sessions increased in the contingent point phase to 1.2. This was followed by a reversal phase in which the average number of hours per student decreased to 0.2. Finally, a reinstatement of the contingent point condition brought about an increase in the number of hours to a mean of 1.4 hours per session. In general, those sessions in which points were made contingent upon work activity showed an increase in community service behavior over those sessions in which points were delivered noncontingently.

The representativeness of the group data was tested by a series of comparisons within individual subjects across experimental conditions. For each subject, the mean score in one experimental condition was compared with the mean score for the subsequent condition to determine whether the direction of the effect was

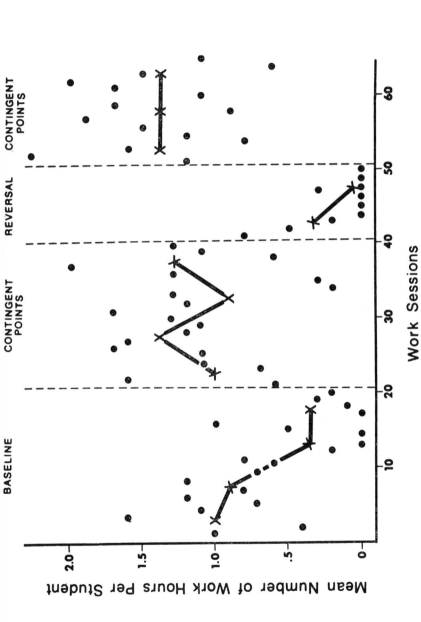

Figure 1-1. Mean number of hours of community service behaviors per student in each work session. The "X's" represent the weekly average number of hours per student in work sessions. Solid lines connect these weekly average points.

the same as for the group data. One hundred percent of the subjects had a lower mean rate of work during the last ten sessions of baseline than during the first contingent point condition. All subjects had a higher mean rate during the first contingent point condition than during the subsequent reversal condition. And, every subject showed an increase in the final contingent point phase from the preceding reversal condition. Thus, the patterns of individual subject responding were totally in agreement with the group data.

DISCUSSION AND CONCLUSIONS

The present study examined the effect of contingent points upon the community service behavior of college students enrolled in a field-work course. The data indicate that when points were made contingent upon community service behavior, the number of hours of that behavior increased. A reversal phase was introduced in the third condition. During this period community service behavior decreased to approximately the baseline level for all subjects. When contingent points were again made a consequence for work activity in the fourth condition, the rate of this behavior once again increased. These findings demonstrate the reinforcing function of contingent points in maintaining community service behavior. The results indicate that contingent points and not some coincidental variable are responsible for the increased rate of responding during treatment.

The Work List procedure employed in the present study assures the inclusion of the community group in the development of work activities for students placed in the setting. Penn House members specified a number of jobs which were written on a Work List for the next student work session. A student attending any work session then chose from among the activities on the Work List for that day. In this way, the field-work instructor drew upon the experience and needs of the community group members and student preferences in the development of a program or well-defined activities for the students. A faculty member, unknowledgeable in group operations, might otherwise be forced to cite non-specific educational objectives, such as bringing the student in "contact" with the community. The Work List procedure is an efficient means of providing students with a selection of structured community service activities of benefit to the placement group.

The recording procedure used in this study provides a practical method of observation for a highly diversified class of responses occurring in both the community group setting and the neighborhood-at-large. The community service behaviors under investigation were recorded by means of a sign-up procedure at specified work sessions. Spot checks by student proctors for reliability required the subject to be present at the stated location and engaged in the particular activity. Reliability checks between the Sign-up Sheet and observed worker activity yielded perfect agreement.

This student-staffed monitoring system was shown to be an effective means of providing an account of the student's work in a nonuniversity setting. A required on-site evaluation would be a problem for many university professors. Since direct observations of student performance are frequently unfeasible without the use of proctors, such field-work instructors are often forced to make indirect observations by means of term papers and other written academic responses. The sign-up system backed up by spot checks proved to be a practical recording procedure for a highly diversified class of behaviors occurring in and around the community setting.

Field-work courses offer a practical means by which university professors may provide community service experience for their students. By contracting with students for work activity, as in the contingent points phases, an instructor may make an hourly estimate of the community service actvity of students in a particular placement setting. For example, at the mean rate of work activity in the second contingent point phase, ten field-work students could provide over nine-hundred hours of service in a thirteen week semester. This information would be useful in the organization and scheduling of community service activities in individual placement settings.

A large number of college students volunteer to work for a variety of social service organizations (Naylor, 1967). A volunteer is ordinarily assumed to act without consequences on his or her behavior. Yet volunteer behavior need not be thought of as uncontrolled. It is likely that unspecified consequences, such as interest in community work, maintain some volunteer work in these settings. The subjects of the present study rated their interest in the activities of the field-work course as "very interested" (4.3 on a scale of 5.0). In spite of this strong verbal expression of interest in community work, the subjects of the present study showed a decreasing trend in the incidence of work behavior during baseline. The subjects' stated interest (perhaps sufficient) to produce some of the initial behavioral output did not sustain work behavior. The results of the present study strongly indicate that external consequences are necessary for the maintenance of community service behaviors by university field-work students.

In summary, the present study examined the effect of reinforcement on the community service behaviors of college field-work students placed with a neighborhood service center. The results show that the number of work hours is higher during treatment than during non-treatment conditions. This experiment demonstrates a practical procedure for the operation of a field-work course involving the community-specification of student work activities as recorded by a student-staffed monitoring system.

READING 2

EXPANSION OF PSI IN ENGINEERING: A PROGRESS REPORT

BILLIE GRACE HERRING

THE PURPOSE OF THIS PAPER is to describe the research on PSI at the University of Texas at Austin under the auspices of the Sloan Foundation and to report some findings from one course that is being developed in that project.[1] Data are incomplete at this time, so that this paper represents a progress report. Statistical analyses remain to be completed on much of the data presented.

The title of the research project is *Expansion of Keller Plan Instruction in Engineering and Selected Other Disciplines.* James Stice, Director of the Bureau of Engineering Teaching, is acting as principle investigator. There are fifteen additional investigators from ten departments in the University. Associate investigators hold rank from assistant professor through professor.

This project is initiating or continuing the development of twelve PSI courses, each of which is described below. Initiation of a new course is called Phase I and refinement of a course which already has been taught at least once is called Phase II.

---

[1] Proposal to the Alfred P. Sloan Foundation for Support of Expansion of Keller Plan Instruction in Engineering and Other Selected Disciplines. James E. Stice, Principal Investigator, University of Texas at Austin, October 9, 1972.

Phase I.

The initial offering of a PSI course requires a considerable commitment of time and effort on the part of a teacher. He must decide what the objectives of his course are and group them into logical, ordered packages called units. He then must prepare recommended reading assignments, write detailed sets of unit study questions and problems, and prepare four to six different readiness tests for each unit. Furthermore, it has been the experience of this program (and Keller's *strong* recommedation) that no more than about two units should be written ahead of time, since students almost never mirror the professor's expectatation. When teaching a lecture course, the teacher chooses the pace and assumes the students are keeping up (even when there is considerable evidence to the contrary). In a PSI course the students are required to learn the material, all of it, and they set their own pace. The students' responses to length of units, difficulty of units, and prior knowledge of course prerequisities rarely coincide with the teacher's expectations. As a result it is better to write most of the units while the course is in progress. Thus instructors are being given one-third released time for preparation of materials the first time the course is taught by PSI.

Phase II.

After a course has been taught by the Keller Plan the first time, revision is always required. Audio modules, TV tapes, interactive computer programs, and laboratory exercises may be added where pictorial displays, motion, and reduction of calculation time will prove helpful. Our experience has been that the first revision of the handout material prepared during the initial offering of a PSI course, while still more demanding than teaching a standard lecture course, requires much less effort than the first writing. The use of mediated materials to facilitate learning, however, makes Phase II about as demanding as Phase I.

In addition to initiating or further developing PSI courses to be described later, this program is trying to obtain information of a fundamental nature to provide answers to a number of questions which appear to be troubling those who teach PSI courses or contemplate initiating them. Interest in the Keller plan is spreading rapidly throughout all levels of education, but most course designers are spending their time solely in developing their own course. With our considerable background in PSI, we feel we may be uniquely qualified to explore some of these questions as a parallel effort to course development. Some of these questions are:

1. Do students learn more (or better) under the Keller Plan than under conventional teaching methods?
2. A Keller Plan course produces very different grade distributions than those seen in conventional courses, as many more students get A's and B's in a PSI course. Are these higher grades justified? (This is a slightly different question than Number 1 above.)
3. Does the "average" student in a PSI course exhibit a significantly different long-term retention of facts and concepts than the "average" student in a lecture course?
4. This program has repeatedly found evidence that students in a PSI course gradually learn how to study efficiently and for meaning, rather than depending on their previous experience that memorizing "gets them by." Documentation on this very important point is needed, and it is important to know if this development of improved ability to learn on one's own transfers to other courses.
5. Can the PSI materials developed by a given professor be used in another university with roughly equivalent results? That is, are well-written PSI courses relatively independent of who is the actual teacher, provided the teacher using them understands how the Keller Plan works?
6. The majority of people who have taught PSI courses have experienced the "procrastination problem," evidenced by a significant number of students who progress through the course at a rate much slower than the average. What are the various causes of procrastination, and how may a course by designed to minimize the problem?
8. Connected with Question 7 is the problem of dropouts. PSI courses regularly produce a higher dropout rate than

other courses (and almost no failing grades). Can this dropout percentage be reduced, and how?

9. What is the effect of class size? The courses being developed will range in size from twenty students to one-hundred twenty students, and Keller suggests that 125 might be the upper limit, since as class size increases the bureaucracy increases, and about twelve proctors may be about all one professor can supervise adequately. Most of the courses we have taught have been in the range of ten to fifteen students. Does the quality of a PSI course suffer as class size increases from fifty to, say, 120?

The answers to these questions are elusive, but they are important indeed. It is felt that more information needs to be obtained about these vital points, and for considerably longer retention intervals.

In summary, this project is initiating or further developing twelve PSI courses and documenting work in an effort to provide answers to several important questions that pertain specifically to PSI courses, but may have broad applicability to human learning at varying educational levels.

Phase I Courses Being Initiated

1. Aerospace Engineering 365-Structural Dynamics (20 students) Roy Craig.
2. Architectural Engineering 362L-Design of Structural Systems in Timber (30 students) David Flowler.
3. Chemical Engineering 376-Process Analysis and Simulation (25 students) D. Himmelblau.
4. Electrical Engineering 321-Electrical Laboratory I (90 students—30 in each of three sections) Charles Roth.
5. Physics 403K-Engineering Physics (40 students) A. Gleeson.
6. Library Science 351-Catologing and Classification (40 students) B. G. Herring.
7. General Engineering 3XX-Introduction to Engineering Mathematics (150 students—50 students per semester for three semesters) Gerald Wagner.

Phase II Courses Being Developed

1. Mechanical Engineering 361-Introduction to Nuclear Reactor Theory (20 students) Billy Koen.
2. Mechanical Engineering 364L-Dynamic Systems Synthesis (30 students) L. Hoberock.
3. Engineering Mechanics 306-Statics (30 students) W. Fowler and P. Nacozy.
4. RTF 321-Principles of Audio and Visual Production (120 students) R. Brooks.
5. Chemistry 302-Principles of Chemistry (100 students) John White.

It is expected that the statics course (Engineering Mechanics 306) will be an important one in answering several of the questions posed above. It is taken by all students in all departments of engineering, and there are fifteen to twenty sections of the course each term. Thus, we have the opportunity to compare PSI sections with others. Since students usually take statics during their freshman year, they will be in residence for three years after completing it so that we can make follow-up studies of retention.

In addition, there is a need to teach the statics course in community colleges. Perhaps half of the engineering students who graduate from The University of Texas at Austin come as transfer students from community colleges. They either do not have the course available, or if it is available, it is often taught by a non-engineering oriented instructor. During the summer of 1973, twenty-eight community college teachers participated in a workshop in which they worked through the statics course with the PSI investigators, and began preparing to offer the course by PSI in their own community colleges during the 1973 to 1974 academic year. Investigators Fowler and Nacozy are maintaining contact with them and giving assistance throughout the year during which they introduce the course. Since the community college teachers are using the materials prepared by Fowler and Nacozy, we expect that we should gain useful data about the transferability of materials from one school to another and from one instructor to another.

Library Science Courses

A basic description of the Library Science Course will serve as an example of how other project courses are conducted and evaluated. The course chosen for development into a PSI course is L.S. 351, Cataloging and Classification. This is a basic course required of all students who earn master's degrees or certification as school learning resources specialists and normally is taken during the first semester of graduate study. A few students in the class each term are not library science students but select the course as an upper division or graduate elective.

The course focuses on the organization of materials and media so that the content can be retrieved for future use. At the end of the course students are expected to be operational in preparing catalog data for input into information systems, whether the system be a card catalog, a computerized data base, a bibliography, or a book catalog. Students are expected to have an understanding of the objectives, principles, and bases for organization of information in any format.

The course moves rapidly from an introduction of objectives, concepts, and principles into an application of them in organizing materials. It lends itself to discrete, fairly precise parts but not to formal linear or branching programming because of the high degree of judgment involved in making a cataloging decision in terms of users, environment, and the data available. There is no satisfactory textbook available for the course. The course is a pre-requisite to an advanced course in cataloging and classification and to a course on developing media collections.

Use of PSI appeared to be appropriate because of the following goals:

1. To take into account previous knowledge and/or experience of students.
2. To offer more opportunities for one to one tutoring.
3. To allow students to cope with personal, family or academic emergencies without penalty for missing class.
4. To determine whether method could be applied to the complex, intricate nature of the course content.
5. To evaluate student potential in terms of self-pacing, mo-

tivating aspects and to predict adaptability to self-directed work in the profession.

In addition, there was some question whether PSI is better suited to particular learning styles, personalities, or educational levels.

Since there was no textbook, it was imperative that the course materials prepared by the instructor carry the full content of the course. In order to avoid excessive amounts of duplicated materials, it was decided to add an audio component using cassette tapes to present background data, explain processes, help students work through some problems initially, and discuss other problems so that students who had difficulty with them would understand how they had been worked.

FACILITIES. It seems that adequate facilities for study and easy availability of materials are important factors in success of PSI course. The entire Graduate School of Library Science is located on the same floor of the Humanities Research Center, providing almost ideal continuing use of facilities for the course. A special cataloging laboratory adjacent to the departmental library provided reference works, cataloging tools, and practice collection materials. Audiotapes and equipment (including headphones) were circulated through the departmental library which has listening and conference rooms. Answer keys to problems were also available in the library.

STAFF. Two doctoral students acting as graduate assistants, three master's students who had taken the advanced cataloging course serving as proctors, and a part-time secretary comprised the project staff during Phase I. Weekly conferences were held with the instructional staff to discuss all readiness tests, clarify and improve unit materials, discuss student progress, and air any other problems. These meetings were a crucial component in the method. The graduate assistants also reviewed all materials as they were written, providing valuable input and suggestions. Each of them also wrote one unit.

COURSE PLAN. The course content was divided into sixteen units. Some were self-contained while others were part of a continuum of several units. There were no formal lectures, but the instructor was available at all study all/testing sessions to assist students. Proctors and graduate assistants were also available at other times to answer questions and to help students. Testing was available at four different times for a total of five hours per week.

PROBLEMS. The problem of procrastination was evident because some students had difficulty pacing themselves without the pressure of deadlines. One student deliberately delayed beginning the course until mid-semester but was able to finish. Another was unable to discipline herself to complete enough units until after the date had passed that would allow completion of the course.

There were two students in the course who felt cheated at not having regular class meetings and lectures by the instructor. Both were older than other students in the class and held advanced degrees. Another similar student in the summer class had exactly the opposite reaction and strongly preferred PSI.

Requiring an achievement criterion of one-hundred percent on all readiness tests also caused some difficulty especially in units where there were as many as sixty to seventy-five small components. Even with subsequent questioning and probing by the proctor, the re-take rate was higher than desired.

Finally, during the course it was discovered that three units were too long and needed to be divided when materials were revised.

REVISION. In preparing to offer the course again, the following revisions were made: re-sequence units, retaining order of only first, second, and last; divide three units each into two separate units; drop one unit and incorporate content elsewhere; revise presentation of content in all units; revise audiotapes and improve technical quality; develop listening guides to accompany tapes.

EVALUATION. This section presents data about the general assessment procedures that are being employed in the total project and the results and data from its application to the library science course in Phase I. During Phase I, considerable attention is being directed toward process evaluation—the continual monitoring of the developing instructional systems. Forms have been developed to elicit systematic feedback from students and proctors with regard to various PSI units. These data, combined with average student time per unit and other related information which can be derived from class unit-progress charts, provide feedback for the unit refinement process. Forms were also designed to facilitate record keeping with regard to instructor and student time. Comparable forms have been designed for use in cooperating control classes in order to provide some means of making cost-time comparisons, although it is recognized that such comparisons can be only approximate. Student time invested in any one unit ranged from one to fifty-four hours.

The mean hours per student per unit was 5.5 hours. It was clear that five units needed revision in terms of length and difficulty according to student time spent on them. Four to five hours seemed to represent a reasonable amount of time spent on each unit. The first revision of units later resulted in a mean of 4.6 hours per unit.

Since several forms of each readiness test were used at the end of the term, the number of times any one form of a test was repeated by students was tabulated and studied in order to determine if some forms of the test were excessively easy or difficult. One form was identified as being more difficult than others in unit 8 and was revised accordingly.

Similar process evaluation procedures are being employed during Phase II of the proposed project, with the resulting unit and test refinement. Since Phase II includes the addition of various technological supplements to the basic Keller Plan format (e.g. displays, TV tapes, etc.) data are being collected with regard to their cost and effectiveness. Two half-time media technicans have been employed to assist in Phase II courses.

At the conclusion of each offering of each course, instruments measuring student achievement and attitudes are administered. The same of parallel instruments are administered in cooperating control classes. A brief attitude inventory was administered to all students enrolled in the library science course, both at the beginning of the semester and again at the end of the semester. PSI students showed a much higher score on the inventory (based on a ten point scale) at the beginning of the semester than did students in the control class: 8.89 versus 7.08 in the control class. At the end of the semester, however, PSI students had a mean score of 9.00 as compared with a mean score of 9.08 for students in the control class. A test applied to the difference in attitude scores between the beginning and end of the term scores for each class showed a significance of .0005 in favor of the control class.

We can account for the wide discrepancy between the "before" scores of the two classes only on the basis of what was said or done by the instructor during the first class session, since the attitude inventory was administered by an outside investigator during the second class session. This semester the inventory was administered on the first class day by an outside administrator before the students even met the instructors.

Final achievement measures will be refined until they meet acceptable standards of content validity and internal consistency. Item analyses are being conducted at the present time. The final criterion tests of student achievement do not contain any of the same items comprising either the readiness tests in the PSI sections or the standard examinations in the parallel control classes. If the same final achievement test is used within a PSI project at the end of Phase I and the end of Phase II, significantly better performance at the conclusion of Phase II might be attributed to course refinements and/or the addition of technological aids—assuming comparable student abilities and test security. No data is yet available since Phase II is now in progress.

The measurement of student reactions to the PSI course at the end of the semester is accomplished by asking students to respond to a set of statements (e.g. "This course caused me to make more effective use of my study time"; "I considered this course intellectually stimulating;" etc.) in terms of a five-step scale definitely yes; yes; uncertain; no; definitely no).

Evaluation items are parallel for PSI courses involved in the project and cooperating control classes. This permits the computation of scores for such dimensions of student evaluation as perceived professional relevance of the course, general "liking" of the course, subjective impressions of effort expended and amount learned, and so forth. Analysis is incomplete at this point, however.

Some Preliminary Data

This section will present preliminary data on the questions pertaining to Keller Plan courses listed earlier in this paper which is pertinent to the evaluation of the experimental courses. Data contributing to their answers will also add considerably to the body of knowledge about PSI in general.

Each of the nine questions will here be considered briefly in terms of evaluation and analysis strategies related to it and in terms of data obtained from the library science courses.

LEARN MORE OR BETTER? Evaluation efforts relating the this question require the existence of control groups taught by more "conventional" methods but using the same textbooks and final examinations as the experimental PSI courses. Such control groups are available for six of the twelve proposed courses. Since the six courses having multiple sections include both elective and required courses, courses from freshman through graduate level, and classes of varying size, it is reasonable to assume that comparisons between student achievment in the Keller Plan courses and the appropriate control courses will lead to some valid conclusion regarding the issue of relative student learning.

Using students scores on the aptitude test of the Graduate Record Examination, a t test was applied which indicated no significant difference between the ability of students in the PSI class (n=20) and in the control class (n=32).

A comparison of examination grades between PSI students and students in a control class showed that the mean score for PSI students was 87.3 and for the control class it was 81.9. Median for PSI students was 87.5, for control students 84. An analysis of variance showed the PSI students' scores to be significant at .054. It must be recognized that the validity of the uniform examination has not been established at this time.

A comparison was also made between the performance of students who took the same course under the same instructor during the previous semester using the lecture method. Two parts of the final examination were identical. Table 2-I indicates the mean error rate on each part, indicating that PSI students performed considerably better. Analysis in terms of factors such as ages, grade

TABLE 2-I

Comparison of Mean Errors on Identical Portions of Final Exam
Between PSI and Lecture Classes with Same Instructor

Part of Exam	Lecture Class, Fall 1972 n = 29	PSI Class, Spring 1973 n = 20
I. Theory, terminology and principles	7.89	4.95
II. Application in cataloging of materials	10.4	4.57

point averages and class rank has not been completed. Analysis is also directed toward attempting to identify the types of students who are most likely to achieve in Keller Plan courses. In addition to aptitude and prior achievement, characteristics such as study habits, motivation for grades, and peer independence are being examined. One observation of instructor and proctors was that there appeared to be a high positive correlation between age of student and discomfort with the PSI method.

ARE HIGHER GRADES IN PSI COURSES JUSTIFIED? The issue involved in this second question is whether the negatively skewed grade distribution which ordinarily results from a Keller Plan course is a valid reflection of student achievement. In terms of evaluation, this issue could be approach in sveral ways. One approach—probably the most realistic one in this situation—is to reanalyze the final achievement test data for Keller Plan courses and their respective control groups (described above) omitting from consideration all students other than those earning A's. If there is no significant difference between mean final achievement criterion test scores of "A" students in the experimental and control groups, it is reasonable to conclude that in terms of content learning as measured by the achievement tests, grades of students taught by the two methods have the same meaning—despite the fact that there are far more high grades in the Keller Plan courses. This analysis has not been done as yet.

DO PSI STUDENTS RETAIN LEARNING LONGER? The evaluation of long-term retention of specific courses poses an extremely difficult measurement problem. The intervention of other organized learning experiences, individual study, work experience and similar variables functions to contaminate practically any attempt to relate a later measure of content retention to the initial learning experience. Therefore, evaluation of long-term retention is being approached by prediction of performance in a subsequent course for which the course under analysis is a prerequisite. The evaluative question, therefore, would be whether the level of actual performance in the later course differs from that of students in control classes.

Approximately forty percent of the students who take the basic catologing and classification course go on to take advanced courses. Their performance in the advanced courses will be compared with that of students who took the basic course in control classes. Only three PSI students have gone on to take advanced courses. In the advanced courses, all performed above the mean for the class as a whole. Four control class students have taken an advanced course; two performed better than the class as a whole, and two did less well. Because the sample is so small at this point, no analysis has been done.

Effect on Study Habits. This question implies a pre- and post-test design, since it would be invalid to attribute improved study skills to a PSI course or to any other experience without having a baseline agent against which change could be assessed. The Survey of Study Habits and Attitudes (Psychological Corporation, 1967) was administered at the beginning and at the end of each semester to lower division students in both PSI and control classes during the first semester of the project. Results show the PSI course had little or no effect on study habits.

Since the Survey of Study Habits and Attitudes was standardized at the freshman and sophomore levels it was not used with the students in the cataloging course. Only subjective reactions from graduate students are as yet available which indicate that twelve students felt that the PSI course had improved their study habits and eight were neutral or felt that it had not.

Transferability of Materials. The transferability issue is being approached by systematic follow-up of the summer institute for community college teachers. While at the University of Texas at Austin, the community college teachers were involved in the various evaluation procedures related to the institute and similar to those previously described. However, those who returned to their respective colleges and began to teach the course in engineering mechanics using the PSI method and materials to which they were exposed will provide an excellent opportunity for studying the feasibility and effectiveness of "transplanting" such instructional packages. Analysis of these community college results at other institutions along with other efforts to use PSI materials designed at the University of Texas at Austin should lead to identification of those elements in the system which have transferability potential. Those variable which consistently hinder such efforts should also be revealed. It will also be possible to use the data collection instruments designed and used locally at the other institutions where the proposed PSI courses are being offered in order to permit inter-campus comparisons.

During the first summer session the library science materials prepared for this project were revised by the instructor and were used by two teaching assistants. We monitored their work closely enough to know that they did not deviate from the basic plan. All students completed the revised course (in spite of eighteen units to be completed in twenty-six days) . Exam performance was lower but not significantly so and possibly could be attributed to the severe time limitations.

Costs. One way that cost analysis may proceed is in terms of differential instructional cost per student per semester or cost per credit hour of registration in the PSI courses and control courses. This will not be completely accurate reflection of cost, however, since in most cases, the control "lecture" course will have been taught many times by the instructor involved. Theoretically, cost per student per semester should decline after the first two semesters of a PSI course.

Time is another cost factor which should not be ignored in the evaluation. Efforts are being made to assess both instructor time and student time spent in instructional activities in the various methods. Accurate measurements with regard to time spent are difficult to obtain at anything beyond a superficial level. It is recognized that nay conclusions in the area of differential time spent must be highly tentative.

Table 2-II summarizes instructor time for the library science courses invested during Phase I. Since audiotapes were used in the

TABLE 2-II
Instructor Time for L.S. 351 Phase 1, Jan. 8–May 21, 1973

Month	Writing Units, Quizzes and Revising	Test-ing Sessions	Proctor Meet-ings	Keys to Problems, Tapes, etc.	Evalu-ation	Meetings and Pre-sentations	Total Hours in Month
January	89	11	7	25	0	2	134
February	72	23.5	5	34	2	1	137.5
March	31	22.5	4.5	14	2	11	85
April	5[1]	15	2.5	9	4	2	37.5
May	16[2]	15	3	0	30	12	76
TOTAL	213	87	22	82	38	28	470

course materials, additional time was involved in preparing them. More instructor time was spent during the early part of the semester with little time in preparation of materials during the last six weeks.

The instructor deliberately chose to be in attendance at all study hall/testing sessions in order to talk with students and obtain feedback on the materials and the work of the proctors. During Phase II, a comparable amount of time will not be spent attending the testing sessions.

Instructor time averaged thirty hours per week. Other cost factors included three proctors who each worked eight hours per week for a total of 288 hours, a ⅓ time secretary, and approximately two-hundred hours of time by the graduate assistants (which was not paid but was a part of field work in another class). During the term we used approximately twenty reams of paper and two-hundred stencils for duplication of materials. The instructor was assigned to spend ⅔ time on the project but actually spent ¾ time. With a total student registration of sixty credit hours and using our cost figures, we find that the first semester development of the course cost approximately $76.00 per credit hour of registration including instructor time but without overhead. Without instructor time, cost was $13.67 per credit hour without overhead.

PROCRASTINATION PROBLEM: The "Procrastination problem is being studied by the inclusion of relevant items on the previously mentioned student course evaluation instrument (e.g. "I frequently found myself postponing the work for this course because of pressure from other courses not taught by self-paced methods; "There were times when I felt prepared to take a readiness test, but the thought of having to make one hundred percent caused me to put it off;" etc.).

Since the Study Habits instrument was not used with library science students, only data from the course-instructor survey are available. Four items related to the procrastination problem are summarized in Table 2–III.

Since several offerings of twelve courses are involved in the project, it is possible to experiment with various approaches to alleviating the procrastination problem (e.g. deadlines, or doomsday dates; guidelines; reminders; etc.) to determine whether any

TABLE 2-III

Library Science Student Responses on Items Relating to
Procrastination in Course-Instructor Survey

Item	Definitely Yes	Yes	Neutral	No	Definitely No
17. I found it frustrating to have to pace myself through this course.	0	2	3	6	9
21. In general, I would have preferred more structure (e.g., scheduling, deadlines, etc.) than this course included.	0	4	4	6	6
34. I felt that I had to hurry over large amounts of material toward the end of the semester in order to complete the course.	1	4	2	12	1
45. In my opinion, the main reason for procrastination by some students in a course taught by this method is:					

8　A.　Work demand and schedules in other courses which they are taking concurrently.
4　B.　The high level of performance required to pass readiness tests.
5　C.　The absence of regular class meetings.
2　D.　The decrease in the need to compete with other students for grades.
0　E.　Personal problems unrelated to the course.

of them is effective in reducing the problem without introducing undesirable effects of its own. Dr. Koen has a study underway concerning the effects of various means of dealing with procrastination. In the library science course (as suggested by Born) a graph with three progress lines was used to help students evaluate their progress; one line was for maximum speed of completion, one for average, and one for the minimal level of progress that a student could pursue and still complete the course. It was found that student progress fell between the average and the minimal lines. Only one guideline date was given. One student deliberately delayed beginning Unit 2 until almost mid term; but he was able to complete the course.

This fall the progress graph was omitted and students were given five guideline dates.

DROPOUT PROBLEM: With regard to the dropout problem, study is directed toward determining if the dropout rate is significantly higher in PSI courses. In those situations where appropriate control groups exist, the proportion of students dropping the PSI course is compared statistically to the proportion dropping the more conventional control course. A z test showed no significant difference between drops in the PSI and control class.

In addition, students dropping either type of course are interviewed briefly with regard to their reasons for dropping and their ideas about modified course procedures and other factors which might have resulted in their completing the course. It is important for the validity of this analysis that all students in experimental and control classes have an equal opportunity to drop if they so desire. Differential means of alleviating the procrastination problem are being evaluated, since dropping out is almost surely related to procrastination.

The data in Table 2-III are not necessarily corroborated by the actual number of drops from the library science course and the reasons given for them. Of the five students who dropped the course, the following reasons were given:

Unable to complete units—1
Illness requiring surgery and long absence from school—2
No reason—2

Since the instructor had taught the same course in previous

semesters using the lecture method, data were available concerning the number of students who dropped the course or withdrew from school. Table 2-IV presents that data.

The percentage of drops is higher than in seven previous semesters but lower than in one semester. It is considerably higher than the mean drop rate for previous semesters, but a z test for a difference between uncorrelated proportions showed that the difference was not significant.

CLASS SIZE: This question is not being treated in the library science course but is being studied in the radio-television-film course and the electrical engineering laboratory. Sufficient time for testing and accurate record keeping are two major problems related to size. In this, as in all the analyses outlined in the preceeding sections, it will be of critical importance to keep in mind other relevant course characteristics such as required versus elective, level and so forth.

Analysis of proctor characteristics and evaluation of the impact of the proctoring experience also afford other potentially fruitful areas for research within the proposed project. Only self-reporting data is currently available.

Revision/Phase II

After having offered the course with revised materials during

TABLE 2-IV

Drops in Cataloging Course with Same Instructor
Nine Sections, 1969–1973

Semester	Number 1 Enrolled	Number Dropped	Percentage Dropped
Spring 1973-PSI	28	5	17.9
Fall 1972	35	3	8.5
Spring 1972			
Section I	28	2	7.1
Section II	21	4	19.0
Fall 1971	47	4	8.5
Spring 1971	34	3	8.8
Fall 1970	38	4	10.5
Spring 1970	28	2	7.1
Spring 1969	28	4	14.3

Mean: 11.3
Mean excluding PSI: 9.1

[1] Includes number who also withdrew from school, consequently number enrolled minus number dropped does not equal population for other data.

the summer with different instructors, feedback will be obtained for further revision prior to offering the course the fall semester. Since student attitudes have been mixed, it is anticipated that after the close of Phase II, two sections of the course will be offered each semester, one by PSI and the other by the lecture method. Students will be allowed to choose the method they prefer.

The staff probably has learned more than the students during Phase I, but it is anticipated that subsequent revisions of the course will result in increased student learning and efficient use of their time. Special attention will be given to the attitudinal factors involved.

READING 3

BEHAVIORAL ANALYSIS OF WOMEN'S ROLES

MARY PETERSON

CERTAIN BODIES OF KNOWLEDGE and certain disciplines seem obvious candidates for the PSI methodology. The striking success of this approach in physical science, engineering and introductory psychology courses is no great surprise (McMichael and Corey, 1969; Mawhinney, Bostow, Laws, Blumenfeld and Hopkins, 1971; Koen, 1971). Once one moves beyond the obvious applications and deals with subject matters that lack a coherent hierarchical organization, the usefulness and relevance of PSI might appear to be less clear. However, more abstract, more nebulous, and more personal material merely provides a greater challenge to the designer of the PSI course.

A course, *Beravioral Analysis of Women's Roles* (BAWR), was designed specifically to meet this challenge, as well as to provide a more scientific framework for the development of a feminist psychology. This second aim is critical. Many feminist courses have covered bodies of anecdotal data with traditional teaching methods, lectures and/or seminars, written papers and examinations and, as a result, have been limited in their scope and effect (Howe, 1970; Howe and Ahlum, 1971). Three immediate goals guided the development of BAWR: 1) to provide students with a working knowledge of the experimental analysis of behavior;

2) to apply this analysis to sex-role specific behaviors; and 3) to expose students to a feminist perspective.

PSI principles were used to design a structure to facilitate mastery of a broad body of readings, to provide proof of mastery of behavioral techniques, and to produce an atmosphere (via small-group/proctor interactions) in which students would be reinforced for exploring and describing their own experiences in behavioral terms.

METHOD
Organization

CLASS COMPOSITION. The class of eighty-six students (seventy-three women and thirteen men) was divided into fifteen groups which were proctored by students who had successfully completed a smaller version of BAWR the year before. These small groups generally met directly after the ninety-minute class session for at least an additional ninety minutes. Attendance at both class and group meetings was monitored by proctors.

CLASSES. Classes were held in the evening, in a large lounge in a student living center. Students often welcomed nonclass members who wished to sit in. Often, cookies and/or wine were served.

GRADING CRITERIA. At the first class meeting, students were given a hand-out describing the structure and content of BAWR. The following explanation of the grading criteria was given to the students:

To receive an A:
1. Class Attendance—one absence
2. Group Attendance—one absence
3. Weekly exercises—one late
4. Pass all reading quizzes
5. Satisfactory participation in class presentation
6. Project on time and approved

To receive a B:
1. Two absences
2. Two absences
3. Two late
4. Pass all reading quizzes

5. Satisfactory participation in class presentation
6. Project on time and approved

To receive a C:

1. Three absences
2. Three absences
3. Three late
4. Pass all reading quizzes
5. Satisfactory participation in class presentation
6. Project on time and approved.

PROCTORS. The proctors were students who had obtained A grades the previous year. All had volunteered for the current course with the understanding that they were to receive four credit hours for carrying out these duties. All proctors also took part in course planning—choosing readings, designing exercises, establishing grading criteria, during the semester preceding the current course.

In addition to utilizing the fourteen student proctors, the instructor proctored a group because she felt constrained by class size and the subsequent lack of opportunity to interact directly with students.

The proctors were responsible for the following duties: 1. checking reading quizzes, providing feedback and readministering portions of quizzes; 2. monitoring weekly exercises, correcting students' use of nonbehavioral language; 3. checking student journals; 4. acting as resource people for the planning of class presentations; 5. providing group leadership, so that discussions were guided in both a personal and behavioral direction; 6. providing role modelling, so that students observed behavioral and feminist principles in action; 7. attending weekly proctor meetings, including planning sessions in the previous semester and ongoing training and course evaluation/modification sessions; 8. communicating to me and the other proctors any particularly reinforcing (plus or minus!) interactions with their students; 9. requesting the instructor's assistance, if necessary; and 10. maintaining student records on a record sheet.

Students were asked to evaluate their proctors both at a six-week general course evaluation and at the end of the term, so that the instructor might determine a grade. These evaluations, attendance, and the instructor's evaluation at weekly meetings provided the basis for a proctor grade.

EVALUATION. A six-week evaluation was administered which served as one of the weekly excercises. Student responses covered many different areas of the course. They were asked to provide in behavioral terms five positive aspects of the course, five negative aspects of the course, and five ways in which the course could be improved.

Content

LECTURES. The first five classes were in the form of lectures covering 1. course structure and criteria; 2. an introduction to the principles of experimental analysis of behavior; 3. an introduction to institutional control of behavior; 4. an introduction to feminism, including a brief history of the movement; and 5. a brief, operant analysis of contemporary "psychiatric" treatment and diagnostic practices administered to women.

The first class meeting was especially important. Most students come to such a course with a history that provokes antipathy toward behavioral language and concepts. To soften the approach I eventually wished to adopt, the course organization and objectives were described in a congenial and informal manner.

After these first five classes, each group (in some cases, two groups combined) was responsible for a full-length class presentation on one of the following topics: Love and Romance, Women: Birth to Kindergarten, Women Kindergarten to sixth grade, Women: Sixth Grade to Twelfth Grade, The Media, Working Women, Black Women, Women and the Law, Gay Women, Aging Women, Women's Liberation: Agent for Change?, Women in Utopian Communities, which were explored in the order listed. In addition, a Latin-American student prepared, with the help of several other non-class member Latin-American women, a presentation on Latin-American Women. Groups presented: verbal reports, slide presentations, in-the-field experiments, experimental questionnaires and experiences in class, panels (of women in the media, Gay women, Women in academe, women in the women's liberation movement), speakers, videotapes produced by a local taping group, on elderly women, both in institutions and their own homes, movies and dramas. When panels and speakers were featured, the group concerned prepared questions, couched in behavioral terms, for our guests. In addition, the instructor attempted to summarize the presentations in behavioral terms.

READINGS. The original list of both required and recommended readings totalled eight pages. Readings ranged from *Science of Human Behavior* (Skinner, 1953), *Analysis of Human Operant Behavior* (Reese, 1966), *The Development of Sex Differences* (Maccoby, 1966) to *Sisterhood is Powerful* (Morgan, 1970), *The Black Woman* (Cade, 1970), *Lesbian/Woman* (Martin and Lyon, 1972), *The Coming of Age* (DeBeauvoir, 1972), as well as, examples from the popular press, i.e. "women's magagines", teenage magazines, newspapers, and contemporary alternative journalism *(Rolling Stone, Los Angeles Free Press)*. Finally, the course used twenty-five to thirty articles published by various feminist journals *(off our backs, Women: A Journal of Liberation, Ms.)* and by Know, Inc., a Pittsburg feminist press.

Readings were organized to precede each class presentation. Student mastery of readings was measured by reading quizzes which were checked on a pass-fail basis. Students were asked to review questions on which they did poorly and were re-interviewed on those points. Students wrote their first attempt at an exam and were personally interviewed in the re-take process. Quizzes were designed by the group responsible for the presentation, were linked to the readings, and were issued one week prior to the presentation. A sample quiz follows:

READING QUIZ #1   PSYCHOLOGY 324   FEB. 13, 1973

Resse—*Analysis of Human Operant Behavior*

1. Distinguished operant behavior from respondent behavior.
2. What is the difference between positive reinforcement and negative reinforcement?
3. Describe the difference between schedules of reinforcement and interval schedules of reinforcement. What are the two main variations of each?
4. What is a baseline measurement? Why is it important to take one, in the experimental situation?

Skinner—*Science of Human Behavior,* Chapters 22, 23, 25, 26.

1. How does Government exert control?
2. What, in behavioral terms, is "superstitious behavior"? Give one example from your experience.

Densmore—*Speech is the Form of Thought*

1. How does Densmore suggest that we deal with sexism in language?

Mainardi—*The Politics of Housework*

1. Describe a political ploy used by males to deal with housework, as defined and/or portrayed by Mainardi. How would you reinforce (positively or negatively) such a ploy?

Exercises. Many of the exercises were designed by the proctors who had participated in similar exercises in the first year of the course and felt that they had been critical in helping to shape verbal behavior and pointing out dramatically the reality of behavior control. Some of the exercises were:

1. Perform three behaviors normally assigned to the opposite sex: record positively or negatively reinforcing responses to them.

2. Listen to one hour each of: Top-40 radio, black radio, Country and Western station. List subject matter of, at least, six songs, noting any references to promise or loss of reinforcement, i.e. "I lost my baby . . . doo wah . . . doo wah . . . what did I do wrong???" Also note sex of performer. Also note items featured in advertisements.

3. Visit a nursing home (we have arranged for visits at five local nursing homes). List available positive and negative reinforcers available to patients over a twenty-four hour span. Contrast them with reinforcers available to you over twenty-four hours.

4. Contrast advertising in *McCall's* and *Ebony,* basing your comments on sex-role stereotyping. Clues: where are male models located in relation to women models and the camera, what are the models doing, where are their eyes directed, how are they dressed? Are there observable differences between men and women, black and white . . . fifteen examples.

Class projects. Students were given a choice of the following projects described in the first class hand-out:

1. *Journal:* Maintain a journal, at least three entries a week, describing (in behavioral terms, where possible) your reactions to class presentations, the readings, other courses, your small group, your friends, the university, television, pop music, your world. Your proctor will check your journal every now and then, which will help you stay out of the bag of frantically inventing twenty-four entries the night before the last class. It's *your* life going down on those pages, treat it with respect.

2. *Tradition:* A five to six page paper on some aspect of Behaviorism and/or feminism and a twenty to twenty-five page paper on a different topic in either category. There will be *no* extensions. It makes sense to discuss the topic you choose with your proctor and other group members . . . they may be able to provide feedback, references and ideas.

3. *Exepriment:* Design and execute an experiment, employing operant principles, which will produce changes in some form of sex-role specific behavior. You must be able to support design with back-up readings. Your back-ground reading list and design must be submitted to your proctor.

4. Suggest your own project: present it to your proctor and group.

All students chose to keep a journal. Since the journals were checked on the above-mentioned unannounced variable interval schedule, students could not fall into the practice of making three weeks' entries the night before a journal check was due. Students were given the choice of having either their proctors or instructor check their journals. All but one chose to use their proctors.

RESULTS

The first aim of this course was simply to equip the students with analytical tools, an aim best reflected by how precisely they employed technical terms as reported by their proctors and revealed in their successes on reading quizzes and exercises. Verbal behavior in class and small groups also provided another useful index. Both of these criteria subjectively indicated a substantive increase by the end of the semester in the use of behavioral terms, not only in sheer frequency but in aptness as well.

The second aim, to apply this technology to an analyses of sex-role related behaviors, achieved an even more notable success, perhaps best reflected in the comments of the students themselves as recorded in their journals. Many of the students became quite accurate in identifying and recording the behaviors with which their boy/girl-friends maintained their behaviors, reinforcing particular styles of clothing with approving, flattering comments, being cute about not being able to do household chores, then providing lavish thanks when chores were done by the controlled, providing negative verbal reinforcement for aggressive behaviors in a girl-friend or "weak" behaviors in a boyfriend.

At the end-of-term evaluation, many of the students rated journal-keeping as the high point of the course; for most of them, this represented their first effort at systematically and consistently recording their own behavior.

The third aim, to provide students with a feminist perspective, was achieved mainly through the orientation of many of the readings and the class presentations; it was reflected in the verbal behavior of the students. For many of them, language and practices which had previously been reinforcing; "Hi, chick, you look fantastic today . . .", having doors held open, for males, being praised by peers for being "cool" and unemotional—became punishments. A male student showed a decrease in the use of the term, "chick", in class meetings over the time-course of BAWR, possibly because he began to be punished with hisses each time he used it.

Out of eighty-six students, seventy-nine received an A, four received a B+, one earned a B and one student received C. The B+ grade is accounted for by superior performance on the class presentation or in small group, as described by their proctor, where a B would have been the assigned grade. One student received an Incomplete with a medical excuse.

The system failed four students, in that they were unable to achieve their *goal-grade*. While they passed the course, they failed to meet their own criteria. In the discussion, I will deal with this failure, as well as the successful majority. All proctors received A's.

DISCUSSION

For this particular course and this particular instructor, failure must be construed as a students' grade falling below their chosen goal, since one of the purposes of the course was to eliminate the ambiguity about grade faced by students in so many college courses. For three students, late exercises and absences contributed to their lowered grade. Perhaps the establishment of pacing deadlines for quizzes and exercises might provide students with the opportunity for less delayed reinforcement for reading. For some students lateness represents a powerful tool for control of the teacher, long, reinforcing lectures and opportunity for interaction around the issue of lateness. The instructor tried, in the first class, to state that she was aware of that phenomenon, would punish it and suggested that students try positively reinforcing methods of control, such as laughter, applause, cheering, etc. For one student, behavioral problems which necessitated psychiatric treatment intruded upon her successful course behaviors. She was given an Incomplete, upon the condition that she audit the course next year, complete the work and demonstrate consistency in class and group attendance.

The proctors contributed many valuable suggestions both during the year and at the end of the semester. They felt a need for more lengthy proctor meetings and for a clearer definition of their roles in helping plan each group's class presentation. Twenty-five students from this year's course have volunteered to proctor next year, and will benefit from the honest and constructive feedback received from this year's proctors.

After the first sex-week evaluation it was concluded that some of the changes suggested by the students cancelled each other out ("more behaviorism" vs. "more feminism") but we did deal directly with suggestions which focused on our behaviors. Students also asked for more direct guidance in performing the weekly exercises. This was given in the form of increased verbal prompting by the proctors and increased probing when exercises were turned in. Finally, students contributed reading suggestions throughout the course which were incorporated into the required reading list. Although student input was generous and was reinforced by observable change in instructor and proctor behaviors.

In general, adapting PSI principles to more "emotional", more abstract, and less well-defined material than is usually covered in Psych 101 or Introductory Chemistry involves different criteria and a slightly altered structure. First, goals such as those outlined earlier, rather than sequential mastery of material may be more appropriate in defining success. Second, smaller groups (five to seven rather than nine to ten members) seem to function better, since much of the material provokes personal responses from all the group members, and discussion (rather than interviews) may be the process most useful in the group experience. Third, diverse methods of eliciting behavior are necessary, since material may be diverse and derive from a multitude of sources, rather than simply from a single text and lectures. Finally, proctors may need a more intensive training period than appears to be the case with more traditional PSI applications. They must be taught to do a great deal of modelling and probing, and they must understand the reinforcement parameters of the group process.

It would seem that this structure can lend itself to a broad range of course material, readings and content, without losing precision and predictable success for the students.

THE USE OF "CONCEPT PROGRAMMING" TO TEACH BEHAVIORAL CONCEPTS TO UNIVERSITY STUDENTS

L. Keith Miller
F. Hal Weaver

THE USE OF CONTINGENCY MANAGEMENT TECHNIQUES in university and college classrooms has been demonstrated to produce a higher level of student achievement than the use of traditional methods of instruction (Bushell, 1965; McMichael & Corey, 1969; Sheppard and MacDermott, 1970; Cooper & Greiner, 1971; Johnson & Pennypacker, 1971; Stallings, 1971; Alba & Pennypacker, 1972; Born, Gledhill, & Davis, 1972; Sapp, Edwards, & Thomas, 1972; Witters & Kent, 1972).

Most contingency management courses specify as target behaviors correct responses to questions based directly on material in an assigned text. Frequently, study guides containing lists of questions about the assigned are provided to the students. The same questions are frequently used to devise quizzes for the students, and a smaller sample of these questions may appear on a final examination. Thus, contingency management procedures

The authors would like to thank Drs. Dave Born and Jim Sherman for their careful reading of the manuscript and their helpful suggestions for revision.

have been aimed primarily at teaching students to display a repertoire of correct responses to a limited pool of questions based directly on the assigned textbook.

Many traditional courses specify as target behaviors correct responses to previously unseen questions based on the same principles as described in lectures or contained in a required text. For example, in mathematics classes instructors may show students how to solve a particular type of problem, and then ask them to solve novel examples of that type of problem. Similarly, a psychology instructor may define "reinforcement," describe several examples of it, and then ask the student to analyze several novel examples of reinforcement by way of testing their understanding of the principle. Thus, many traditional courses have aimed at teaching students to display a repertoire of correct responses to an unlimited pool of questions based on the principles described in an assigned text.

The type of target behavior specified by traditional courses has been termed "abstraction" (Skinner, 1952), "abstract stimulus control" (Ferster & Perrot, 1968) or "conceptual behavior" (Whaley & Malott, 1971) by behaviorists. In its broadest meaning, conceptual behavior can be said to exist when a subject makes a particular target response in the presence of a new stimulus from a particular stimulus class while not making that particular target response in the presence of stimuli from outside that stimulus class (Whaley & Malott, 1971). An example of conceptual behavior might involve describing a series of new situations to a student and asking him to label them as examples of "reinforcement" or of "nonreinforcement." If he correctly applies the label "reinforcement" to some examples while not applying it to examples that do not involve reinforcement, then his behavior can be said to be under the control of the abstract concept of "reinforcement."

This paper reports an experiment that analyzes a behavioral procedure designed to generate student performance characteristic of conceptual behavior. The procedure adds what we have termed "concept programming" to the usual textual materials found in an introductory course in applied behavior analysis. Students are given textual material describing a series of fictitious examples of everyday behavior that or may not illustrate a particular behavioral concept. They are required to designate what concept is illustrated. If they are to produce correct responses, they must generalize to a wide variety of examples of each concept while discriminating these from examples of other concepts. They are, of course, provided corrective feedback on their answers.

The textual material and concept-programs given to the students are grouped into four major units. To determine whether this material generates conceptual behavior, four generalization subtests were devised. Each subtest contains twelve novel examples of concepts that were taught in a corresponding unit of the generalization program. By repeatedly administering the four subtests, and by introducing the four course units in a staggered fashion, it is possible to examine the effect of each unit of the concept-program on the corresponding subtest. This defines a multiple baseline experimental design capable of determining whether the concept-program units produce an improvement in the corresponding generalization subtest (Miller & Weaver, 1972).

METHODS

Subjects

The seventy subjects were all students in a personalized, undergraduate course covering the basic principles of behavior analysis. They were primarily freshmen and sophomores representing a variety of majors. The course is an introductory course in the Department of Human Development at the University of Kansas. Miller's *Principles of Everyday Behavior Analysis* (in press) was used as the textbook.

Textbook Description

The textbook was designed to use the principles of discrimination and generalization to develop abstract conceptual behavior in the students. The book contains twenty-six lessons, each lesson stressing one major behavioral concept or several related major concepts. Thus, there are chapters on such topics as "methods of behavioral observation," "reinforcement," and "discrimination training."

Each lesson is divided into three parts: an "introduction," a "concept-program," and a "self-quiz."

The introduction typically concists of one to four pages introducing the student to the concept of that lesson. This introduction includes a definition of each concept, several illustrations of that concept occurring in everyday behavior, and instructions on how to identify whether or not a situation exemplifies that concept. Thus, this part of the lesson is similar in structure and intent to the major portion of most typical textbooks.

The "concept-program" consists of twenty fictional examples of everyday situations. About 65 percent of the examples exemplify the concept under study in that chapter while the remaining examples exemplify similar concepts from previous chapters. These latter examples are included to help the student learn to discriminate examples of related concepts from one another as well as provide a review of earlier material.

The task of the student in the concept program position of the book was to identify the concept exemplified by the example. To assist the student in doing this, the first few examples were accompanied by several questions that pointed out how the example did or did not conform to the definition contained in the introduction to the lesson. These questions were included to prompt the correct identification of the example. These prompts were gradually faded out during the first ten examples so that there were no prompts in the last ten examples. Answers to all of the questions relating to the first ten examples were provided to the student in the back of the book for immediate feedback. All questions called for one-word fill-in answers.

The examples were all based on common everyday situations that would be familiar to most university students. For example, 20 percent of the examples dealt with the social interactions between adults. This would include friends drinking beer together, lovers quarreling, and a friend helping another to lose weight. Another 17 percent dealt with group living situations such as occur among university students in dorms and communes. Another 17 percent of the examples dealt with professor-student interaction in university classrooms. About 11 percent of the examples dealt with students engaged in political behaviors. Another

25 percent dealt with examples of parent-child interactions, many of them involving university age children. Only 10 percent of the examples dealt with pupil behavior in public school settings. Thus, perhaps 80 percent of the examples dealt with the behaviors of normal young adults in everday social settings. None of the examples dealt with animal behavior or the behavior of such abnormal populations as retardates, schizophrenics, or adults with severe clinical problems such as phobias and the like.

The third part of each lesson consists of a "self-quiz." The self-quiz contains ten questions relating to the introduction and twenty questions relating to the examples contained in the concept-program portion of the text. The questions relating to the examples included short, four to six line summaries of the examples with the requirement that the student identify the behavioral concept exemplified by it. All self-quiz questions required one word answers. No answers were supplied to the student for any of these questions.

Course Description

The course was run along the lines of a standard personalized course. The self-quiz portion of the textbook served as a study guide for the students. Students were required to take a quiz based on a sample of ten self-quiz items to demonstrate mastery of each lesson. If they did not pass the quiz with a score of ninety percent or better, they were required to write out the answers to the concept-program portion of the text before retaking the quiz. When they handed in those answers they were eligible to take additional forms of the quiz until they attained a score of ninety percent. Their grade in the course depended upon their average score in the first form of the quiz for each lesson—a "B" being earned by an average of 90 percent of more, a "C" by an 80 percent average and so on. They could earn a one letter grade increment by completing a special project assigned by the instructor. Student proctors were available to answer questions on the introduction and the examples (but not on the self-quiz items) and to grade their quizzes. Students had to progress through the course by keeping up with a series of target dates assigned by the instructor (Miller, Weaver, & Semb, in press).

Thus, the course involved the use of study guides, frequent quizzing, mastery criteria, and student proctors.

Generalization Test

The generalization of the students' responses from the examples in the textbook to novel examples was measured by a means of a Generalization Test. This test consisted of forty-eight questions that had never been seen before by the students. These questions consisted of examples of sixteen concepts in three different concept areas. In order to increase the novelty of the items, the content areas were ones that did not appear in the textbook: Sixteen examples involved animal experiments, sixteen involved the research behavior of a psychologist, and sixteen involved the behavior of welfare clients and caseworkers.

The forty-eight example-questions were scored in four separate subtests based on the four major units of the textbook. Thus, the percentage of correct responses was computed separately for the twelve items that involved concepts from the "Methods of Behavioral Research" unit; for the twelve items involving concepts from the "Reinforcement Control" unit; for the twelve items involving concepts from the "Stimulus Control" unit; and for the twelve items involving concepts from the "Aversive Control" unit. These four subtest scores were used to define four different baselines for the subject's example-analyzing behavior.

This test was administered to all students in the class at one-week intervals for thirteen weeks during the semester. At no time did the students receive feedback on their performance.

Experimental Design

The experiment examined the effect of the textbook on the students' ability to answer questions on the Generalization Test correctly. For this purpose, each of the four major units of the textbook, plus the associated procedures employed in the personalized course, were treated as separate treatment packages designed to teach the student how to answer questions in that content area. Thus, the scores of the students on each of the four baselines was examined before, during, and after they were assigned and tested on that portion of the textbook. Specifically, each student was given the Generalization Test once a week for the thirteen weeks of the semester.

This procedure defined a multiple baseline design across the four question-answering baselines where the treatment was the associated part of the textbook. This defined six experimental conditions:

BASELINE: During the first test all four question-answering behaviors were in pre-treatment or baseline condition.

TREATMENT FOR METHODS: During the second and third weeks, the teaching package was applied to questions relating to methods of research. The three other areas were in a baseline condition during this period.

TREATMENT FOR REINFORCEMENT CONTROL: During the fourth through sixth weeks, the teaching package was applied to questions relating to stimulus control; methods and reinforcement were simultaneously in a post-treatment condition while aversive control was still in baseline.

TREATMENT FOR AVERSIVE CONTROL: During the tenth through twelfth weeks, the teaching package was applied to questions relating to aversive control. The other three areas were in a post-treatment condition.

POST-TREATMENT: During the thirteenth week a final test was administered. All four areas were in a post-treatment phase at the time of this test.

Thus, the use of each set of questions as a seperate baseline permitted the experimental analysis of each major unit of the textbook in a multiple baseline design.

RESULTS

Figure 4-1 shows the effect of the four teaching packages on the mean percent of correct responses on each generalization subtest. During baseline, the mean percent of correct answers ranged from 8 to 35 percent correct for the four subtests. During treatment for the Methods subtest, this percent jumped to about 70 percent while very little change occurred in the other three subtests. During treatment for the Reinforcement subtest, the mean percent increased to 80 percent with little change in the other subtests still in baseline. During the treatment for the Stimulus subtest, the mean percent increased to about 60 percent with no change in the Aversive Control subtest. When the treatment package was applied to the Aversive Control subtest, the mean percent of correct responding increased to about 70 percent. During posttreatment condition, the mean correct responding for the four subtests ranged from 65 percent to 85 percent correct. Thus, not only was an increase noted in each of the subtests, but that increase was clearly associated with the introduction of the teaching package for that specific area.

Figure 4-2 shows the mean pre-test (week #1) and the mean post-test (week #13) scores for the "animal," "research," and "welfare" examples appearing on the generalization test. As can be seen, the students' correct responses generalized approximately equally well to all three types of examples.

An analysis of the individual scores made by students reveals that all but seven students out of forty-six showed a gain in all four subtests on the post-test compared to the pre-test. Thus, an analysis of the individual data reveals that the group effect described in Figure 4-1 is also a reliable effect of the behavior of individual students.

DISCUSSION

The results of this experiment showed that the percentage correct responses to novel questions increased after the treatment package was introduced. The treatment package consisted of the textual material for a major unit of the textbook plus the contingency system implemented in the personalized course. The fact that the percent of correct responses for each unit increased only after the introduction of the treatment package provides evidence that the package produced these increases. Further, the individual data indicates that this effect was reliably observed in the behavior of individual students.

It is our contention that the observed gains in individual scores represent a measure of the extent to which the students' use of behavioral terms generalized from the definitions and examples on which they were initially instructed to new examples on which they were never instructed.

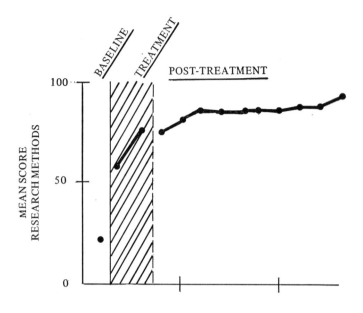

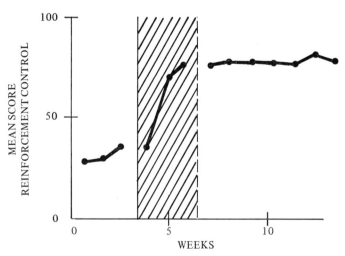

Figure 4-1A, 1B. The mean percentage of questions answered correctly by seventy undergraduate students on each of four subtests of a generalization test. The

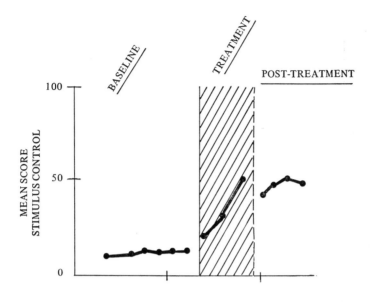

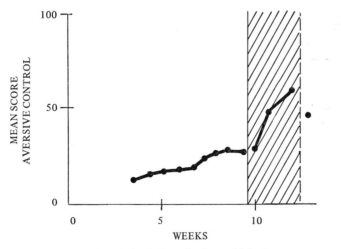

striped bars represent the period of time during which the concept program correlated with each sub-test was made available to the students.

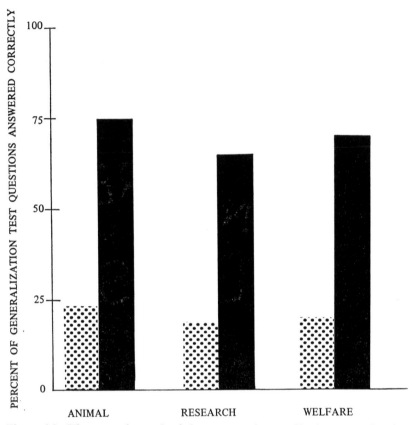

Figure 4-2. The mean for each of three types of generalization examples that were answered correctly during a pre-test and a post-test administration of the Generalization Test.

It might be argued that this is not a case of "generalization" because the examples were not novel once the students had first taken the Generalization Test. However, virtually all tests of generalization used in the animal literature use generalization stimuli repeatedly. What makes a stimulus suitable for a generalization test is that consequences are never applied to the response in the presence of that stimulus (Blough, 1961). Thus, in the present experiments, students at no time received feedback on their answers to the items on the Generalization Test. Thus, it seems reasonable to regard these items as a valid test of the generalization of student responses.

It might be also argued that there was nothing new about the items of the Generalization Test, and that it was, therefore, not a test of generalization. For example, the items required the same type of response to the same type of stimulus situation. This was, of course, by design. The usual tests of generalization of a response are designed to determine whether the same physical response generalizes to a new stimulus condition. In the present case, the same sixteen terms were investigated to see if they were applied to new examples. Furthermore, the examples were intentionally designed for maximum difference from the items used in the teaching materials. The most dramatic case of this was the use of animal experiments because all of the textbook examples referred to everyday behavioral situations involving normal humans. The use of research behavior and welfare examples, while not as dramatic, were also entirely different in content from the examples used in the textual materials. Furthermore, all cues of wording, use of terms, and the like were also eliminated from the Generalization Test items. Thus, it seems that a strong case can be developed for those items being completely unlike any that the students were trained to answer.

Thus, the methodology strongly points to the Generalization Test as a valid test of the generalization of the students' response to novel stimulus situations. At the same time, the students continued to discriminate examples of one behavioral term to examples of another. This is implied in their high test scores in that improper discrimination would result in a low Generalization Test Score. Thus, the present results indicate that students generalized their response to novel stimulus situations while discriminating these from examples of other terms.

The results of the experiment may also be interpreted as evidence that the students were taught conceptual behavior. "Concept" may be defined behaviorally as a class of stimulus situations that have a defined similarity (Whaley & Malott, 1971). Thus, the unlimited set of verbal examples of "reinforcement" that all conform to the definition of that term would constitute a concept. Behavioral evidence of conceptual behavior requires the demonstration that students' use of the term "reinforcement" is applied correctly to representative examples of other behavioral terms. The results of the last administration of the Generalization Test provided just such evidence. Thus, the present experiment may be interpreted to support the contention that a treatment package including concept programming provides a behavioral procedure for producing conceptual behavior with respect to academic material.

The concept programming procedure would seem to be one that could easily be applied in many academic courses. All that it requires is the formulation of a set of examples that both illustrate and contrast a definition or principle. The examples that illustrate should presumably contain as many irrelevant differences as possible so that the student will learn to attend to the essential characteristics of the examples. And the examples that contrast should be as similar to the illustrations as possible while failing to be the same in at least one important aspect.

When the concept program for the "Reinforcement" lesson was developed, these principles were observed. The names, behaviors, settings, and other irrelevant features of examples of reinforcers were varied. Further, some examples that were contrary to common sense were used when an example of spanking included the information that the rate of a behavior that it followed increased. The contrasting examples were similar in the use of names and behaviors to examples of reinforcement. However, these examples included cases of a prior event that produced an increased behavioral rate; cases of pleasant events that did not produce an increase, and so on. The principle was to design examples that required the students to focus on the essential elements of a "reinforcer."

The procedure as we used it also involved a fading technique. The first few examples were accompanied by questions designed to prompt the correct response. For example, with respect to examples in the "Reinforcement" lesson, one prompting questions might ask "Did the event in the example *follow* the response?" and another question might ask "Did the even *increase* the rate of the response?" Finally a prompting question might ask "Since the event followed the response and increased the rate of the response, it would be called a _____." Such prompting questions were designed to draw the student's attention to the critical features of the example, thereby greatly increasing the probability of the student emitting the correct response. Such prompting questions were used at a decreasing rate during the first ten examples. They were eliminated entirely for the last ten examples. The second ten examples contained nonprompted questions such as "The event is an example of what behavior process?"

All questions used in the concept program were analyzed one semester by requiring students to complete and hand in answers to them. The questions were then graded and questions having an error rate of over 10 percent were revised. Thus, the final generalization program permitted students to progress through it with a minimum of errors.

A set of illustrative and contrasting examples involving a gradually faded sequence of prompting questions such as these could be developed as supplementary material for use with any standard textbook. Such material might be developed and handed out with a study guide.

In summary, this experiment demonstrated that a teaching package that includes concept programming produces a higher percentage of correct responses to a generalization test. These results suggest that concept programming may be a powerful technique for developing conceptual behavior in standard academic courses.

EXPERIMENTAL COMPARISONS

THE PAPERS IN THIS SECTION are all efforts to compare along various dimensions the relative effects of PSI or similar individualized methods to the effects on students of more traditional teaching procedures. At the same time, these comparisons are conducted with applications of PSI to such varied content areas as psychology, microeconomics, elementary dynamics, business personnel administration, sociology, and French. Individualized teaching methods have already been applied to virtually every kind of subject matter traditionally a part of higher education curricula.

A COMPARISON OF TWO TEACH-ING FORMATS AT THE COLLEGE LEVEL

COLLIER COLE
SANDER MARTIN
JOHN VINCENT

EVALUATIVE STUDIES ARE now firmly establishing the Keller method (Keller, 1966; 1968) as a systematic behavioral approach to teaching (McMichael and Corey, 1969; Sheppard and MacDermot, 1970; Born, Gledhill, and Davis, 1972; Alba and Pennypacker, 1972; Whithurst, 1972). However, these studies have not been devoid of problems. Methodological problems that have faced these studies include:

1) Matching experimental and control groups for GPA/academic skills and ability (McMichael and Corey, 1969; Sheppard and MacDermot, 1970; Whitehurst, 1972)
2) Control of differences in teaching experience of instructors (McMichael and Corey, 1969)
3) Equating course procedures (Born, Gledhill and Davis, 1972; Whitehurst, 1972)

This investigation was based on a thesis submitted by the senior author to the University of Houston in partial fulfillment of the requirements for the M. A. Degree.

4) Pre-exposure to test items (McMichael and Corey, 1969)
5) Use of same instructors to teach both experimental and control sections (Sheppard and MacDermot, 1970; Born, Gledhill and Davis, 1972; Whitehurst, 1972)

The purpose of this study was to compare a Keller format class with a traditional lecture class. The methodological problems outlined above were considered and steps were taken to control for them.

A further problem with earlier studies was the fact that student performance under a Keller format has been investigated solely on the basis of identical final exams administered to both experimental and control sections at the end of the course. It is possible that the Keller format produces initial positive class differences (i.e. significantly higher results on final exam scores) only to be lost over time. Hence, another major purpose of this study was to investigate retention of course material over time. A follow-up exam was designed and administered to samples selected from both classes two months following the end of the semester.

This study also systematically as well as retention of material, investigated other dependent variables. These included study patterns, student satisfaction, grade expectations, student interaction, final exam scores.

METHOD

Subjects

Subjects were students enrolled in two undergraduate psychology courses entitled "Behavior Modification." Each course was taught by a different professor: one was using the Keller format and the other a "lecture" format. Both instructors were male and had recently graduated from the same university. The course materials and content were similar and textbooks and readings were identical (Both sections used *Behavior Principles* by Ferster and Perrott, Appleton-Century-Crofts, 1968, and *Control of Human Behavior, Volume II* by Ulrich, Stachnik, and Mabry, Scott, Foresman and Company, 1970). The students were mainly undergraduate juniors and seniors and were unaware of the class differences. They were administratively assigned to one of the two-class sections, both of which were taught at the same time on the same days. After obtaining the overall grade-point average for all students from the registrar, both classes were tested for differences in GPA and none were found (t = .14). In an attempt to avoid contamination of results (each class competing for a better position, or comparing of data between students in different sections) neither class was informed of the nature of the present study. (However, there was no way to control for hypotheses generated on their own.) They were simply told that over the course of the term for the benefit of the instructor they would be submitting weekly study reports, and a course questionnaire would be filled out at the end of the semester. No mention was made of a follow-up exam. Also, the two instructors were not informed of the results on the weekly data reports or course questionnaire until the semester was over.

PSI Class Organization

This section (N = 46 plus 6 proctors) met on Monday-Wednesday-Friday for one hour per session. Mondays were reserved for "interviews." Students could come to class and find other students or teaching assistants (undergraduate students who had taken the course the previous semester) who would "listen" or "talk" on a section. Each student was required, a) to "talk" on a section and demonstrate his proficiency by answering discussion questions covering the material, and b) after demonstrating his own proficiency, the student then "listened" to another student and evaluated his mastery of the material. Wednesdays were reserved for guest speakers, lectures, and films. Psychologists and educators from the community were invited to speak on their areas of interest and research. Attendance at these lectures, as at all class meetings, was optional. On Fridays the class broke up into small discussion groups, each with one of the teaching assistants, and covered material of interest in greater detail. These groups also planned visits to local institutions and generated behavioral exercises.

The course content was divided into four levels. Each level had four sections over which a student talked and listened before taking a written exam. There were four level exams made up from a sample of the discussion questions, each one having to be passed before the student could go on the next level. To pass an exam, the student needed to answer ten of the twelve short essay questions correctly. A final exam was also given but did not count toward the final grade. Students were instructed not to prepare for the final exam, it was used by the professor more as an index of recall of material.

Grades were assigned on the basis of how many levels were completed by a student. Completion of all four levels earned an A, three levels a B, two levels a C, one level a D, and zero level an F. Deadline dates for completing a level were also assigned. This was designed to alleviate procrastination, a problem which has been reported in some PSI format courses (Sherman, 1967; 1971; 1972). As an example of this particular system, a student going for an A would have to complete the first level by the appropriate deadline date (usually the 4th week) . . . students not meeting the deadline would automatically drop to a lower grade level.

Lecture Class Organization

This section (N = 39) also met on Monday-Wednesday-Friday morning for one hour per session. Mondays and Wednesdays were reserved for lectures and demonstrations. Lectures were almost entirely supplementary, being employed mainly to clarify course concepts and present related materials on clinical application of behavior modification. Lectures often included the areas of interest and expertise of the particular professor; attendance at lectures was not mandatory. Fridays were reserved for small group discussions and films.

Grades were based on a term project ($\frac{1}{3}$), a book critique or midterm exam ($\frac{1}{3}$), and a required final exam ($\frac{1}{3}$). All exams were made up by the instructor and composed of items never seen before by the students. A low grade on any of the three course requirements could be supplemented by doing an extra-credit term paper on a negotiated topic. Final grades were distributed on the basis of a liberal normal curve.

Procedure

The study investigated four major dependent variables:
1) self-reported student study hours
2) student attitudes
3) final exam scores
4) scores on follow-up exam

Self-reported Study Hours

At the end of each week's final class meeting, students in both sections submitted the number of hours spent studying for the class during the previous week. No names were required on the paper and students were encouraged to be as honest as possible.

Student Attitudes

One week prior to the end of the term, both sections were asked to fill out a questionnaire consisting of sixteen items sampling course satisfaction and interest. The items were constructed in the manner of a Likert scale of the type: Not applicable—Strongly agree—Agree—Disagree—Strongly diasagree. For purposes of tabulation and analysis, each response was assigned a numerical value. (Not applicable—1; Strongly agree—2; Agree—3; Disagree—4; Strongly disagree—5.)

Final Exam Scores

Both sections were administered a final exam consisting of both multiple-choice (the type used on the lecture format exams) and short essay (the type used on the PSI format exams) questions. The exam was prepared by the lecture format instructor and covered lecture material and assigned readings. The section of the exam used to compare both classes was based on material common to both groups (assigned readings) .

Scores on Follow-up Exam

A sample of students from each class section was administered a follow-up exam two months after the official end of the course. The exam was prepared by the senior experimenter and consisted of forty-five multiple-choice items covering all the identical assigned reading materials for the course.

RESULTS

Self-Reported Study Hours

An overall t-test between the PSI group (Grand mean = 5.46 hours per week) and the lecture group (Grand mean = 5.36 hours per week) resulted in no significant difference $(t = .09)$. Weekly study counts were tabulated, and Figure 5-1 shows a graph of the average number of study hours reported by members of both sections on a weekly basis throughout the semester. Arrows indicate those points at which exams were administered to each section (PSI group—four exams plus final exam; lecture group—one exam plus final exam). Similarly, Figure 5-2 presents a cumulative record of the self-reported study hours for both groups.

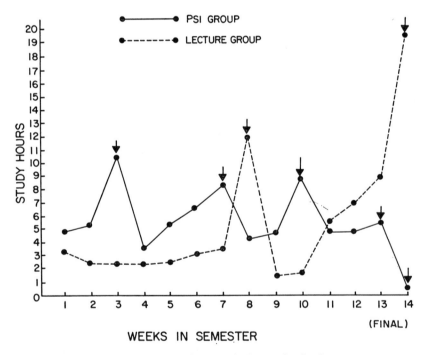

Figure 5-1. Weekly report of student study hours for both groups.

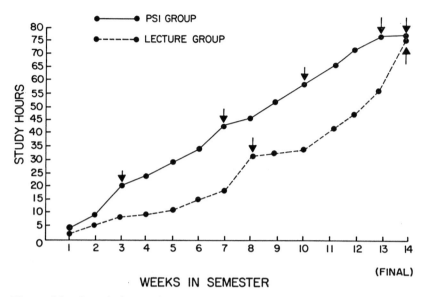

WEEKS IN SEMESTER

Figure 5-2. Cumulative student self-reported study hours.

T-tests were performed to compare each class on a weekly basis. Significant differences at the .01 level were reported for weeks 2, 3, 5 to 10 indicating more studying by the Keller group. The lecture group was significantly different (at the .01 level) for weeks 8 and 14 (Final exam). No differences were found for weeks 4 and 11 to 13.

Student Attitudes

A sample of students from the PSI group (N = 32) and the lecture group (N = 32) were administered a sixteen-item course questionnaire. Both groups were asked: "What grade do you expect to receive in this course?" The results were significant at the .001 level (t = 4.07) in favor of the PSI plan.

EXPECTED GRADE

	A	B	C	D	F	Underter-mined
PSI:	29	2	1	0	0	0
Lecture:	10	16	2	0	0	4

T-tests were performed to compare both groups on all sixteen questionnaire items.

A t-test between groups on the perceived "overall value of the course" was significant at the .001 level (t = 4.00) in favor of the PSI group.

OVERALL VALUE

	Excellent	Good	Fair	Poor
PSI:	27	5	0	0
Lecture:	13	14	4	1

In order to verify this finding, a t-test was performed to compare students in both groups expecting to receive the grade of A for the course on the variable of "overall value." Again the results were significant at the .01 level (t = 3.12) in favor of the PSI group.

Final Exam Scores

Scores on the final exam administered to student samples from the PSI group (N = 40) and from the lecture group (N = 17) were tabulated (Table I). A scoring key was used for grading the objective portion of the exam; the essay portion was scored by the senior experimenter using a list of acceptable criteria. All exams were scored "blindly"—the examiner unaware of each student's class assignment. (The reason for the small N in the lecture group was that two forms of the final exam were used. The lecture group had the option of taking the final exam on one of two days. Form A was administered on the first day while Form B was administered on the second day. All of the PSI group took the Form A exam on the first day while only part of the lecture group did the same. The comparison was based only on these two samples).

The two groups were compared on final exam performance. Results were significant at the .05 level (t = 2.54) in favor of the PSI group (Table 5-I). A breakdown of the final exam into essay and objective sections was reported.

Relative to the total possible points on the final exam (i.e. 50), the difference between groups was 8 percent (the PSI group

TABLE 5-I

Comparison of Final Exam Scores

PSI	Lecture
N = 40	N = 17
Mean	Mean
Total = 38.55	Total = 34.76
Objective = 14.00	Objective = 12.94
Essay = 24.55	Essay = 21.82
SD	t
Total = 1.49	Total = 2.54*
Objective = .90	Objective = 1.22
Essay = .99	Essay = 2.76**
	*$p<.05$
	**$p<.01$

scoring 77 percent and the lecture group scoring 69 percent of the total possible points).

Scores on the Follow-up Exam

Scores on the follow-up exam administered to samples from the PSI group (N = 15) and from the lecture group (N = 15) were tabulated and reported (Table 5-II). A scoring key was used for grading these objective questions.

Dut to the badly skewed nature of the final distribution of grades for the two courses, it was impossible to match students for the follow-up exam on the basis of final grade received. The final distribution of grades for both sections was as follows:

FINAL GRADE

	A	B	C	D	F	Incom-plete	With-draw
PSI:	35	2	4	1	0	3	1
Lecture:	9	18	5	0	0	0	7

In order to insure randomness of the follow-up sample from the Keller group, a comparison of seven A students randomly selected from the sample with remaining A students in the sample yielded no differences (t = 1.27).

A post hoc analysis was then performed (Table 5-III). The seven A students from the lecture sample were matched with the random selection of seven A students from the Keller sample.

TABLE 5-II

Comparison of Follow-up Exam Scores

	PSI				Lecture		
S	Score	Final Grade	GPA*	S	Score	Final Grade	GPA*
1	34	A	1	1	22	A	2
2	30	A	3	2	20	A	3
3	24	A	1	3	28	A	2
4	34	A	2	4	25	A	2
5	33	A	2	5	16	A	1
6	37	A	3	6	21	A	3
7	27	A	4	7	33	A	3
8	28	A	2	8	31	B	1
9	30	A	2	9	22	B	3
10	38	A	3	10	20	B	2
11	27	A	1	11	21	B	4
12	38	A	2	12	23	B	3
13	34	A	3	13	24	B	2
14	34	A	1	14	26	B	3
15	32	A	2	15	23	B	3

* Key to GPA:
  1 = 3.50–4.00
  2 = 3.00–3.49
  3 = 2.50–2.99
  4 = 2.00–2.49
  5 = 1.50–1.99
  6 = 1.00–1.49
  7 = less than 1.00

A t-test was performed to compare the two groups. The results were significant in favor of the Keller group at the .01 level ($t = 4.01$).

Further analysis indicated that relative to the total possible points on the follow-up exam—45—the difference between samples was 22 percent (the Keller sample scoring 74 percent and the lecture sample scoring 52 percent of the total possible points).

DISCUSSION

Results show that the actual amount of study over the semester did not differ under the two formats. The striking difference,

TABLE 5-III

Post-Hoc Analysis of Follow-up Scores for Students
Receiving Grade A in Course

PSI	Lecture
N = 7	N = 7
Mean = 33.4	Mean = 23.5
SD = 2.44	
t = 4.01* 　　　　　*p<.01	

however, was in the *style* of study. Rather than a "massed" learning approach, as under the lecture format where the student studies wildly just prior to exams, the PSI format allows for more "distributive" learning; material is covered in equal chunks at less massed and more regular spaced intervals.

Responses on the course questionnaire indicate that even though the amount of work required under a PSI format is perceived as greater, students unanimously agree that the amount of pressure is less and the feeling of achievement is higher. There is less anxiety prior to exams and less worry about final grades. Students feel they have more recognition as individuals under such a self-paced teaching format. Interaction among students is greatly increased; they feel they get to know fellow students, as well as the instructor, better under this format than in other courses of equal size and credit. Also, the higher the grade expectation, the greater is mastery of course material and perceived enjoyment of the course. Rather than simply being a function of grade expectation (i.e. the higher the expected grade, the better the course is liked), results indicate that the "overall value" of the course was rated higher by those students expecting an A in the PSI format class than by students expecting an A in the lecture format class.

Final exam scores denote a higher level of mastery of material under a PSI format. Although the two sample sizes differed on this variable, there was a significant difference in favor of the PSI group on the combined final exam (at the .05 level). This is especially impressive when one keeps in mind that the final exam was a key determinant for final grades for students in the lecture group; consequently they studied a great deal for this exam (Figure 5-1). And, the PSI group was instructed *not* to study for the final exam for it did not count toward the final grade. One might argue that students under the lecture format were subject to test anxiety, greater pressure to perform well. This is speculation and warrants further study. One could compare final exam results between a Keller group and a lecture group where both were required to study for the exam.

A breakdown of the final exam into essay and objective sections shows that the PSI performed significantly better (.01 level) on the essay portion of the exam (Table 5-I). This was to be expected since all of the semester exams for this group were of a short-essay nature. The lecture group's experience was on objective (multiple choice) exams. However, they failed to score significantly higher than the PSI group on the objective portion of the final exam. With this fact in mind (no difference between groups on objective portion) the follow-up exam was composed of objective items in order to provide no advantage to either group (or possible a slight advantage in favor of the lecture group; one could not safely argue that experience on essay type exams automatically facilitates better performance on objective exams). It is of note to remember that the final exam was prepared by the lecture format instructor, and built-in bias (if any existed) would have favored the lecture format group.

Results on the follow-up exam clearly demonstrate that the PSI format fosters greater retention of material over time. This finding is supported by the literature on classical animal/human learning experiments which outlines the advantages of "distributive" as compared to "massed" learning (Mednick, 1964). "*Spaced practice*, or the allowance of frequent rests, causes less work decrement than *massed practice* since it permits accumulated response fatigue to dissipate. Consequently, the learning of verbal and motor tasks is usually aided by space practice (page 87)." Demonstratively a large part of the success of the Keller format rests on the principle that covering course material in spaced chunks increases mastery over the traditional massed method of study (intensive study only prior to exams).

It is also of interest to look at the correlation between grade received and grade-point average for both student samples receiving the follow-up exam. Table 5-II presents the distribution of follow-up exam scores; also included is the final grade received and the overall grade-point average for each subject in both samples. The correlation for the PSI group is .00 (due to the fact that *all* subjects in this sample received an A in the course) while that for the lecture group is .21. This would indicate that under a PSI format, grade-point average does not predict grade received in the course. In other words, it would appear that motivation to work is greater when students have control over the outcome. Students with differing grade-point averages can work for and earn the "A" grade they want. This would certainly contribute toward the perceived feeling of more recognition as an individual under such a teaching format.

One final subjective point can be mentioned. Students from both classes were selected at random, telephoned, and asked to participate in the follow-up exam. For the PSI group, seventeen people were contacted in order to reach the criterion of fifteen for the sample (88%). For the lecture group, thirty-two people were contacted before the criterion of fifteen was reached (46%). By far, students in the Keller sample were more enthusiastic, anxious, and on time to take the follow-up exam.

It is highly appropriate to mention here that carrying out comparison studies of this nature involves anticipating and resolving numerous methodological problems. No matter how hard one tries to equate and control for all factors, there will always be some difference between the two groups compared. With respect to the present study, one can control for assigned readings such that text material (lectures, demonstrations), especially when taught by different instructors, can only be highly similar, not identical. Students will not ask the same question in both classes and subjective experiences may not be comparable. It is often difficult to completely control for individual instructor differences. The only way to resolve this problem is to have each instructor teach two classes, one under the PSI format and the other under the lecture format. However, this is often not economically feasible from the standpoint of a university department's allocation of teaching assignments. There also may be no need for four sections of the same course. Even then there still exists the possibility of instructor bias toward one format or the other. Another difficulty lies in being able to match students on some variable and then administer a called-for test. In this study it was impossible to match students on the basis of grade received for the follow-up exam. This was due to the badly skewed final distribution of grades. There simply were not enough A's (in the lecture group) and B's (in the Keller group) to carry out this statistical procedure. Future comparison research of these two formats will have to address itself to more controlled emphasis focused on this variable of retention of material.

A few verbatim comments from students in the Keller course appear below. They come from the course questionnaire and the tone of the comments is typical.

"I learned so much by this method of teaching, and I extremely enjoyed it."

"Hurrah for behavior modification."

"Fantastic! Greatest course I've ever taken."

"Wish more courses were taught like this."

"I really liked the idea of no penalty for failing tests. It helped to reduce a lot of pressure."

"For the first time in any college course, I felt responsible for what I learned—and was treated like a responsible individual."

From the author's perspective, this study would indicate that a self-paced, personalized style of instruction—like the PSI format —is valuable at the college level. Course material is covered as well, if not better than under the lecture format. Of equal importance, the student is allowed a certain amount of "freedom and dignity" in mastering assigned materials and receiving credit for required/elective courses. This would appear to be more in line with what one expects from a college level course.

READING 6

TEACHING INTERMEDIATE MICRO-ECONOMICS USING THE PERSONAL-IZED SYSTEM OF INSTRUCTION

Thomas H. Tietenberg

INTRODUCTION
An Overview

THE PERSONALIZED SYSTEM OF INSTRUCTION (PSI) represents an alternative method of instruction to both conventional lecturing and programmed instruction. Various features of this method have made it appealing to a growing number of disciplines and schools.

In economics few evaluations of this technique have been reported in the literature. These have been conducted within the environment of a large university and have evaluated the application of the technique to an introductory economics course.

The purpose of this paper is to report on an experiment which is differentiated from previous studies in two ways: (1) the PSI technique was employed on a microeconomics course in which a one semester introductory course was a prerequisite and (2) the experiment was conducted within the enviroment of a small liberal arts college.

The author acknowledges the benefit of helpful comments on a previous draft from Allen Kelley, Arthur Welsh, Stephen Buckles, David Booth, William Moomaw, Andrew Crider and Paul Clark.

METHOD

Background

The types of educational objectives which characterize an economics education range in complexity from the memorization of simple definitions and facts to the acquisition by the student of the ability to reason analytically in an unstructured environment. While the PSI seems perfectly appropriate to satisfy the simpler educational objectives it is less clear that the method is appropriate for achieving the more complex objectives. The questions used to test the depth of understanding on these more complex and unstructured applications are by their very nature essay questions which are not quickly graded and which are certainly much less amenable to proctor grading than more objective tests. These characteristics make it difficult to incorporate essay questions into the unit tests. Since the unit tests are the main means of reinforcing what the student learns, this raises the question as to whether the use of the PSI might preclude this important form of learning.[1]

The PSI course designed for this experiment attempted to stimulate this type of learning by taking two steps. First the discussion questions in the units which are designed to guide the student in his mastery of the material included unstructured essay questions. Secondly, it was emphasized that although this kind of question would not appear on the PSI unit tests it would appear on the final. The plan was that the discussion questions would focus the student's thinking on this type of learning and the promise that essay questions would appear on the final examination would drive the student to the professor to see how one might go about dealing with these kinds of questions. From there the professor could capitalize on the opportunity for a one-to-one relationship provided by PSI to think through these problems with the student.

---

[1] A more serious concern would be that the faculty member's behavior would be altered as well. When the faculty member discoverd what kinds of learning were best accomplished under the PSI he may well be tempted to eliminate all other forms of learning to improve the performance of his students.

Procedure

A total of ninety-two students were allocated to three sections of microeconomics. Two of the sections were taught in a conventional lecture format and the final section was taught in the PSI format. All three sections met for two one and one-half hour periods a week. Each student was exposed to the same body of material. The course was based on a conventional test which all sections used. The PSI section students had the text supplemented by written handouts which consisted of the kind of elaboration and/or clarification that would ordinarily occur in a lecture.

All students were administered a common final examination. The experiment was designed to compare the lecture with the PSI section on input variables (student time, faculty time, material cost) and on output variables (final exam scores and student perceptions of the value of the educational experience). The empirical testing was based upon two instruments—the final examination and the course evaluation. These instruments are so central to this evaluation that they are separately described below, but first their role in the experiment will be discussed.

The first analysis was performed on the final examination scores. The technique of regression analysis was used to isolate insofar as possible the unique effects of the teaching method on final exam score. Specifically the answers for two questions were sought:

(1) Were there observable differences between the students in the PSI section and the students in the lecture sections in their performance on the final examination after controlling for other various measurable influencing factors?

(2) Is this differential, if any, uniform across students of different avilities or is the performance differential higher for students with a record of successful past performance in economics? Or higher for students with a somewhat lower level of performance in the past?

The second unit of analysis is the course evaluation form. Since these are filled out anonymously, it is not possible to link the response to a particular student. Therefore, the analysis of these forms is restricted to comparison of mean scores across sections.

Two constraints were imposed on the experimental design which made the analysis somewhat more difficult than would have been the case if it were a completely controlled experiment. Manpower considerations dictated that no professor could teach more than one section. This made the isolation of the technique differences more difficult because they were intertwined with differences in teaching ability among the faculty members. The method of controlling for faculty teaching differences is discussed below.

The second constraint resulted from the desire to be fair to the students. Fairness in this case translated into freedom of choice. Students were notified in advance which section was to be the PSI section and within the limits were allowed the choose the type of instruction they would receive. The impact of this on the analysis was that it was not possible to isolate differences in attitude before the course from attitudes acquired during the course of instruction.

The final examination was worth a total of one-hundred twenty points and consisted of three parts of equal weight. The first part consisted of eight short answer questions in which the students were given eight false statements and asked to explain why they were false. The second part consisted of four questions which represented a combination of two numerical problems and two ten minute discussion questions. The final part consisted of two twenty minute questions, the first of which was a complex application of general equilibrium analysis and the last question was a multipart question in which the student was faced with successively more difficult questions concerning the impact of alternative taxes on consumption.

The examination was put together from a pool of questions submitted by the three faculty members. To avoid possible biases in grading each faculty member graded one part of the examination for all ninety-two students without knowing which student's paper was being graded. Before the grading commenced scales were drawn up for each of the three parts to insure that an A answer on Part I would be worth roughly the same amount of points as an A on Part II and so forth. The course evaluation form used in this report is the standard instrument administered to almost all courses at Williams College. On this form students are asked to rate the professor on various traits usually associated with good teaching and the course in terms of its educational value. These ratings are based on an ordinal scale from one to seven, with a score of seven carrying a connotation of outstanding. In assigning these ratings the students are asked to compare the professor and course being rated with other faculty members and courses they have had at Williams.

Table 6-I presents information which is useful for two purposes.[2] It portrays the means of some of the characteristics of the students in each of the sections.

To test for a difference in student composition between the two types of sections resulting from allowing students to select their own method of instruction, a series of difference of means tests were run on the four variables given in Table 6-I and the resulting t ratios are given. It is not possible to reject the hypothesis at the 90 percent level of confidence that these two samples were drawn randomly from the same parent population. Apparently no clear advantage to either method was perceived uniformly by a single type of student as defined by the four variables in Table 6-I.

---

[2] Out of the ninety-two students who took the course only eighty had complete background records which were usable for the analysis.

TABLE 6-I

Mean Values of Selected Student Characteristics
for Lecture and PSI Sections

Variable	PSI Section	Lecture Sessions	Difference of Means t-ratio
Mean Economics Grade Point Average[1]	8.34	7.82	1.290
Mean S.A.T.—Math[2]	680.5	682.8	0.165
Mean S.A.T.—Verbal[2]	635.9	625.4	0.632
Mean Age	19.2	19.2	0.000

[1] This grade point average is based on a 12 point scale. An 8 is a B and a 7 is a B—.
[2] These are the scores received on the Scholastic Aptitude Test of the College Entrance Examination Board.

RESULTS

The often cited advantages of using a PSI method are (1) enhanced student performance, (2) better retention of material for longer periods of time, (3) the students are enthusiastic about taking PSI courses and (4) the students are allowed a much greater flexibility in allocating their study time. In this section the first, third and fourth of these potential advantages will be examined within the context of the above described experiment. Retention will be examined in a follow up study in a couple of years.

The evaluation of student performance, based on the testing instrument described above, is concerned with three questions: (1) does the PSI lead to superior performance? (2) what group of students seemed to benefit most from the PSI—students entering the course with high grade point averages? students entering the course with low grade point averages? neither? both benefit equally? (3) to what extent are these results sensitive to the form of the testing instrument?

The first hypothesis is that the introduction of the PSI method made no difference in the final examination scores of equally experienced faculty members. The verification of this hypothesis translates into a test that the coefficients on the last two variables in Table 6-II are simultaneously zero. With a F value of 0.45 for the test statistic it is impossible to reject the hypothesis at any conventional level of confidence. The introduction of the PSI method made no statistically significant difference in final examination scores.

The second hypothesis is that the PSI method has not discernible differential impact among students who have experienced varying degrees of success in economics in the past. The verification of this hypothesis translates into a test that the coefficient for the interaction variable (the last variable in Table 6-II) is zero. The results of this conventional t-test are presented in Table 6-II. Once again it is not possible to reject the hypothesis for any conventional level of confidence.

Although the differences were not statistically significant, they were present. The question of interest being two identical students who took the course with one being instructed by the

TABLE 6-II
Estimates of the Parameters of a Linear Model to Predict
Final Examination Scores
$(N = 79 \quad R^2 = .416)$

Variable	Estimated Coefficient	t value
Economics grade point average	3.136	3.478**
S.A.T.—Math	0.064	2.796**
S.A.T.—Verbal	−0.003	−0.156
Early final[1] (1 = early final; 0 = regular fiinal)	−3.692	−0.693
Age of student (in years)	−1.659	−1.055
Mad math course at Williams	−0.161	−0.058
Sex (1 = female; 0 = male)	−3.602	−1.034
Teaching experience of professor (in years)	2.672	2.673**
P.S.I. (1 = P.S.L.; 0 = Lecture)	−2.743	−0.197
P.S.L. X Economics grade point	0.686	0.392

[1] The final was given a month early to all PSI students who had finished the course and who wished to take the early final.
[2] This interaction variable is defined as the economics grade point average for PSI students and 0 for all other students.
** Statistically significant at the 99% level of confidence.

PSI method and the other by the lecture method. How much better would the PSI student have done on the final examination? We can estimate this percentage improvement for pairs of students with strikingly different past performance records in economics using the coefficients presented in Table 6-II. The result, presented in Table 6-III, is puzzling and discouraging because one hope for the PSI would have been that it would have been a boon for the previously less successful student. Because the course is based on mastery, one would expect a compacting of the final grade distribution for the PSI section.[3]

---

[3] The variance of final examination grades for the PSI section was smaller than the variance in the final grade in the two lecture sections combined and smaller than the variance in each lecture section separately; however, these differences were not statistically significant.

TABLE 6-III
Estimated Percentage Improvement in Final Examination Score
Resulting from PSI for Students of Differing Abilities

Past Economics Performance	Percentage Improvement
Highest Quartile	6.5%
High Middle Quartile	5.4%
Low Middle Quartile	4.2%
Lowest Quartile	2.3%

In order to refute or substantiate these suspicions empirically it was necessary to translate them into hypothesis tests. As a first step the score on the final examination was disaggregated into four sub-scores. The first three scores were the mutually exclusive scores achieved on each of the three parts of the examination. The main element of difference among these parts was the complexity of the questions and the time allocated to doing them. The fourth subscore was the total number of points accumulated by the student on the three questions which were less oriented toward problem solving and more oriented toward a discussion of the issues. These questions were in an essay format and clearly more subjective.

For each of these four component parts of the final examination the model was reestimated with the dependent variable being the score on that portion of the test and the independent variables remaining as they were described in Table 6-II. Then the two hypotheses described above were tested on these four new sets of data. The test that the PSI method did not make any difference could not be rejected for any conventional level of confidence.[4] Similarly, the test that improvements in final examination scores attributable to the PSI technique were the same for students with differing past performance records in economics could not be rejected for any conventional level of confidence.[5]

While these findings are consistent with the more general hypothesis that the PSI method is not severely hampered by the necessity for the unit tests to be of the short, objective variety, it is important to report the measured differences so that future experiments can determine whether or not they persist under repeated experimentation.

The information in Table 6-IV points out that the distribution of educational benefits was affected by the type of question asked. On the short answer questions, which were the ones most similar to the format of questions found on the unit tests, the students with the poorest past performance record were benefitted marginally more than students with superior past performance records.

---

[4] The F values were respectively—.401, .445, .054, and .106.
[5] The t-values were respectively—.050, .488, .262, and .420.

TABLE 6-IV

Estimated Percentage Improvement Attributable to the PSI Method
by Students of Differing Abilities on Component Parts
of the Final Exam

Past Performance in Economics	Components of the Examination			
	Short Answer	Medium Answer	Long Answer	Essay
Highest Quartile	5.6%	10.8%	1.1%	5.8%
Upper Middle Quartile	5.9%	8.4%	−0.4%	3.3%
Lower Middle Quartile	6.1%	5.8%	−2.5%	0.5%
Lowest Quartile	6.5%	2.0%	−4.7%	−4.2%

This effect, however, was offset by the rest of the examination. As the examination questions become longer, more complex and less structured the poorer students did relatively less well. For the essay questions and the long answer questions apparently the poorer student would have been better off in a lecture section.

Performance on final examinations is not the only criterion by which the educational process can be or should be judged. Other significant facets include the degree to which the course taught the student to pursue the subject matter on his own, the degree to which the course taught the student new ways to understand and evaluate problems and the degree to which the course provides a basis for discussion outside the classroom. The course evaluation instrument used at Williams, which was described above, provides one considerably less than perfect, but nonetheless useful, vehicle for assessing these other dimensions.

Table 6-V summarizes the information from the course oriented questions in this evaluation form. The table gives the mean for each method of teaching and the value of the t-ratio which is the statistic used to test whether these means are different in a statistical sense. The PSI section received a higher rating on all dimensions. In four of the five dimensions the PSI mean was significantly higher using a 95 percent level of confidence and in the remaining dimension the PSI mean was significantly higher using a 90 percent level of confidence.

As one thinks about these questions keeping in mind the method used in PSI, the statistical superiority of the PSI may be surprising. For example, one hypothesis could have been than

TABLE 6-V

Student Perceptions of Their Educational Experience in the
PSI and Lecture Sections

Course Characteristic	PSI[1] Mean	Lecture[1] Mean	Difference of Means t-ratio
Taught me to pursue subject on my own	5.59	4.36	2.93**
Stimulated me to discuss the subject in general conversation	5.07	3.81	3.69**
Increased my appreciation of the subject	5.79	4.33	4.12**
Course has taught me new ways to understand and evaluate problems	6.00	5.45	1.70*
Overall rating of the Educational Value	6.30	4.96	4.35**

[1] These are based on an ordinal scale from one to seven with seven connoting outstanding.
** Significant at the 95% level of confidence.
* Significant at the 90% level of confidence.

one of the costs of the highly individualized approach embodied in the PSI would be a drop in the interaction among students since the students could conceivably be proceeding at quite different paces. As shown in the second row in Table 6-V the students in the PSI section perceived themselves as being more stimulated to discuss microeconomics out of class than did their colleagues in the lecture sections.

In the final question the students were asked to subjectively rate the educational value of the course. The PSI sections perceived the course to be of greater educational value than did their colleagues. The course evaluation form also asks the students to describe their degree of motivation for the course by categorizing it as very high, high, moderate or low. The responses to this question by method of teaching are given as Table 6-VI. About

TABLE 6-VI

Student Perceptions of Their Degree of Motivation in the
PSI and Lecture Sections

My motivation in this course can best be described as:	PSI	Lecture
Very high	37.0	13.5
High	55.6	42.3
Moderate	7.4	30.8
Low	0.0	13.4

92 percent of the students in the PSI section proclaimed them-selves as either highly or very highly motivated while only 56 percent of the lecture sections recorded a similar degree of motiva-tion. While it cannot be determined, given the way the question was asked, how much of this difference in motivation was already present at the beginning of the semester, the differences are strik-ing. The students in the PSI section perceived themselves to be on the whole much more motivated than did their colleagues in the lecture sections.

The final piece of information contained in the course evalua-tion was a question which asked the students in retrospect to choose the method of teaching which they would believe to be the best for conducting the microeconomic theory course. The tabulated responses are presented in Table 6-VII. Of course in a question of this sort there is probably always a tendency to prefer the method chosen, but once again the differences are striking. Only one person who took the PSI would have preferred a variant of the lecture method, but almost one quarter of those in the lecture sections felt, in retrospect, that the course would be best taught by the PSI method.

One of the desirable aspects of a PSI method is that it provides any student who can master the material at a rate faster than the pace taken by the traditional lecture method with the opportunity to allocate his study time in a manner consistent with his indi-vidual program. The records kept on when each student passed each unit indicate considerable diversity among students in the time phasing of mastering the course material. Nine of the thirty-two persons finished at least one month early. Four more finished three weeks early. Two did not complete all the units, but one

TABLE 6-VII

Percentage Responses on Desired Teaching Technique
for PSI and Lecture Sections

This course would best be conducted as:	PSI	Lecture
Formal Lecture	0.0	44.0
Informal lecture with discussion	3.7	32.0
PSI	96.3	24.0
	100.0	100.0

of these was bedridden with mononucleosis during a good share of the semester.

An analysis of the person who finished at least a month early reveals, not surprisingly, that they were all B+ or above students in economics in the past. Not all such students, however, chose this rapid pace. The student who had completed the fewest number of units (5) when the first person to complete the course had finished was a straight A student in economics. This once again makes the point that the self-pacing feature of PSI is a feature which appears to benefit mostly the students who have already demonstrated a superior capability in economics.

Another of the alleged benefits of the PSI method is that is fosters a beneficial individualized contact between the student and the professor. It fosters this kind of contact by (1) releasing faculty time from lecturing and making that time available to students and (2) by meeting with the students in the classroom where any reluctance to visit the professor in his office can be circumvented. The course evaluation form allows us to test whether this benefit is empirically supported by this experiment. One of the questions on the evaluation instrument asked the student to rate the value of individual discussions with the instructor on a seven point scale as to how much they had learned from these discussions. Those who had not had such discussions were to check "doesn't apply." This question allows us to check both the degree of faculty-student interaction and the perceived value of this interaction to the learning experience. The results are presented in Table 6-VIII.

It would appear that at least for this experiment the PSI

TABLE 6-VIII

A Comparison of the Degree of Participation in and the Mean Ordinal Value of Individual Discussions with the Instructor in Lecture and PSI Sections

	PSI	Lecture
Percentage Reporting Individual Discussions	74.1	47.4
Mean Ordinal Contribution to Learning (on a Seven Point Scale	5.75	3.74

method is not the same as in a regular lecture course. Most of the input differences would be reflected in differences in the monetary cost of running the course, but two would not—faculty time and student time. Faculty time is not fully reflected in the cost because the instructor is paid in terms of the number of sections taught and his salary is not systematically related to the amount of time that he or she puts in preparing for that class. Thus two teaching techniques may appear to cost the same when in fact one, by its very nature, takes much more time to prepare. For this reason faculty time will be considered separately.

Similarly student time is not part of the monetary cost. Since the PSI method requires the student to take a more active role in his education, he or she may well have to work harder, which may affect his or her other courses. Therefore, the demands on student time made by this PSI course and its impact on other courses will also be examined separately below.

Faculty Time

Of interest to faculty members is the question, "how much time does it take to prepare a PSI course as compared to a lecture course?" The first difference between these two techniques is that for PSI sections the workload tends to be redistributed more toward the beginning of the course. Generally it is recommended that at least one half of the units and unit tests be completed before the class starts.

The comparison of the total amounts of time involved depends on the circumstances. After running this experiment it is clear that the total time devoted to setting up a course of this type was on the order of one and one-half times as much as if devoted to setting up a lecture course the first time one teaches it. For instructors who have been teaching the same course for some years and who intend to teach it again with only minor modifications the initial additional time required to switch to a PSI method would be much greater.

The main dimension of the PSI method which leads to this differential is the necessity for writing up to four different tests for each unit (to allow for multiple failures). Writing this number of test questions which are comprehensive, fair and which satisfy the educational objectives is a difficult proposition. However, once the materials have been developed the time devoted to the PSI method would appear to be only minimally higher as long as the basic structure of the course remained the same. The reason for its being minimally higher is that modifications of the course are slightly more difficult in a PSI course since they have to be carefully rewritten for the student, whereas in a lecture course it is possible to jot down the change on the lecture notes and deliver the embellishment extemporaneously.

Student Time

The course evaluation form provides some information on student perceptions of the workload in a PSI course as compared to the perceptions of students in the lecture sections. As reflected in Table 6-IX it is clear that more of the PSI students perceived their workload as being heavier than average than did the students in the lecture sections.

Although the students seemed to find this extra work educationally well spent, the question remains as to whether or not this increased workload would lower student performance in other courses. To answer this question the grade point average for the other courses taken during the same semester as the microeconomics class was computed for every student in the sample. Then for the total population this other course grade point average was regressed against (1) the cumulative grade point average at the beginning of the semester and (2) a binary variable indicating whether or not the student was a member of

TABLE 6-IX

Student Perceptions of Workload (Percentage)

The workload for this course in relation to other Williams Courses was:		PSI	Lecture
Much lighter		0.0	2.0
Lighter		10.7	11.5
About the same		21.4	57.7
Heavier		64.3	25.0
Much Heavier		3.6	3.8
	Total	100.0	100.0

a PSI section. The PSI students did better in their other courses than would have been expected purely on their grade point average, but the difference is not statistically significant. It would certainly appear that the PSI method does not detract from the other courses.

In conclusion neither the most damaging arguments against the PSI system nor the most compelling arguments for it were upheld by this experiment. It does not appear to be inherently biased toward the accomplishment of simple educational objectives. Neither the areas on which it achieved better results than the lecture method nor the areas on which it fell behind the results for the lecture method were characterized by differences large enough to be statistically significant. It does not appear to provide a boon for the below average student as long as the course must be completed within a deadline.

It does, however, provide an alternative educational option which, while not dominating the other methods, does seem to offer students a choice which they value. Used prudently the PSI method can make a valuable addition to our arsenal of teaching techniques in economics. This contribution can either take the form of replacing certain lecture courses by PSI or by adopting one or more of the PSI features for incorporation into a conventional lecture course.

A COMPARISON OF THE PERSON-ALIZED SYSTEM OF INSTRUCTION WITH THE LECTURE METHOD IN TEACHING ELEMENTARY DYNAMICS

P. A. Rosati

As a direct result of the great success that many college teachers had experienced with the Personalized System of Instruction, it was resolved in 1972 to develop the second year dynamics course at the University of Western Ontario into the PSI format. An intermediate step in the transition from the lecture method to the PSI method was accomplished during the academic year 1972/73, in which the Dynmaics course was presented to half the students as a lecture course and to the other half as a PSI course.

This paper describes the comparison of the lecture group with the PSI group on the basis of examination performance, time spent on the course and student opinion as expressed in questionnaires.

METHOD

The second year Dyamics course was divided into fourteen equal difficulty units. Each unit contained detailed references to three standard texts together with notes and sample problems. Five readiness tests were written for each unit.

The seventy-five students who registered for the course were divided into two equal ability groups on the basis of their performance in the first year Mechanics course. The two groups were designated the PSI group and the lecture group and the average mark in each group is shown in Table 7-I under the heading of original mark. Despite considerable opposition, no student was permitted to change groups.

The lecture group, taught by the author, was given two lecture hours and one tutorial hour each week. The PSI group was proctored by three undergraduates (one third year and two fourth year) and there were three one-and-a-half hours sessions each week. Although the author attended many of these sessions, he purposely refrained from tutoring.

The course was twenty four weeks long. All student wrote a common Christmas examination at the end of the eleventh week and a common final examination at the end of the twenty-fourth week. The final mark which a student received for the course was generally the average of these two examinations together with the coursework mark. A student in the PSI group attained a coursework mark of 100 percent if he completed all units.

TABLE 7-I

Summary of Average Marks and Times for Both
Lecture Group and PSI Group

	PSI Group		Lecture Group	
	Mean	Standard Deviation	Mean	Standard Deviation
Original Mark (%)	67.6	12.0	66.2	14.0
Christmas Exam Mark (%)	69.5	14.6	67.0	15.8
Improvement (%)	1.9		0.8	
Final Exam Mark (%)	73.6	14.2	67.3	16.8
Improvement (%)	6.0		1.1	
Time (Hours)				
First Term	51.1	17.3	50.9	12.1
Second Term	46.1	18.4	50.2	20.0
Total	97.2		101.1	
Number of Students	38		37	
Withdrawals	3		1	
Did Not Write Final	1		1	

The lecture group was required to produce a record each week of the time they had spent on Dynamics. The PSI group declared the time they had spent on each unit when they requested a readiness test. The opinions of the PSI group were sought in three questionnaires which were submitted during the second, twelfth and twenty-second weeks of the course.

RESULTS AND DISCUSSION

The results of the study are described below under the separate headings of performance, times and student opinions.

Performance

The results of the two common examinations, the Christmas examination and the final examination, are stated numerically in Table 7-I and plotted as histograms in Figure 7-1. The PSI group performed 1 percent better than the lecture group on the Christmas examination and 5 percent better on the final examination. This difference is significant at the 5 percent level. It seemed, in the second term that the PSI group accepted the new teaching method as a valid one, but nevertheless, in their questionnaire responses, did not express any marked preference for the method.

The correlation between the original mark and the final examination mark was 0.18 for the PSI group and 0.64 for the lecture group. These correlations would support the contention that the PSI group had been effectively encouraged to break their previous work patterns and make independent efforts. The lecture group, who spent approximately the same time on the course, continued to work in their accustomed, less effective manner.

An attempt was made to compare the effectiveness of the PSI method with the bright students to the effectiveness of the method with the dull students. The students in each group were further divided on the basis of their original mark into "above mean" and "below mean." The final examination student performance in each of these sub-groups is shown in Table 7-II. It is noticeable that the below average student in the PSI group improved ten percent more than the below average student in the lecture group. This was a surprising and humbling result for the lecturer who

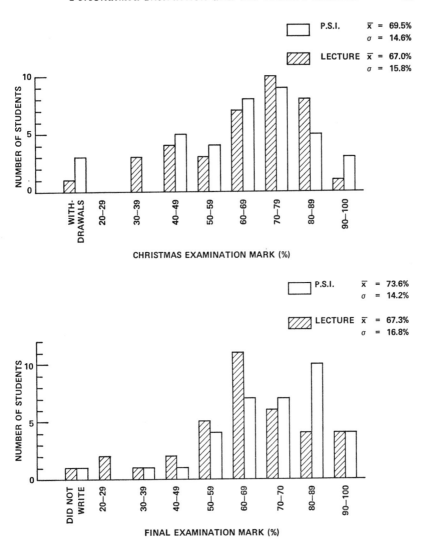

Figure 7-1. Comparative performance of the two groups in common examinations

had considered that his lectures were particularly useful for the below average group. Figure 7-2 shows the final examination performance in terms of the original student grade. There is little difference in performance between the lecture group and the PSI group for those students who originally were grade A or

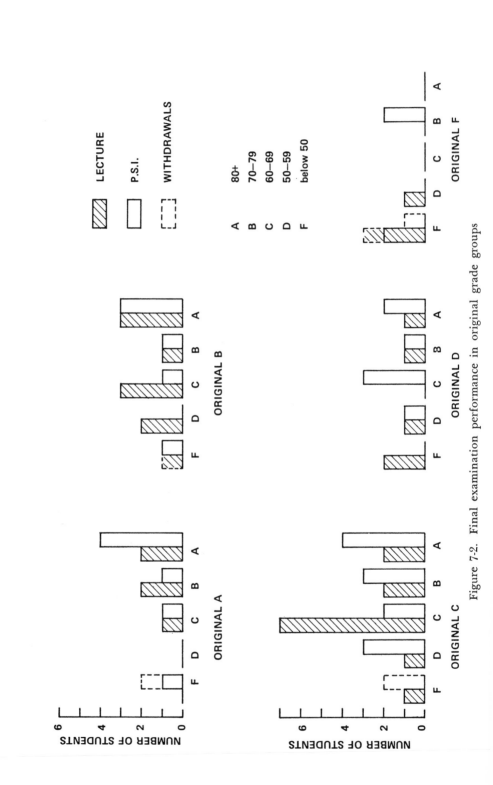

Figure 7-2. Final examination performance in original grade groups

TABLE 7-II

Performance of Above Average Students Compared with
Performance of Below Average Students

	PSI		Lecture	
	Above Mean of 67.6%	Below Mean of 67.6%	Above Mean of 66.2%	Below Mean of 66.2%
Number of Students	16	18	16	19
Original Mean Mark	77.7%	58.7%	77.0%	57.0%
Final Exam Mean Mark	74.7%	72.5%	75.4%	60.5%
Improvement	−3.0%	13.8%	−1.6%	3.5%

grade B. For those students who were originally in the lower grades (C, D, and F) it is noticeable that the PSI group performed better.

Three students withdrew from the PSI group whereas only one student withdrew from the lecture group. It should be noted, however, that all these withdrawals were withdrawals from the complete Engineering program and not just from the Dynamics course.

Times

Histograms of the times spent on the course by each of the two groups are shown in Figure 7-3. Contrary to the findings of other experimenters[1,3,5,7,9] there is little difference in average time between the two groups and, in fact, the PSI group spent about four percent less total time than the lecture group. Possibly the out-of-class communication between the two groups tended to constrain them to spend approximately the same time on the course.

In order to check the veracity of the times quoted by the students a short questionnaire was anonymously completed by them in the subsequent academic year. The questionnaire results claimed overwhelmingly that the original time estimates had been accurate and that there was "absolutely no advantage to the student misquoting his time."

In the first term, as expected, the standard deviation of the times for the PSI group was 30 percent higher than for the lecture group. However, the second term, the standard deviation of the times for the lecture group was about 10 percent higher

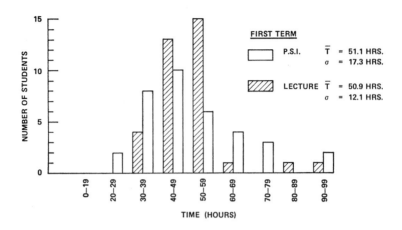

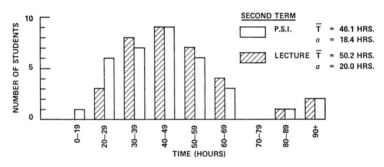

Figure 7-3. Comparative times spent on the course by the two groups

than for the PSI group. This reveals that by the second term the lecture group developed a degree of self-pacing and allocated to the course only that amount of time they considered necessary for success. The rate at which the PSI students proceeded through the course is shown graphically in Figure 7-4. It is noticeable that the class average curve is forced towards the uniform progress curve by the Christmas examination of the twelfth and the final examination of the twenty-fourth week. Similarly the examinations prevented the procrastinator from going unchecked throughout the whole course. On the other hand it was felt that the fast student would have finished the course in about ten weeks if there had been no examinations.

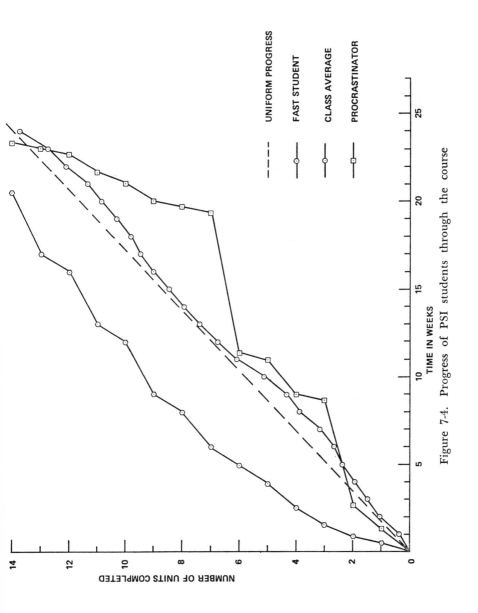

Figure 7-4. Progress of PSI students through the course

The rate at which the PSI group wrote the readiness tests is shown in Figure 7-5. Apart from peaks before the Christmas and final examinations, the number of tests written each week were surprisingly uniform at about twenty-two. This uniformity successfully disguises the fact that there was no regular pattern in the way any individual student wrote his tests. Each students' tests record clearly expresses the go-at-your-own-pace feature of the course, and the composite record of all students demonstrates clearly the individual manner in which each student progresses through the course.

The average time spent on each unit by the PSI group is shown in Figure 7-6. With the exception of unit 3, which proved cumbersome, the graph confirms that the author was successful in writing equal difficulty units. The vast difference between the lowest and highest time curves accentuates the students' individuality.

The distribution of the recycles on the readiness tests is shown

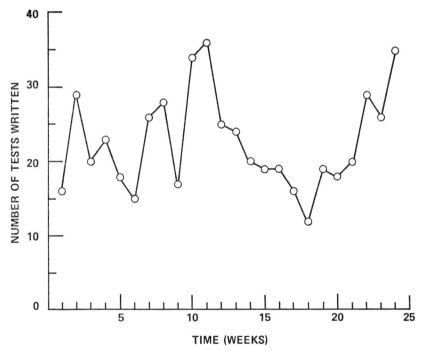

Figure 7-5. Rate at which PSI group wrote readiness tests

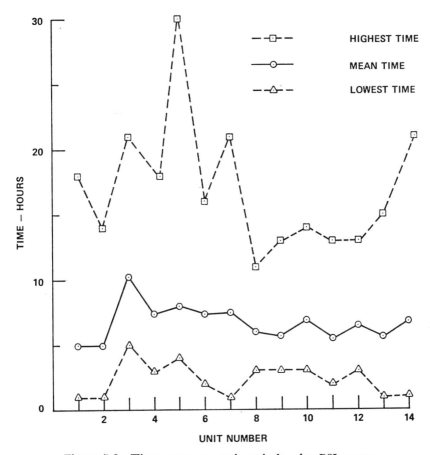

Figure 7-6. Time spent on each unit by the PSI group

in Figure 7-7. Most of the recycling (70 %) was done in the first term: by the second, most of the students used the unit objectives carefully and did not present themselves unprepared for a readiness test. Also, by the second term, the proctors developed a more lenient marking technique and allowed the student to "patch up his math and calculations."

Student Opinion

The PSI group expressed their opinion of the new teaching method by completing three separate questionnaires during the second, twelfth and twenty-second weeks of the course.

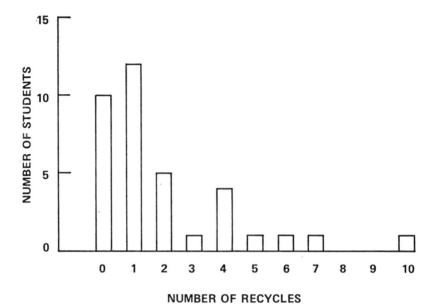

NUMBER OF RECYCLES

Figure 7-7. Distribution of the readiness test recycles in the PSI group

The students were not markedly impressed with PSI; 50 percent of them thought it was a better teaching method, yet sixty-six acknowledged that it had improved their study skills and would be willing to take another PSI course.

The most enthusiastic responses related to the undergraduate proctors: about 90 percent of the students enjoyed working with the proctors, thought the proctors were efficient, and that they did indeed "personalize" the course. Teaching was a new experience for the proctors, and they worked very hard to make the course a success. The students inevitably sensed and responded to this enthusiasm.

The author was not directly involved in proctoring the students, for he was teaching the "rival" lecture group, but he was frequently present in the PSI study room and was most impressed by the general industry and enthusiasm of the students.

The PSI experiment in the second year Dynamics course was considered successful in that the PSI group outperformed the lecture group by 5 percent at a significance level of 5 percent on a common final examination. Unlike previous experiments the PSI group achieved their success without spending extra time on the course. The students were not overly enthusiastic about the new teaching technique but expressed great praise for the student proctors.

It is felt that the PSI group in this experiment were limited by some of the constraints of the lecture group. The author certainly was constrained not to unduly interfere with the PSI group, and he welcomes the opportunity next year to conduct the whole Dynamics course using the PSI approach.

PSI IN A BUSINESS PERSONNEL COURSE

MARK HAMMER

AFTER AN INITIAL CONTACT with PSI in the Fall of 1972, a decision was made to implement it the following spring semester in a junior-level course in personnel administration enrolling about 150 students. Gearing up for a full PSI implementation in such a short time was only possible because the previous semester's approach in this course included a well-developed program of performance objectives, student-scheduled repeatable testing, and personalization (Hammer & Henderson, 1973; Hammer, Henderson & Johnson, 1972).

In designing the PSI procedures to be used benefit was derived from the experiences reported by Keller (1968), Green (1971), and Dressler (1972), and from the workable techniques developed and described by Born (1971). This report will describe the course procedures used, report some results measured and observed, and discuss briefly some possible implications.

The author would like to acknowledge the helpful comments on an earlier draft of this paper made by Professors Obert Henderson, James Horrell, James Johnston, and Chem Narayana. The project upon which this paper is based was made possible by grants from the Business Development Fund and the SHBl51 Innovation Development Funds at Washington State University.

METHOD

Course Organization

The topics to be covered in the course were divided into thirteen units consisting of one orientation unit, nine content units, and three review units. For each of these units, written objectives were prepared for those concepts considered sufficiently basic to justify requiring mastery by all students; these were referred to as "basic objectives." Basic objectives were distributed in the form of one-page handouts, each of which included between six and fifteen performance objectives for the nonreview units.

The minimal requirement for all students to earn a passing ("D") grade was that they master the basic objectives specified for each of the thirteen units of the course. Demonstrating this mastery required the student to pass each of thirteen basic objectives unit tests with 100 percent correctness, and a basic objectives final examination at 90 percent. Unit tests were administered by proctors, and the final exam was administered by the course instructor.

Students could qualify for "C" or "B" course grades by pursuing optional learning activities, mainly written reports on articles from a readings book, in-depth tests over single chapters of the text, and attendance at optional enrichment activities such as films, guest speakers, and lectures. Completing these activities earned "grade points," and students aspiring to a "C" or "B" course grade were required to maintain a minimum pace of grade points completed *week by week* throughout the semester.

Since the "D" grade requirement was quite arbitrary and highly structured, and the "B" and "C" requirements gave some freedom but were still quite structured in specifying the possible options available, it was decided to give students wide freedom of possible projects and activities to earn the "A" grade. Proctors were delegated the responsibility for approving proposals by their students, for supervising progress, and for evaluating the final products and recommending a grade. A one-pace set of broad guidelines was provided to both students and proctors concerning amount of effort expected and general criteria for evaluation.

Basic Objectives Tests

For each basic objective unit, a series of computer-generated parallel test forms was prepared (cf. Hammer & Henderson, 1972a; 1972b), with each form having objective and short-answer essay questions which together covered all objectives contained in the unit. Students could take a unit test at any time from their proctors, and were allowed to take as many tests as necessary (with no penalty for failure) to obtain their proctor's certification of 100 percent mastery for a particular unit. Each student's cumulative progress in passing basic objectives tests was charted on a 5x8 card which showed clearly the units to be completed versus the weeks remaining in the course.

Pre-printed forms for appealing test questions were made continuously available to students and their use was encouraged by awarding grade points to students who used them to point out erroneous or misleading questions or to suggest improved versions. The instructor answered all appeals in writing, and both the appeals and his answers were entered in a three-ring binder where they were available to all students for inspection.

Undergraduate Proctors

Applications for course proctor were solicited from among students who had completed the course earlier with a grade of "B" or better. The prospectus accompanying the application blank described the terms and conditions: proctors would be expected to spend four "duty hours" per week in the learning center, to attend weekly proctor meetings, to do advanced readings and submit written reports, to accept responsibility for tutoring ten to thirteen students, to grade tests and reading reports from these students and provide fast, constructive feedback, to keep accurate records on the progress and problems of each student, and to work closely with the senior instructor and the course manager (an undergraduate assistant who was paid to manage records and materials) to evaluate course structure and student reactions. In return for this, proctors received three semester hours of credit in an upper-division course.

Criteria for selection of proctors included ratings of dependability, personal integrity, desire to help others in a tutoring role, emotional maturity and stability, and academic achievement, in roughly that order of importance.

Recorded Mini-Lectures

For each of the nine content units of the course the thirteen proctors and a "mini-lecture" was taped for the benefit of students who preferred the aural mode of learning or who needed additional assistance in understanding the text and other materials. These tapes addressed the basic objectives specified for that unit and attempted to explain each of them. Since the proctors were responsible for reviewing their mastery of basic objectives prior to the taping session, they were freshly aware of the ambiguitis of the printed material and of the places where help was most needed, and were ready to provide helpful suggestions and elaboration. The resulting mini-lecture tapes were between ten and twenty-five minutes in length. Duplicate copies were made available in the library's listening laboratory and in the learning center.

RESULTS AND DISCUSSION

Attendance at the final examination period was required of all PSI students even though most of them had previously completed all requirements for the grade to which they aspired. This requirement served the purpose of obtaining course evaluations from students and of gathering final test performance data to compare with that of the previous semester's students.

Subject Matter Mastery

Two forms of the final examination were prepared for the PSI class in order to schedule an alternate exam period. Forms A and B of the final test each contained four parts: Parts 1 and 2 had forty objective questions apiece, and Parts 3 and 4 each had one comprehensive essay question. Form A was identical to the final test given the previous semester. The forty true-false, multiple-choice, and fill-in questions in Part 1 were drawn from a bank of some five thousand questions which had been previously written by the author and a colleague in connection with a program of computer generated repeatable testing (Hammer & Henderson, 1972a; 1972b). Part 2 of the final test consisted of forty of the eighty true-false, multiple-choice, and matching questions contained in a pre-printed achievement test supplied by the textbook publisher. Test Form A contained the odd-numbered questions from this achievement test and Test Form B contained the even-numbered questions.

For both Part 1 and Part 2 of the final exam, mean test scores on Forms A and B were nearly identical; neither difference approached significance. These scores were subsequently combined for analysis. Composing essay questions for Parts 3 and 4 of Form B which were parallel in score and difficulty to those on Form A proved more difficult; mean essay scores for Forms A and B differed significantly. Consequently, only the scores from Form A, which had questions identical to those asked a semester earlier, are reported here. This meant that all data gathered for the PSI students was based on questions which had been composed prior to the PSI course and prior to the formation of any plans to use them for comparative purposes.

Student performance scores on comparable questions of the final tests for fall 1972 (pre-PSI) and spring 1973 (PSI) are summarized in Table 8-I. The scores of PSI students were significantly lower than those of pre-PSI students on Part 1 objective questions, and nonsignificantly lower on the publisher's

TABLE 8-1

Mean Final Exam Scores, PSI v. Pre-PSI

	Fall 1972 (Pre-PSI)	Spring 1973 (PSI)	t (2-tail) p (t)
Part 1: 40 Objective Questions	31.1 (N = 100)	28.6 (N = 126)	5.08 $p < .001$
Part 2: 40 Objective Questions	25.3 (N = 100)	24.4 (N = 126)	1.648 $p < .05$
Part 3: Essay Question "A"	12.2 (N = 100)	16.2 (N = 75)	$p < .001$
Part 4: Essay Question "B"	7.3 (N = 100)	12.9 (N = 75)	$p < .001$

objective achievement questions in Part 2. In contrast, PSI student performance on the essay questions of Parts 3 and 4 was considerably better than that of pre-PSI students.

Interpretation of Table 8-I data should be made in light of several considerations which reflect the fact that formal evaluation of the PSI approach was secondary to concerns of implementation and survival during this first-semester experience. First, PSI students had no formal grade-related motivation for performing well on the exam; their grades had been determined by the time the exam was given, and they knew it. In contrast, 25 percent of the course grade was determined by final exam performance in the pre-PSI course.

Secondly, pre-PSI students had considerably more exposure during their course to objective test questions of the type used in Parts 1 and 2 of the final exam than did the PSI students; for the pre-PSI students performance on such objective tests was the largest factor determining final course grades, and thanks to the then-existing program of student-scheduled repeatable testing, they received lots of practice.

Third, many PSI students exhibited unexpected hostility toward the requirement of taking a final exam. Many of them were not convinced that there was a good reason, and were consequently very casual about taking the test. They also expressed their displeasure on the course evaluation forms.

Finally, the instructor graded all the essay questions for these two groups. While he followed closely a structured set of rules for scoring various responses in order to improve reliability, he of course knew that the most recent group was all PSI students. Methodologists would correctly point to the possibility of experimenter bias at this point; ideally, the essay exams should have been scored by raters who were blind to the experimental condition. Unfortunately, the exam papers of the pre-PSI students were readily distinguishable from those of the PSI students, and an unbiased rating would have required the transcription of all responses, plus grading. It was decided that the added credibility to be gained did not justify the effort since this is basically a description report of a first-semester PSI experience and not a tight empirical comparison.

Performance on the comprehensive essay questions of Parts 3 and 4 was heavily dependent upon thorough understanding of basic course concepts. Since one of the major differences between the PSI and pre-PSI groups was the mastery learning requirement applied to basic objectives, the comparison of the PSI students' performance on these questions to that of their predecessors was important. Figures 8-1 and 8-2 show how the distribution of essay scores differed between the PSI and the pre-PSI classes. It can be seen that for both questions the proportion of students receiving low scores was substantially lower among the PSI group. This would seem to be a natural consequence of the application of the mastery learning philosophy.

Student Attitudes

The four-page form which solicited student evaluation of instructional techniques asked for both open-ended comments and quantifiable ratings on various aspects of the course.

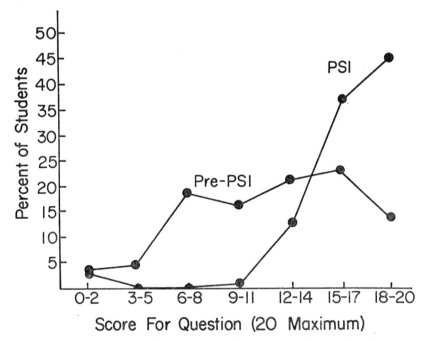

Figure 8-1. Distribution of exam scores for essay question "A" PSI v. pre-PSI students (PSI course spring 1973, n=75. Pre PSI course fall 1972, N=100

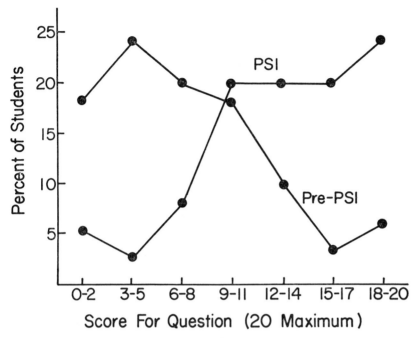

Figure 8-2. Distribution of Exam scores for essay question "B" PSI v. pre-PSI students (PSI course spring 1973, n=75 Pre PSI course Fall 1972 N=100

An "overall evaluation" of basic objectives tests was solicited on a seven-point rating scale. Students were asked to compare these tests with testing procedures used in the "typical" or average course. A total of five students (7.1%) rated the basic objectives tests as "slightly worse," "considerably worse," or "much worse." In contrast, 109 students (85.8%) rated them as "slightly better," "considerably better," or "much better."

Open-ended comments on basic objectives tests indicated that students especially liked the repeatability feature, the immediate grading of tests by the proctor, and the fairness in evaluation and grading. The 100 percent grading standard drew criticism from a few, but the majority indicated that they felt this to be a fair requirement as long as tests were repeatable and immediate feedback and tutoring were available.

Each student was asked to rate his own proctor, using a seven-point scale, on each of the following characteristics: fairness in grading, helpfulness, provision of encouragement and recognition, availability, honesty, knowledge of subject matter, and ability to explain difficult concepts. The average rating given by 127 students to proctors on all of these characteristics was highly favorable; for all but one, the mean ratings exceeded 6.0. The characteristic receiving the lowest average rating, "knowldege of subject matter," still received a distinct modal rating of 6, or "very good."

Student ratings of other course features on the seven-point scale were mixed. Generally favorable ratings were given to the basic objectives mini-lectures (mean ratings: 5.9), the basic objectives hand-outs (6.5), and the learning center (6.0). On the other hand, relatively unfavorable ratings went to depth tests (4.4), readings reports (4.6), and enrichment activities (4.8), and each of these is being revised in light of the accompanying student comments. Finally, favorable overall evaluation was reflected in the ratings for "amount of useful information learned" (6.1) and "overall evaluation of this course" (5.6)

Students were asked to estimate the average time requirements of the course, to compare this time with the requirements of other courses, and to indicate whether or not they felt the requirement was reasonable. Time estimates varied widely between one and twenty hours per week. Sixty-five percent of the students indicated that they spent either "slightly more" or "much more" time, 17 percent indicated "about the same," and 18 percent checked "slightly less" or "much less." In spite of these heavier-than-average time requirement estimates, a two-to-one majority of the students indicated that they thought the time required was reasonable.

When asked if they would like to be a course proctor if they had the opportunity, students responded forty-nine yes, fifty no, twenty-eight undecided. Finally, in response to the question, "would you recommend this course to a friend?", the tally was ninety yes, sixteen no and twenty-one undecided.

Proctor Performance

The most gratifying aspect of this adaptation of the PSI approach was the performance of the thirteen undergraduate proctors—they were *magnificent*. Several indicators can be cited to suggest the extraordinary nature of their contribution to the course.

One index of proctor response would be the amount of time which they voluntarily spent in the learning center during "off-duty" hours. Whereas each proctor was formally obligated to be available in the learning center for four scheduled hours weekly, in actuality they averaged between twice and three times that much time. During an evaluation interview at the end of the semester one proctor proctor estimated that he had *averaged* thirty hours a week in the learning center during the semester. Each one of the thirteen exceeded not only my formal requirements but my expectations in his willingness, or rather eagerness, to be available to provide help when needed.

A second index of proctor response is the previously-mentioned ratings they received from their students on anonymous course evaluation forms. Considering the diversity of personalities and backgrounds existing among thirteen proctors and 150 students, it seemed amazing that the students were so uniformly positive in rating their proctors. Only a handful of students gave below-average ratings on any dimension to their proctors, and overall, proctors fared much better than did instructor-controlled variables.

A third indication of proctor response was their enthusiasm during the weekly proctor meetings. Despite the fact that these meetings frequently lasted for over two hours, they were constantly an enjoyable occasion for all concerned.

A fourth indication of proctor response was evaluations by the proctors themselves of the value of the proctoring experience. While objective data was not collected from them, as a result of close informal contact with them it is strongly felt that each of the thirteen would subscribe to all of the following statements:

> I have put considerably more time in this (proctoring) course than I have in typical three-hour courses;
>
> In spite of the extra time I am glad that I have been a proctor this semester, and would recommend it to a qualified friend;
>
> I feel that I have gotten as much or more out of this than the students I have helped;

I feel sure that I will remember this experience as one of the most rewarding and worthwhile of my undergraduate career;

I feel that my involvement in this course, along with that of the other proctors, has made the course a substantially stronger educational experience for the students involved than most other college courses;

I feel that my understanding of the course content is much better than it was just after I finished the course as a student.

A final subjective reflection of proctor performance is the course grades which they received. They were told at the beginning of the semester that the baseline grade for satisfactory fulfillment of the requirements of the proctor role was "B," that a proctor who "let me down" once would be put in the "C" grade category, that a repeated failure to meet formal requirements would result in dismissal with a "W," and that "A" grades would be given only to proctors who exceeded my expectations for contributing to the fulfillment of course goals. At the end of the semester "A" grades were given to all thirteen proctors with no qualms whatsoever.

Tapes, Appeals, and "A-Level" Projects

The semester was begun with some apprehension about prospects for the taped mini-lectures as a result of earlier unsuccessful attempts to create tape recorded learning materials for use in mini-courses (Hammer, Henderson, & Johnson, 1972). Thus it was gratifying to see that the mini-lecture tapes were being used regularly by a majority of students enrolled. It is estimated that about thirty percent of the students used the tapes religiously as primary learning sources, another 40 percent used them most of the time to supplement other resources, and thirty percent used them seldom or never. It seems that they provided a preferable alternative learning resource for a substantial segment of students, and that they were an effective use of both instructional time and low-cost hardware.

Students made heavy use of the forms provided for appealing test questions. Some 250 appeals were received during the semester, of which roughly 80 percent were awarded grade points.

This meant that a considerable amount of time was spent responding to test question appeals and revising questions, but a much stronger test item bank also resulted. The most important outcome though, is that the appeal opportunity provided a constructive outlet for frustrations related to test questions, and probably greatly reduced the likelihood of tests being perceived as arbitrary or aversive. The amount of learning reflected in an appeal was impressive. In order to bolster their cases students often combed the text thoroughly, checked alternate sources, and even consulted other faculty members.

Another source of uncertainty going into the course was the decision to delegate responsibility for "A-grade" projects to the proctors. Happily, occasional nightmares of several possible versions of disaster were not realized and this feature worked out very well. After reviewing and reflecting upon the sixty-eight projects which were submitted for "A" grades, the following conclusions seem appropriate:

a) There was no way for the instructor to have personally supervised the sheer number of projects which were undertaken by students in my class.

b) The quality of projects ranged from marginal to outstanding. The instructor would have denied credit to about 10 percent of them.

c) The proportion of "unconventional" projects was impressive, and included field trips, surveys, interviews with business executives, creation of audio tapes, photography, collections of sample forms and tests used by various organizations, and even a dramatic production to illustrate course principles.

Despite repeated pleas for more guidance on "A"projects, it is strongly felt that the benefits of providing wide freedom and minimal structure outweigh the costs. For one thing, highly gifted students are more likely to apply their best efforts when precise requirements or expectations are left unspecified. For another, the students collectively embody a large reservior of talent, experiences, group memberships, and business contacts having potential for unique applications of course concepts. Only by providing an environment supportive of innovation can this diversity be usefully related to academic work.

One Hundred Percent Mastery Requirement

The requirement for 100 percent mastery on basic objectives tests frequently attracts comment. Both students and teachers who first learn of this requirement frequently respond with disbelief: "You've gotta be kidding," or "That's impossible," or "You must ask terribly easy questions."

A key characteristic of the basic objectives tests which made 100 percent mastery feasible was that they were graded by the students' proctors immediately after being taken. The significant difference is that proctors are able to discuss any questions missed with the student and may give credit on the spot for errors due to ambiguous test questions or simple misunderstandings. Each question missed on a basic objectives test thus becomes a cue for the proctor to quiz the student further to discover whether in fact he has mastered the learning objective to which the question relates. Thus technically the 100 percent requirement does not mean that a student who missed one question fails, but that he fails if he can't convince his proctor that he understands the related objective.

The reasonableness of 100 percent mastery requirements seems to depend upon three conditions: 1) the identification of truly essential concepts through written objectives, 2) the close coordination of test questions to objectives, and 3) proctor grading. Given these three conditions the conclusion of an earlier PSI developer that one should not compromise on the 100 percent requirement seems appropriate. The difference between 100 percent and 90 percent requirements may not sound like much, but in fact the philosophical and psychological differences are major.

Course Grades

The distribution of final course grades given to the PSI class contained 48 percent "A's," 27 percent "B's," 5 percent "C's," 14 percent "D's," 6 percent "F's," and no incompletes.

It should first be pointed out that higher course grades were not earned by following the numbers or by sheer perseverence through highly structured learning materials. Nor were higher grades based on the quantity of units completed, as is the case in many PSI courses. In this class lower levels of learning (memory, retention, and recall) were the concern of the basic objectives, and students mastering these earned a "D" course grade. Earning credit toward higher grades involved higher levels of learning (analysis, synthesis, and critical evaluation) and also involved a shift in emphasis away from content and toward process.

At the lower end of the grade scale, most of the "D's" given were to students enrolled in the course "pass-fail," and the minimum grade requirement to earn a "pass" was a "D." In the past some teachers have frequently felt a mixture of anger and guilt about pass-fail students—anger that they qualified for a "pass" with so little effort, and guilt that others had been cheated by awarding passing grades to these students after such little achievement. In contrast, each passing student in the PSI course mastered all basic objectives and demonstrated that mastery by passing thirteen basic objectives tests at 100 percent and a final basic objectives exam at 90 percent. These students then elected not to pursue optional enrichment activities for a higher course grade.

In many courses students enrolling pass-fail end up with marginal understanding of a haphazard assortment of concepts covered by the course. The philosophy of allowing students to enroll pass-fail makes more sense under a PSI arrangement— students can elect minimal effort or involvement in a certain area but can still be assumed to have understood the basics if they pass the course.

Keller and Postlethwait, among others, have suggested that instructors of self-paced courses should be prepared to be generous with the incomplete grades, arguing that a course in not truly individually-paced unless a student has the freedom to go at a slower-than-average pace and finish after the end of the semester. This permissive stance toward incomplete grades was not adopted for several reasons. First, an important distinction needs to be made between macro-scheduling and micro-scheduling. Allowing students to schedule their own learning activities within each day, week, or even each month no doubt constitutes a major improvement over traditional instructional practice. However, one problem is that the ready availability of incomplete grades allows (or maybe even invites) students to postpone self-paced work in favor of other less flexible classes. Another problem is that it allows students an easy escape from attaining their own goals. Allowing an easy escape from a self-imposed crunch may not be the best thing to do for students. At the macro-scheduling level students already have self-pacing—they may choose to take five courses, or three or six courses, with each new term.

In summary, the following generalizations reported to be emerging from other applications were confirmed by this experience:

a) students in PSI courses report spending considerably more time than in traditional classes, and they also drop out in greater numbers;

b) students who finish PSI courses are usually given higher grades than in traditional classes;

c) final examination performance of PSI students is mixed, some reports of no differences and some of superior PSI performance;

d) students are highly favorable in their ratings of the PSI approach;

e) undergraduate proctors seem especially to benefit from the system.

AN INNOVATION FOR INTRODUC- TORY SOCIOLOGY: PERSONALIZED SYSTEM OF INSTRUCTION

Susan G. Clark

In the fall of 1972 an experimental section of introductory sociology was introduced into the curriculum at Georgetown University. The course, modelled on Keller's (1968) Personalized System of Instruction, was self-paced (within the confines of a semester), mastery-oriented, and student proctored.

The purpose of this paper is to describe the Keller plan as applied to sociology, and the replicate earlier studies (McMichael and Corey, 1969; Sheppard and MacDermot, 1970) which had demonstrated PSI student's superior performance on final examinations when compared to students in Lecture sections.

The Keller plan has not been frequently adapted for teaching sociology. Perhaps one reason for this is that many assume the emphasis on mastery requires a coherent and consistent body of material to master. Within the field of sociology there is little agreement about "correct theories or even true facts." This need not be limiting, however, for the instructor can alert the student to controversies within the discipline by his or her choice of reading materials and through notes incorporated in the study

Reprinted from *Teaching Sociology*, volume 1, number 2 (April 1974) (c) by permission of the Publisher, Sage Publications, Incorporated.

guides. The student, of course, must be informed that the material in the study guides is of equal importance to the readings, and that he is responsible for this material in the unit tests. Thus lectures, or at least mini-lectures, can be communicated to the student in written form. Without this flexibility, the PSI could not easily be made suitable for teaching sociology.

METHOD

During the first year of teaching with the PSI method, one text book and four paperback books constituted the course materials. The text was in the traditional format, and the paperbacks were chosen to reflect differing points of view within the discipline. Each of the paperbacks equalled one unit. Two of the unit tests on the paperbacks were conducted orally with groups of three to six students. This worked well with a class of sixty, but proved too time consuming in the second semester with a class of eighty. In the fall semester first day of class, the students received a syllabus and a general information sheet which included operation and study procedures, grading specifications, and a chart for recording individual progress. Then the students picked up the study guide for Unit I and left. This was the only time the class was together.

Since there were no funds to pay proctors, the first four students who successfully completed Units I and II were invited to become proctors. This follows Sherman's (1971) suggestion to use students taking the course as proctors. Those four students became so interested in the course that they continued to proctor throughout the semester. This situation does not often occur; usually students progressing most rapidly fluctuate during a semester. During the spring semester, when the PSI method was again used in a larger class, five students proctored during each class period, but twelve students participated in proctoring throughout the semester.

The question of the capability of undergraduate proctors has been raised. Much of the course does depend on how well the proctors perform. There are several checks on the proctors. First, each proctor has detailed answer sheets for each test prepared by the instructor. Also proctors sign each test paper which they grade. All proctors knew that the instructor would occasionally reread test papers. This tended to keep them from being too lenient and provided the proctors with an excuse to give students who might be pressuring them.

The student response to student proctors was quite favorable. In response to a questionnaire[1] students agreed with the statement, "I took advantage of the opportunity to ask questions of the proctors." Somewhat more strongly, they agreed, "I have no objection to being graded by proctors who are my classmates." Students tended to disagree with the statement, "I would have studied harder if proctors were faculty rather than students."

In addition to the proctors, one undergraduate assistant was paid by the department. He handed out quizzes and filed each student's completed tests in folders. All tests (both passed and failed) were kept in a separate folder for each student. This filing took several hours each week. The assistant was also responsible for checking that all unit tests and all proctor answer sheets were accounted for at the end of each class period.

RESULTS AND DISCUSSION

Three members of our department, including myself, drew up a sixty-question multiple-choice final exam.[2] Four sections of introductory sociology took this test; three of these were lecture courses, each taught by a different instructor using different texts. The results presented in Table 9-I show the PSI section receiving the highest average and are consistent with McMichael and Corey (1969) and Sheppard and MacDermot (1970).

During the spring semester, one section of Introductory So-

---

[1] Kent R. Johnson administered a questionnaire to the students following the final exam. These results are being evaluated and are contained in Johnson's unpublished manuscript. On a 5 point scale (1 = strongly agree, 5 = strongly disagree), the class average for the statement about asking questions of proctors was 2.04. The average regarding objection to being graded by other students was 1.73 and the average concerning using faculty as proctors was 3.98 (slightly disagree).

[2] Priorities established by a University of North Carolina departmental survey concerning introductory sociology were used as a guide for including questions on our test.

TABLE 9-I

Section	Number of Students	Relation of exam score to course grade	Mean score out of 60 and percent correct	Inter-quartile range
Lecture 1	75	Exam equals 25% of course grade	36.9 (60.2)	8
Lecture 2	40	Exam carries no weight on course grade.	34.2 (57.0)	11
Lecture 3	47	Exam given as "bonus", approximately 2% could be added to course grade.	37.4 (62.3)	8
PSI—fall	58	"Pass" on exam (70%) means keeping grade earned on units. Fail means grade reduced.	45.3 (75.5)	6
PSI—spring	71	"High pass" on exam (80%) means keeping grade earned on units. "Pass" (70%) means grade on units reduced. Fail means grade of C is maximum for course.	43.7 (72.8)	6

ciology was again offered using the PSI method. Other than changing a few unit test questions for clarity and weighing the final more heavily, the general procedures of the first semester were retained. The same test was given as a final exam with the same results as with the Fall PSI section. An analysis of variance of the means of these five sections proved significant beyond the .001 level ($F = 32.6$, $df = 4,286$).

Sheppard and MacDermot (1970) tested students in their experimental (PSI) and control groups with a standard exam. The students in the PSI section were told that the test was not part of their final exam, while students in the control section believed the test would determine 50 percent of their final grade. The control and experimental conditions in the present study are different. Lecture 2 (control) took the standard test as a review which counted nothing toward their final grade. Lecture

3 took the test for bonus points toward their final grade (but not as part of their final exam). Only Lecture 1, among the lecture sections, believed the test to be part of the final exam. If this kind of motivation is a determining factor, Lecture 1 would receive the highest scores on the test. Yet the scores of the three lecture sections do not vary greatly (60.2%, 57%, and 62.3%). Students in fall and spring PSI sections performed significantly better (75.5% and 72.8%).

Other factors might also be expected to influence exam scores. For example, the type of tests to which the students were accustomed could influence the outcome. However, students in the PSI sections and in Lecture 3 had been tested during the semester by means of multiple choice tests. The variation between these classes cannot simply reflect adeptness at taking this type of test. Another factor which could have contributed to the results was the lower proportion of freshmen in the fall PSI course. To test for this, freshmen scores were averaged separately. The freshmen in the fall PSI section averaged eighteen wrong, and in the spring, freshmen averaged 17.4 wrong. Freshmen in Lecture 1 averaged 22.2 wrong. Class breakdown was not available for Lecture 2 or 3; however, all but 10 to 14 students in each of those sections were freshmen. Average wrong was 25.8 in Lecture 2 and 22.6 in Lecture 3. The consistency of the results over two semesters lends credence to the notion that those in the PSI sections learned more by all objective measures during one semester of sociology. In sum, it seems that the similarity of the fall and spring PSI results and the similarity of the scores among the fall lecture courses are difficult to explain with these arguments.

As was found in other PSI courses, the students rated the course highly. Students' evaluations included such comments as, "this is the first time I was motivated in an introductory course," and "I found the sense of accomplishment from passing a test most rewarding." On a standard form in the fall semester, 14.3 percent of the students rated the class outstanding, 71.4 percent rated the class above average, 14.3 percent rated the class average and none rated the class below average or poor. Although this form was distributed before final grades were known, students were fairly sure of their final grade. Certainly some satisfaction stems for the high proportion of A's given in the class. Myers (1970) found that knowing that they would receive an A to be among the top ranked reasons given by students concerning important aspects of a PSI course. It might be noted that the ratings received in the PSI course do not vary greatly from ratings the same instructor received when offering a lecture course in introductory sociology.

The final exam can be used as a check on students who may cheat, consistently use a lenient proctor, or simply try to memorize the material. During the first semester, the power of the final exam as a tool to combat cheating on unit tests was not recognized. This final was graded pass/fail where failure meant reduction of the earned grade by one full letter. Thus one student failed the final and still received a B. During the spring semester the final was weighted more heavily. Three essay questions were added to the exam. (Scoring on the essay was not computed as part of the comparison with fall semester.) The exam was graded high pass (100% to 80%), pass (79% to 70%), or fail (69% and below). High pass meant that the student maintained the grade earned according to the number of units passed. Pass reduced their grade by .5 credit points. Thus a B became a C+. Failure meant a reduction of one full letter grade or a maximum of C. This change, plus the fact that the student assistant was aware that cheating occurred during the fall semester seemed to reduce the incidence of known cheating.

The cheating problem must concern all who use the PSI method. Although one would hope that removing sanctions from failing tests would remove the motivation to cheat, this was not the case. In fact, the prospect of an "easy A" seemed to increase the temptation to cheat. Extreme care was taken to account for all the tests at the end of each class, and it was not known how students could cheat given the fact that they sat in the front of the room to take tests, left their books in the back of the room, and did not know which of three forms of the unit test they would receive. At the end of the first semester a lengthy discussion with two students about how a student *might* cheat uncovered several ingenious methods all of which required a buddy system. The first student would take a test, say Unit III, Form C, and fail. He would then write all the test questions down that he could recall. Then he would try to pass, perhaps Form B was given to him. He would again write down all the questions. His buddy would now appear for Unit III and tell the student assistant that he had failed Form A and would receive Form B or C. The pair would reverse after three or four units so that the other would do the greater share of the work. Another less complex method described was simply correcting the answers while waiting in line for a proctor. Certainly the effort put into the system raises doubts about the effectiveness of the system in saving time for the student. Unfortunately, the fact that a student completing all sixteen units and failing the final exam would still receive a B encouraged a few students to try the easiest ways to complete the units. The amount of cheating however was never high. In retrospect, it seemed possible to identify five or seven students out of sixty who cheated during the fall semester. Various methods of weighing the final exam could be examined for the impact on cheating.

PSI offers the possibility of exciting variations. Audio visual equipment may be used while still permitting students to progress at their own speed. The PSI course currently being offered (now team taught) has 135 students. There are two videotape cassette machines; three films are required as an integral part of the course.

The object of teaching is to enable students to learn a particular body of material and to help them develop their thinking ability. The PSI method succeeds admirably in this, especially when compared to the lecture method. Some students and faculty state a preference for the "lecture method" when they actually prefer a small class, where some teacher-student interaction is possible. Rarely do they mean a class of 100 to 150 where little discussion is possible. With PSI one faculty can teach at least one-hundred students with more face-to-face discussion than would be possible in a lecture class of comparable size.

An unexpected result of PSI is the amount of student interaction generated by this teaching method. A great deal of discussion occurs between students and student proctors. It was assumed that students studied more with other students outside of class because the class was non-competitive in grade distribution. The questionnaire administered after the last class, however, suggests that students study less with other students.[3] The students progressing through the class most rapidly studied least with others. Apparently the fact that students are studying different materials during any one week of the semester tended to decrease interaction outside the classroom.

Questions arising from unintended consequences of the method should be researched. How does the student perceive the professor and the professor's concern for the individual student? How does the student perceive the proctor, and how does it influence his self concept to have a peer placed in a position of power over him? Finally, assuming the students reported satisfaction with a PSI introductory course, does this mean the student liked the subject, the method of teaching, or the teacher? Many students report choosing a major because of the influence of a charismatic professor in introductory courses. Will many students major in a field if their introduction to that field is by means of a PSI course? Answers to these questions would significantly expand our understanding when choosing to teach by PSI.

With the evidence that now exists, however, is seems that the benefits of PSI far outweigh any costs. This system of teaching is an exciting experience for the instructor and for the students. Others interested in innovation in sociology would do well to experiment with PSI.

---

[3] Johnson, Kent R., unpublished manuscript. "The format of this course induced me to study more with my fellow students than in other courses I have taken." Class average 3.58 (slightly disagree) .

CONTINGENCY MANAGEMENT IN COLLEGE FOREIGN LANGUAGE INSTRUCTION

Leona G. Bailey

THE APPLICATION OF METHODS of instruction and contingency management to higher education has become increasingly widespread in recent years. At least two effective management systems (Keller, 1966; McMichael and Corey, 1969) are being used more and more (Born, *et. al.* 1972; Johnston and O'Neill, 1973). These and similar systems have not yet been applied to subject fields outside of the social sciences, although the instructional problems (large classes, heterogeneous student population, large amounts of material, difficulties in testing and grading) are essentially the same in other content areas.

There are several such instructional problems inherent in the area of foreign language education, a field which has undergone radical changes in teaching methodology (from translation to Berlitz to aural-oral) but which has not yet seriously responded to questions of instructional management. College language classes, even with thirty-five students are much too large to provide the individualized imitation and feedback necessary to learn an oral skill. The students enter basic courses with a wide variety of native and foreign language learning backgrounds and all are required to be proficient in the new language at about the sixth grade level at the end of two semesters. Infrequent and often subjective testing procedures usually leave the students in doubt as to their abilities and progress in the course.

The purpose of the present study was to develop a system of individualized instruction and contingency management for a first year college French course. The students in the course were to master the foundations of the foreign language in such a way as to cover at least as much material as the control group and to gain a number of additional measurable benefits.

Little or no quantifiable and replicable research has been done in the field of foreign language education to substantiate the validity of innovative language learning programs in higher education. New programs have ranged from total immersion learning (thirty hours a week of hearing, speaking and reading the foreign language) to multi-track instruction (a distinct emphasis on one of the language skills or foreign cultures in each track). Of those programs which contain elements of contingency management systems, very few have been described in enough detail and with sufficient supporting data to be evaluated.

Brown (1971) reported that the accelerated elementary German course he directed completed four semesters' work within two semesters. There were no tests or exams; instead, the students were given "daily challenges" (dictations, exercises and drills). All the students received an A or a B for the course.

At Dartmouth College, (Kraft, 1972) an intensive (fifteen hours a week) team-teaching course in basic French resulted in the students achieving higher scores on achievement tests than did a control group. According to the author, the essential features of his program were having a foreign language dormitory (to stimulate real-life situations) and small classes (fourteen students per class). It would be impossible to replicate either of these systems or to determine which variable controlled the students' achievement.

There have been reports in other fields of systems of instructional management which are effective and replicable. Per-

sonalized instruction (Keller, 1966), which includes a requirement of mastery of small units which the students typed responses
into the terminal for questions, drills, fill-in-the-blanks, etc.
The program would advance after a correct response and would
recycle to an earlier phase after an incorrect response. Each
program took twenty to forty minutes to complete and was
followed by a test section for which answers were provided.
The students were able to do the CAI assignments after receiving training on the program at any of the terminals located
in the library and in the student union.

In order to enrich the students' cultural experiences of
France and the French language, some materials from a variety
of media were acquired and presented to the students within
the context of the class work or in special enrichment activities.
Several slide programs were used, some with an accompanying
record or tape (chateaux of the Loire, monuments of Paris,
the life and works of Albert Camus, a student tour of France).
Filmstrips included a French family at home, French overseas
possessions, and French Canada (Quebec). A number of films
were available to the students from the university film library
(the Provinces, the French Revolution, the Louvre, Charle-
magne's Empire). Posters were used to illustrate talks on trav-
elling in France and a French version of Scrabble was procured
for the class.

Procedure

The basic French class which was used as the experimental
group consisted of a two quarter sequence of courses (referred
to as French 111 and French 112) in which each student could
choose one of two tracks of study (oral or reading-composition)
befitting his interests and abilities. At the beginning of French
111, the students were given a course description in which
the two tracks were outlined. The students then chose which
track they wished to pursue; they could switch tracks of material
with the aid of proctors who administer quizzes and provide
feedback to the students, has clearly been shown to produce
higher grades (Keller, 1968) and superior final exam performance
(McMichael and Corey, 1969). The role of the proctors in

the Keller system has been analyzed by Farmer, *et al.* (1972) who found that proctored students were superior to non-proctored students of final exam performance and in their rate of progress through the course.

An equally effective system developed by Michael (Cooper and Greiner, 1971) does not require that the students pace themselves or that the proctors play as essential a role as in the Keller system. Instead the students follow the pace established by the instructor. However, by having more than one opportunity to pass each exam, the mastery requirement can still be met. These and other researchers have demonstrated quite convincingly that systems of contingency management and individualized instruction can be developed and applied to solving the problems of instruction in higher education.

Method

Subjects

Two classes of a multi-sectioned basic French course were chosen at random as the experimental and control groups. Since the selection of the two groups was not made until after enrollment was closed, the students had no prior knowledge of any instructional differences in the various French classes.

The experimental and control groups each consisted of thirty-five students, 62 percent of whom were freshmen. The average age of the experimental group was 19.2 years; for the control group, it was 19.7 years. The mean GPA of the experimental group was 2.95; the control group's GPA was 3.1. Many students in both groups had had some foreign language training in high school (approximately one year for both groups), but the students had had no previous formal or informal training in French at either the college or high school level.

Setting

Both lecture and seminar classes were held in regular university classrooms during winter and spring quarters (1973). The departmental language laboratory was used for lab exercises and recording oral tests. The students also made use of the listening and viewing area of the main library where video tape recorders and computer terminals were available.

Equipment and Materials

The basic text for the course was a standard first year French book, *Parole et Pensée* (Yvone Lenard, Harper and Row, 1970). Although the text taught all four skills (listening, speaking, reading and writing) to the students, there was a definite emphasis on conversation by means of the verbal-active method of instruction (questions and requests posed in French by the teacher to which the students responded). The text was accompanied by a lab workbook in which the students wrote dictations and exercises during the lab period. There was also a set of audio tapes which were played (one tape per week) during the regular lab session in which native French voices were heard.

Although the experimental students choosing the reading-composition track used the regular course textbook *(Parole et Pensée)*, the written exercises and reading passages contained therein were found to be inappropriate formats for the presentation of the structures and vocabulary of basic French to students in a conversational track. Thus a series of weekly student packets was written which incorporated the same text material but presented in an oral format (questions and answers, substitution exercise, topics for dialogue, etc.). These packets (five to ten pages apiece) were duplicated and distributed to the students in the conversational track and to the assistant instructors.

There were two other types of instructional guides written for French 111 and 112. The experimental students choosing the conversation track attended the language lab at least once a week where they listened and responded to the professionally prepared tapes. A lab guide which included the oral exercises the students heard was produced and distributed to the students. Teachers' guides for both tracks were developed which included specific suggestions on how to handle and how much time to devote to specific grammatical points and exercises in the text and in the student packets.

There was produced a series of twelve videotape instructional programs to be used as extracurricular teaching aides for students in the conversation track. Each program attempted to present a real life situation in which the grammar and vocabulary taught each week was demonstrated. After several types of programs had been created, the final format for the videotapes (each lasting from five to ten minutes) included a dramatic sequence, a question and answer drill (correct answers supplied) and a short oral test (student answers to be recorded on cassette tape). The subject matter consisted of such scenes as a visit to a clothing boutique, shopping for groceries, a television news broadcast, and student campus life. The students viewed the tapes at their convenience in the Listening and Viewing area of the library at any time during the day.

For the students in the reading-composition track who would not have profited from watching videotapes of spoken French, there was devised a computer assisted instructional program (CAI) which was presented in weekly units corresponding with the class work. A program based on the first twenty chapters of *Parole et Pensée* was written in or return to the regular one during the first week of the quarter.

In the oral track, the students attended three hours of class per week in which pronunciation and intonation exercises, repetition of pattern sentences, verb drills, dialogues, and question and answer periods were conducted. The reading-composition track consisted of English presentation of basic grammatical structures, reading and discussing passages written in French, and a number of written exercises (translations, paragraphs, dialogues and letters).

A course management system for this basic French class was devised which included the following components: a point system for grading purposed, a weekly testing procedure, a method of remediation and requizzing, a rotating schedule of activities for the assistant instructors (proctors).

The students were informed on the first day of class that they would earn their grade for the course by earning points each week for several activities. There was a maximum of fourteen points available each week: ten exam points, three class points, and one homework point. The homework point was given upon successful completion of specific homework assignment such as attending a videotape or language lab lesson, completing a computer assisted instruction program, or turning in written exercises or a composition. For the activities which required mere attendance, the students knew that they had received their homework point. With written work, the students were awarded a half or whole point (depending upon the quality of the assignment) by the instructor within one day of receiving the assignment. The instructor recorded the homework points for the class each week.

The class points were earned by attendance at and participation in classroom activities. Since the class met three times a week, each day's participation was worth one point; mere attendance would normally earn the student one-half point. In order to earn a full class point the student was required to engage actively in the class work including answering questions when called on, volunteering information or questions, and engaging in written activities when requested. The instructor recorded one point, one-half point, or no points (absent) for each student in the class after each session. Since the students did not know if they had received a full point for participation each day, they were informed of this once a week by means of a cumulative point chart.

The students earned the ten exam points by successfully completing an examination over each week's work. The examinations were criterion referenced and were given in three forms on three successive days (Wednesday through Friday). The following points were awarded for performance on each exam:

First Exam	90–100%	10 points
(Wednesday)	50– 89%	2 points
	0– 49%	0 points
Second Exam	90–100%	8 points
(Thursday)	50– 89%	2 points
	0– 49%	0 points
Third Exam	90–100%	6 points
(Friday)	50– 89%	2 points
	0– 49%	0 points

It should be clear from this point system that the students were encouraged to do their best on the first exam, thereby relieving themselves of any further responsibilities for the class after

Wednesday. However, a student could make his ten points in several ways, including earning two points on Wednesday and eight points on Thursday (90–100%) etc. The system was designed so that a student could not earn his ten points by waiting until Thursday to begin his exams. If a student once scored in the 90 to 100 percent bracket, he could not add points in a subsequent exam for that week. Students carried their points from week to week and received written verification of their cumulative points each week .

During French 112, a slight but significant change was made in the point system by offering bonus points. One bonus point per week could be earned by attendance at and participation in an enrichment activity. Students who were "down" several exam or class points could thereby find a way to improve their grade. By mid-quarter of French 112 almost every student in the program had taken advantage of this "bonus" opportunity on at least one occasion.

In order to provide maximum flexibility, consistency, and security during the weekly testing sequence, a set of exam procedures was developed. The students were offered three separate class periods on the testing days in which to take their exam. These three periods immediately followed the last class session on Wednesday. Thus a student could complete the required exam as soon or as late as he wished, depending on his schedule and/or his confidence in his abilities.

Each week, three versions of the exams for both tracks were prepared by the instructors. The same format was used for all exams, and the same structures were tested in each version. When a student completed an exam, the version that he used was recorded on a test roster. If, based on the results of his first exam, a student chose to take one or more requizzes, he was given the alternate versions of the exam.

Security of the exams was maintained in a number of ways. The exam papers and testing tapes were in the possession of the instructors until just before the first exam period each Wednesday, Thursday, and Friday. An assistant instructor picked up the testing materials and took them to the testing room and language lab. Since a different proctor monitored each hour of the exam period, the proctors were told not o leave the room until the next proctor arrived. Students were separated and no notes or textbooks were permitted in view. Two instances of cheating were discovered, and a point penalty was levied against those students.

A weekly test roster was prepared which listed the student's number the week, the test form, points earned on the exam, equivalent test points, and total test points for the week. The students were informed that all test results would be available by 6:30 p.m. each testing day and that a copy of the test roster would be posted on a conveniently located departmental bulletin board. The students were required to check the results to decide if they should take the required to check the results to decide if they should take the requiz on the next day.

Another important segment of the instructional management system of this program was the remediation and requizzing procedures. In order to aid the students in their attempts to improve before taking the Thursday and Friday requizzes, remediation sessions were set up to teach individuals or small groups of students those concepts that had proved to be the most difficult on the exam. At least three assistant instructors (and occasionally the course instructor) were available to work with students who attended these optional remediation sessions. Since many students passed the first or second exam leaving usually 75 percent or less of the class (the average was about 50%) eligible to be remediated, there was a most favorable instructor to student ratio. At Friday's remediation session there was often a one to one ratio because most of the students had already passed Wednesday's or Thursday's exam.

The remediation sessions were individualized to the greatest degree possible. The assistant instructors reviewed the students' written and oral exams, made notes on their deficiencies, and found exercises in the text to assist the student. The assistants divided the students among themselves in advance and prepared to work only with the three, four, or five students they had chosen from those eligible. The students worked in small groups asking and answering questions about the test questions and the class exercises after having examined their test paper from the previous day.

Requizzing was carried out in essentially the same way as the first exam. The students signed up for one of the three testing periods and were informed of the results by 6:30 p.m. on Thursday or Friday. The students took alternate versions of Wednesday's exam on the requizzes. For the few students (10 to 15%) who did not pass at criterion on Thursday, there was a second remediation session offered prior to the third exam on Friday. If any student did not pass the exam after three attempts, they were advised to contact the course instructor before the next Monday's class for personal counseling. On an average one or two students a week fell into this category.

Since the assistant instructors played such a large role in the implementation of the program it would be helpful to descirbe how they became involved in the course and what their explicit duties were. Several weeks before the quarter began upper division French majors and minors were invited to attend a meeting of prospective assistant instructors. At the meeting they were given an overview of the program, a description of the duties and the benefits of joining the program. (The assistant instructors received three hours of course credit for work in addition to on the job training and experiences which we felt would be invaluable to these potential language teachers.) A group of seven (eight for French 112) assistant instructors was chosen from the dozen or so who expressed interest.

The assistants were asked to attend the first week of class as observers while at the same time receiving instructions and training for their various duties. They were required to attend one class per week of either track throughout the quarter and to fill out a classroom observation form, which emphasized the classroom presentation, the instructor's attitude, and interaction with the students. In addition to familiarizing themselves with the work studied each week, the classroom observation helped to teach methods of foreign language instruction to the assistants.

There was a weekly meeting held for the assistant instructors, the instructors, and the program director. Rotating assignments were given out at the meeting along with a general description of the week's work. Questions and problems about the previous week's activities were discussed and informal feedback from the students was given to the whole staff. The weekly meeting was very important in keeping the spot; rumor and hearsay were kept to a minimum.

The assistants were present for two or three hours a week at unstructured office hours during French 111 to answer questions a student might have. Due to poor attendance, these hours were changed to help sessions scheduled Tuesday night and Thursday morning, and about 10 percent of the students attended help sessions each week.

The assistants proctored all the examinations for both tracks. They were in charge of giving out the tests, setting up the language lab to record the oral exams, and keeping track of which version of the exam each student took. The assistants also graded about 90 percent of each exam according to answer keys which were provided by the instructors; they then recorded the students' results and posted the test roster. The assistants' duties in remediation and requizzing have been outlined above.

The assistant instructors were also assigned the responsibility of monitoring and/or directing the weekly enrichment activities. Since most of these activities relied on the use of media, the assistants were trained in the operation of slide, film strip and film projectors, tape recorders and the language lab console. The activities ranged from showing a film on the Louvre to giving a slide show of a trip to France to giving a demonstration of how to make French onion soup; the assistant instructors were most imaginative in suggesting topics for the enrichment.

During the course of the experiment, several measures of student achievement and attitude were taken. Comparisons of number of chapters studied and final grade scores between the experimental and control groups were made. A standard language achievement test (*Pimsleur Language Aptitude Battery*, 1966) was administered to both groups at the end of French 111 and French 112. There were several attitude surveys taken: a university testing instrument (SIRS), a departmental teaching evaluation, and a feedback form developed specifically for the experimental program.

The control class was conducted in standard fashion including a lecture presentation of grammar, student written and oral responses and weekly lab work. Students attended class five days a week, were given a written exam every two to three weeks, and were informed of their progress in the course at mid-term and at the end of the quarter.

RESULTS

The research conducted to measure the effects of the various contingency managment procedures indicated that the experimental class derived a number of positive benefits from the program. The students in the experimental group spent an average of 3.63 hours per week engaging in class activities; the control

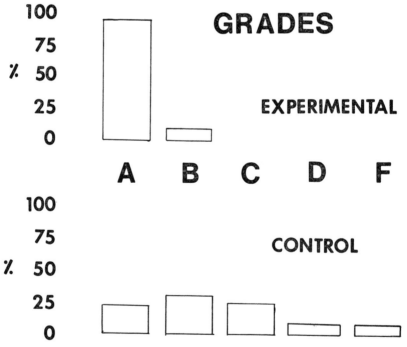

Figure 10-1. Distribution of grades for experimental and control classes.

students averaged 4.92 hours in French class. The students in the contingency management program covered as much material (67% of the chapters of the text) as the control group (65% of the text). The students in the experimental class had a significantly higher percentage of superior grades than the students in the control group in both French 111 and French 112. Figure 10-1 shows that in French 111 there were 93 percent As and 7 percent Bs; no other grades were received. The control class received 22 percent As, 29 percent Bs, 24 percent Cs, 13 percent Ds and 12 percent Fs. In French 112, the results were similar (21% As, 30% Bs, 28 percent Cs, 14 percent Ds, seven percent Fs in the control group) although there was a small percentage of Cs (81% As, 12% Bs, 7% Cs) earned in the experimental class.

Feedback from the students in the experimental group derived

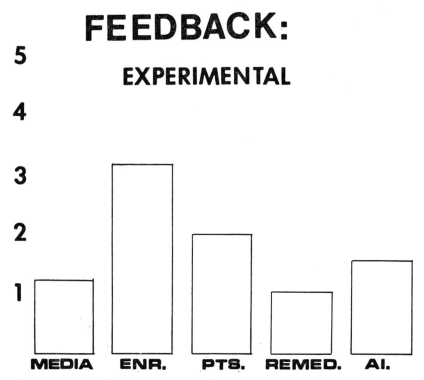

Figure 10-2. Questionnaire responses of experimental students to course components (1 = high and 5 = low agreement).

from a questionnaire indicated that they preferred the unique features of this program. Several questions were asked in each of five major categories (media, enrichment, point system, remediation, assistant instructors). The results seen in Figure 10-2 show that the students liked four out of five components of the program. (A low score indicates strong agreement.) Only the enrichment activities were not rated as strongly favorable.

Students in both the experimental and control groups completed the university's teaching evaluation questionnaire, the Student Instructional Rating System (S.I.R.S.). The composite profile of this evaluation form identifies five major rating areas: instructor involvement, student interest, student-instructor interaction, course organization, and course demands. Figures 10-3

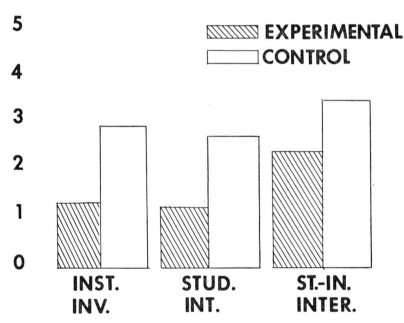

Figure 10-3. Responses of experimental and control students to the university questionnaire in instructor involvement, student interest, and student-instructor interaction.

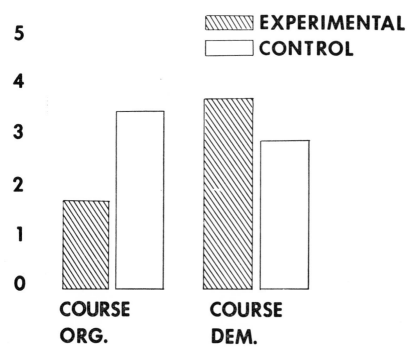

Figure 10-4. Responses of experimental and control students to the university questionnaire in course organization and course demands.

and 10-4 show that all categories received quite favorable ratings for the contingency management program. In the course demands category, a high score is interpreted as a positive evaluation.

The experimental and control groups took a standard language achievement test with the following results (expressed as gain scores on the three sub-tests from pre-test to post-test).

Figure 10-5 shows that the experimental group achieved greater gains in listening and writing; the control group improved more in reading.

CONCLUSIONS

In this study, we have shown that principles of behavior analysis can be applied to the development of instructional man-

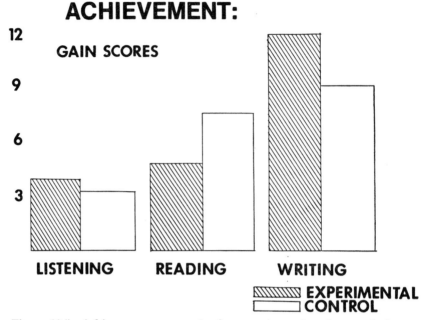

Figure 10-5. Achievement test results for experimental and control classes.

agement systems in college foreign language teaching. Students were able to spend less time (75% of the time spent in regular classes) engaging in class activities while covering the same amount of material and achieving higher grades. Students in the contingency managed course liked the various management procedures and rated their course instruction as superior along several dimensions. Achievement test gain scores gave the students in the experimental group a slight edge over those in the control group.

Several problems areas were identified during the course of the study. First, the recruitment and training of the assistant instructors was a large and time consuming task which could be alleviated by retaining many of the undergraduate tutors for more than one quarter. Second, the students were less than enthusiastic about the culturally-based enrichment activities even when bonus points were awarded for attending those sessions. Perhaps the cultural materials should be more closely integrated with the formal class work in the future. Last, except for some student choice of subject matter and weekly activities, the program is primarily instructor controlled and paced. It may be that, at least in the reading/composition track, written materials for the entire course can be made available to the students at the beginning of the quarter and completed at the student's own rate.

This program has implications for foreign language instruction in many settings and at several levels. Secondary school teachers might very well use their third and fourth year students as assistant instructors for the first and second year classes. Multiple testing and remediation need not be restricted to basic college language classes; language majors at the most advanced levels could profit from the frequent testing and high performance criteria. The use of contingency managed instruction could well be directed to other, more esoteric, subject matters in languages such as literature survey courses and seminars. The principles of behavior analysis have been successfully applied in the teaching of foreign languages; instructors and researchers in other areas of the humanities should be encouraged to apply these principles to their own disciplines.

STUDENTS TEACHING STUDENTS

ONE OF THE MOST CONSISTENT FEATURES of individualized teaching methods is the use of students in a teaching capacity in order to assist in making individualization possible. Some of the many facets of the use of students to assist in teaching and testing other students are treated in the three papers in this section. "An Analysis of Student Manager-Student Inter-actions During Performance Sessions" describes a detailed method for investigating exactly what goes on between the "student-teacher" and the student. The second paper, "Proc-tors' Discussion of Students' Quiz Performance with Students" examines the effects of discussions between these two parties. Finally, "The Effects of a Proctor Training Package on Uni-versity Students' Proctoring Behaviors" describes a training program for these student-assistants.

AN ANALYSIS OF STUDENT MANAGER-STUDENT INTERACTIONS DURING PERFORMANCE SESSIONS

PATRICK A. QUIGLEY

THE BEHAVIORAL APPROACH TO COLLEGE TEACHING as developed by Johnston and Pennypacker (1971) affords its users numerous possibilities with regard to the examination of variables contributing to student success or failure in the process of teaching. Multiple score comparisons (Alba and Pennypacker, 1972), student study behavior (Johnston, Roberts, and O'Neill, 1972) and performance criteria defining grades (Johnston and O'Neill, 1973) have been assessed with regard to student performance. Since this system requires oral responses for a fill-in sentence completion item, a variety of responses is permitted the student to which the student manager must judge the correctness or incorrectness of the responses. As described by Johnston and Pennypacker (1971), the test items required up to two or three words, the items were one or two sentences long, and there was little or no dialogue between the student and his manager during the performance part of the session.

The author wishes to express his thanks to Norma Badford, Barbara Bryant, Cameron Cavin, Ed Cox, Carol Jenkins, John Jordan, Debi Stasny, and Mike Weaver for serving as student managers and to Chuck Hogarth and Cheryl Goodman for coding the tapes. Dr. Gene Moffat assisted in structuring the tables.

With the adoption of Biehler's *Phychology Applied to Teaching* (1971) and Littlejohn's file of fill-in-items (1972) for an undergraduate, junior level course in educational psychology, the materials themselves suggested changes in procedure and presented new possibilities for extending work in this area. The questions from Littlejohn's file are often longer than two sentences, no cues with regard to the number of words expected for a correct response are given, and generally a number of items could be answered appropriately without technical language and thus require a full sentence response. A question concerning student manager reliability for these items rose quite early during the implementation of the behavioral approach to college teaching for these materials. The following study produced data to answer this question and provided the observations which recommended a second, more complex investigation of the student manager-student interaction during performance sessions.

METHOD

Subjects

Thirty-one undergraduates and one graduate student enrolled in the undergraduate education psychology course for students in teacher education programs participated as subjects.

The eight student managers were students who had taken the course previously and demonstrated their knowledge of the material at an A level. They received three hours course credit for "Applied Behavior Analysis" in which serving as a student manager is the most frequently chosen means to fulfill a lab requirement. The grade in this course was determined on the basis of fulfilling requirements as a manager and attending twice weekly discussions of pertinent readings, the procedures, and any difficulties encountered by their proteges which should be brought to the instructor's attention.

Procedures

The sign-up procedures and recording techniques were similar to those described by Johnston and Pennypacker (1971) with a few exceptions. There was only one mandatory session per week. If a student did not notify his manager in advance of missing an appointment or skipping the once weekly session, the correct criterion rates for the next session and for that session alone were raised by .5 responses per minute. Table 11-I contains the grade letter equivalents for all response rates as announced at the first class meeting. The text was divided into seven units of two chapters apiece (two chapters were omitted for this study because no data with respect to the mean trials to criterion were available). Mastery of these units to the student-selected criterion rates assured him 8 percent of the total grade at the appropriate letter grade equivalent. The remaining 20 percent was determined either by volunteering to participate in a tutoring program offered to the local schools or by participating in discussions on selected readings and performing a behavioral monitoring project. The readings were taken from Biehler's *Psychology Applied to Teaching, Selected Readings* (1972). Class meetings were scheduled three times a week. Mondays and Wednesdays were used for the nontutors to discuss the readings and review their data and Fridays were used for the tutors to review the behavioral data collected during the meetings with the school children. Performance sessions were scheduled outside of class time.

In order to achieve a full description of many possible types of events occurring during the ten minute test portion of the twenty minute performance session the Student Manager Reliability Report (SMRR) was developed to permit a survey recording of many possible types of interactions and supply the basis for assessing reliability of student manager judgements. Table 11-II contains the first form of the SMRR.[1] The form permits the recording of sessions without manager supplied information (A1,

---

[1] The terms used for this report, in part, are the same as those used in Lindsley, O., *Handbook of Precise Behavior Facts*, Kansas City, Behavior Research Company, 1971.

TABLE 11-I

Letter Grade Equivalents to Response Criterion

Letter Grade	Correct Rate	Incorrect Rate
A	≥ 3.0	$\leq .4$
B	≥ 2.5	$\leq .4$
C	≥ 2.0	$\leq .4$
F	< 2.0	$> .4$

TABLE 11-II

Definitions for Student Manager Reliability Report

Category	Subcategory
A. Programmed Event	1. Question read by student. 2. Further hint from manager, eg. "Refine answer" or "Use your own words."
B. Program	1. Response to response, no hints. 2. Correct response to correct response, hints.

C. Movement	1. Verbal a. Correct
	         b. Incorrect or Irrelevant,
	          eg. "I don't know."
	 2. Nonverbal, eg. student gestures that answer is unknown, short silence—scored as incorrect.

D. Arrangement	1. CRF 2. Other
E. Arranged Event	1. "Go" response, eg. Praise from manager, "Proceed", "Come back to it later", student flips card to view answer. 2. "No go", response, eg. "Stop and think", "Reread", or any A2 from manager.
F. Movement Double Check (after performance test)	1. Correct 2. Incorrect
G. Recording Plan	1. 10 minutes. 2. 5 minutes. 3. > 10 minutes, "Time out"from scoring correct or incorrect responses. 4. "First come", either time elapses or number of responses occur to terminate the test.

B1, D1, E1, combinations) or with manager supplied information (A1, B1, D1, E1, A2, B2, D2, and so on). The information supplied by the manager (A2's) consisted of hints with regard to the type of answer required (technical or nontechnical terms) rather than a hint with regard to the specific answer required. The B2 type of program was used to describe a procedure in which the manager could keep supplying the A2, types of programmed events until the student supplied the correct response (C1a). C2 responses were scored as incorrect. D2 was entered to permit the recording of intermittent schedules (however they were never used). The E1, and the E2 were "go" and "no-go" responses with respect to the next A1 or programmed event. The E1 was achieved either by the student turning the flash card to view the answer or by some signal from the manager to proceed to the next question. The record plan sections were included to describe various ways of terminating the sesion. G1 was typical and consisted of a ten minute session. G2 was a five minute session which was used by the managers when it was obvious during the early minutes of testing that the student knew the material and could easily produce the criterion rates for a shortened time period. G3 occurred as a result of a student emitting various forms of anxious behavior. In this situation, the student manager would initiate the test by giving the student about three minutes of reading the cards, and any responses produced at this time would not be counted as correct or incorrect, but merely serve to relax the student and orient him to the material. At the end of this short period, the manager would tell the student that the timing and counting would begin. G4 occurred when a student produced many more correct responses (>30) than were needed under G1 condition and only a few incorrect responses. Rates under this condition were calculated according to the time actually taken to produce the responses, rather than the ten or five minute basis. These definitions were then placed on another form, with letters and numbers serving as columns; spaces for noting the item were left as rows.

To collect the reliability data, the managers recorded three to four performance sessions on a small cassette recorder. Typically, the manger knew what student and which unit would be upcoming for a test. The manager shuffled the item file, recorded the order of items being used on the SMRR, recorded the session itself on tape, and then supplied the appropriate check marks to the SMRR immediately after the student left the room. The manager could refer to the tape for recalling details of the session, if necessary. In order to assure an objective selection of students to be recorded, the managers were not informed in advance of receiving the recorder and were only told to tape the very next session. Another advanced student, familiar with the approach to teaching, collected the SMRR and the tape recording completed by the student manager, noted the item order on another SMRR, listened to the tape, and supplied the appropriate checks while listening to the tape independently of what the student manager had scored on the original SMRR.

RESULTS

The total number of check marks is derived by adding those obtained by the manager to those noted by the independent listener. Subtracting the number of discrepancies between both reports leaves the number of agreements. This number, divided by the total number of tallies, yields a percentage of agreement for all items on the SMRR. The percentages of agreement for the different managers ranged from 85 percent to 99 percent with a mean of 94.8 percent agreement. While this figure was felt high enough to assure reliable judgements, and inspection of SMRR's-by-manager revealed wide differences with regard to the use or non-use of the A2-B2-E2 combinations versus the straight forward A1-B1-E1 combinations as reported by Johnston and Pennypacker (1971). These procedures were labelled as Extra Programmed Event (EPE) or as non-Extra Programmed Event (non-EPE) conditions, respectively. Since the managers were not encouraged to run sessions one way or the other, the differences were not surprising. When these data were compared to the data on student performance for trials to criterion and amount of time needed to complete the materials, it was found that the one manager who consistently used the non-EPE condition had students who typically finished faster than other students, never dropped out of the course, took fewer trials to meet criterion, and finished the units by the end of the quarter. These data are contrasted in Table 11-III for the manager using the non-EPE sequence and another manager representative of those who used the EPE sequence. These last observations provided the basis for a much more elaborate investigation as reported in the following ex-

TABLE 11-III

Comparison of Student Data from Managers Using or
Not Using Extra Programmed Events

	EPE User[1]	Non-EPE User[2]
Mean Weeks to Completion	7.8	6.2
Mean Trials to Criterion Per Unit	3.2	2.3
Drop outs	0	0
Incompletes	0	0

[1] n = 5 for this manager.
[2] n = 6 for this manager.

perimental study. The procedures in this pilot study provided the following grades for the thirty-two students enrolled: 72 percent A's; 6 percent B's (all units completed at an A level but failure to attend discussions or turn in a project) ; 1 percent C's (one student who worked at the C level criteria all term) ; 9 percent I's; 9 percent G's (Withdraw Passing or Drop). Of these data, it should be noted that with the exception of one student, all those enrolled either completed all units at the A level criterion, or requested I's or G's. Those three students requesting I's were seeking A's in the course with one or more units left unmastered. All have since completed the course.

METHOD

Thus with the assurance that there was high agreement between raters and that the SMRR was sensitive to procedural differences between managers, it seemed logical to pursue a more controlled study which would assess the effects of these differences on student behavior. This experimental investigation represents merely the first use of the SMRR in a formal study, and its usefulness is not thought to be coextensive with this study alone. As the literature to date has emphasized numerous variations characterizing the performance sessions, a closer look at the content of these sessions themselves seemed promising.

Subjects

Forty-two students enrolled for the summer session in the same course participated in this study. When asked by the instructor how many enrolled in this section because of the manner in which it was run, only one student replied in the affirmative. Thus any selective bias due to interstudent communication was not present prior to the first class meeting. Six advanced undergraduates meeting the same criteria as before served as student managers. Five of the six were repeating the experience for a second quarter.

Procedures

The procuedures for meeting student managers, rate criteria for letter grade equivalents, and the SMRR recording were the same as in the pilot study. An additional unit was inserted to extend the coverage to the entire text. In order to determine the effects of extra programmed events in the form of hints on student performance, each manager was asked to vary the EPE and non-EPE sequence with every other student who showed up for the first scheduled appointment. The student placed in the EPE group was then to receive up to four hints upon making an incorrect response (either Clb or C2). This treatment continued through the terminal performance on the third unit. At this time (which varied from student to student due to self-pacing) a reversal occurred; the students receiving the non-EPE sequence were placed in the EPE condition and those who had been in the EPE condition were then placed in the non-EPE condition. This phase continued through the terminal performance on the sixth unit, at which time a final reversal occurred for the last two units. Thus each student manager implemented an ABA or BAB design, depending upon the order in which the students showed up for initial performance sessions. This design was selected for two reasons. First, it was felt that the contrast would be better evidenced by having each manager control both treatments. Second, the feasibility of using the techniques would be better assessed by having each manager try both, thus precluding the possibility of overlooking a significant manager-by-treatment inter-action. Since it was observed in the pilot study that the EPE sequence tended to slow response rates and thus require additional trials to criterion, review tests were inserted after the third, sixth, and eight units to determine if the additional studying and subse-quent extra trials enabled students to learn the material better than those who went uninterrupted through the performance sessions. Many of the review test items from the 1973 version of Biehler's Instructor's Manual. Generally they tended to represent case situations which require the recognition of applications and analysis of key points within the chapters. In the case of three chapters for which no items were available, the instructor con-structed items which reflected the same emphasis. The difference in test item construction between those used in the performance sessions and those for review was intended to control for the effects of learning as a result of familiarity with items in performance sessions alone. These tests contained twenty-one questions each and could not be retaken.

Student managers recorded sessions as in the first study; however, two recordings per manager for each treatment phase were made. The recordings comprised one of each type of treatment per phase. An independent observer assessed the percentage of agreement, as before.

Finally, with the addition of the review tests, the weights of various activities in relation to the final grade were 70 percent for unit performance, 15 percent for review tests (5% each), 10 percent for the behavioral monitoring project, and 5 percent for participating in discussions on the selected readings. The grade equivalents for scores on the review tests are 90 percent = A, 80 percent = B, 70 percent = C, 60 percent = D, 60 percent = F. As the schools were closed, the tutoring program was not in operation. The class was scheduled for Monday, Wednesday and Friday. One third of the class met on each of these days to discuss the readings and present their behavioral data. As before, performance sessions were scheduled outside of class time.

RESULTS

The collection of tapes from student managers provided data for assessing the reliability of their judgements and the extent to which the EPE and non-EPE treatments were administered. The percentages of agreement for each of the student managers by treatment type within each of the treatment phases was consistently high, with the overall mean being 98.2 percent.

The ratios of extra programmed events to incorrect responses in Table 11-IV indicated that with few exceptions the EPE and non-EPE conditions were handled appropriately by the managers. Individual ratios were obtained from the same SMRR tapes used to assess agreement. These ratios were computed by dividing the total number of extra programmed events by the total number of incorrect responses for each recorded session. Thus, for ratios greater than 1.00, a student manager supplied more than one extra programmed event before the student could emit his next response. Ratios equal to 1.00 indicated that not all incorrect responses

TABLE 11-IV

Ratios of Extra Programmed Events to Incorrect Responses[1]

Manager	Treatment Phase						Overall Manager Ratio[2]	
	I		II		III			
	EPE	Non-EPE	EPE	Non-EPE	EPE	Non-EPE	EPE	Non-EPE
1	.23	.00	.20	.25	.60	.00	.28	.04
2	.62	.00	1.58	.00	.95	.00	1.00	.00
3	5.00	.07	.00	.00	1.67	.00	.68	.06
4	1.70	.00	1.14	.05	.64	.00	1.00	.03
5	1.20	.00	.82	.00	.82	.*	.92	.00
6	.71	.00	1.00	.50	1.20	.00	.92	.06

[1] Ratios are reported as fractions of extra programmed events to one incorrect response.
[2] Overall ratio for EPE condition = .88; overall ratio for Non-EPE condition = .04.
* Recorder not on during session.

earned extra programmed events. The overall manager ratio was computed by adding the extra programmed events and incorrect responses across phases for each condition and then dividing the extra programmed events by incorrect responses. The overall ratio were obtained by adding the raw totals for each manager and then dividing one grand total by the other.

Table 11-IV indicated the only exception to a higher ratio in a non-EPE condition than in an EPE condition was for the first manager during the second treatment phase. The ratio for the sixth manager during the second treatment phase revealed a relatively high number of extra programmed events. However, given the other data for this manager, this ratio remained well contrasted for the appropriate delivery of extra programmed events under EPE conditions. In general, the overall manager ratios indicated that only four of the six managers achieved or were relatively close to the optimal ratio of 1.00 for the EPE condition. It should be noted that even these managers permitted degrees of variability from one treatment phase to the next. The optimal ratio for the non-EPE condition was .00. There was less variability between and within managers for this condition. Part of the variability under both conditions was attributable to the students themselves either by asking for the extra programmed events or by telling the manager not to supply them. In the former case, the hint was usually supplied. Thus the ratio was inflated. In the latter case, the hint was withheld and the student proceeded to the next question. Then the ratio was less than optimum.

Table 11-V summarizes overall student performance under both conditions without reference to the order or frequency of the treatments. All rates were compiled in terms of answers (correct or incorrect) per minute. Speed measures were obtained by adding correct rates to incorrect rates. Accuracies were computed by dividing gross speed into the correct rate for each session (initial or terminal) over all units. This quotient indicated percent correct.

As Table 11-V indicates, the treatments differentially effected student behavior to a limited extent. Students initially performed at a slower rate and higher accuracy under the EPE condition. The trials-to-criterion data and the terminal rates revealed this difference to be short-lived and inconsequential with respect to mastering the course content during the quarter. The mean percent correct on review tests showed a slight advantage under non-EPE conditions. However, the most significant finding from the review scores under both conditions was the relatively low

TABLE 11-V

Numerical Summary of Student Performance Under Conditions With and Without Extra Programmed Events

Source	With	Without
Mean rates of reading and correctly/incorrectly answering items on the first attempt on each unit.*	1.54/1.15	1.41/1.51
Mean rates of reading and correctly/incorrectly answering items on the final attempts on each unit.	3.30/.26	3.30/.26
Mean speed of reading items on the first/final attempt on each unit.	2.69/3.56	2.92/3.57
Mean accuracy of reading items on the first/final attempt on each unit.	57%/93%	48%/92%
Gains in speed/accuracy from first to final attempts on all units.	.87/36%	.65/44%
Mean trials to criteria for all units.	2.19	2.26
Mean per cent correct for all Review Tests	50.8	55.9

* All speeds are based on movements per minute.

percentages. In comparison to the data from the pilot study (Table 11-III), the trials-to-criterion data were similar for non-EPE conditions for both studies regardless of the design (between subjects versus within subjects). This was not the case for the EPE conditions in both studies. The data for the EPE conditions in the experimental study more closely approximated the non-EPE data for both studies. At this point, the only explanation possible is the fact that five of the six managers participated in the program for the second term. An examination of the trials-to-criterion data for the only new manager added for the second study revealed 3.6 trials-to-criteria in the EPE condition and 3.4 trials-to-criteria in the non-EPE conditions for his students over all units. Thus the managers' history must also be considered in addition to their interactions during performance session. Practices which reduce delays between performance sessions may account for some of the differences. While all managers were encouraged to have their students attend performance sessions as frequently as possible, it seems possible that some managers take a longer period of time to learn what techniques will accomplish this feat. Put another way, there may be a correlation between the delay of subsequent performance session and trials-to-criterion which deserves formal study.

The grade distribution under the contingencies in this second experiment was: 53 percent A's; 31 percent B's; zero percent C's; 14 percent G's (Withdraw Pass or Drop) and 2 percent I's. This last student attended one performance session and was never seen again. The smaller percentage of A's in this study was attributable to review test scores.

DISCUSSION

This study has pinpointed several topics worthy of further consideration. These are both subjects relevant to further interaction analyses and subjects treated as empirically extraneous until present. Each will be handled in turn.

First, with the development of a reliable measurement device to study manager-student interactions, more detailed parametric investigations may be attempted. For example, the relationship of hints to incorrect responses may be extended by varying the ratios used in this study. Also the types of hints themselves may be varied to investigate the possibilities of better programming. In either case, the methodology will enable researchers to assess the extent to which treatments are being reliably and differentially administered. This study indicated some variability between and within managers. Thus rehearsal or role playing practices could be tried to reduce variability and assure stable ratios of any manager supplied events to student responses. Further, the methodology may provide the basis for assessing therapeutic techniques for reducing test anxiety. The high frequency of tests alone in the behavioral approach and personalized approaches to college teaching resembles "flooding" therapies. At present, only the alternate recording plans on the SMRR reflect attempts in this direction. As this and similar methodologies are adopted and refined, perhaps a greater understanding of those emotional behaviors concurrent with the academic, verbal behavior of students will be achieved.

Second, with regard to empirically extraneous variables, the accuracy of student performance under EPE and non-EPE conditions for review tests must be considered. The test items used from performance sessions were items which demanded the direct recall of information or recall (fill-in-the-blank) of slightly interpolated information (putting an answer in nontechnical terms or presenting the gist of slightly larger bits of information). The test items for the review tests required the recognition (multiple choice type) of applications and analyses of the very same information contained in the text. Thus two variables were involved: question type and question complexity. Gronlund (1973) has illustrated the necessity of lower mastery requirements for the more complex items. Given this suggestion the accuracies preset for grade equivalents in the present study should be interpreted as unreasonably high. Thus the obtained accuracies are probably within a desirable range given the complexity of the questions. The data has lent support to the necessity of arranging educational contingencies which prompt information mastery enroute to application, analysis, synthesis, and evaluation skills. However, the data have also indicated the insufficiency of information mastery alone to assure induction to more complex levels.

A solution to this problem would entail some additional investigation of student manager training and their interactions with students. The basic question then becomes one of student manager reliability for correct, more complex responses. Often these complex items represent divergent products, and as such, the recall (fill-in) items will tend to heighten this divergence. However, if items for formative evaluations (unit performance) and for summative evaluation (review tests) are placed in a recognition mode (multiple choice), the divergence should be reduced and reliability for any level of question would be restored. Initially the untested preference for fill-in items within the Johnston and Pennypacker (1971) approach must be examined at the level of information or knowledge mastery (formatively and summatively) and then for the more complex levels. Vargas (1972) has written an excellent guide for those interested in examining and classifying levels of learning in a taxonomic form.

PROCTORS' DISCUSSIONS OF STUDENTS' QUIZ PERFORMANCE WITH STUDENTS

Daniel E. Hursh
Jan Wildgen, Bonnie Minkin, Neil Minkin,
James A. Sherman and Montrose M. Wolf

Since the personalized system of instruction (PSI) format was first proposed and implemented by Keller (1968), many studies have been carried out to compare its effectiveness with the more traditional lecture-exam format (Alba & Pennypacker, 1972; Keller, 1968; McMichael & Corey, 1969; Sheppard & MacDermot, 1970). The results of these studies have indicated that the PSI format (or slight variations of it) produced higher student performance on final exams and higher student ratings of the course than the same materials presented in a lecture-exam format.

One of the consistent features of these PSI courses is the

The research reported in this article was conducted when the first author was a predoctoral trainee and supported by NICHHD Grant No. 5T01HD00247-04 to the Department of Human Development at the University of Kansas. The authors wish to thank Rod Conard, Nancy Conyers, Andi and Paul Plotsky for their invaluable help with the development of the course materials and for doing such fine jobs as the course's first proctors. Reprints may be obtained from the first author c/o Department of Psychology, Western Carolina Center, Morganton, North Carolina 28655.

use of student proctors. Keller (1968) emphasized the importance of using proctors by noting that it allows for frequent quizzing, immediate feedback, discussion with students and tutoring of students. The data (Farmer, J., Lachter, G. D., Blaustein, J. J., & Cole, B. K., 1972) appear to support Keller's (1968) emphasis. However, proctoring involves many behaviors and it is not clear which of these many behaviors are functionally related to student's performance. The present study evaluated whether proctors' discussions with students about their incorrect answers facilitated their test performance and whether or not the students preferred to have such discussions. Further, this study evaluated whether the students were able to apply the specific information they were required to learn during the course to general questions concerning the subject matter.

Method

Students and Proctors

Thirty-four students at the University of Kansas who were enrolled in a PSI course entitled "The Principles and Procedures of Behavior Modification" took part in the present study. Four other undergraduates who had completed the course materials served as proctors for the course.

Setting

A university classroom served as the setting for the class meetings. Class met for one hour, three days a week throughout the semester. With the exception of the first and last two days students were free to attend class for the purpose of studying and/or taking quizzes whenever they chose.

Procedures

Students in the course were required to pass all quizzes over the course readings with at least nine out of ten correct in order to receive an "A" grade for the course. On each quiz the students were allowed as many retakes as necessary to achieve the ninety percent criterion. If a student failed to complete all seventeen quizzes by the end of the semester he was given a withdrawal instead of an "A" grade.

The thirty-four students were divided into two groups. With one group of students the proctors discussed incorrect answers on the first five quizzes but not on the second five quizzes. With the other group of students, the proctors did not discuss incorrect answers on the first five quizzes but did on the second five quizzes. On the final seven quizzes all students chose, on each quiz, whether or not to have the proctor discuss the incorrect answers with them. If a proctor was to discuss an incorrect answer to a quiz question with a student, he gave the student prompts, discussed relevant information and/or asked leading questions until the student correctly answered the question or it became obvious that the student could not answer the question. If the student could correctly answer the question during the discussion he was given credit for it. If the proctor was not to discuss the incorrect answers with the student, the proctor merely told the student his score and pointed out which answers were incorrect. A graduate student

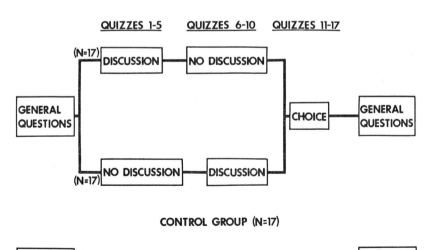

Figure 12-1. The experimental design depicting the sequence of conditions each group of students experienced.

or professor was always available in the classroom to answer any questions the student had about the readings, study questions or their answers to quiz questions. The graduate student or professor, however, did not change the grading done by the proctors. After finishing the course, students completed a course evaluation that asked them which components of the PSI package they found helpful and how they would rate the course in comparison to the other courses they had taken.

Before beginning the course and then again after they passed their last quiz, all students in the course answered general questions over the course materials. These questions asked the student to describe behavior modification programs (e.g. to toilet train a child), design studies (e.g. to experimentally analyze the effects of a behavior modification procedure) and describe the circumstances that would lead one to use a punishment procedure to modify behavior. Another group of students enrolled in a PSI course in Nutrition also answered the general questions. From this group seventeen students were chosen such that the mean of their scores matched the mean of the experimental class's scores and their individual scores matched the scores of seventeen of the thirty-four students in the experimental class. Each of these seventeen control students then answered the general questions a second time after an interval equivalent to the time it took the student they were matched with to complete the course. All students were simply asked to complete the test both times. There were no contingencies for completeness or accuracy.

Data was collected on both quiz scores and answers to the general questions. Periodically interobserver reliability was assessed. On an answer-by-answer basis mean intergrader reliability was 98 percent for the quizzes and 88 percent for the general questions.

RESULTS

All students on their first attempt on all quizzes scored a mean of 96 percent correct. For quizzes on which students discussed their incorrect answers with the proctors, they scored a mean of 98 percent correct on their first attempts. For quizzes

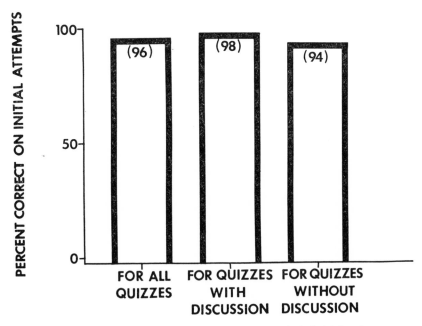

Figure 12-2. The students' mean percent correct on their initial quiz attempts on all quizzes, quizzes with discussion and quizzes without discussion.

on which students did not discuss their incorrect answers with the proctors, they scored a mean of 94 percent correct on their first attempts. Thus, the discussion of incorrect answers produced only slightly higher scores on first attempts than did no discussion. However, when given a choice between discussion and no discussion students chose to discuss their incorrect answers with a proctor on 237 of the 238 occasions to choose (seven choice quizzes × thirty-four students). In addition, students had to retake 18 percent of their quizzes when they were not given a chance to discuss their incorrect answers, whereas, when given a chance to discuss and potentially change their incorrect answers students had to retake only 3 percent of their quizzes. However, if students' initially incorrect answers had not been corrected during the discussions they would have had to retake 35 percent of their quizzes.

In the experimental course, students' answers to the general questions contained a mean of 7.9 of the possible twenty-six

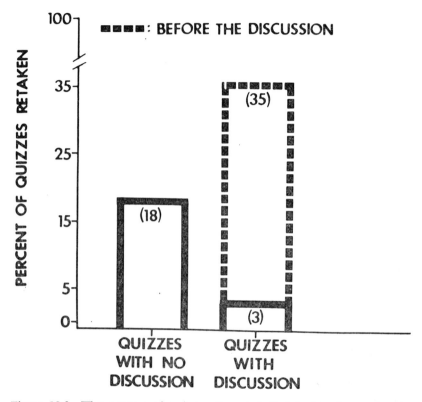

Figure 12-3. The percent of quizzes attempted that had to be retaken by students when they had no discussions and when they had discussions. The dashed bar represents the percent of quizzes that would have had to be retaken if the students had not had the chance to change initially incorrect answers during the discussion with the proctors.

points before they experienced the course and a mean of 11.5 after they had completed the course. The students not in the experimental course scored a mean of 7.8 initially and 7.4 on their second attempt. Thus, students in the experimental course increased their performance on the general questions, whereas, the other students did not.

A supplementary finding was that all students took and passed quizzes more frequently as they progressed through the course. Thus, a cumulative record of their quiz passing performance resembles the scallop-like pattern of responding char-

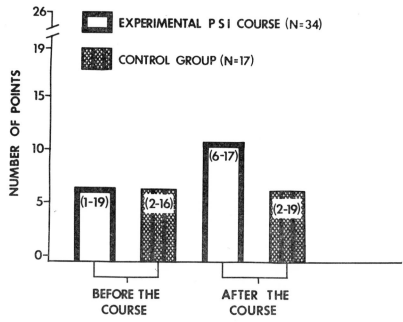

Figure 12-4. The experimental PSI class and the control group's mean and range (the numbers within the bars) of scores on their answers to the general questions.

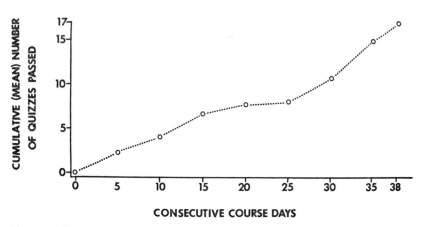

Figure 12-5. The cumulative (mean) number of quizzes passed by all students at five day intervals throughout the experimental PSI course.

acteristic of animal (Ferster & Skinner, 1957) and human (Maw-hinney, Bostow, Laws, Blumenfeld, & Hopkins, 1971) responding when under a fixed-interval schedule of reinforcement.

On the course evaluation the students rated the experimental course as more interesting than other courses they had taken (5.9 on a seven-point scale where 1 = much less interesting than and 7 = much more interesting than) and more work than other courses (4.9 on a seven-point scale where 1 = much less than and 7 = much more than). On a seven-point scale (where 1 = a hindrance and 7 = very helpful), students rated the helpfulness of having proctors as 6.4, being able to pace themselves at 6.9, having study guide questions at 7.0 and being required to pass quizzes with at least nine out of ten correct at 6.5.

DISCUSSION

Discussions produced almost no increase in students' mean accuracy when initially answering quiz questions. However, it appears that students were better prepared to initially provide correct answers to the quiz questions when they were not given any chance to discuss and potentially change their incorrect answers. They had to retake 18 percent of their quizzes when they had no discussion but would have had to retake 35 percent of their quizzes if they had not been able to change some of their initially incorrect answers during discussions with the proctors. Giving the students the chance to change their initially incorrect answers in discussions with their proctors almost eliminated the need for retakes (only 3%). Another important finding was that, after having experienced both discussions and no discussions, students almost always chose to have discussions when given the option.

One potential criticism of PSI is that it appears to teach only a specifically defined and limited repertoire rather than setting the occasion for a more general repertoire with respect to subject matter. The general questions in this study were used to test whether this PSI format could produce a more general repertoire than that which was specifically required as part of the course itself. The results from these general questions appear to indicate that PSI can teach a more general repertoire. Having students from another course answer the same questions only provided a control for the possibility that the passage of time itself could account for the increased scores of students in the experimental PSI course. Further evaluations of this issue will need to include comparisons between PSI techniques and other teaching methods.

The results of the course evaluations indicated, as did earlier studies, that students report finding PSI more interesting, even though is requires more work, than other courses they had taken. In the present study students were also asked how helpful the different PSI components were. Their responses to these questions indicated that the students found each of the components very helpful.

THE EFFECTS OF A PROCTOR TRAIN-ING PACKAGE ON UNIVERSITY STUDENTS' PROCTORING BEHAVIORS

F. HAL WEAVER

L. KEITH MILLER

R ECENT INVESTIGATIONS of Keller's (1968) method of Personalized Systems of Instruction has indicated that the PSI methodology produces measurably better learning in higher education (McMichael & Corey, 1969; Sheppard & MacDermott, 1970; Johnston and Pennypacker, 1971; Alba & Pennypacker, 1972; Born, Gledhill & Davis, 1972).

An important feature of the PSI method is the use of undergraduates as proctors. These are usually students who have previously completed the course and demonstrated mastery of the material. In general, each student is assigned to a proctor for the duration of a PSI course. Each proctor is available to help his students with any questions over the assigned material. When a student is ready to take a quiz, the proctor administers and grades each quiz.

There is some evidence that proctors are an important component of the PSI method. Recently, an investigation by Farmer, Lachter, Blaustein & Cole (1972) showed that proctored students performed better on final examinations than did nonproctored students and that proctored students progressed through the course at a faster rate. Nelson & Scott (1972) found that interactions with proctors are a highly rated part of their PSI course. Thus, the importance and usefulness of proctors seems to be reasonably well established.

The organization of a course using the Personalized System of Instruction procedures requires the selection and training of student proctors. To date there has been little specification of desirable proctor behaviors beyond reading the course assignments and interacting with their students in a nonaversive way (Gallop, unpublished). The basic tasks of proctors might be described as: 1) monitoring the course progress of those students assigned to him/her; 2) assisting the students with questions they have over the course material through explanation and prompting correct responses; and 3) scheduling reinforcing consequences following correct responses to increase the likelihood of developing the behavioral repertoire of the students. These three behaviors will be referred to in the rest of this paper as preparation, prompting and praise.

The present experiment reports a single subject analysis of the effectiveness of a "proctor training package." This package consisted of a manual describing how to be a proctor and a simulated student-proctor interaction in which the student received immediate feedback on his appropriate use of three proctor behaviors. A further role playing situation was used to permit observation and measurement of each of three proctoring behaviors before and after training.

Method

Subjects

Three undergraduate students, enrolled in an introductory behavior analysis course at the University of Kansas, served as subjects. Two of the students were sophomores and one was a freshman.

The introductory course was taught using Personalized System of Instruction procedures. Each of these students was assigned to and met with a course proctor during the semester. Since the experiment was conducted during the last month of the semester, each student had the opportunity to interact with their proctor for about three months prior to participating in the experiment.

Setting

The experiment was conducted in a classroom. Four persons were present during each role-playing session: a proctor trainee, a person playing the role of a student, an observer and a reliability observer. The observer sat at a desk approximately five feet to the left of the trainee and the reliability observer sat approximately five feet to the right of the student.

The trainee was provided with the materials required of a proctor during the sessions. These materials consisted of the text used in the course, *Principles of Everyday Analysis* (Miller, 1974) ; a proctor's answer key containing a glossary of all terms taught in the course and answers for all study guide and quiz questions. The person playing the role of the student also had a copy of the text, a copy of a "script," and a filled-in quiz over one of the regular course lessons.

The text used in the course is divided into twenty-six lessons, each covering one behavior concept. The first part of each lesson gives an introduction to and definitions of the concept to be taught. The second part consists of twenty examples of everyday behavioral situations. The student is supposed to answer a set of questions about each example. The questions are sentence completion, the answers to which are behavioral terms reinforcement, extinction, avoidance, etc.). The third part is a "self-quiz" which consists of an average of thirty questions that are based on the definitions and examples contained in that lesson. A sample of ten self-quiz items make up each lesson quiz.

Role Playing Sessions

The purpose of each session was to permit observation and measurement of the three proctoring behaviors as they occurred during a scripted interaction between the trainee and student.

At the beginning of each session the student was given a script to use. Only the student was given the script. The script consisted of a total of thirty-five statements by the person playing the role of the student, each of which served as probes for appropriate proctor behavior. The student recited each script probe to the trainee while maintaining as much eye-contact with the trainee as possible. The trainee was instructed to respond to each probe. Following the trainee's response the student recited the next scripted probe. Thus, the trainee's responses to each scripted question recited by the student permitted measurement of the trainee's proctoring behaviors.

Before each session the trainees were given the same written instructions:

> In order for you to proceed you should review your student's folder to see how she or he is progressing in the course. Your task is to help your student with any questions over the lesson material prior to taking the quiz and once the quiz is completed, you should grade it and answer any questions about the answers.

A session began when the student was seated in the desk facing the trainee. Each student was instructed to allow the trainee to review his progress record before reading the scripted questions. If the trainee did not begin by reviewing the record the student read the first scripted question to the trainee.

Response Definitions

During each experimental session a trainee was observed for his use of three different proctoring behaviors: "Preparation Behaviors;" "Prompting Behaviors," and "Praise Behaviors."

Preparation Behaviors consisted of the trainee greeting his student by name; verbally reviewing the student's progress record and asking the student if he had any questions over that day's lesson.

Prompting Behaviors consisted of the trainee making an appropriate verbal prompt to assist a student to answer their own questions. Prompting consisted of any or all of the following sequence of responses. First, getting the student to attempt an answer to his question; next asking the student to provide a definition of the key terms in the answer; and then asking the student to provide an explanation of how the term applies to the example in the text.

Praise Behaviors consisted of a trainee giving his student positive feedback over his course standing to date, e.g. "You're doing very good work," "I see you have an A so far;" and giving the student positive feedback for correct or partially correct responses during the prompting sequence, e.g. "You gave a very good definition of reinforcement."

Using a data sheet, the observer during each session recorded the occurrence and nonoccurrence of the five possible preparation behaviors; the thirty-five possible prompting behaviors and the occurrence and nonoccurrence of the twenty-nine possible praise behaviors.

Mean percent occurrence of preparation, prompting, and praise behaviors was determined for each trainee by dividing the number of occurrences of those behaviors as recorded on the observer's data sheet by the total number of occasions that the behaviors should have occurred and computing a mean.

Training Package

On three different occasions during the experiment, each trainee participated in a training program. Each session of the program lasted about an hour and was conducted in the same classroom where the role-playing sessions took place. This training program was designed to teach the use of the three proctoring behaviors.

One day prior to each scheduled training session, a set of written instructional materials were given to each trainee. A different set of materials was prepared for each of the three proctoring behaviors. Each set consisted of a description of the proctoring behavior to be trained; a self-quiz that consisted of a description of the proctoring behavior to be trained; a self-quiz that consisted of an average of fifteen fill-in questions based on the description; and a set of hypothetical examples for each set of instructional materials before beginning a training session. After the answers were collected the trainer then gave the trainee a ten item quiz. The questions on the quizzes were selected directly from the self-quiz questions. Each trainee was required to score at least 80 percent correct on a quiz. If a score of 80 percent was not made, the trainee was required to re-read the instructional material and take a different form of the quiz.

After the quiz was completed, the trainer and trainee entered into a simulated student-proctor interaction where the trainer assumed the role of the student. A training script similar to the role-playing script was used during this interaction. The content of the training script was different than the role-playing script used during the regular experimental sessions. Note that simulated situations were used for two functions in the experiment: First, to observe proctoring behavior; and second, to train each proctor behavior.

When the session began, the trainer instructed the trainee to proceed with the interview. The trainee was allowed to respond and the trainer provided immediate feedback after each correct response ("That's correct, well done."). For each incorrect response, the trainer used a correction procedure. This procedure consisted of the trainer modeling the correct response, having the trainee repeat the response and then beginning the interaction again.

Reliability

The observer and a reliability observer made simultaneous but independent observations of each trainee's proctoring behaviors and responses to the questions contained on the script used during the experimental role-playing sessions. Reliability observations were made during each session for each trainee. At the end of each session the observers' data of the occurrence and nonoccurrence of each of the three proctoring behaviors were compared to obtain a measure of reliability. Total reliability was determined from the observers' data sheets made during each session for each trainee. This measure was computed by dividing the number of agreements of each proctoring response by the number of agreements plus disagreements. Total reliability for preparation behaviors was 90 percent with a range of 50 to 100 percent; for prompting behaviors, total reliability was 85 percent with a range from 60 to 100 percent; for praise behaviors total reliability was 90 percent with a range from 66 to 100 percent.

Experimental Design

A multiple baseline design across the three proctoring behaviors was used to evaluate the effectiveness of the training package. Preparation Behaviors were trained first, Prompting Behaviors trained second and Praise Behaviors trained last.

Baseline. For the first six sessions pre-training observations were made of each trainee's Preparation, Prompting and Praise Behaviors.

Training: Preparation Behaviors. For sessions 7 to 12 preparation behaviors were observed for the effect of this training while prompting and praise behaviors remained untrained in baseline.

Training: Prompting Behaviors. After session 12, the training package was used to train prompting behavior. For sessions 13 to 18 prompting behaviors were observed for the effect of training, while baseline observations were continued for the praise behaviors and post-training observations were made on the preparation behaviors.

Training: Praise Behaviors. After session 18 the training package was used to train praise behaviors. For sessions 18 to 24, praise behaviors were observed for the effect of training, while post-training observations were made on the preparation behaviors and prompting behaviors.

Two generalization tests, Test A and Test B, were scheduled both before and after training for each trainee. Each of the tests was conducted in the same classroom where the role-playing sessions occurred. The purpose of these tests was to permit observation of each trainee's use of the three proctoring behaviors to obtain a measure of generalization.

GENERALIZATION TEST A. A generalization script was used during these two tests. The questions contained on this script were "novel" since they were over a lesson different than the lesson covered by the experimental role-playing script. Thus, the content of the questions were new with respect to the concepts and terminology covered. However, the generalization script was functionally the same as the script used during the experimental role-playing sessions since it contained a total of thirty-five statements to the trainee each of which served as probes for appropriate proctor behavior. The same role-playing procedures during this test were followed as during all other experimental sessions. In addition, the trainees were provided with the same written instructions, materials and the same participants were present during the tests as for the experimental sessions.

At the end of each generalization test the observers data sheets were compared to obtain a measure of reliability for each trainee's use of the three proctoring behaviors. This yielded a mean total reliability of 100 percent for preparation behaviors; and 87 percent with a range from 77 to 94 percent for prompting behaviors and 92 percent with a range from 73 percent to 100 percent for praise behaviors.

A composite mean percent occurrence of each trainee's use of the three proctoring behaviors was computed from the observer's data sheet before and after training.

GENERALIZATION TEST B. One of three students from the course were each assigned to a trainee. During these tests the trainee assisted the student with any questions he had over the lesson he was preparing to take the next class quiz over and then administered and graded the quiz. Each trainee was provided with the students progress record from the class and the same written instructions and materials used for the experimental sessions.

Audio tapes were made of the trainee and student's interaction. Using an inch recorder contained in the tape recorder, the observer and reliability observer independently but simultaneously recorded the inch number during which the trainee made appropriate eye contact with his student. The tapes were later scored by the observers to obtain a measure of reliability for each trainee's use of the three proctoring behaviors. This yielded a mean total reliability of 100 percent for preparation behaviors; and 98 percent with a range from 90 to 100 percent for prompting behaviors and 94 percent with a range from 85 to 100 percent for praise behaviors.

A composite mean percent occurrence of each trainee's use of the three proctoring behaviors was computed from the observers' scoring of the audio tapes.

RESULTS

Figure 13-1 is a summary graph showing the session by session average of each trainee expressed as a composite mean percent occurrence of the three measures of proctoring behaviors before and after training.

During baseline the mean percent occurrence of preparation behavior was 14 percent. After the training package for preparation behaviors was introduced the mean percent occurrence of those responses increased to a mean of 80 percent. At the same time baseline observations were continued for prompting and praise behaviors; the mean percent occurrence of those responses remained stable with some decrease in the occurrence of prompting behavior.

When the training package for prompting behavior was introduced the mean percent occurrence of prompting behavior increased from 52 percent to a mean of 90 percent. At the same time, praise behavior remained stable in a baseline condition; the mean occurrence of preparation behavior during post training observation remained stable at about 80 percent.

Finally, when praise behaviors were trained the mean percent occurrence increased from 5 to 88 percent. Post training observations of the other two behaviors showed that the occurrences of those responses remained stable.

These data show that each behavior increased after the introduction of the training package but remained stable during baseline and pre-training observations.

Figure 13-2 presents the individual data from which the summary data were derived. These data show that the post training occurrences of each of the three proctoring behaviors increased for each trainee after they had completed the components of the training package. Thus, the composite mean percent occurrence of each of the three proctoring behaviors is representative of each trainee's behavior.

Figure 13-3 shows the composite mean percent occurrence of the trainees' proctoring behaviors observed during Generalization Test A in which a different script was used. The diagonal bar represents the mean percent occurrence of proctoring behaviors before training and the solid bar represents the occurrence of the

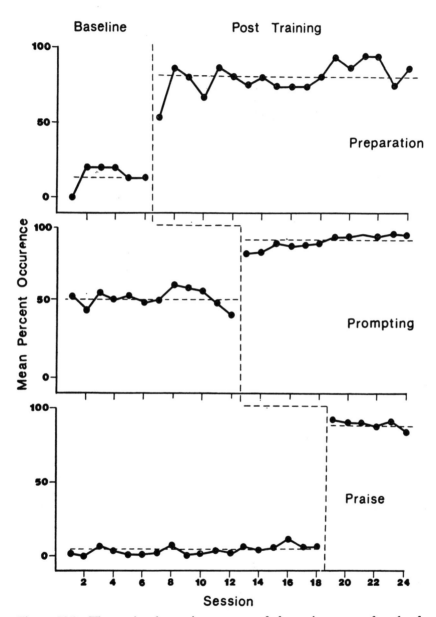

Figure 13-1. The session by session average of the trainees use of each of the three proctoring behaviors expressed as a composite mean percent ocurrence during baseline after training.

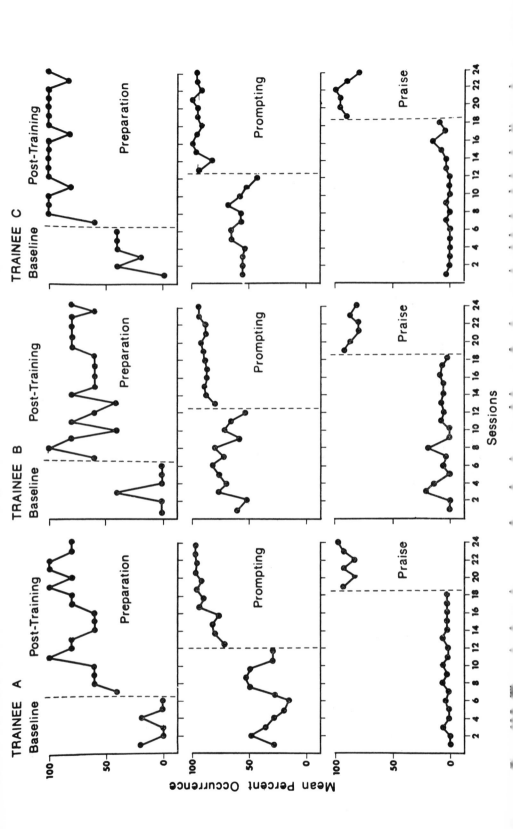

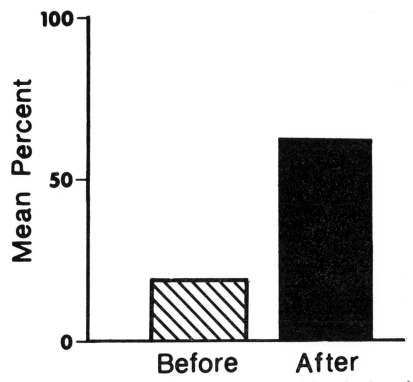

Figure 13-3. The composite mean percent occurrence of the trainees' use of proctoring behaviors observed during generalization Test A (where a novel script was used) before and after training.

behaviors after training. Before training the composite mean percent occurrence was 21 percent and after training it was 83 percent. These results indicate that the training package had the effect of increasing the trainees' appropriate use of proctoring responses to the novel questions contained on the generalization script.

Figure 13-4 shows the composite mean percent occurrence of the trainees' proctoring behaviors observed during Generalization Test B in which an actual student was proctored in a nonscripted situation. The diagonal bar represents the mean percent occurrence of proctoring behaviors before training and the solid bar represents the mean percent occurrence of the behaviors after training. These data show that before training the composite

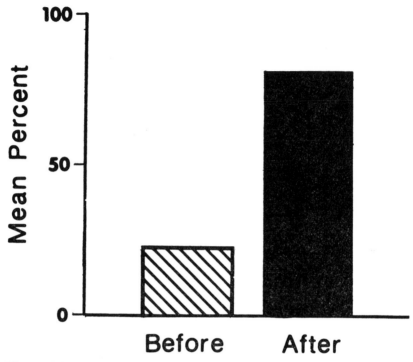

Figure 13-4. The composite mean percent occurrence of the trainees' use of proctoring behaviors observed during generalization Test B (where an actual student was used) before and after training.

mean percent occurrence was 19 percent and increased to 62 percent after training. These results indicate that the training package also had the effect of increasing the trainees' appropriate use of proctoring behaviors during an interaction with a student from the course.

Taken together, the results from the generalization tests suggest that this training package was effective in increasing the trainees' use of appropriate responses to novel questions asked of him/her during an unscripted interaction with a student from the course.

DISCUSSION

The results of the experiment clearly indicate that the proctor training package was effective in producing increases in proctoring responses of three undergraduate students. The fact that the occurrence of each behavior did not increase until after training indicates that the training package was responsible for the observed increases. Further, the individual data showed that the summary data is representative of each trainee's performance.

Further investigations may lead to a determination of whether both components of the proctor training package are necessary. The manual was effective in teaching the behaviors as measured by the quizzes administered over that material during the training sessions. However, it is not known if both the manual and role-playing training were necessary to produce the appropriate responses observed during the experimental sessions. On the other hand, experience with the simulated proctor-student interaction suggests that it is an integral component of the training situation.

The results further indicate that the training package was effective in producing some generalization of the entire class of proctoring behaviors to a set of novel questions and to a novel student. The results of Generalization Test B, where a student from the course interacted with the trainees in an unscripted interaction, were not as impressive as the results of Test A where a generalization script was used. Although no special techniques to increase generalization were used in the training procedures, the generalization sessions were similar enough to the experimental sessions for generalization to be expected. It may be that the role-playing component of the training sessions did not provide sufficient practice for the trainee with respect to integration of the prompting and praise behaviors. Steps are now being taken to incorporate many alternative ways of asking a proctor questions as well as different responses to a proctor's delivery of praise.

One question about the experiment should be discussed. Are the three behaviors: Preparation, prompting and praise valid proctoring behaviors?

It has been suggested by at least one source that important proctor behaviors are the scheduling of reinforcing events to follow the desired variants of a student's behavior (Farmer, Lachter, Blaustein & Cole, 1972). This suggests that some technique for prompting and reinforcing the variants of a student's behavior is needed. Clearly the prompting sequence used in this study begins to specify a procedure designed to produce the desired responses of a student. Similarly, the praise component begins to specify a procedure for proctors to schedule the occurrence of positive feedback with respect to a student's standing in the course and to his behavior during the prompting sequence of the interaction. Further, past experience with the Keller Method suggests that monitoring each student's progress through the course is an important dimension in maintaining the teaching staff's contact with each student's performance and ensuring that each student is informed of his academic achievement.

The fact that the training package was shown to be effective in teaching student proctor behaviors that have been pointed out as important and useful indicates the package to be a useful tool to extend the efficiency and effectiveness of the teaching staff. In addition, the specification and measurement of at least three proctor behaviors may provide a criteria for defining and evaluating good student proctors.

ACADEMIC PERFORMANCE AND GRADES

ONE OF THE MOST IMPORTANT INFLUENCES on how the student reacts to the demands of a course is the way in which standards of performance are defined and the way grade labels are related to these criteria. The first paper, "Mastery Test Proficiency Requirement Affects Mastery Test Performance," examines mastery criteria and some of their effects. The second paper, "Comparison of Graduated and Fixed Point Systems of Contingency-Managed Instruction," shows the influence of grade-related point systems on performance. The last paper, "Forced Excellence Versus 'Free Choice' of Grades in Undergraduate Instruction," looks at the combined effects of grading standards and grade labels. The conclusions of these studies suggest that grading practices in higher education may be in need of some substantial changes.

MASTERY TEST PROFICIENCY RE- QUIREMENT AFFECTS MASTERY TEST PERFORMANCE

MICHAEL L. DAVIS

DICKINSON COLLEGE

A NUMBER OF EDUCATORS HAVE RECENTLY described variations on traditional systems of college instruction. Some of these fit under the name Personalized System of Instruction (PSI) coined by Keller (1966, 1968). Although specific applications of the Keller method may differ, most variations require the student to demonstrate mastery by mastery test covering one unit of material before proceeding to the next unit in the sequence. The student passes the mastery test when his performance meets the proficiency criterion defined by the instructor. Also, the student is given considerable freedom to pace or schedule his progress through the course materials.

The mastery testing features of the PSI procedures have been described as a mastery learning procedure by Wilson and Tosti

This study was conducted as a Ph.D. thesis while the author was at the University of Utah and was supported by the Department of Psychology.

I thank Mike Corley, Mary Alice Rudelich, Paul Lund, Katie Hawk, Michelle Buchanan, Eddie Parker, Joanne Ushio, and Kim Kannel who served as proctors and/or helped to reduce the data, and Dr. David G. Born who was my thesis advisor.

(1972). Mastery learning occurs when some instructional procedure is used that ensures that students reach a predefined high quality of performance. Mastery learning is a discriminating concept in instructional technologies. Instructional procedures that produce mastery learning presumably do so in spite of differences in students' academic histories, aptitudes or entering behaviors (Block, 1971).

The PSI procedures attempt to produce mastery learning by the use of a performance or proficiency criterion. For instance, in Born's (1970) version of PSI students are required to produce an acceptable answer to all items in each mastery test. This is a 100 percent proficiency criterion. The experiment reported here was designed to assess the effects of lowering the proficiency requirements from 100 percent to 50 percent to determine if mastery learning was occurring in students with different aptitudes or entering behaviors. As a second interest, data were obtained indicating the amount of contact time students had with textbook materials in a special study setting. Students with differing academic histories (either a high cumulative grade point average or a low grade point average in previous university courses) were selected. If mastery learning was occurring, then students from both grade point levels would be expected to meet the proficiency criterion at either the 50 percent or 100 percent levels. Finally, it was anticipated that a lower proficiency requirement might affect students' rates of proress through the course.

METHOD

Subjects

The subjects were selected from 150 students who enrolled in a section of general psychology at the University of Utah, Spring quarter, 1972. The highest twenty students, in terms of grade point average (above 3.04 on a 4.00 scale) and the lowest twenty-six students (below 2.20 on a 4.00 scale) were selected to be subjects. Of the original list of forty students, eight high GPA and eleven low GPA students did not complete the course or withdrew. Each student was randomly assigned to be supervised by one of six undergraduate course assistants called *proctors*.

Course Procedures

Generally the students were enrolled in an introductory psychology course that employed a version of the PSI format described by Born (1970) and used in a previous quarter at the University of Utah (see Born, Davis, Jackson, & Whelan, 1972).

Progress Through the Course and Text Materials

A student progressed through the course by reading one unit of material, passing a mastery test covering that unit, reading the next unit, taking a test, and continuing this sequence until all sixteen units were covered. When a student failed a mastery test, he was required to restudy the assignment and take an alternate form of the test.

The textbook materials were organized into sixteen units. Because the experiment was designed to obtain data about student contact time with the textbook, the students were not in possession of their own textbooks. Instead text materials were available to be checked out and used in the study center, a library-type setting. The library setting (Study Center) was a large room with no windows and was capable of seating approximately sixty students. To prevent students from studying for other courses, talking about other courses, etc. they were asked to leave all briefcases and books on shelves near the monitor's station, and only students enrolled in the introductory phychology course from which the subject sample was drawn were allowed to use the study center. Also, data from a previous course indicated that students using the study center spent a high percentage of their time looking at the text materials and writing (see Born & Davis, submitted).

Time in Study Center

The study center monitors recorded the time of day each student entered and left the study center using a wall clock as the time standard. From these records each student's total time per entry was obtained by subtracting the entry time from the exit time. Reliability checks on this time datum were made by a reliability checker who was frequently in the study center, near the monitors reducing the time of day data to study time form.

She obtained reliability data by recording the student's name and time of day as students entered and left the center. By comparison with the times recorded by the monitors reliability estimates were made. The times obtained by each monitor were correlated with those obtained by the checker during reliability checks, and a minimum of ten observations were made on each monitor. The product-moment correlation coefficients were all above $= .990$.

Mastery Tests

When a student was ready to take a test he reported to a testing room any weekday during the scheduled class hour and requested the appropriate unit test from the instructor. Test items were of completion and short answer types. Following completion of the test, an undergraduate student proctor scored the test and interviewed the student. The interview included asking the student to restate written answers that were incorrect or ambiguous. Written answers that were unacceptable could be clarified or revised orally during the interview. Revised, acceptable oral answers were counted as "correct" inasmuch as the student was allowed to pass the test. For purposes of later data analysis, only written performance data as scored by the proctors were analyzed.

The course was divided into four phases, each phase consisted of four unit mastery tests and terminated with a comprehensive review examination. To insure that no student fell too far behind in taking tests and to ensure equal numbers of test opportunities at each phase deadline, dates were set by which all students were required to take the examination. Each phase could consist of as many as, but no more than eleven testing opportunities.

A validity check on the proctors' scoring relative to acceptable prototype answers previously defined by the instructor was made by having the instructor blindly score thirty randomly sampled mastery tests that had been scored by each proctor, that is, a total of 180 tests. Product-moment correlations were computed using the total number of correct items assigned by each proctor and by the instructor as the variables. These correlation coefficients ranged from $= .867$ to $= .959$. In all comparisons the instructor's mean score was lower than the proctor's mean score for the thirty tests; the greatest difference was 0.9 item out of an average of 11.8 items per test scored. That is, on the average the greatest percentage disagreement between the instructor and any proctor was 7.6 percent.

Experimental Design

TREATMENT PROCEDURES AND ASSIGNMENT OF SUBJECTS. Two mastery testing procedures were employed. One procedure required students to pass mastery tests by providing an acceptable answer to each mastery test item; this was the 100 percent or high proficiency requirement (HP). The other procedure required students to pass mastery tests by providing acceptable answers to at least one half of the items; this was the 50 percent or low proficiency requirement (LP). Students in each of the GPA categories were randomly assigned to a group that progressed through the course under the HP or to another group that progressed through the course alternating between the LP and the HP.

The sequence of treatments for each group of students are shown in Table 14-I.

RESULTS AND DISCUSSION

Mastery Test Performance

The number of correctly written answers (as scored by the proctors) provided by each student to mastery test items were totaled for the four units in each phase of the course. The total number of correct answers in each phase was divided by the total

TABLE 14-I

Summary of Sequence of Treatments and Assignment of
Groups to Treatment Sequences

Groups	GPA***	Phases of Course			
		1	2	3	4
1	High	HP*	HP	HP	HP
2	High	LP*	HP	LP	HP
3	Low	HP	HP	HP	HP
4	Low	LP	HP	LP	HP

* HP–High (100%) Proficiency on Mastery Tests.
** LP–Low (50%) Proficiency on Mastery Tests.
*** GPA–Cumulative Grade Point average based on at least twenty attempted quarter units.

number of possible answers to obtain a percent correct score. These percentage scores were calculated (1) on the basis of all the tests students attempted and (2) on the basis of only the tests students passed.

Group mean percentages were calculated for each group of students at each phase of the course; these means are shown in Figure 14-1. The upper panel means were calculated on the basis of all attempted tests, and the lower panel means were calculated on the basis of only the mastery tests students passed.

First, high GPA students provided a higher percentage of

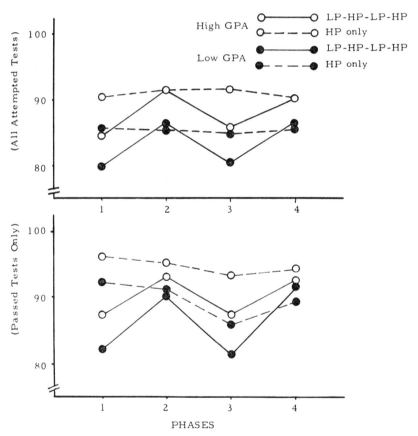

Figure 14-1. Mean number of unit tests successfully completed for each group during the three point intervals of the semester.

correctly written mastery test answers than low GPA students and this was found to be statistically reliable.[1] Secondly, for all students assigned to the low proficiency condition there was a lower percentage of correct answers (1) than when the same students were assigned to the high proficiency conditions or (2) than the students concurrently assigned to high proficiency. Statistical analyses supported these results. The GPA X Treatment Group interaction was statistically reliable.[2] This indicated that the proficiency requirement was effecting some differences in student mastery test performance even though low GPA students were not performing near the level of the high GPA students, and students from neither GPA level were performing at mastery (100% correct written performance).

The mastery testing procedures that were employed were very similar to those used by Born (see Born, Gledhill, and Davis, 1972). The present results indicated that at least Born type applications of the PSI do not necessarily result in mastery learning, that is, 100 percent correct answers. Further, these data do not support the contention by Wilson and Tosti (1972) that PSI type mastery testing is necessarily a mastery learning procedure. First, students rarely provided one-hundred percent correct written answers, and secondly, low GPA students did not perform at a level generally comparable to that of the high GPA students.

However, a higher proficiency requirement clearly resulted in superior mastery test performance. Therefore, assuming mastery tests to be an appropriate measure of learning, a higher perfor-

---

[1] By reference to Table 14-I, it should be clear that there was an extreme groups design where the GPA level was the concomitant variable. The other factors in the design included phases of the course (four levels) and the Treatment Sequence to which students were assigned (two levels). Because unequal numbers of students were in each group an unweighted means analysis of variance (ANOVA) was computed using procedures suggested by Winer (1972, pp. 241–244), and mean comparisons were made using the Newman Keuls test. The ANOVA yielded a GPA main effect $F = 8.500$. $df = 1, 23$, $p < .01$, and the Newman-Keuls test indicated that the means were different ($p < .05$).

[2] The ANOVA described in footnote 3 yielded a GPA X Treatment Sequence Groups interaction $F = 5.000$, $df = 3, 69$, $p < .01$, and multiple comparisons using the Newman-Keuls test indicated that the means of students (groups) assigned to 50 percent were lower than when the same students were assigned to 100 percent or than the means of students always assigned to 100 percent ($p < .05$).

mance criterion would seem desirable. On the basis of data from courses with slightly different contingencies and behavioral measures Johnston (Johnston and Pennypacker, 1971; Johnston and O'Neill, 1973) has made a similar suggestion. In the present data, it would appear that a 90 percent proficiency criterion could be used since during the 100 percent criterion phases students typically wrote at least that percentage of answers correctly. It is further interesting to note that a 90 percent proficiency level approximates the empirically determined criterion described by Johnston and Pennypacker (1971).

In their analyses Johnston and Pennypacker (1971) emphasized the importance of individual student performance records. Individual student records of mastery test performance in the present study were constructed by cumulatively totaling each student's percentage correct mastery test answers at each testing opportunity. The top panel of Figure 14-2 shows the cumulative percentage of correct answers for two prototype low GPA students who were assigned to the 50 percent criterion during Phases 1 and 3 of the course. The diagonal lines extending below the functions indicate the date when the student took a comprehensive examination. The most apparent differences would be in terms of the overall rate of answering mastery test items per opportunity. Student DT performed at an overall rate that was higher than that of DS. During the first three phases of the course, performance similar to that of DS was more typical of low GPA students than of high GPA students. Because of this an analysis was attempted of these cumulative records relative to time deadlines that were established as course procedure. Students were allowed no more than eleven testing opportunities to pass four mastery tests and to take the comprehensive examination covering those four units. The lower panel of Figure 14-2 shows the students' performance records plotted relative to the eleven-day deadlines. Because student DS consistently took the examinations on the last possible day, her cumulative record is unchanged. However, student DT consistently took his examinations before the deadlines. His record for each phase of the course has been offset by an amount shown with

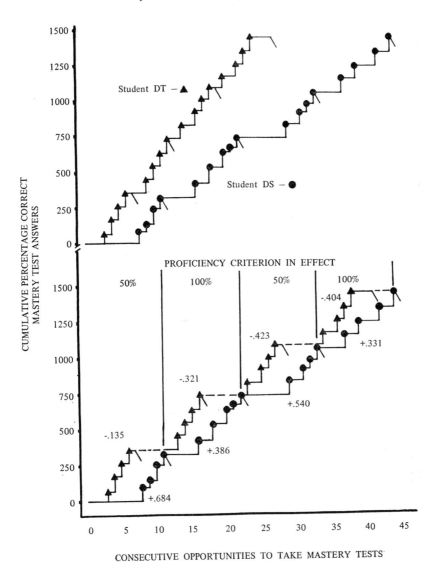

Figure 14-2. Proportion of students in each group categorized as Early, Steady, and Late Responders.

dashed lines so that each phase on the figure is effectively eleven days long. That is, student DT's data is plotted relative to the eleven-day deadline.

It is apparent that student DT was completing his required tests and examination before the deadlines and that student DS was completing the required work just in time to meet the deadlines. In language that is typical of behavior analysis DS was procrastinating or responding with a "scallop" that is sometimes typical of behavior under control of time-based contingencies.

To quantify the differences in the cumulative performances shown in the lower panel of Figure 14-2 a mathematical index of curvature described by Fry, Kelleher and Cook (1960) was computed for each cumulative record at each phase of the course. Figure 14-3 includes some cumulative records to illustrate the types of curves that are associated with different values of the index. The index can theoretically range from −1.000 to = 1.000. When the curve is negatively accelerated as in the first curve in Figure 14-3 the index has a positive value. When the curve is nearly a straight line the index is of near-zero value as in the second record in Figure 14-3. As a general rule, the greater the

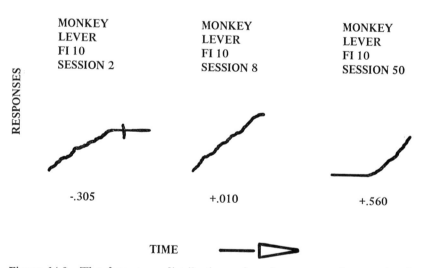

Figure 14-3. The frequency distributions of students per units completed during the three intervals of the semester. Cross-hatched bars represent the completion of eight or more unit tests during the interval.

curvature (departure from a straight line) the greater the magnitude of the index.[3]

Returning to the bottom panel of Figure 14-2, the values of the indices of curvature for each phase have been shown. Because DT completed the testing very early the indices for DT's curves are negative while the indices for DS's curves are positive. Also, the magnitude of the indices of DS's curves are informative. During 100 percent criteria phases of the course when DS began testing earlier and answered a higher percentage of items correctly the indices of curvature are of a lower value than during 50 percent criteria phases. In general, a lower valued index indicated that a student began testing earlier and/or finished testing sooner relative to the time deadlines associated with each comprehensive examination.

The indices of curvature of all student cumulative records of mastery test performance are in Table 14-II. Students who consistently had lower valued indices during 100 percent phases (Phases two and four) than during adjacent 50 percent phases have been indicated by an asterisk. Most of the low GPA students who alternated between 50 percent and 100 percent had lower indices during the 100 percent phases as compared to the adjacent 50 percent phases. This suggested, and in fact visual examination of the cumulative records verified, that a larger proportion of the low GPA students began or finished the testing later when the fifty percent criterion was in effect than when the 100 percent criterion was in effect. Similar performances by students not assigned to the 50 percent criterion or who had a "better" academic history (higher GPA) were far less frequent.

---

[3] In fact, the magnitude of the index suggested by Fry, et al. (1960) is determined both by the curvature (best fit) of the function to which the index is fit and by the number of time intervals into which the function is broken when the index is calculated. As the number of time intervals approaches infinity the absolute magnitude of the index approaches 1.00. At less than infinite numbers of intervals the limited of the absolute magnitude of the index is given by the quotient $\dfrac{(n-1)}{n}$, where n is the number of time intervals. In the present study $n = 6$, and the limits of the index were $\pm .833$.

TABLE 14-II
Index of Curvature for Cumulative Percentage Correct Mastery Test
Answers for Each Student at Each Phase of the Course

GPA	Students	Phase of Course			
		1	2	3	4
	Group I	100% Only			
	JH	+.264	+.409	+.341	+.482
	PH	+.153	+.156	+.244	+.096
	MM	−.151	+.134	+.396	+.176
	JM	+.133	−.022	−.328	+.322
	RAS	+.246	+.150	+.322	+.307
High	Group II	50%	100%	50%	100%
	DB	−.347	−.420	−.326	−.272
	PF	+.037	+.254	−.169	+.011
	BH	−.009	+.187	+.306	+.184
	RK	+.428	+.663	+.255	+.232
	LIL*	+.249	+.197	+.500	+.292
	ML*	−.068	−.339	−.083	−.340
	FP	+.069	+.160	+.081	−.410
	Group III	100% Only			
	SA*	+.232	+.197	+.605	+.479
	BB*	+.667	+.591	+.695	+.054
	AG	+.167	−.034	−.060	−.092
	KL	+.272	+.428	+.400	+.184
	LEL	+.156	+.443	+.374	+.467
	KM	+.308	+.214	−.073	+.149
	SM	+.507	+.489	+.476	+.509
Low	Group IV	50%	100%	50%	100%
	JK*	+.447	+.345	+.403	+.064
	BM*	+.307	.000	+.104	−.006
	ER	+.219	+.300	+.530	+.095
	MS*	+.625	+.583	+.640	+.494
	ROS*	+.354	+.342	+.733	+.574
	DS	+.684	+.368	+.540	+.331
	DT	−.135	−.321	−.423	−.408
	KW	−.493	−.328	+.005	−.097

Time in Study Center

The total daily time in the study center for each student was
cumulatively summed over successive days when the study center
was open yielding a distribution of cumulative study time for each
study opportunity. In the upper panel of Figure 14-4 are the
cumulative study time distributions for each study opportunity
for two prototype low GPA students who were assigned to the 50
percent criterion during Phases 1 and 3. The index of curvature
described in the previous section was calculated on these cumula-

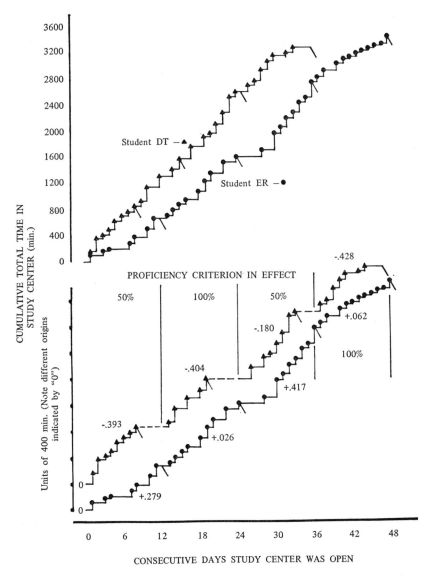

Figure 14-4. Proportion of students in each group who completed more than twenty-five units, exactly twenty-five units, and less than twenty-five units.

tive distributions, and these indices are shown in the lower panel of Figure 14-4. In terms of time in the study center, Student DT began using the study center early, studied consistently and finished early relative to the examination deadlines. By comparison, Student ER either did not study consistently or began to study later when the 50 percent criterion was in effect as compared to when the 100 percent criterion was in effect. When the 100 percent criterion was in effect ER appeared to use the study center fairly consistently over the study opportunities. Under both ER completed studying on the examination deadline dates.

Again, the indices of curvature reflect curvature in the time in study center records. Indices calculated on DT's studying are all negative in value. On the other hand, indices calculated on ER's studying are either noticeably positive in value (during 50 percent criterion) or near zero (during 100 percent criterion).

Table 14-III shows the indices of curvature calculated on the cumulative records of time in the study center for all students. Students whose indices were lower during the 100 percent criterion phase as compared to adjacent 50 percent criterion phases have been indicated with an asterisk. A large proportion of the low GPA students assigned to alternate between the 50 percent and the 100 percent criteria obtained indices of curvature that were lower when the 100 percent criterion was in effect.

Incidentally, during 100 percent criterion the same low GPA students in Group 4 appeared to have a lower index of curvature for both mastery test performance (Table 14-II) and for time in study center (Table 14-III). That is, the distribution of mastery test performance over test opportunities and the distribution of time in study center both suggest that low GPA students began studying and testing and finished studying and testing later under the 50 percent criterion than under the 100 percent criterion. The similarity in the shape of the cumulative records of mastery test performance and studying was suggested by Johnston and Pennypacker (1971). The present data clearly support their suggestion. The correlation between students' index of curvature of mastery test performance and index of curvature of time in study center was +.798, +.796, and +.709 respectively for each phase of the course. On the other hand, correlations of total mastery test scores and total time in the study center ranged from +.28 to −.41.[4]

---

[4] The critical value of r in a test of r being different than zero at $p = .05$ is $r = \pm .374$ with twenty-six degrees of freedom.

TABLE 14-III
Index of Curvature for Cumulative Total Study Time for
Each Student at Each Phase of the Course

GPA	Students	Phase of Course			
		1	2	3	4
	Group 1	100% Only			
	JH	+.107	+.149	−.026	+.549
	PH	−.031	−.267	+.185	+.106
	MM	−.256	−.015	+.234	−.094
	JM	−.237	−.427	−.475	+.501
	RAS	−.058	+.283	+.149	+.337
High	Group 2	50%	100%	50%	100%
	DB*	−.514	−.545	−.171	−.428
	PF	+.133	+.191	−.097	+.221
	BH	−.291	−.300	−.041	+.077
	RK	+.203	+.646	+.267	+.472
	LIL	+.215	+.040	+.173	+.173
	ML*	−.418	−.504	−.288	−.308
	FP	−.035	+.024	−.266	−.308
	Group 3	100% Only			
	SA	−.029	−.123	+.111	+.349
	BB	+.536	+.653	+.551	+.159
	AG	+.050	−.085	−.140	−.243
	KL*	+.163	−.003	+.253	+.044
	LEL	+.007	−.415	+.196	+.238
	KM	+.009	+.302	−.257	+.082
	SM	+.090	+.061	+.091	+.283
Low	Group 4	50%	100%	50%	100%
	JK*	+.212	−.100	+.270	−.133
	BM*	+.108	−.201	+.342	−.245
	ER*	+.279	+.026	+.417	+.062
	MS*	+.606	+.507	+.526	−.030
	ROS*	+.414	+.289	+.696	+.356
	DS*	+.334	+.263	+.389	+.116
	DT	−.393	−.404	−.180	−.428
	KW	−.066	−.150	−.186	−.261

Conclusions

The goal of this study was to discover what effects changing the instructor-defined proficiency criterion would have on mastery test performance and time in a study setting for two groups of students, one with a very good academic history and another with a considerably poorer academic history. First, the percentage of correct mastery test answers was lower under the 50 percent criterion than under the 100 percent criterion. Secondly, students with a poorer academic history obtained lower percentage correct mastery test scores than did students with a superior academic history. Third, the way in which students with a low GPA distributed their mastery test performance and time in the study center over the opportunities to be tested or to study tended to be adversely affected by the 50 percent criterion. That is, low GPA students tended to begin studying and testing earlier, to study and test at more regular rates, and to meet test and examination contingencies earlier under the 100 percent criterion than under the 50 percent criterion.

These results suggest certain procedures be employed in Keller type courses. First, other things being constant a higher proficiency requirement would typically be desirable since it should result in superior performance. Where empirical determination of the proficiency criterion is not possible because students are allowed some margin of error in definition and short answer items that can be clarified during an interview with a proctor, the instructor's stated criterion may not be met.

Secondly, the present data indicated that cumulative records of mastery test performance may, as Johnston and Pennypacker (1971) suggested, also reflect the way a student distributes his studying over the time available. If so, instructors may use cumulative records of mastery test performance as a diagnostic to detect students who (1) are more likely to have difficulty meeting course deadlines and (2) may not be studying sufficiently or may not begin studying early enough to meet course deadlines. From that point other descriptive techniques (e.g. Johnston, Roberts and O'Neill, 1972) or management techniques (Miller and Gimpl, 1972) should be employed to effect appropriate changes in the student's study behavior.

Thirdly, there was some indication that students with a poorer academic history (low GPA) were affected differently by a Keller-type course than students with a superior academic history. On the average, low GPA students answered a lower percentage of mastery test questions than high GPA students. Further, they tended to wait until later, relative to course deadlines, to begin taking mastery tests and use the study center. It would seem that these are precisely the students who should be encouraged and induced to begin testing earlier so that course deadlines do not continue to be such aversive contingencies. Again, in this respect cumulative records of mastery test performance may be a particularly useful diagnostic for low GPA students.

Finally, while the index of curvature was a useful technique for quantification of mastery test cumulative records, it may not be too practical for courses that are not specifically designed as research settings. First, the index is time-consuming to calculate. Secondly, the relationship between the value of the index and student performance records is not easy for undergraduate course assistants to understand. For practical purposes with both course assistants and students, it would probably be more useful to emphasize the importance of continuous progress through the course.

A COMPARISON OF GRADUATED AND FIXED POINT SYSTEMS OF CONTINGENCY MANAGED INSTRUCTION

STEPHEN C. BITGOOD

KERRY SEGRAVE

THIS PAPER IS CONCERNED with procrastination, the most frequently observed problem of student behavior. Procrastination refers to a response pattern of students in which less work is completed early compared to the greater amount completed late in the semester. In both coventional and contingency managed courses students who earn low grades often demonstrate a low initial rate of work (Lloyd & Knutzen, 1969; Sheppard and Mac Dermot, 1970; Powers and Edwards, 1972). Several investigators have addressed themselves to the procrastination problem. For example, Lloyd (1971) attempted to overcome the slow start of procrastinating students by offering bonus points for work completed early in the semester. This technique appeared to be successful in establishing work in the semester since eleven of the

This course was completed at McMaster University, Hamilton, Ontario, Canada. We gratefully acknowledge the assistance of the following individuals who served as proctors: Chris Crowley, Joel Hundert, Marg Brevik, Bob MacFarlane, and Jane Salhani. We also wish to thank Dr. G. D. West, Dean of the School of Adult Education for his cooperation.

sixteen students from the bonus point group turned in work during this same period. Bitgood and Kuch (1971) used a graduated point system in which the value of successfully completed tests decreased during the semester. Over 90 percent of the students completed at least one unit test during the first week and the percentage of students completing at least one unit per week did not fall below 80 percent until the sixth week, at which time the majority of students had completed the required number of points for an "A". While the results were encouraging, there was no experimental comparison in this study and it was not possible to attribute student performance to the graduated point system. Powers (personal communication) at Utah State University reported similar results using a procedure which he calls an adjusting point system. The paper presented by Scott Wood and Ruth Wylie at this conference describes yet another procedure designed to reduce procrastination. The Wood-Wylie technique gives bonus points several times during the semester for maintaining a minimum rate of test completion.

The present course was designed to provide an experimental comparison between an Increasing Graduated Point System, a Decreasing Graduated Point System, and a Fixed Point System. In the Increasing Graduated Point System a successful performance earned eight points during the first interval of the course, ten points during the second interval, and twelve points during the final interval. In the Decreasing Graduated Point System a successful test performance earned twelve, ten, and eight points for successive intervals of the course. Finally, in the Fixed Point System successful tests earned ten points throughout the course.

METHOD

Subjects

The subjects were ninety-six undergraduate students enrolled in the summer evening general psychology course at McMaster University during the summer of 1973. Thirty-two students were assigned to each of the three groups. A total of nine students dropped from the course, two from the Fixed Point Group, three from the Decreasing Graduated Point Group, and four from the Increasing Graduated Point Group.

Materials

The source material used in the course was a general survey introductory psychology text (Kendler, 1968). The text was divided into thirty units averaging approximately twenty pages each. For each of the units students were provided with study outlines (Corey & McMichael, 1970) which reviewed the main points of the units and required written responses for definitions, identifications, and exemplifications. Behavorial objectives for the units were also described in the outlines. For each unit there were four test forms samplinig the material emphasized by the study outlines. A course evaluation form developed by Koen (1970) was also used.

Procedure

At the first class meeting students were randomly divided into three groups. This division was accomplished by giving each student a slip of paper which directed him to one of three smaller classrooms. Students had no prior knowledge that each class would be treated differently. Course outlines describing the structure and objectives of the course were distributed, and questions regarding the course procedures were answered. Students were told that attendance at proctoring sessions was optional and that they could proceed through the course at their own pace. Proctoring sessions were available during the two-hour class periods on Tuesday and Thursday evenings. Proctoring sessions involved studying the unit outlines, discussing the course material with proctors, and takiing unit tests. The six proctors rotated among the three groups from week to week in order to control for biases in grading.

The semester was divided into three equal intervals for the purposes of assigning test points. Group 12-10-8 (Decreasing Graduated Point Condition) received twelve points for each successful test during the first third of the semester, ten points for each successful test during the second interval, and eight points during the last interval. Group 10-10-10 (Fixed Point Condition) received ten points for each successful test throughout the semester; and finally, Group 8-10-12 (Increasing Graduated Point Condition) received eight points during the first interval, ten during the second, and twelve during the last interval of the semester.

Twenty-five of the thirty text units were covered on the final exam and students were required to complete these twenty-five units in order. A total of 250 points earned from unit tests comprised 50 percent of the final grade and the final exam accounted for the other 50 percent. Students were allowed to complete the remaining five units for points. Each point in excess of 250 was multiplied by .1 and added to the students' final grades. Thus, students were given extra credit for work beyond the requirements of the course.

RESULTS AND DISCUSSION

Several findings in the present study suggest that the tendency of students to procrastinate was modified by the graduated point systems. These findings include (1) the number of successful unit tests completed by each group during the three point intervals of the semester; (2) the proportion of students in each group exhibiting Early, Steady, and Late response patterns during the semester; and (3) the frequency distributions of students per units completed by each group during the three intervals of the semester.

Figure 15-1 graphs the mean number of successful unit tests completed for each group during the three point intervals of the semester. The fact that Group 10-10-10 increased its mean response rate during the semester indicated the tendency of many students to procrastinate when the point value remained fixed throughout the semester. Procrastination was more pronounced in Group 8-10-12 where a small number of unit tests were taken during the first point interval and a large number were taken during the third interval.

Response rates were high during the first two point intervals in Group 12-10-8; this group actually completed more work during the ten point interval than during the twelve point interval. This latter finding may suggest that although procrastination was attenuated somewhat, it was not completely offset by the greater payoff of the twelve point interval. The lower rate of responding in the third interval was due to the fact that the majority of students had completed all their course work at this time. In summary, compared with Group 10-10-10, procrastination was increased in Group 8-10-12 and decreased in Group 12-10-8.

Figure 15-1 also indicates that the number of successful unit tests completed during the first and third point intervals was an increasing function of the number of points earned per test. In the first interval Group 8-10-12 averaged fewer unit tests (3.89) than did Group 10-10-10 (6.47) and Group 12-10-8 (9.55). During the second interval when all groups received ten points per test,

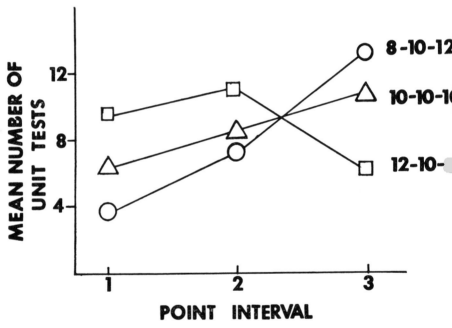

Figure 15-1. Mean percent mastery test answers at each phase of the course for each of the four treatment sequence groups. The means in the upper panel were computed on the basis of all tests students attempted, and the means in the lower panel were computed on the basis of only the tests students passed. At Phases 1 and 3 the groups shown in solid lines were required to answer only fifty percent of the test items correctly (the low proficiency requirement—LP) to pass a test. At other phases these students were required to answer 100 percent of the items correctly (the high proficiency requirement—HP), and the other groups were assigned to HP during all phases.

the same ordering between groups was found with Group 8-10-12 averaging 7.29, Group 10-10-10 averaging 8.30, and Group 12-10-8, 10.93. By the last point interval Groups 8-10-12 and 12-10-8 had reversed their order. Group 8-10-12 had a mean of 13.11; Group 10-10-10, a mean of 10.60; and Group 12-10-8, a mean of 6.03. The number of unit tests successfully completed for each group during the three point intervals of the semester was submitted to an analysis of variance for a mixed design, one variable between-subjects and one within-subjects. A significant group X point interval interaction was found; $F (4,78) = 77.37$, $p<.001$; as well as a significant effect of point interval; $F (2,78) = 4.05$, $p<.05$. The point interval effect indicates that students tended to complete more work late than early in the semester. No point schedule resulted in a significantly greater number of total unit tests than either of the other schedules; $F (2,78) < 1$.

The results of Figure 15-1 support a conclusion that is consistent with the principles of reinforcement: students' rate of work is dependent upon the payoff. It is difficult to understand why this principle is not applied more often in the classroom.

Since group means rarely describe the behavior of individuals, the patterns of responding for individual students were divided into three mutually exclusive categories: Early, Steady, and Late Responding. If A equals the number of units completed in the first point interval, B equals the number of units completed during the second interval, and C equals the number of units completed during the last interval, then the categories of responding can be defined in the following manner:

Early Responders: $\dfrac{A + B}{2} > C$, where $|A - B|$ or $|A - C|$ or $|B - C| > 2$

Steady Responders: $|A - B|$ or $|A - C|$ or $|B - C| \leqq 2$

Late Responders: $\dfrac{A + B}{2} > C$, where $|A - B|$ or $|A - C|$ or $|B - C| > 2$

Note that for both Early and Late Responders the absolute value of at least one of the differences among point intervals (i.e. A − B,

A – C, or B – C) was greater than two unit tests. Students whose point interval differences resulted in an absolute value of 2 or less were classified as Steady Responders. Early Responders completed more work during the first two thirds of the course than during the last third, and Late Responders completed more work during the last third than during the first two thirds of the course.

Figure 15-2 show the proportion of students in each group categorized as Early, Steady, and Late Responders. It is apparent from this figure that the particular point schedule had a substantial

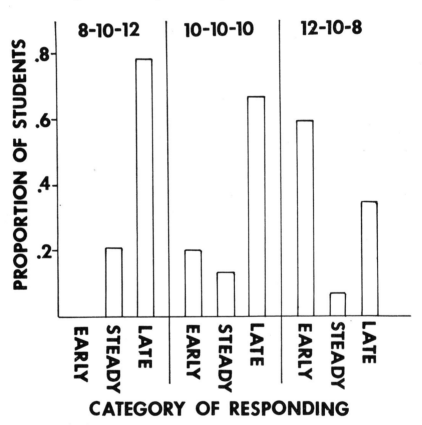

Figure 15-2. Upper panel shows two students' cumulative percentage correct mastery test answers at each opportunity to take a test. Lower panel shows the same data plotted against the eleven-day examination deadlines (see text for explanation) and also shows the index of curvature at each phase of the course. Both students were assigned to alternate between the 50 percent and the 100 percent requirement.

effect of the pattern of responding observed by individuals in each group, X^2 (4) $= 26.23$, p $< .001$. The most striking finding from this figure was that no Early Responders in Group 8-10-12 were observed, while fifty-nine percent of the students in Group 12-10-8 were placed in this category. In addition, the proportion of Late Responders was a function of point schedule: .79 for Group 8-10-12, .67 for Group 10-10-10, and .34 for Group 12-10-8.

Two conclusions can be drawn from Figure 15-2. First, students do not always respond in a similar manner. Although the majority of students can be classified as Late Responders, there is a substantial number of other patterns of responding. The other conclusion is that there is little tendency for students to complete work at a high rate early in the semester unless there is a large payoff for this work.

Figure 15-3 illustrates the rates of test completion for each group by the use of frequency distributions. Cross-hatched columns indicate the completion of eight or more units during the interval. A rate of about eight units per interval enabled a student to complete the course at a steady pace. It is apparent that the distribution of students per units completed changed during the semester for all three groups. The extreme case was found in the distribution of Group 8-10-12 in which two students completed more than eight units during the first point interval, but by the third interval twenty-seven of twenty-eight students completed more than eight unit tests. Group 10-10-10 exhibited a similar but less extreme pattern of a greater proportion of students completing more work later in the semester than early in the semester. A large proportion of students in Group 12-10-8, on the other hand, completed more work in the first two intervals than in the last point interval. This figure, similar to the last two figures, illustrates that the point schedule exerted powerful control over the rate of work of students.

The above results demonstrate that point schedules control *when* students complete their work. Another question of interest is, "Do the point schedules control *how much* work the student will complete?" Remember that students were allowed to earn extra credit by completing more than the twenty-five units covered on the final exam. It was possible for students to

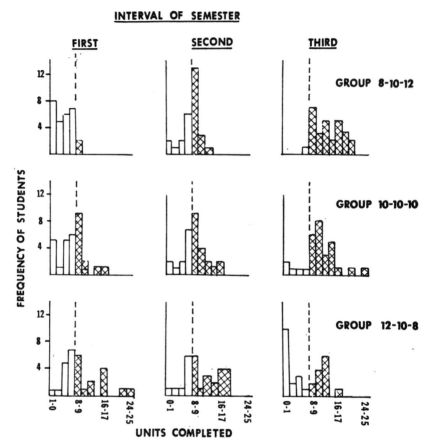

Figure 15-3. Three prototype graphs showing the relationship between the form of the function and the magnitude of the index of curvature (after Fry, Kelleher, and Cook, 1960).

complete up to thirty total units. The proportion of students in each group who completed greater than twenty-five units, exactly twenty-five units, and less than twenty-five units can be compared to see if the three point schedules resulted in differences in the amount of total units completed. This comparison is shown in Figure 15-4 which graphs the proportion of students in each group for each category of total units. Group 12-10-8 resulted in the completion of more than either Group 10-10-10 or Group 8-10-12. The proportion of students

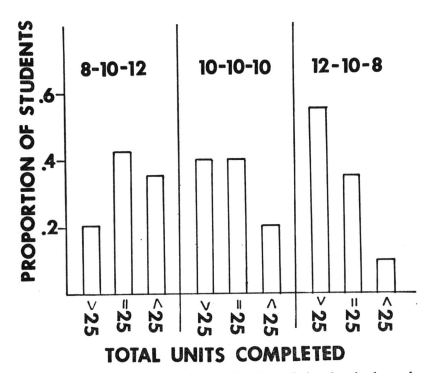

TOTAL UNITS COMPLETED

Figure 15-4. Upper panel shows two students' cumulative time in the study center at each opportunity to study. Lower panel shows the same data plotted against the eleven-day examination deadlines (see text for explanation) and also shows the index of curvature at each phase of the course. Both students were assigned to alternate between the 50 percent and the 100 percent proficiency requirement.

completing more than twenty-five units was .55 for Group 12-10-8, .40 for Group 10-10-10, and .21 for Group 8-10-12; $X^2 = 25.46$, $p < .001$, df = 2. In addition, a greater proportion of students in Group 8-10-12 (.36) failed to complete at least twenty-five units compared with .20 for Group 10-10-10 and .10 for Group 12-10-8; $X^2 = 19.92$, $p < .001$, df = 2. Since Group 12-10-8 resulted in both high rates early in the semester and a greater number of completed unit tests, the present results are consistent with the notion that reducing procrastination results in an increase in the total amount of work completed.

Final exam scores were submitted to a one-way analysis of

variance. Point schedules did not result in significantly different final exam scores between the three groups, F (2,84) = 1.02. Final exam performance was apparently insensitive to the fact that Group 12-10-8 completed more work.

A course evaluation form was given to students when they completed the twenty-fifth unit. Seventy of the eighty-seven students completed these forms. Unfortunately, the students who did not complete at least twenty-five units did not have the opportunity to complete course evaluations. Thus, the responses may have been biased. Of the students who completed course evaluation, the results were very favorable. For example, sixty-seven students indicated they would take another course taught by a similar method, but only two students said they would not. In addition, forty-eight students said the self-paced method was better than the lecture-discussion method, seven students considered it as good but not better than the traditional methods, and one student stated it was inferior to traditional methods. Results of the course evaluation were similar in all groups.

The Decreasing Graduated Point System is only one of many possible solutions to the procrastination problem. Several alternative techniques were noted previously in this paper (Lloyd, 1971; Powers, personal communication; Wood & Wylie, 1973). In addition, the most popular technique has been to administer compulsory tests at fixed times, such as daily or weekly (Cooper & Grenier, 1971; Malott & Svinicki, 1969; Mawhinney, Bostow, Laws, Blumenfeld & Hopkins, 1971; and Stalling, 1971). One disadvantage of the fixed-test-time procedure is that there is less flexibility regarding the scheduling of student study time. Students generally prefer to schedule their own study time, although it is often argued that many students are poor schedulers and must be given deadlines. A counterargument asserts that students should be trained to schedule their study time. It is not readily apparent that the Decreasing Graduated Point System assists in this training process. Another disadvantage of the fixed-test-time technique is that students are not encouraged to work faster than the specified minimum rate. Many students prefer to complete the required work as fast as possible to free their time for other activities. In addition, fast work rates are often considered desirable in our society. Whether students are overly concerned about either of these disadvantages of the fixed-test-time technique, remains to be demonstrated.

In summary, the present study demonstrated that the schedule of work payoff controlled both *when* the students completed the greater proportion of their work and *how much* total work they completed. The tendency to procrastinate was increased when a lower point value was given for tests completed early compared with tests completed late in the semester and the tendency to procrastinate was decreased when a higher point value was given for tests completed early. Finally, a higher proportion of students in the Decreasing Point Condition completed extra work than of students in the other point groups.

FORCED EXCELLENCE VERSUS "FREE CHOICE" OF GRADES IN UNDER-GRADUATE INSTRUCTION

Carol Whitehurst
Grover J. Whitehurst

O NE OF THE OUTCOMES OF INTRODUCING contingency management techniques into the college classroom is a grade distribution that is highly skewed due to a large proportion of A's as compared with other grades (Born, Gledhill, and Davis, 1972; Ferster, 1968; Keller, 1968; Meyers, 1970; Whitehurst, 1972). Such an outcome has been justified on the basis that students learn more in programmed courses and therefore should get higher grades, and that programmed methods reduce individual differences in performance and thus result in a tighter distribution of marks. There is evidence to support the premise of both these points (Born, et al. 1972; McMichael and Corey, 1969; Alba and Pennypacker, 1972).

If narrower distributions of performance with higher means are indeed desirable and if grade distributions are designed to reflect performance distributions, then students who drop or get grades of less than A in behaviorally managed courses represent failures of the management system. In fact, these failures occur quite frequently. For example, in the grade distributions presented in Keller's (1968) seminal paper on personalized instruction (which were drawn from several behaviorally managed courses) grades of less than A, withdrawals, and incompletes constitute, in one case, over 60 percent of the total grade distribution and in no case less than 40 percent. In a report of a behaviorally managed course by Sheppard and MacDermott (1970), 73 percent of the students who enrolled in the course fell in the non-A category. These cases should not be taken as representative for there is a broad range of results on this variable. For example, only 22 percent of the students in Ferster's (1968) study of personalized instruction did not receive A's. Two of the most "successful" reports are by Meyers (1970) and Whitehurst (1972). In the Meyers study, only 3 percent of the enrollees received grades of less than A, while the analogous figure was 8 percent and 4 percent for the two classes by Whitehurst.

There are, of course, many variables which might account for the differences previously discussed. The amount and complexity of the required work, the pre-course background of the students, the amount of remedial instruction available, and the performance criteria of the instructor are some factors which might contribute to the obtained differences. One salient difference between the Meyers (1970) and Whitehurst (1972) study, as compared with the many procedures which have produced a larger range and less skewed distribution of grades, lies in the range of performance made available to the students. Students in the Whitehurst (1972) study were told that they could either meet the criterion for an A or they would receive an F. Meyers (1970) told his students that they could receive an A or an incomplete. How this incomplete was to be resolved was ambiguous (in fact one student received a B). Johnston and O'Neill (1973) recently demonstrated that altering the minimum performance criteria for a grade of A is functionally related to students' academic performance. The authors defined their grade criteria in terms of a minimum number of test items to be read and answered incorrectly per minute in a proctoring session. In contrast, other programmed courses have typically defined criteria for various letter grades in terms of number of units completed (Sheppard and MacDermott, 1970).

The present study was designed to investigate the role of "free choice" of grade in a behaviorally programmed college course. Two principal questions were asked. First, does a contingency which allows only A's actually result in superior performance as compared with a structure which allows a full range of grades? This question cannot be answered by comparing previously reported studies for they differ on a host of variables in addition to the grades made available to the students. In the Johnston and O'Neill (1973) study, the authors demonstrated that the letter grade of A exerted stimulus control over students' academic performance, regardless of the performance criteria attached to the grade label; but they did not investigate the comparative effects of an A-F versus a traditional grading system. If, in fact, an A-F system results in superior performance, the second question is whether it is more desirable than allowing a range of grade choices. At first exposure, the answer to this question would appear affirmative. Why should an instructor institute a contingency which results in mediocre performance if he can as easily assure that nearly all students will master the material and perform at a superior level? If academic history is to be the only criterion for assessing a teaching technology, then an instructor cannot ignore a procedure which produces more mastery. Indeed, Johnston and O'Neill (1973) strongly advise that an instructor define minimum performance criteria and caution against defining performance criteria for grades of less than A. However, mastery is not the only consideration, as Keller has noted: "The kind of change needed in education today is not one that will be evaluated in terms of the percentage of A's in a grade distribution . . . it is one that will produce a reinforcing state of affairs for everyone involved . . . (1968, p. 86)." One could quarrel with the implication of Keller's statement that a student's "happiness" with a course is more important than what he learns in it, but surely his evaluations are important. Students, who dislike a method of teaching might be less likely to use the course content in new situations, more likely to harm interactions between the instructor and other students, and more likely to cheat.

An attitude measure was included in the present design as a way of evaluating what Keller called "a reinforcing state of affairs." If in fact an A-F system produces higher grades and higher student evaluations, or at least no lower evaluations than a range of grade procedure, it would be the method of choice. However, if it produced more mastery but reliably lower evaluations, its use may be contra-indicated for those who value positive student reactions as well as mastery. Such results would necessitate devising ways of making A-F systems more acceptable.

Method

Subjects

In the fall semester of 1971, 164 students enrolled in one of five sections of an undergraduate course, titled Child Psychology, taught by the first author at C. W. Post College, Greenvale, New York. The three sections (N = 92) comprising the experimental group were scheduled as follows: one class met on Monday, Wednesday, and Friday mornings; two classes met on Tuesday and Thursday afternoons. The two control group sections (N = 72) were scheduled at noon on Monday, Wednesday and Friday; and at midday on Tuesday and Thursday.

Students who had registered for the course were not informed as to the method of instruction, conduct, nor purpose of the study (since the instructor had not previously taught the course).

Procedure

COURSE CONTENT. The philosophical orientation and textual materials employed in the course were similar to those described by Whitehurst (1972) except for the following modifications: The Holland and Skinner (1961) text was not used, nine articles from a readings book by Gelfand (1969) were assigned, and only ten other journal articles were required. Twelve formally outlined lectures were delivered by the instructor; five films and two slide shows were also presented by the instructor. Discussion sections were conducted under a specified set of rules regarding the nature and content of information provided.

COURSE ORGANIZATION. At the first class meeting all *S*s received a syllabus listing reading assignments for each of the eleven test units, and dates for scheduled activities. In addition, a handout describing the purpose and rules of the course was presented. At the close of class, a twenty item multiple choice pretest (composed of questions which were parallel to scheduled exam questions and sampling the whole content of the course) was administered to assess whether initial differences obtained for the experimental and control groups.

Students attending class three times a week had the option of attending a lecture or presentation on Mondays, participating in a group discussion of assigned materials on Wednesdays, and taking unit exams on Fridays. Students attending class twice weekly had the optional attendance lecture on Tuesdays, and group discussion, followed by testing, on Thursdays.

Examinations were composed of twenty-five multiple choice items drawn solely from the assigned unit readings. On scheduled test days, unit exams were handed out at the beginning of the class. Students recorded their answers on a response sheet which was graded, upon completion of the test, by a graduate assistant. Students who chose to attend the discussion period after the test were required to wait outside of the classroom until all *S*s had completed the exam.

Passing a unit was defined as obtaining a score of twenty-one or above on a test. Students who attempted the exam on the scheduled test day and failed were allowed to take an alternate form makeup quiz at any of ten scheduled retest sessions during the following two week period. If *S* failed two written tests, a one-to-one oral tutorial was administered by the instructor, or one of three graduate assistants, until the *S* was judged to have met written criteria for passing the unit. Students who chose not to attempt the first scheduled unit exam were required to take the alternate form exam at one of two scheduled evening hours and were not allowed the option of a make-up exam or a tutorial. Students were allowed two weeks (from the date of the scheduled unit exam) in which to complete a unit. If an *S* did not master the unit within the definite period, he did not receive credit for having passed the unit. The twelfth unit of the course required a short paper with specifications similar to those described by Whitehurst (1972). Students in the experimental group sections were told on the first class day that they could receive either an A (equivalent to passing all twelve units) or an F (equivalent to passing less than twelve units) as a course grade. Control group Ss were informed that they could receive any of the following grades: A (pass twelve units), B+ (pass eleven units), B (pass ten units), C (pass eight or nine units), D (pass seven units), F (pass less than seven units).

On the last day of class, students completed a twenty-three variable, anonymous questionnaire in which they were asked to evaluate several aspects of the instructor's behavior as well as the content, structure, and instructional method of the course. The questionnaire was mailed with a self-addressed, stamped envelope and letter of explanation to all Ss who either dropped or earned failing grades in the course. In addition, the twenty item multiple choice pretest was readministered as a posttest comparison measure.

RESULTS

Data for all Ss were coded onto data cards and analyzed by computer employing a Datatext program (Armor, D. J. and Couch, A. S., 1970). Since a random distribution of Ss into the experimental and control groups was not possible, the initial question concerned the equality of the Ss in the two groups. This question as first assessed by comparing undergraduate grade point averages for all enrolled Ss except entering freshman and transfer students (N = 124). Although a t-test indicated that the control group had a statistically significant (p = .03) lower grade point average than the experimental group, the actual mean differences were quite small (experimental group mean = 2.8, control group mean = 2.6). However, to rule out the possibility that the independent manipulation was confounded with entering grade point average, the latter variable was entered as a covariant in subsequent analyses of treatment effects. Supporting the hypothesis of initial S equality was the finding of no significant difference (p > .05).

Four Ss officially dropped out of the experimental sections and one S dropped out of a control group section. Of the mailed questionnaires, one of five was returned for the control group, whereas five of sixteen were received from experimental group Ss.

The first experimental question concerned the proportion of A's versus lower grades earned by the experimental and control Ss. Eighty-six percent of the experimental group Ss earned a grade of A as compared with 66 percent A's earned by control group Ss. (See Fig. 16-1). An analysis of convariance indicated these differences to be statistically significant (p < .01). A t-test analysis of pretest-posttest difference scores yielded results which did not reach significance (p > .05).

The finding of superior grades in the experimental subjects is an important one. These results can only be evaluated in relationship to the attitudinal reactions produced by the two instructional methods. A comparison of the two treatment groups on the attitude survey variables did not reveal a striking pattern of differences. Although control group Ss rated the instructor as having been clearer in stating the course rules than did the experimental group (p = .02), and the experimental group rated the instructor as having clearer enunciation than did the control group (p = .03); no significant differences be-

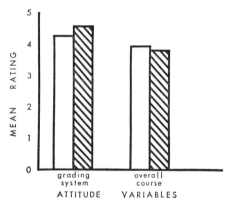

Figure 16-1. Bar graph of percent grade distribution for "forced excellence" experimental group (hatched marked) and "free choice" control group (open).

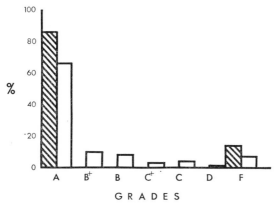

G R A D E S

Figure 16-2. Bar graph of mean response for "forced excellence" experimental group (hatched mark) and "free choice" control group (open) on rating course grading system and rating of course overall.

tween the two groups held on the overall rating of the professor (p = .22). The control group Ss reported attending more lectures (p = .02) and more discussion sessions (p = .01) than the experimental group. Attitude survey differences on the questions relating to the type of grading system employed (p > .05) and overall rating of the course (p > .05) were insignificant (see Fig. 16-2). Nevertheless, reported differences between the two groups with respect to how much they got out of the assigned readings approached significance (p = .06) and favored the control group.

DISCUSSION

The results of this investigation suggest that an A-F procedure is preferable to the more frequently encountered range-of-grade provision. These findings are in keeping with the suggestion of Johnston and O'Neill (1973) that defining performance criteria for the highest mark will likely produce better academic performance than defining performance requirements for the whole range of grades. Grades were reliably and significantly higher in the A-F classes, and the attitude measures indicated that both procedures were reacted to positively and nondifferentially (with very few exceptions). The fact that the control classes did not indicate that they got more from the assigned readings than the experimental class is of some interest. However, the absolute differences in responses to that item of the attitude survey were quite small (experimental group mean = 4.35, control group mean = 4.42) and taken in the context of the total attitudinal response, this difference is probably unimportant. The non-significant posttest differences may be attributed to the fact that many of the test items, though randomly selected, bore heavily on generalizations of concepts presented in the first three units of the course. Furthermore, there was no grade-related contingency for "doing one's best" on the posttest.

These attitude results are somewhat surprising based on an analysis of the motivational characteristics of the A-F procedure. Many students who receive an A when it is the only alternative to failure report that they would have been satisfied with a lower grade (Meyers, 1970). While the exact percentages will be specific to a particular course, the current study would suggest that approximately twenty percent of the A students in the experimental group would have obtained less than an A if that alternative had been available. If, in fact, it is the promise of an F contingent upon quitting (the "doomsday contingency" as Malott (1971) has called it) which motivates these twenty percent of the students, then their behavior is strongly analogous to discriminated avoidance; the discriminated stimulus in their particular case being the statement by the instructor of the rules of the course and the avoidance behavior being study and perseverance above their baserates. If the behavior of these students is avoidant in character, then one might expect negative emotional reactions that are said to be generated by aversive control techniques (Skinner, 1953). The fact that such reactions were not obtained could be explained in two ways. First, while the A = F method may be aversive to students who normally get grades lower than an A, the receipt of a grade higher than that usually obtained may have a counter-active influence so that the attitude statements are unchanged from what they would otherwise be. The second possibility is that perhaps there are no emotional concomitants of behavior generated by certain types of aversive control which are different from those generated by certain types of aversive control which are different from those generated by positive reinforcement schedules. Recent research with animals (Schuster and Rachlin, 1968) would support the possibility of the latter statement. Which of these two possibilities is correct cannot be presently determined. Nevertheless, one might expect the experimental group's attitude statements to be more positive under the latter hypothesis on the assumption that, all other things being equal, higher grades should increase positive evaluation.

ASSIGNMENTS AND TESTING

THIS GROUP OF RESEARCH STUDIES concerns both testing and the amount of material to be tested. The first two papers, "The Combined And Differential Effects Of Two Types Of Preparatory Quizzes On College Student Behaviors" and "An Analysis Of The Effects Of Hour Exams And Student-Answered Study Questions On Test Performance," address different means of testing and the resulting effects on how well students learn. "The Comparative Effects Of Self-Grading Versus Proctor Grading On Class Efficiency And Student Performance" approaches the novel idea of letting students grade themselves. The last two papers, "Exam Performance And Study Behavior As A Function Of Study Unit Size" and "The Effects Of Quantity Of Assigned Material On College Student Academic Performance And Study Behavior," investigate the amount of course material which is assigned and tested.

THE COMBINED AND DIFFERENTIAL EFFECTS OF TWO TYPES OF PREPARATORY QUIZZES ON COLLEGE STUDENT BEHAVIORS

RANDY LEE WILLIAMS

M OST INVESTIGATORS OF CONTINGENCY MANAGED COURSES have focused their research on variations of PSI which have typically de-emphasized the lecture and have allowed students to determine when they will take unit exams (Keller, 1968; McMichael and Corey, 1969). One problem is these student-paced systems has been that during the semester students procrastinate the taking of unit exams. To obviate this problem some researchers have instituted contingency managed courses that are instructor-paced (Malott and Svinicki, 1969; Cooper Greiner, 1971). Typically unit exams occur once a week with a remedial exam for students not passiing the first exam on each unit (Bostow and Blumenfeld, 1972). Though students within the weekly exam format are less likely to procrastinate studying over long periods

This research was based on a Master's thesis completed at Western Michigan University. I especially wish to thank Dr. Jack Michael who has been a close friend and constant source of new knowledge. In addition, I owe him my gratitude for his advice and criticisms regarding this study and for allowing me to use his course, Verbal Behavior. I also wish to thank Dr. Rob Hawkins and Dr. David O. Lyon for their suggestions and criticisms.

of time within the semester, there is nothing to prevent procrastination of studying within the week. One aim of the present research was to determine the effects on major exam scores of a quiz which tested students over material outlined in course study objectives.

Keller believed lectures to be a relatively inefficient method of teaching, but there may be courses or occasions during courses when lectures can be important. An instructor may use lectures to supplement written materials with more current research findings or to supplement deficient units that he has not had time to rewrite. Assuming that lectures can be important, it is then essential that students attend lectures in order to learn from them. Another aim of the present research was to determine the effects on attendance and major exam scores of a quiz which tested students over material presented in lectures. In summary, this research was conducted to determine both the combined and differential effects of two types of quizzes on major weekly exam scores, attendance at lectures, and study time of college students.

METHOD

The students were sixty-one undergraduates who completed a course in verbal behavior at Western Michigan University. Skinner's *Verbal Behavior* was the primary text for the course. Classes were scheduled for 10:00 a.m. to 11:50 a.m., Monday through Friday.

For each week's unit, students received a set of study objectives relevant to the week's reading assignment. On Monday and Tuesday of each week the instructor supplemented written objectives through lecture. At the beginning of each of these class periods a short five-minute quiz was given which tested students on material outlined in course study objectives. Following each of the two lectures was a short five-minute quiz which consisted of one question covering material presented in lectures.

On Wednesday of each week a major exam was given which consisted of five essay questions and which took students approximately one hour to complete. The pass criterion for the major weekly exam was such that a student could lose only two exam points out of twenty-five possible and still pass the exam. A pass would give a student ten grade points, the maximum possible for one week. If a student lost from three to six exam points of the twenty-five possible he would receive only two grade points. If more than six exam points were lost on an exam the student would fail the exam and would receive no grade points. Since there were fifteen weeks in the semester a student could earn 150 grade points. A total of 140 grade points earned a student an A, 130 a B, 120 a C, 110 a D, and less than 110 an F.

Each correctly answered quiz question was worth one bonus point to be applied against points lost on the Wednesday major exam. For example, if a student lost four points on the unit exam but had correctly answered three of the four preparatory quizzes, then the resultant exam points lost was one. The student would then receive a pass on the unit exam.

On Thursday students were given the opportunity to look over their exams to see that they were correctly graded. If there was any ambiguity in an answer grades were to count the answer or sub-part of the answer as incorrect. If a student believed some answer was incorrectly graded then he submitted the exam for regrading along with a written explanation of why he felt the answer was correct.

After submission of regrade requests a remedial lecture was given to students not passing the exam. The instructor focused on major points with which students were having difficulty. At the end of this remedial lecture a one question quiz over the lecture was given which was worth two points that would be applied against points lost on the Friday remedial exam. The remedial exam was similar to the Wednesday exam, except a student could only earn up to eight grade points on this remedial exam.

During the first week students were told that a self-report form would accompany each new set of study objectives. On this form students were instructed to record the amount of time they studied in preparation for the Wednesday exam and the days that that study occurred.

At the end of the fourth week students were rank ordered on the basis of their raw scores on the Wednesday exams. Next they were divided into high, middle, and low levels of performance on

Weekly Activities

Monday	Tuesday	Wednesday	Thursday	Friday
Quiz On Objectives	Quiz On Objectives	Exam	Return Exams	Remedial Exam
Lecture	Lecture		Regrade	
Quiz On Lecture	Quiz On Lecture		Remedial Lecture	
			Quiz On Lecture	

Figure 17-1.

the basis of these raw exam scores. Individuals in each group were then randomly assigned to one of four conditions. In the first condition students continued to take both the quizzes over the study objectives and quizzes over the lectures *(QS/QL)*, in the second condition subjects took only *QS* quizzes, and in the third, subjects took only *QL* quizzes, and in the fourth condition subject no longer took any of the preparatory quizzes (No. Q.). If a subject was not required to take a particular quiz, he received the bonus free as though he had answered the question correctly. These procedures resulted in twelve experimental groups.

Free bonus points were never made contingent on lecture attendance. However, if a student attended lecture he was asked to hand in a quiz sheet with his name on it. If a student returned at least one quiz sheet he was counted as present. Attendance was recorded for the first four weeks and for the last five weeks of the study. As a reliability check, during the middle of one of the class periods subjects were asked to enter their names on a roll sheet.

RESULTS

Data from each experimental group for the first four weeks of the course were used as baselines. Baseline data were then compared with data from the experimental phase. For each subject the amount of study during the experimental phase was given a percentage value based on the amount of study in baseline. If a subject studied the same amount in the experimental phase as in the baseline his study in the experimental phase was given the value of one-hundred percent. A three-way analysis of variance with weighted means showed no significant differences in amount of study between groups. Looking at the amount studied across conditions and across levels of performance showed that subjects tended to study approximately the same amount during the experimental phase as they had in baseline.

For each subject the distribution of time spent studying during the experimental phase was compared with the distribution of time spent studying during baseline. For purposes of this research study prior to Tuesday was considered *early* study for the major exam, whereas study on Tuesday or Wednesday morning was considered *late* study. The overall trend of the class was an increase in the percentage of late study. However, the increase in late study was not the same for all groups. Of the study by subjects who took *QS*, 56 percent was late study in baseline. For the experimental phase these subjects averaged an 8 percent increase in the percentage of late study. Of the studying by subjects who did not take *QS*, 62 percent was late study in baseline. These subjects, therefore, had a lower ceiling on the amount that late study could increase, yet they averaged a 19 percent increase in late study. Figure 17-2 shows that this trend was found in high, middle, and low performers. Towards the end of the experiment late study was no longer increasing for subjects who took *QS*. However, Figure 17-3 shows that late study continued to increase for subjects who did not take *QS*. A Mann-Whitney U was computed and showed that the subjects not taking *QS* increased their late study significantly more than those taking *QS*. Significance was beyond the .01 level.

For each group of weeks shown in Figure 17-3 at least two self-report forms were returned for 97 percent of the possible occasions for returning them. If one or no self-report was returned for one of the groups of weeks then an interpolation method was used to supply or supplement data for those weeks.

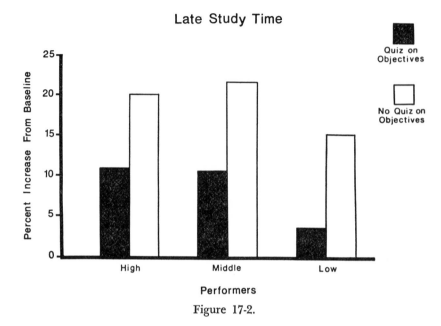

Figure 17-2.

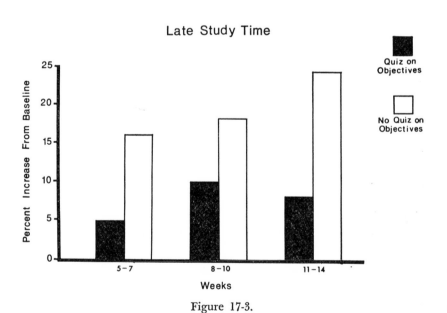

Figure 17-3.

For each group the mean number of points lost per major exam was computed. A three-way analysis of variance showed no significant differences due to the effects of either type of preparatory quiz. Median number of points lost on the major exams was also computed. Figure 17-4 shows this data.

Based on median data subjects who took both QS and QL tended to lose the fewest number of points on the major exams. Those subjects who took no quizzes lost the greatest number of points. Subjects who took only QS or only QL tended to lose an intermediate number of points.

During baseline the mean attendance of subjects in each of the four conditions was 96 percent. However, during the last five weeks of the experimental phase there was a large decrease in attendance for subjects in two conditions.

Figure 17-5 shows that mean attendance for subjects who took both QS and QL or only QL remained at approximately baseline level. The mean attendance for subjects who took only QS was decreased by twelve percent. The mean attendance for subjects

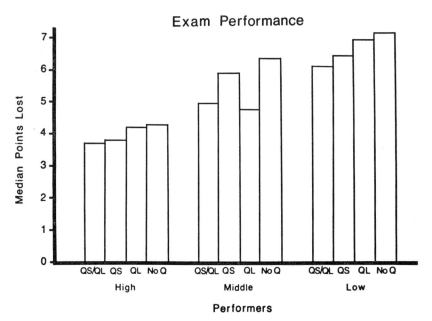

Figure 17-4.

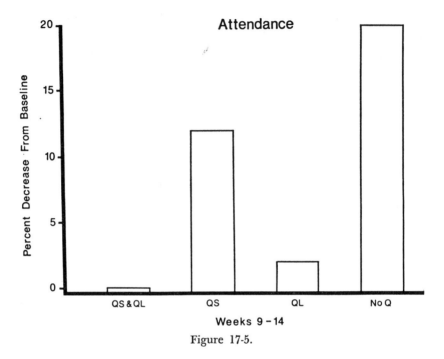

Figure 17-5.

taking no quizzes decreased by 20 percent. A three-way analysis of variance with weighted means showed significant main effects attributable to QL beyond the .001 level. The one reliability check on attendance showed a 98 percent agreement.

DISCUSSION

Lloyd (1972) and his associates found that students attended lectures more often when lectures were relevant to questions asked on exams than they were not. In the present study all lectures were relevant to questions that would be asked on major exams. This may be the reason for such high overall attendance in the present study even though lectures were nonmandatory. For those subjects who took quizzes during lecture periods, attendance at lectures gave these students the opportunity to earn points on quizzes that would result in a more lenient grading criteria on the major exams. This could be one probably reason for the greater attendance by subjects who took preparatory quizzes. For subjects who took *QL*, attendance at lectures and attending to what was said in lectures was the only preparation needed to perform well on *QL*. This may have been a major factor in their attendance remaining so high. For subjects who took *QS*, study over course material prior to attending lectures was needed in order to perform well on *QS*. If subjects did not prepare for the quiz there would be a smaller probability of earning quiz points and therefore less reason to attend lectures. Subjects who took no quizzes did not have the opportunity to earn a more lenient grading criteria by attending lectures. Therefore, these subjects had less reason to come to lectures than those subjects who took quizzes; in fact, these subjects attended lectures the least often.

Though differences in median data for points lost on major exams by subjects in the various conditions were small, the trends in these data were found across all three levels of performance. It should be emphasized that in this course a difference of only one point on the major exam often meant the difference of a student needing to take an exam a second time or not.

Though amount of study remained approximately the same for all experimental groups the distribution of time spent studying was not the same. Subjects who took *QS* distributed their study more evenly throughout the week than subjects who did not take *QS*. The percent of increase in late study by subjects who did not take *QS* was over twice that of those who did.

On an anonymously answered questionnaire ninety percent of the subjects said that the self-reports on study were completed with more than moderate accuracy. Also 75 percent said that the self-reports reflected the same time that was actually studied. Only 2 percent stated that the self-reports showed much more or much less time than was actually studied. The various experimental groups tended to respond to these questions similarly. These responses by subjects would seem to lend some support to the validity of the data gotten from the self-report method.

These two types of preparatory quizzes appeared to be responsible for controlling several student behaviors. It took less than thirty minutes for one undergraduate to grade seventy quizzes. The course instructor made the quiz by simply taking one question from the study objectives. These were relatively small and convenient changes to make which appeared to control college students' attendance, distribution of study time, and performance on exams. Therefore, these two types of preparatory quizzes may be quite valuable and efficient techniques to be used by college instructors for controlling these student behaviors.

READING 18

AN ANALYSIS OF THE EFFECTS OF HOUR EXAMS AND STUDENT-ANSWERED STUDY QUESTIONS ON TEST PERFORMANCE

GEORGE SEMB

INSTRUCTORS IN TRADITIONAL COLLEGE COURSE frequently use hour examinations to evaluate student learning and to determine course grades. There is, however, no experimental evidence to suggest that *students* benefit from such exercises. In a recent study, Semb (1973) found that hour examinations by themselves produce much poorer performance than hour exams preceded by a series of short, unit quizzes which are characteristic of personalized systems of instruction. Experiment I was designed to determine whether or not hour exams, when preceded by a series of quizzes, have any functional value for student learning or retention. If hour exams enhance student learning, they ought to be included as part of the personalized instruction package. If, how-

This research was supported in part by the General Research Fund (3317-5038), Office of Research Administration, University of Kansas, and in part by the University of Kansas Computation Center. The author wishes to thank several individuals who served as assistants in the course—Dan Conyers, Rich Feallock, Steve Fawcett, Juan Jose Sanchez Sosa and Robert Spencer. Reprints may be obtained from George Semb, Department of Human Development, University of Kansas, Lawrence, Kansas 66044.

ever, they do not help students master the material any better or improve retention, instructors would be well-advised to eliminate them and rely solely on unit quizzes.

Along a similar dimension, several instructors who use personalized instruction rely heavily on study questions or study objectives to emphasize major points in the course readings (McMichael & Corey, 1969; Born, Gledhill & Davis, 1972; Semb, Hopkins & Hursh, 1973). Semb, et al. (1973) and Semb (1973) have reported that students perform better on study question items than on nonstudy, probe items, and furthermore, that performance on both types of items can be manipulated by the kind of training the student receives. Experiment II was designed to determine whether or not study questions answered by students outside of class could be used to replace unit quizzes in a personalized instruction course. If unit quizzes can be eliminated, instructors stand to gain a great deal in terms of the amount of time student proctors have to spend with students, and the amount of time and money spent to produce unit quizzes.

EXPERIMENT I

Experiment I was designed to determine if hour exams, preceded by a series of unit quizzes, have any affect on subsequent student test performance.

METHOD

Subjects, Setting, and Course Personnel

Students enrolled in an introductory child development course served as subjects. During enrollment, students were randomly assigned an identification number between 001 and 657. Students 001 − 007, 101 − 107, 201 − 207, 301 − 307, 401 − 407, and 501 − 507 met during one class period (8:30 MWF). Students 008 − 014, 108 − 114, 208 − 214, etc., met during another class hour (9:30 MWF), and so forth. Each class (N = 16) met for 150 minutes a week, either during three fifty minute sessions (MWF) or two seventy-five minute periods (Tuesday-Thursday).

Each section had forty-two students and was managed by one graduate teaching assistant, one undergraduate teaching assistant and six undergraduate student proctors. Each proctor had previously received an A in the course and received course credit for his work. The ratio of students to proctors was 7:1. Students met in a small lecture room to take quizzes, to receive feedback on their performance and to interact with course personnel.

Students 001 — 098 and 601 — 607 (N = 105) were defined as Group 1. Students 101 — 198 and 611 — 617 (N = 105) were defined as Group 2. Ten students from Group 1 and nine from Group 2 withdrew from the course during the semester, leaving a total of ninety-five students in Group 1 and ninety-six in Group 2 that participated in Experiment I.

Procedure

The course was divided into four major content areas and each part was further subdivided into four units. A unit consisted of a thirty page reading assignment and twenty-five short-answer, essay study questions.[1] The course was both student-paced and instructor-paced in that the student could work as fast as he wished, but he had to maintain a minimum rate of progress (on the average of 1.5 quizzes passed per week) or withdrew from the course (Miller, Weaver & Semb, 1973). The semester lasted for fourteen weeks (forty-two class days for MWF sections and twenty-eight class days for Tuesday-Thursday sections).

To progress through the course, students had to master sixteen quizzes corresponding to the unit assignments and four hour examinations which covered each of the content areas. The mastery criterion was defined as 100 percent correct on all quizzes and hour exams. Students could take each quiz or hour exam (different forms) as many times as necessary to meet the mastery criterion.

Each quiz consisted of ten items randomly selected from the student's set of twenty-five study questions. Hour exams consisted of twenty study questions; five of the twenty-five study questions were randomly selected from each of the four content units. Study questions were designed to emphasize major points in the course

---

[1] Course materials included *Readings in Developmental Psychology Today* (Cramer, 1970), *Elementary Principles of Behavior* (Whaley and Malott, 1971) and *Human Development Lecture Notes and Study Guide* (Semb, 1973).

readings and to help students integrate major concepts and ideas. All items were short essay questions.

When a student completed a quiz or hour exam, he or she took it to his proctor who graded it immediately. The proctor graded each item as either correct, partially correct, or incorrect on the basis of how closely it matched answers provided in the instructor's manual.

The student was given an opportunity to justify or explain answers which the proctor marked as partially correct or incorrect. If the student's oral explanation satisfied the proctor, the item was graded as correct. Progress to the next unit depended upon whether or not the student's performance met the 100 percent mastery criterion.

After the student had completed the last assignment of the course, he was eligible to take a final examination. The final consisted of forty-eight multiple-choice items. Three items were sampled from each of the sixteen content units which made up the course. Two of the items were based on the student's study questions (recall items). The third item was a generalization question which required the student to integrate major aspects of the course (probe items). The instructor and three graduate students determined whether each item should be categorized as recall or probe. If consensus was not reached, the item was eliminated or revised until consensus was achieved.

Ninety-six final exam questions (sixty-four recall and thirty-two probe) were constructed. Four different forms of the final were prepared by randomly assigning items from the two pools until each unit was represented by two recall items and one probe item. Students took the final on Thursday evenings throughout the semester, or the last day of class, dependiing upon when they completed the last hour exam. Answers were recorded on IBM answer sheets and machine graded.

Performance on the final determined the student's entire grade in the course. Thirty-six points were required for an A, thirty for a B and twenty-four for a C. If a student scored less than an A, he was allowed to retake an alternate form of the final during exam week at the end of the semester.

Experimental Design

Experiment I used a counterbalance, within-group, reversal design. Each of the four course parts constituted a separate experimental condition. The two conditions were:

Hour Exam (HE) —Students were required to master the four unit quizzes *and* the hour exam with 100 percent correct.

Quiz Only (QO) —Students mastered the four unit quizzes with one-hundred percent correct, but no hour exam was administered.

Group 1 went through the conditions HE-QO-HEQO. To control for changes in course content and item difficulty, Group 2 went through the conditions in the opposite order, QO-HE-QO-HE.

Grading Reliability

At least once during each class period, one of the teaching assistants observed a proctor while he or she graded a student's quiz. The assistant observed the proctor as he graded each item and listened to the student's explanation of partially correct or incorrect answers. If the assistant agreed with the proctor's evaluation of the student's answer, it was scored as an agreement. If there was any discrepancy between the assistant's grade and the proctor's grade, it was scored as a disagreement. Reliability checks were made on sixty-nine unit quizzes and six hour exams for Group 1. Of the 810 items checked, there were 774 agreements and 36 disagreements. Reliability, calculated by dividing the number of agreements by the number of agreements plus disagreements, was 0.955. The assistants checked eighty-six unit quizzes and ten hour exams for Group 2. Of the 1060 items checked, there were 998 agreements and sixty-two disagreements (reliability = 0.945).

RESULTS

Sixty percent (N = 57) of the students in Group 1 earned a grade of A the first time they took the final examination as compared with 64.6 percent (N = 62) of the students in Group 2. Of the thirty-eight students in Group 1 who earned less than an A, twenty-nine received Bs and nine received Cs as compared with twenty-seven Bs and seven Cs in Group 2.

Only performance on *first-attempt* finals were analyzed. The final was separated into four parts corresponding to the four content parts of the course. Percentages correct on each part are plotted in Figure 18-1 for groups 1 and 2. Percent correct was derived by summing the total number of items correct across students and dividing the total number of responses emitted. Each recall point in Figure 18-1 represents eight recall items (two per unit), and each probe point represents four items (one per unit).

Group 1's performance on recall items during the four parts of the final average 81.4, 81.7, 84.2 and 78.1, respectively. Mean percent correct on probe items was 70.3, 63.4, 64.5 and

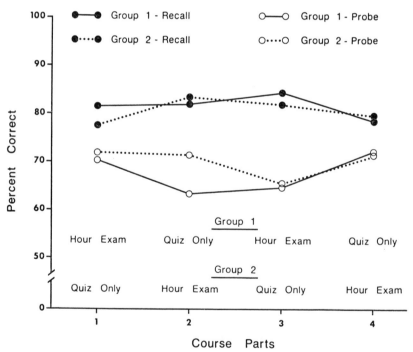

Figure 18-1. Mean percent correct for Group 1 (solid lines) and Group 2 (broken lines) on first-attempt final examinations for each of the four parts of the course. Recall items are indicated by closed circles and probe items by open circles.

72.3. For Group 2, mean percent correct on recall items was 77.7, 83.6, 81.8 and 79.0, and on probe items, 71.1, 71.4, 65.1 and 72.3. These data indicate that there were no consistent differences between the two experimental conditions on either recall or probe items. That is, hour exams did not influence performance on final exams; otherwise, one would have expected differential effects in the within-group comparisons between Parts 1 and 3 *versus* Parts 2 and 4. The only consistent difference shown in Figure 18-1 is that students answered recall items correctly 10 to 15 percent more frequently than probe items, a finding that is similar to that reported by Semb, Hopkins and Hursh (1973) and Semb (1973).

In terms of individual performances on Parts 1 and 3 versus Parts 2 and 4 (recall and probe items combined), thirty-four students in Group 1 performed higher during the hour exam conditions, forty-six performed higher during the quiz only conditions and fifteen remained unchanged between conditions. A t-test comparing mean performance between conditions revealed no statistically significant differences ($t = 0.54$, $df = 94$, NS). Forty-nine students in Group 2 performed higher during the hour exam conditions, thirty-six did better during the quiz only conditions and eleven remained unchanged. Again, a t-test comparing mean performances revealed no significant differences ($t = 0.65$, $df = 95$, NS).

EXPERIMENT II

Experiment II was designed to determine whether student-answered study questions could be used to replace unit quizzes as part of the personalized instruction package.

METHOD

Subjects, Setting and Course Personnel

Subject selection, setting and course personnel were identical to those described in Experiment I. Group 3 consisted of students 201–298 and 621–627 and Group 4 consisted of students 301–398 and 631–637. Eleven students from Group 3 and ten from Group 4 withdrew from the course leaving ninety-four students in Group 3 and ninety-five in Group 4 that participated in Experiment II.

Procedure

All procedure and materials described in Experiment I were the same with two important exceptions. First, all students in both groups took hour exams at the end of each part of the course. Mastery was again defined as 100 percent correct. Second, during units when students were required to hand in written answers to study questions instead of taking unit quizzes, the student proctors randomly graded ten of the twenty-five study questions. To insure randomness, proctors graded those questions numbers that the student would have answered had he been in the unit quiz condition by referring to the unmarked, computer-generated quiz. As in the quiz condition, items were marked as correct, partially correct, or incorrect. Students could justify partially correct or incorrect answers. If the student did not master the study questions, he was instructed to redo the assignment and present the questions again for random grading. In those instances, the proctor graded a new set of ten questions, again by referring to a computer-generated quiz.

Proctors also recorded the amount of time the student spent taking each quiz (during applicable units) and the amount of time he or she spent grading the quiz or study questions. The proctor recorded the time the student received a quiz, the time he or she started grading it (or the time he started grading the study questions) and the time the grading process stopped. The difference between the first two times was defined as student test time, and the difference between the last two items was defined as grading time.

Experimental Design

Experiment II used a counterbalanced, reversal design. Each of the four parts of the course constituted a separate condition. The conditions included:

Unit Quizzes (UQ) —Students mastered the four unit quizzes before taking the hour exam, which also had to be mastered. Mastery was defined as 100 percent correct.

Study Questions (SQ) —Students presented written answers to study questions, ten of which were randomly selected and graded. Mastery of the ten study questions allowed the student to progress to the next unit. After mastering the four units, the student could take the hour exam, which also had to be mastered with 100 percent correct.

Students in Group 3 went through the conditions UQ–SQ–UQ–SQ. To control for changes in course content and item difficulty, Group 2 went through the conditions in opposite order, SQ–UQ–SQ–UQ.

Grading and Timing Reliability

Reliability checks identical to those described in Experiment I were made on unit quizzes, student-answered study questions and hour exams. Checks were made on thirty unit quizzes, forty-two sets of study question answers and twenty hour exams in Group 3. Of the 1120 items checked, there were 1067 agreements and 53 disagreements to produce a reliability of 0.952. The assistant checked forty-one unit quizzes, fifty sets of student-answered study questions and fifteen hour exams in Group 4. Of the 1210 items checked, there were 1156 agreements and 54 disagreements (reliability = 0.955).

Reliability checks were also made on sixty-six unit quiz test times, sixty-six quiz grading times and fifty-two study question grading times. Reliability, calculated by dividing the number of minutes of agreement by the number of minutes of agreement plus disagreement, was 0.904 for content quiz times, 0.978 for quiz grading times and 0.941 for study question grading times.

RESULTS

Seventy-four percent (N = 70) of the students in Group 3 earned a grade of A the first time they took the final examination as compared with 67.4 percent (N = 64) of the students in Group 2. Of the twenty-four students in Group 3 who earned less than an A, sixteen received Bs and eight received Cs as compared with twenty-four Bs and seven Cs in Group 4.

Percentages correct on each of the four parts of the final are plotted in Figure 18-2 for both groups. Group 3's performance on recall items averaged 82.8, 84.4, 88.3 and 82.5 percent correct, respectively, on the four parts of the final. Mean percent correct on probe items was 77.1, 73.4, 64.6 and 68.7. For Group 4, mean percent correct on recall items was 82.2, 84.7, 85.0 and 81.4, and on probe items, 71.3, 70.3, 63.9 and 72.8. There were no consistent differences between the two experimental conditions in terms of performance on both recall and probe items. The only consistent difference shown in Figure 18-2 is that students answered recall items correctly 10 to 15 percent more frequently than probe items, a finding that is identical to that reported in Experiment I.

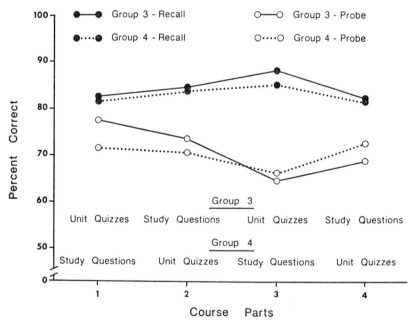

Figure 18-2. Mean percent correct for Group 3 (solid lines) and Group 4 (broken lines) on first-attempt final examinations for each of the four parts of the course. Recall items are indicated by closed circles and probe items by open circles.

In terms of individual performances on Parts 1 and 3 *versus* Parts 2 and 4 (recall and probe items combined), thirty-seven students in Group 3 performed higher during the quiz condition, forty-five did better during the study question condition and twelve remained unchanged. A t-test comparing mean performances between conditions revealed no significant differences ($t = 0.21$, df = 93, NS). Forty-five students in Group 2 performed higher during the quiz conditions, thirty-seven did better during the study question conditions and thirteen remained unchanged. Again, a t-test revealed no significant differences ($t = 0.54$, df = 94, NS).

Students in both groups combined took a mean of 18.2 minutes (SD = 7.6) to complete unit quizzes. It took proctors 9.4 minutes (SD = 4.6) to grade unit quizzes as compared with 8.1 minutes (SD =4.6) to grade study questions. The difference in grading times between quizzes and study questions was not statistically significant ($t = 1.47$, df = 116, NS), although it appears that it took proctors a little longer to grade quizzes than it did to grade study questions. To demonstrate the comparability between the two experimental conditions, students averaged 28.8 minutes to take an hour exam during the Study Questions conditions as compared to 26.1 minutes during the Unit Quiz conditions ($t = 0.91$, df = 34, NS). Grading time for hour exams was 11.1 minutes during the Study Question conditions and 11.7 minutes during the Unit Quiz conditions ($t = 0.34$, df = 34, NS). Performance on hour exams averaged 96.2 percent correct during the Study question conditions and 97.4 during the Unit Quiz conditions ($t = 0.64$, df = 88, NS).

GENERAL DISCUSSION

The results of both experiments have important implications, not only for instructors who use personalized instruction, but also for instructors who use more conventional teaching procedures. Experiment I demonstrated that hour examinations, when preceded by a series of unit quizzes which had already been mastered (a typical procedure in most personalized systems of instruction), do not improve retention as measured by performance on a comprehensive, final examination. That is, given the procedures used in Experiment I, hour exams did not appear to have any functional value for student retention. It should be pointed out that the unit quiz procedure used in Experiment I used two components, the use of study questions as a source for quiz items and a 100 percent correct mastery criterion, both of which have been demonstrated by previous research (Semb, Hopkins & Hursh, 1973; Semb, 1973) to be important factors in producing high levels of student test performance. It is impossible to say whether the same results would have been obtained had either or both of these components been eliminated.

The results of Experiment I are also related to a study (Semb, 1973) which demonstrated that hour examinations (several unit quizzes combined) cannot be used to replace unit quizzes without sacrificing high levels of student test performance. Students in the Semb (1973) study performed approximately 20 percent worse on a comprehensive course examination when they were required to master several unit quizzes at the same time. The results of Experiment I and the Semb (1973) study indicated that there is little empirical support for the use of hour examinations either to replace unit quizzes, or in addition to them.

The results of Experiment II indicated that student test performance does not decrease if student-answered study questions are used to replace unit quizzes. If instructors rely on study questions or study objectives to emphasize major points in a course, and if they use those questions or objectives as a basis for constructing quiz items, it may be possible to eliminate unit quizzes entirely. Although many instructors do not use test items which are repeated directly from study questions, it stills stands to reason that student-answered study questions ensure that students have responded to the material. Furthermore, the results of Experiment II indicate that exam performance is not adversely affected by the use of student-answered study questions. If performance on probe items (Fig. 18-2) had decreased during the Study Question conditions, there might have been a cause for alarm. However, performance on probe items during both the Study Question and Unit Quiz conditions was nearly identical, which suggest that student-answered study questions do not hinder generalization. It is possible that the study questions themselves, which were common to both procedures, were an integral component of the generalization achieved, as measured by probe items. That remains an empirical question. At least, the procedures investigated in Experiment II did not affect performance on either probe or recall items differentially.

Instructors stand to gain a great deal by using student-answered study questions rather than unit quizzes. First, there is no need to construct and produce unit quizzes. Second, class time can be used more efficiently. Students in Experiment II averaged 18.2 minutes per unit quiz to answer the ten short-answer, essay items as compared with zero minutes of class time to complete answers to study questions. The time saved could easily be used by proctors to grade and interview students over important material covered in the study questions. A common phenomenon in the present course is that many students arrive in class at the same time (the beginning of the class period) and complete unit quizzes at approximately the same time. Thus, it is not uncommon for two or three students to be waiting for a given proctor to grade his or her quiz. During this time (on the average, the initial 18.2 minutes of a fifty-minute class period), proctors wasted valuable time, time which could be devoted to interacting with students. Such a situation could be attenuated if students arrived at different times throughout the class period ready to discuss written answers to study questions. Finally, if a proctor can grade several sets of study questions during the class period, it may be possible to increase the ratio of students to proctors above the ratio of 7:1 used in the present course. Given that performance did not differ under the two conditions in Experiment II, it would appear as if the use of student-answered study questions might be an effective way for instructors to improve the efficiency of personalized instruction by increasing the ratio of students to proctors.

THE COMPARATIVE EFFECTS OF SELF-GRADING VERSUS PROCTOR GRADING ON CLASS EFFICIENCY AND STUDENT PERFORMANCE

Tim Blackburn
George Semb
B. L. Hopkins

SEVERAL STUDIES (Keller, 1968; McMichael & Corey, 1969; Sheppard & MacDermot, 1970) have compared the effects of personalized systems of instruction as a procedural package outlined by Keller (1968) to the traditional lecture-examination methods. In each of these studies, students in the PSI courses have received higher scores on final exams than in lecture courses and, in addition, have tended to rate the PSI courses more favorably than the lecture courses.

Even though PSI has been demonstrated to be effective, it is often not efficient in terms of the number of personnel needed to administer the course. One important aspect of Keller's plan is the feedback students receive on their work. The use of proctors, as outlined by Keller, was to allow for immediate scoring of tests, frequent tutoring, and enhancement of the

Portions of this research were supported by a grant from the Office of Instructional Resources through the University of Kansas Endowment Association (71-2294), Lawrence, Kansas 66045.

personal-social aspect of the educational process. The role of proctoring in personalized instruction was investigated by Farmer, Lachter, Blaustein, and Cole (1972). They compared the final exam scores of four different groups of students who during the semester received varying amounts of proctoring on their tests, ranging from no proctoring to all tests proctored. Their results indicated that a) the proctored students were superior to the nonproctored students as measured by final examination performance, and b) the amount of proctoring (for the proctored groups) did not differentially affect final examination performance. Even though Farmer, et al. have demonstrated that not all parts of a course need to be proctored, some proctors are still needed to grade quizzes taken by the student and, with increased class size, this becomes a fairly formidable problem. One alternative not yet explored is self-grading by the student of his own quiz materials.

The present study compared two applications of self-grading within the PSI format. One study investigated self-grading with no proctor feedback. This procedure provided the students with immediate feedback on their quiz questions from an answer guide, but did not provide for proctor evaluation of the student's written answers or verbal skills. The second study investigated self-grading with proctor evaluation. Proctors, in this case, evaluated the students' accuracy of grading and verbal skills on two randomly sampled interview questions. If self-grading can be demonstrated to be effective, the number of people needed to successfully conduct large PSI classes could be substantially reduced.

EXPERIMENT I

Experiment I compared the effects of self-grading with no proctor feedback and proctor grading of quiz material on class efficiency and student test performance. To assess the effectiveness and efficiency of the procedures, four dependent variables were measured. 1) student performance on instructor graded tests, 2) accuracy of student self-grading, 3) student test taking time and self-grading time, and 4) proctor grading and interview time.

In addition, students were asked to evaluate self-grading to other forms of instruction. A second experiment was also conducted to compare self-grading with proctor feedback to proctor grading. However, procedures and results for Experiment II are presented later.

METHOD

Subjects, Setting, and Course Personnel

Students enrolled in an introductory child development course served as subjects. During enrollment, students were randomly assigned (forty-two students each) to one of two sections. However, five students withdrew from the course sometime during the semester and one student failed to report to class, leaving forty-one students in one class and thirty-seven in the other. A classroom was available during three fifty-minute class periods on Monday, Wednesday, and Friday; however, students were not required to come to class every day. The semester lasted for fourteen weeks. One graduate teaching assistant, an undergraduate teaching assistant (coordinator) and six proctors managed each section. Each proctor was responsible for approximately seven students. Proctors had completed the course during the previous semester with a grade of A and received course credit for their work as student assistants.

General Procedures

The course was divided into four major content areas (parts), and each part was further subdivided into four units. Each unit consisted of a set of reading assignments[1] and twenty short-answer study questions.

To progress through the course, students had to master sixteen unit quizzes, take four hour exams and a final. The unit quizzes corresponded to the unit assignment and consisted of eight items randomly selected from the student's set of twenty study questions. The mastery criterion for each unit quiz was

---

[1] Course materials included *Readings in Developmental Psychology Today* (Cramer, 1970), *Elementary Principles of Behavior* (Whaley and Malott, 1971), and *Human Development Lecture Notes and Study Guide* (Semb, 1973).

defined as 100 percent correct. Students could take as many different forms of a unit quiz as necessary to reach the mastery criterion. Each unit quiz mastered contributed four course points to the student's grade in the course.

The course was both student paced and instructor paced. That is, students were allowed to work at their own rate as long as they maintained a minimum rate of progress specified by the instructor (about 1.5 days per quiz). For each day a student fell below the minimum rate required, twenty-five points were deducted from his total number of points. This is equivalent to lowering the student's grade one half grade level for each day he was below the minimum rate required.

On the first day of class, students were required to take a pretest which sampled all parts of the course equally. However, a student's score on the pretest did not count towards his grade in the course. The pretest and hour exams contained two types of items, study items, questions taken directly from the students' set of study questions, and nonstudy items, questions which students were not given in advance. Nonstudy questions items generally required the student to integrate major concepts, ideas, or procedures from the readings. Twenty-four nonstudy items were constructed for each of the four parts of the course. Each nonstudy item was checked by the teaching assistants and instructor to ensure that it did not match any of the students' study questions items.

The pretest and four hour exams were arranged as part of a multiple baseline testing procedure (Miller and Weaver, 1972; Semb, 1973). The hour exams occurred at the end of each part and consisted of twenty-five short-answer, essay items. Tables 19-I and 19-II outline the source and number of study and nonstudy items for each test.

Hour exams were graded outside of the classroom by the teaching assistants. Each question was scored as either correct, partly correct, or incorrect with points of 2, 1, and 0, respectively, given for each question. To earn an A for the hour exam, students had to score twenty-four points on the Part 1 hour exam, twenty-eight on the Part 2 hour exam, thirty-two on the Part 3 hour exam, and thirty-six on Part 4. The number

TABLE 19-I

Multiple Baseline Testing Procedure: Source and Number of
Pretest and Hour Exam Study Question Items

Conditions .... Pre-Training		Post-Training			
Exams .... Pretest	Pretest	Hour 1	Hour 2	Hour 3	Hour 4
Source of Items					
Part 1	4	14	2	2	2
Part 2	4	2	14	2	2
Part 3	4	2	2	14	2
Part 4	4	2	2	2	14
Total Study Question Items per Test	16	20	20	20	20

of points required for an A increased during each successive
hour exam because the number of items previously trained also
increased (see Tables 19-I and 19-II). Points needed for a
B on each of the hour exams can be derived by subtracting
three points from the number of points needed for an A.
Points for a C can be derived by subtracting six points from the
number of points needed for an A.

The final exam was available after a student had completed
all unit quizzes and hour exams. The final consisted of sixty-
four multiple-choice items. Four items were sampled from each
of the sixteen units which made up the course. Two of the
items were based on the study questions (recall items) and

TABLE 19-II

Multiple Baseline Testing Procedure: Source and Number of
Pretest and Hour Exam Non-Study Question Items

Conditions .... Pre-Training		Post-Training			
Exams .... Pretest	Pretest	Hour 1	Hour 2	Hour 3	Hour 4
Source of Items					
Part 1	2	2	1	1	1
Part 2	2	1	2	1	1
Part 3	2	1	1	2	1
Part 4	2	1	1	1	2
Total Non-Study Items per Test	8	5	5	5	5

two required the student to integrate major aspects of the course (probe items). Probe items which appeared on the final, however, were not the same as the nonstudy items which appeared on hour examinations. Each item on the final was worth 1.5 points and contributed to the student's final grade in the course. Points earned on the final were added to hour exam points and unit quiz points to determine the student's course grade. For course grades of A, B, and C, students needed 248, 212, and 184 points, respectively. Following the final exam, students were asked to "rank the following procedures in order of preference, most preferred first: A) Lecture-exam type classes; B) PSI with proctor grading; and C) PSI with self-grading."

Experimental Procedure and Design

PROCTOR GRADING—During the proctor graded parts, students received a quiz from the proctor and upon completion of the quiz, returned it to the proctor for grading. If all questions were correct, the proctor would choose two questions over which he interviewed the student. Interviews were intended to further sample the student's knowledge on the material covered by the questions chosen. In addition, it was hoped that by requiring the student to verbalize his answer, the student's repertoire concerning the material would improve. However, no data were collected to substantiate this point. If a student failed any of the eight items on the quiz or the interview, he was told he would have to retake an alternate form of the quiz covering the same unit before he would be allowed to progress further in the course.

In addition to grading and interviewing students, proctors recorded three times on the student's quiz: 1) the time a student began taking the quiz, 2) the time a student finished taking the test and the proctor began grading the quiz, and 3) the time the proctor completed grading and interviewing the student. For example, when a student received a quiz the proctor would record the time to the nearest minute at the top of the student's quiz paper. A second time would then be recorded when the quiz was returned to the proctor for grading and a third time when the proctor completed his grading and interviewing.

SELF-GRADING. During the self-grading parts, quizzes were again distributed by the proctor. Following the completion of the quiz the proctor gave the student an answer guide which contained the answers to all questions on the unit quizzes. The student would then return to his desk to grade his own quiz. Students were asked to mark either a "C" for correct answers or an "X" for incorrect answers. It was the student's responsibility to decide on the correctness of his own answer. Each answer guide contained all questions and answers for the unit being covered by the student. Students were instructed to use the portion of the answer necessary for grading their quiz and that copying answers from the book or changing an answer on their test constituted cheating which would result in an "F" in the course. However, this never occurred.

If the student graded all eight items as being correct, he would return his quiz, along with the study guide answers, to the proctor who would in turn record the student's progress. If a student failed himself, he was required, as in the proctor graded parts, to take another quiz over the same unit. No interviews were conducted in the self-graded parts. Proctors were asked to record the times when a student started and finished a quiz. A third time was recorded when the student completed grading his own quiz.

DESIGN: A counterbalanced ABAB design was used to evaluate the effectiveness and efficiency of the self-grading procedure. That is, students in one section used the self-grading procedures in Parts 1 and 3 and proctor grading procedures in Parts 2 and 4, while students in the other class used the self-grading procedures in Parts 2 and 4 and proctor grading in Parts 1 and 3. All students covered the same material and took the same quizzes and exams as specified in the General Procedure section.

TABLE 19-III

Part	1	2	3	4
Class 1	Self-Grading (A)	Proctor-Grading (B)	Self-Grading (A)	Proctor-Grading (B)
Class 2	Proctor-Grading (B)	Self-Grading (A)	Proctor-Grading (B)	Self-Grading (A)

Reliability

Reliability measurements were recorded on 1) Proctor grading of unit quizzes; 2) Proctor's grading of sample items during the self-grading procedure; 3) Teaching assistants' grading of hour exams; 4) Proctors' recording of times; and 5) Students self-grading.

Reliability measurements of proctor grading of unit quizzes were taken by one of the teaching assistants at least once during each class period. The teaching assistant or coordinator observed the proctor as he graded each item and listened to the student's partially correct answers. If the observer agreed that an item was either correct or incorrect, it was recorded as an agreement. However, if there was a discrepancy between the observer and the proctor, it was recorded as a disagreement. Reliability checks were made on a total of 119 unit quizzes taken from both Experiment I and II. Of the 872 items checked, there were 811 agreements and 61 disagreements. Reliability, calculated by dividing the number of agreements by the number of agreements plus disagreements, was 93.00 percent.

Reliability grading of sample items during the self-grading procedures was again taken by either the teaching-assistant or coodinator who would observe the proctor while he graded the two items. The definition of reliability is the same as for proctor grading of unit quizzes and was similarly calculated. Reliability checks were taken on a total of seventy-one unit quizzes from both Experiments I and II. Of the 142 observations, 131 were agreements and eleven were disagreements, yielding a reliability score of 92.25 percent.

To check reliability on the hour exams, a second grader scored items on the same basis as did the primary grader, that is, 0, 1, and 2 points for an answer. Agreement was defined as both graders scoring an individual answer exactly the same way. Any discrepancy was defined as a disagreement. Reliability checks were taken on ninety-six review tests. Of the 2400 items checked, there were 2210 agreements and 190 disagreements. Reliability was again calculated by dividing the number of agreements by the number of agreements plus disagreements and equaled 92.20 percent.

Reliability on the proctors' recording of test taking times, grading times, and proctors' grading and interviewing times was recorded by either a teaching assistant or coordinator. The proctor and observer simultaneously recorded the time a student began a quiz, the time he completed a quiz, the time he finished grading a quiz, and, when appropriate, the time the proctor completed an interview. Two different forms of reliability were calculated. First, total number of minutes difference between each time recorded was calculated. This was done for each observation. This total was then divided by the total number of observations and multiplied by sixty to give the total number of seconds difference in observation. Of the 796 observations, there were 248 minutes difference or a mean of 18.6 seconds difference across all observations.

Secondly, the length of time recorded by the two observers for test taking, grading, and interviews was compared. The larger number would then be divided into the smaller to yield a percent reliability for that observation. These times were then averaged to give a total percent reliability. Five hundred and thirty-five pairs of observations were considered with a mean percent reliability of 94.8.

Reliability on students' self-grading was recorded after all students had completed the course. A second grader randomly selected 10 percent of all quizzes taken during the semester that were self-graded. Each answer was graded as being either correct or incorrect on the basis of how closely it matched answer in the instructor's answer guide. Of the 1014 items graded, there were 998 agreements and 16 disagreements. Reliability was calculated in the same way as review and proctor graded tests and had a mean of 98.42 percent.

RESULTS

The mean amount of time for student test taking and student and proctor grading is presented in Figure 19-1. During the proctor grading procedure, proctors' mean grading time was 5.88 minutes, while during the self-grading procedure, proctor time was essentially zero with their performing the administrative

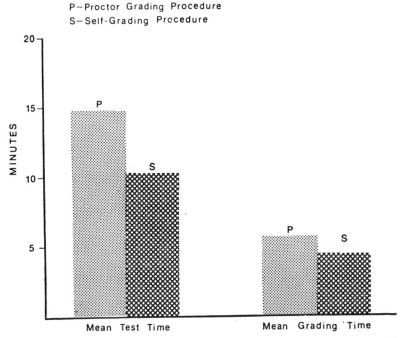

Figure 19-1. The mean test time for student and mean grading time for students and proctors during self-grading and proctor grading.

tasks of handing out tests and answer guides and maintaining student records.

While using the proctor grading procedure, an approximate mean of twenty-one minutes was need by the student to both take a test and have it graded by the proctor. Of that time approximately 14.88 minutes was spent taking the test while the remainder was spent having the proctor grade the test. In comparison, during the self-grading procedure, students needed only approximately sixteen minutes in the classroom, five minutes less than during the proctor grading procedure. During this procedure, a student spent a mean of 11.46 minutes taking the test and 4.54 minutes grading the test. Again, no proctor time was required other than for administrative functions.

A comparison of test scores for both groups is presented in Figure 19-2. Study items and nonstudy items were analyzed separately. Review test scores are plotted such that the two

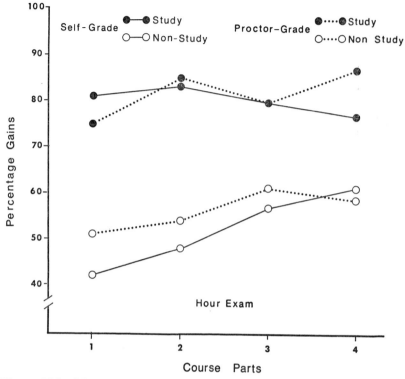

Figure 19-2. Mean percentage gains over pretest levels for both proctor graded and self-graded students. Study question items are represented by solid circles and nonstudy items by open circles. The self-graded students are connected by solid lines and proctor graded students by dotted lines.

different procedural conditions (as opposed to classes) are connected across all four units. Each data point represents the percentage gain for each part of the course as measured on the hour exams. That is, student's pretest score over each part was subtracted from the hour exam score to control for material previously answered correctly by the student on the pretest. No difference in percentage gain on study items answered are apparent when either was used. Students whose tests were graded by a proctor had a mean gain of 82.50 percent on study-question items repeated on the review test across all four review tests. Students who graded their own tests and never received feedback from the proctors had a mean percentage gain of 81.25 on study question items. However, there was a 5 percent difference on nonstudy items (questions not previously seen by the student) between students whose tests were proctor graded and those that were self-graded. Proctor graded students scored a mean percentage gain of 56.25 while self-graded students had a mean of 52.26 percent gain across all non-study items on the hour exam.

Figure 19-3 presents the final exam scores for both groups. The final exam scores are broken down into recall and probe items from each part. Each data point represents the percent of

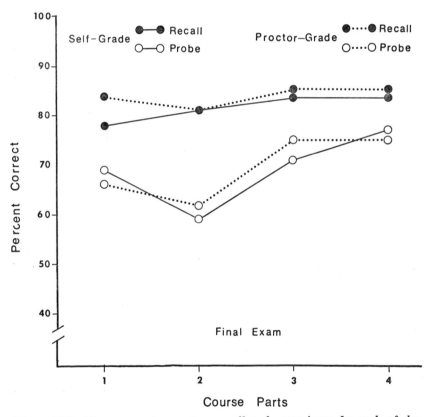

Figure 19-3. Mean percent correct on recall and prose items for each of the four parts of the course as measured by the final examination. Recall items are represented by the solid circles and probe items by the open circles. The self-graded students are connected by a solid line and proctor graded students by a dotted line.

questions answered correctly across the four parts of the course. Proctor graded students had a mean of 83.75 for recall items and 69.50 percent for probe items. Students who self-graded exhibited equivalent performance with a mean of 81.75 percent correct on recall items and 69.00 percent for probe items.

Ninety-six percent of all students in the self-graded sections completed the rating form following the final exam. Ninety-seven percent of all students rated self-grading more favorably than lecture-exam type classes while 80 percent of the students rated the self-grading procedure more favorably than the manager grading procedure.

Results for the multiple baseline testing procedure are not presented in this paper; however, sample data are available in Semb (1973) which demonstrate the contingent relationship between student's test results and the teaching procedure.

EXPERIMENT II

Experiment II investigated the comparative effects of student self-grading with proctor feedback and proctor grading of quiz material on student test performance. The setting, course personnel, general procedure and design are specified in Experiment I.

Subjects

Subjects were selected at the same time as were subjects for Experiment I, with students being randomly assigned to one of two sections (forty-two students per class). However, two students failed to report to the class and five students withdrew from the course sometime during the semester, leaving thirty-nine students in one section and thirty-eight in the other.

Experimental Procedure

PROCTOR GRADING. Procedures for proctor grading were the same as specified in Experiment I.

SELF-GRADING. During the self-grading parts, quizzes were distributed by the proctor. Following completion of the quiz, students obtained an answer guide from the student manager. Students then graded the correctness of each answer on the basis of the answer given in the answer guide. If all eight items were correct, the student would return his quiz and answer guide to the proctor. The proctor would then choose *two* questions on the basis of a random number table. He would check these two questions for correctness and accuracy of student grading. If either of the answers were judged to be incorrect or if the student had graded either of the two incorrectly, he required to retake a quiz over the same unit. If both answers and student grading were correct, the proctor would then interview the student over the same two questions. Again, interviews were intended to further sample the student's knowledge of the material.

Proctors were required to record four times on the student's quiz form: 1) the time a student began taking the quiz, 2) the time the student finished a quiz, and began grading his quiz, 3) the time the student completed grading a quiz, and the proctor began his check and interview, and 4) the time the proctor completed the interview.

RESULTS

The mean testing time for students, grading time for students, and grading and interview time for proctors of both groups, if presented in Figure 19-4. During the proctor grading procedure, proctors spent a mean of 6.15 minutes grading per test in comparison to 3.71 minutes grading and interviewing per test, about half the time, during the self-grading procedures.

Total time by the student in the classroom during the proctor grading procedure was about twenty-two minutes. Of this time, a mean of 14.70 minutes was needed for taking the test with the remainder spent being graded by the proctor. During the self-grading procedure, students also needed an average of twenty-two minutes in the classroom for both test taking and grading. Of that time, students spent a mean of 13.54 minutes taking the test and 4.78 minutes grading the test. The remaining time was spent in the interview with the proctor.

The review test scores for students who self-graded and received proctor feedback and students whose tests were proctor graded are presented in Figure 19-5. As in Experiment I, no difference

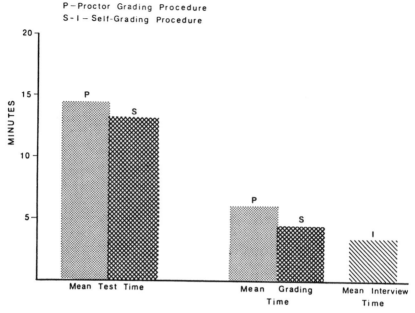

Figure 19-4. The mean test time for students during self-grading and proctor grading. Mean grading time by students and mean grading time and interview time by proctors.

between groups was demonstrated on study question items. Students who self-graded had a mean percentage gain of 84.00 across all four tests, on the study items, while proctor graded students had a mean percentage gain of 82.00 across the four different parts. Also, differences in scores is apparent with the nonstudy items. Self-graded students performed with a mean gain of 53.00 percent, while proctor graded students had a mean gain of 54.75 percent across the four hour exams.

Final exam scores are present in Figure 19-6. As in Experiment I, the final exam scores are broken down into recall and probe items from each part. Each data point represents the percent of items correct from each of the four corresponding parts. Students whose tests were graded by a proctor had a mean of 82.25 percent while students who self-graded had a mean of 82.75 percent correct on recall items, taken from the four different parts. For probe items (items not previously seen by the student) proctor graded

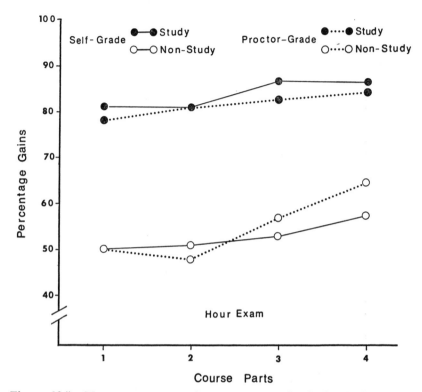

Figure 19-5. Mean percentage gains over pretest levels for both proctor graded and self-graded students. Study question items are represented by solid circles and nonstudy items by open circles. The self-graded students are connected by solid lines and proctor graded students by dotted lines.

students had a mean of 67.75 percent, while self-graded students had a mean of 71.75 percent correct for all four parts.

Ninety-eight percent of the students completed the rating form following the final exam (see Experiment I, Procedures). Ninety-eight percent of the students rated self-grading more favorably than lecture-exam type classes and 82 percent rated the self-grading with proctor feedback procedure more favorably than the manager grading procedure.

GENERAL DISCUSSION

The results of both experiments suggest that self-grading can be useful for those instructors who do not have a large population

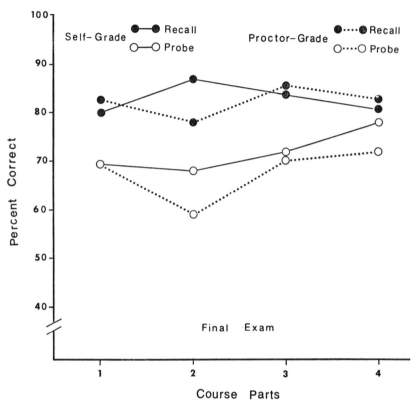

Figure 19-6. Mean percent correct on recall and probe items for each of the four parts of the course as measured by the final examination. Recall items are represented by the solid circles and probe items by the open circles. The self-graded students are connected by a solid line and proctor graded students by a dotted line.

available for their classes, but who still wish to use personalized instruction as a means of teaching. Recording of times allowed for analysis of the amount of time used by both students and proctors during the three different procedures and thus the efficiency of each procedure. The hour exams sampled the student's repertoire over all parts of the course and, in particular, over the part just completed, thus, any differences in student performance should be apparent of these tests (Miller & Weaver, 1972; Semb, 1973). In addition, the counterbalanced reversal design should have controlled for any sequencing effect and for the difficulty of material from each part, thus attributing the results directly to the grading procedures used. These two procedures allowed for analysis of comparative effectiveness of both self-grading and proctor grading.

During self-grading with no proctor feedback procedure, proctors performed essentially administrative tasks, that is, handing out test forms and answer guides and maintaining student records. In addition, students needed less time in the classroom for taking tests and self-grading, than when proctors graded their tests.

Experiment I further demonstrated that self-grading was effective in maintaining student performance on the hour exam study-question items, but that proctor graded students' performance was slightly better on non-study items. However, this difference was not apparent on the final exam which sampled all parts of the course equally. On the final exam, both proctor graded and self-graded students performed equally well on both recall and probe items across all parts of the course. It is conceivable that, using this procedure, instructors could use personalized instruction in a class of thirty to forty students with only one or two proctors to assist in the administrative functions.

Experiment II demonstrated that self-grading by students with proctor feedback was both efficient and effective when compared to a more "traditional" approach to personalized instruction (Keller, 1968). While students needed approximately the same amount of time in the classroom, proctors were required to work only about half as much during the self-grading procedure as compared to the proctor grading procedure. In addition, students received verbal feedback on their written answers and verbal explanations of the two sample questions. This seems to maintain the personal interaction and tutoring aspect that Keller deemed necessary in his original plan. Experiment II further demonstrated that self-graded students with proctor feedback performed as well as did proctor graded students on all hours exams on both study and nonstudy items. The final exam again demonstrated that students' performance on both recall and probe items was essentially the same for either procedure.

Given this procedure, instructors could conceivably teach a course using personalized instruction with not decrement in student performance. At the same time, the number of proctors necessary to run the course with self-grading could be reduced to about half that needed to run the course with proctor grading. In comparison to self-grading with no proctor feedback, self-grading with proctor feedback seems to offer both efficiency in teaching with no decrement in student performance on either type of questions asked.

Finally, results from student rating forms indicated that students preferred personalized instruction to lecture-exam type classes. These findings are similar to those of Keller (1968), McMichael and Corey (1969), and Born, Gledhill, and Davis (1972). In addition, students tended to prefer the self-grading procedure to the more "traditional" PSI format in both experiments.

In conclusion, self-grading seems to be a plausible technique for use in personalized instruction. It is important that efficiency in use of new teaching methods keep pace with increases in effectiveness. Although actual manipulation of the student-manager to student ratio needs to be investigated, data from these two experiments tends to indicate that self-grading can be used in those classrooms where availability of student help is minimal.

EXAM PERFORMANCE AND STUDY BEHAVIOR AS A FUNCTION OF STUDY UNIT SIZE

DAVID G. BORN

ALTHOUGH THERE ARE MANY major ways that the personalized system of instruction (PSI) described by Keller (1968) is different from more traditional forms of college instruction, one of the most important from the student's point of view is the self-pacing feature which allows students to complete course requirements at their own rate. While the freedom offered by self-pacing is highly valued by most students, many students may commence work slowly under self-pacing conditions, fall seriously behind early in the course, and eventually withdraw (Born & Whelan, 1973). To discourage procrastination many instructors have added a contingency to the self-pacing feature which is designed to guarantee some minimum rate of progress through the course, but which allows the student the freedom to work faster than the minimum rate. Examples of such procedures are the *doomsday contingency* of Malott and Svinicki (1969), the *minimum rate line* of Miller, Weaver, and Semb (1973), and the *instructor initiated withdrawal procedure* described by Born (1970). The reader should note that each of these examples attempts to generate student progress with the threat of aversive consequences.

Frequently, in a discussion of student procrastination, someone will suggest that the problem could be largely avoided if at least the initial study units were very short. The rationale underlying this suggestion seems to be that with smaller units students could prepare more quickly, they would be more likely to perform successfully when tested, successful test taking would promote more study, etc. On the other hand, for a constant amount of course material to be learned, smaller units will require more units and progressively less flexibility for student self-pacing in the typical course of fixed duration. Although small units may get the student started more quickly, with smaller units the student has a tighter regimen to follow if he is to successfully complete the course. In any event, it seems likely that the size of study units (or number of tests) may have a marked effect on the way in which students progress through a PSI course.

To determine the effect of study unit size, the present experiment utilized three small sections of a beginning psychology course. All sections were taught using the PSI format, and all students used exactly the same course material presented in the same way. The difference among the sections was in the amount of material which had to be mastered for each test: one section had to pass eighteen tests over the eighteen units in the course, a second section was required to pass nine tests over two units each, and a third section had to pass only six tests over three units each. Several dimensions of student study behavior and test completion were monitored during the course of the experiment.

METHOD

Students

The seventy-two students who enrolled in the beginning psychology course at the University of Utah during Spring Quarter, 1972 served in the present experiment. Two students asked to be transferred to another section of the course immediately upon hearing the course procedures described (see below), leaving a total of seventy students.

Procedures

At the first class meeting all students were told that the course would be taught in an unconventional manner. The procedures and rationale of PSI (Keller, 1968) were then described briefly, and students were given a written statement of course policies and procedures which covered basically the same information described in class. Then the students were told that we had developed some special study materials for a new type of textbook that was soon to be released, that we had obtained several pre-publication copies of this textbook that would have to be used in a special Study Center in the Behavioral Sciences Building, and that we were trying to determine the most efficient way to package the course material so that students could most conveniently learn the content of the course. Because of the interest in packaging material we would be asking different groups of students to take different numbers of tests, although all students would take a final examination. Each student was then assigned to one of three classrooms where she/he would report for future testing. The assignment of students to testing rooms was haphazard, and was accomplished by dividing an alphabetical listing of names into three equal parts and assigning each of the three sections of the alphabet to a different testing room. Finally, in concluding this first class meeting students were told that if they would prefer to be enrolled in a section of the course taught in a more traditional way by a different instructor the author would help them transfer to another section. Two students requested a transfer on the grounds that they would find it very difficult to do their studying in the Study Center because of part time employment.

The written course material was located in the Study Center and was unavailable elsewhere on campus. This material was divided into eighteen units and was presented to students in folders which they could check out for use in the Study Center. Each folder contained a ten to thirty page reading assignment stapled on the right side of an opened folder and a study guide stapled to the left side of the folder. The study guide introduced the reading assignment and presented a list of items and questions intended to help the student master the material.

The Study Center was a large room equipped with tables and chairs and capable of seating about sixty students. Just inside the door a monitor was seated at a desk and received student requests for specific units of course material, noted the time on the request card, and received the folders when they were returned by students. The difference between the time a student received a folder and the time it was returned was used as a measure of textbook contact time (Study Center time). The Study Center was open for student use from 8:30 a.m. to 5:30 p.m. and from 7:00 to 10:00 p.m. Monday through Friday, and from 9:00 a.m. to 12:30 p.m. on Saturday.

Generally speaking, the course procedures were like those described by Keller (1968) and have been reported in detail elsewhere (Born, 1970) ; (Born & Zlutnick, 1972) . Students were required to pass a series of tests over the written course material. These tests were evaluated by a student proctor who judged each item as correct or incorrect and conducted a brief interview with the testee over the crucial points in the written material. If the student's performance was unacceptable he was asked to restudy the material and return at a later date to take a different examination.

Accompanying each of the eighteen units of course material was a set of three to four short quizzes. Each quiz consisted of eight to ten short-answer questions that could usually be answered in a couple of sentences. Students in Section 1 were required to pass a quiz over each study unit. Students in Section 2 were required to pass a quiz over two units at a time. These tests were produced by simply stapling together a pair of quizzes for the appropriate two units. Similarly, for students in Section 3, tests were produced by stapling together three unit quizzes.

The most notable exception to Keller's procedures employed in the present experiment was the lowering of the master criterion for passing tests from 100 percent to 90 percent; students in Section 1 could have one unsatisfactory answer per test, students in Section 2 could have two unsatisfactory answers, and in Section 3 students could have as many as three unsatisfactory answers.

On the first day of class all students were told that they could progress through the course material at their own rate, but they were warned that it is very easy to fall behind schedule and difficult to catch up. There was no contingency employed by the author to force progress through the course. Tests could be taken only on Monday, Wednesday, and Friday, and with twenty-seven days scheduled for testing there was considerable room for self-pacing even by students in Section 1 (eighteen tests). To permit students to finish the course early, they were told that an early final exam could be taken by students who finished early, but it would not be scheduled until it was clear that at least five students would have completed the test series (which made them eligible for the final). This early final was administered about a week and a half before the last day of regular classes.

On Tuesday and Thursday of each week students could attend a series of lectures, films, and demonstrations which were intended to supplement the written course material. With a few exceptions these activities were concerned with applied psychology and emphasized behavior modification programs. Students were not held responsible for any material presented during these class meetings.

The final examination consisted of a section of forty multiple choice items where one or more answers could be correct, and sixty short answer questions which required anything from drawing simple graphs to writing several sentences. None of the items on the final exam had been used previously in the course. On a previous occasion when this examination had been given in a different course, the correlation between score on multiple choice and short answer items was $r = +0.78$. Thus, although multiple choice items had not been used in the course prior to the final examination there is no reason to believe these items could have "washed out" differences between class sections (see Alba & Pennypacker, 1972).

The short answer portion of the final examination was independently scored by members of the proctor staff and by the author. Each answer was scored as being worth 0, 1, or 2 points, and the sum of the points awarded by the proctor and by the author were subsequently correlated to get an index of grader agreement. The resulting correlation was $r = +0.86$.

RESULTS

Although there was no deliberate attempt to match class sections on the basis of cumulative grade point average (GPA), Table 20-I shows that among students originally assigned to the

TABLE 20-I

Entry	Section 1 One Unit/ Test	Section 2 Two Units/ Test	Section 3 Three Units/ Test
Total number of testing days	27	27	27
Number of tests to be completed	18	9	6
Extra testing days	9	18	21
Number of students registered	23	22	23
Number of students withdrawing	5	4	3
Number of students finishing	18	18	20
Percentage of students withdrawing	22%	18%	13%
GPA* of students registering for class	2.69	2.71	2.74
GPA range	1.10–3.87	1.64–3.85	1.44–4.00
GPA of students completing class	2.90	2.79	2.75
GPA range	2.11–3.87	2.23–3.85	1.44–4.00

* Maximum GPA range: 0.00–4.00.

three class sections there was little difference in either the mean or range of student GPAs. However, because some students withdrew from these sections over the academic term the mean and range of GPAs for students completing each of the sections was slightly different.

The major findings of the present experiment appear in Table 20-I and Figures 20-1a, 20-1b, and 20-1c. All of these data were obtained only from students completing the course. Generally speaking, size of the test package had virtually no impact on major features of student performance, although some perhaps trivial measures were affected in obvious ways. Both the mean and range of scores on the final examination were very similar for all three sections. Furthermore the mean number of entries into the Study Center and mean total time in the Study Center were comparable for the three sections. Finally, Table 20-II shows that even the rate of progress through the course, as measured in terms of time to complete six, twelve, and eighteen unit tests, is strikingly similar for all sections.

Figures 20-1a, 1b, and 1c show a cumulative record of Study Center hours for individual students in the three class sections over the academic term. The records displayed in the figures are from the two students in each section who had the highest total

TABLE 20-II

Entry	Section 1 One Unit/ Test	Section 2 Two Units/ Test	Section 3 Three Units/ Test
X̄ final examination score	81.4%	82.1%	82.8%
Exam score range	62–92.5%	66.5–91%	70–91%
Number (and percent) of students taking the early final examination	7 (39%)	4 (22%)	8 (38%)
X̄ number of Study Center entries	33	29	26
X̄ number of Study Center (Hrs.)	39 Hrs.	38 Hrs.	42 Hrs.
Range total time in Study Center	15.6–69.8 Hrs.	21.0–78.3 Hrs.	19.7–80.2 Hrs.
X̄ time to write answers to test questions in class	16.4 min.	30.2 min.	46.5 min.
X̄ number of testing days to complete course units			
6 units	10.1	12.3	11.3
12 units	17.8	20.0	18.2
18 units	24.7	25.5	24.6

Study Center time, the two students with the lowest total Study Center time, and a student with the middle rank of total Study Center time. Although there are no gross differences in these records by class section, careful inspection of the records does suggest that the procedure of frequent testing over small units tends to regularize studying. Note for example that very long periods of study (4-5 hours) occur rarely in the study records of students in Section 1, but they occur several times in the study records of students in Sections 2 and 3. Similarly, long breaks between visits to the Study Center are uncommon for students in Section 1 relative to students in Sections 2 and 3. Thus, as one might expect, frequent testing over small units of material seems more likely to lead students into regular study routine.

Figure 20-2 shows the Study Center records and the examination patterns for students who withdrew from each of the three sections. Only three of the four students who withdrew from Section 2 (two units/test) are shown because the study records of the fourth student are missing. Also, one of the withdrawals

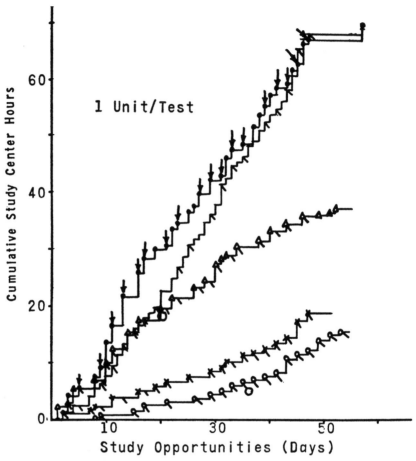

Figures 20-1a, 20-1b, 20-1c. Records of cumulative hours of time in the Study Center by five individual students in each of three different sections of a PSI course. The days on which tests were taken in the testing room are indicated with either a "hash" mark or an arrow. Tests failed are indicated with a circle at the end of the test mark.

in Section 3 (three units/test) is not plotted because it involved a special case (a student who was injured in an automobile accident with only one remaining test to complete two weeks before the end of the course). Although the number of student withdrawals in each section is insufficient to draw any firm conclusions about test package size and its affect on withdrawals,

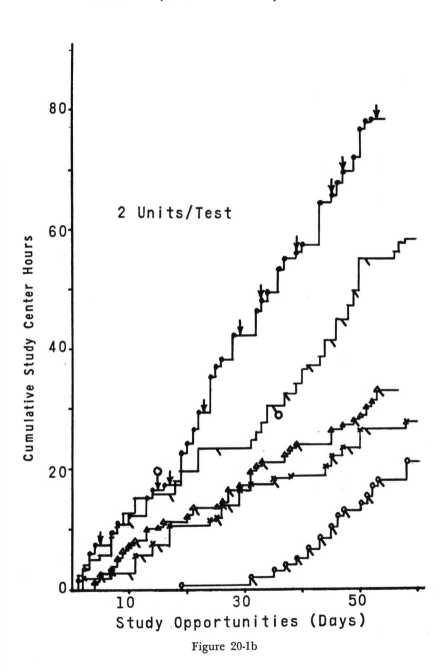

Figure 20-1b

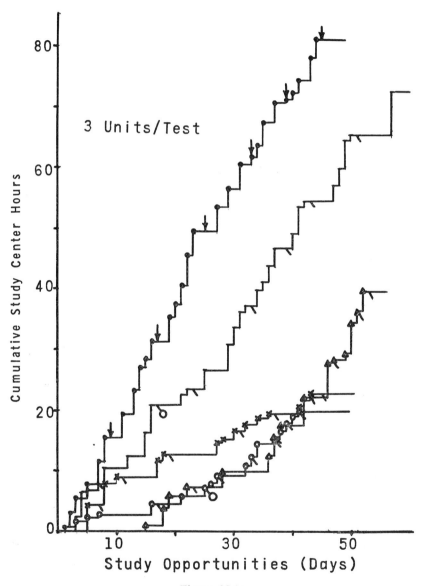

Figure 20-1c

there are some interesting things to be noted in the collection of data shown in Figure 20-2. First, it may be noted that there are few test failures which appear in the records of these students. Second, all but two of the ten students shown in Figure 20-2 made their first appearance in the Study Center reasonably early in the academic term. Third, it may be noted that most of the students passed the last unit test they took in the course. Fourth, none of the records reflect an excessive amount of Study Center time per unit, suggesting that these students were not having great difficulty with the course material. Finally, the reader should note that most of these records show one or more long periods of absence from the Study Center which occur just prior to the student's last appearance in class.

DISCUSSION

The remarkable similarity in the performance of students in all three sections is the greatest surprise in the present experiment. Given the same mastery levels for all sections, use of student proctors, etc., the size of the required study package (or number of tests) seems to be of little consequence over the range of values used in the present experiment. Although number of tests to be taken would intuitively seem to be a powerful variable in developing general patterns of study, for the measures of student behavior in this experiment this variable appears to have had little effect when immersed in the constellation of other variables comprising PSI.

The similarity of effects which appear in Table 20-I and Figures 20-1a, 1b, and 1c, should not be taken to mean that the size of the study unit (number of tests) is unimportant in PSI. Indeed, there is an entirely different dimension along which this variable may be extremely important. From Table 20-II it may be seen that mean time to complete a test in Section 1 was 16.4 minutes, whereas in Section 3 a test required on the average 46.5 minutes. In Section 1, where students reported often for brief testing, the atmosphere of the class was light and friendly, and there was much active discussion of subject matter between students and between students and teaching staff. This discussion

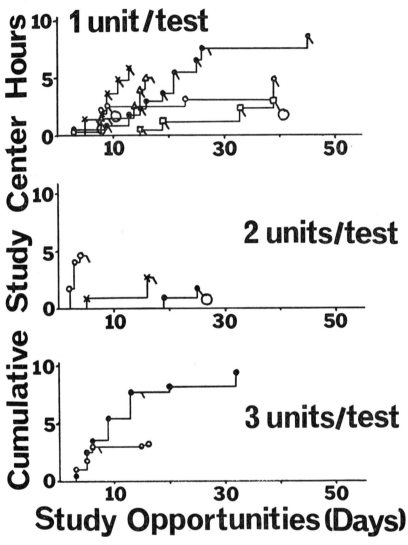

Figure 20-2. Cumulative hours of time in the Study Center for students who withdrew from the three sections of the course. As with earlier figures, the days on which tests were taken are indicated with diagonal "hash" marks, and a test failure is indicated with a large circle at the end of the hash mark.

sometimes occurred before testing, it occurred during the interview, and sometimes it occurred after the test evaluation was completed. In Section 3 on the other hand, the testing room was simply not fun for either students or the proctor staff. The room was very quiet for most of the class hour, and the length of the test to be evaluated, combined with the small amount of time remaining in the class hour when the test was completed made the interview very intense and sometimes not as thorough as it should have been. The friendly and informal atmosphere in Section 1 likely developed in large part because of the frequent proctor-student/student-student contacts necessitated by the frequent testing schedule. In other words, frequent tests over small units may contribute in a major way to the highly favorable ratings reported for many PSI courses (Born & Herbert, 1971; Gallup, 1969).

The individual records of students who withdrew from the class sections of the present experiment generally support and extend the findings and suggestions of Born and Whelan (1973) about student withdrawals. Generally speaking, there is nothing in the data shown in Figure 20-2 to suggest that these students have an unusually difficult time with the course material—in spite of the fact that students who withdraw tend to come from the lower end of the GPA distribution (Born and Whelan, 1973). The data on Study Center time help to clarify the observation that students who withdraw progress slowly through the required series of unit tests. By showing that these students do not study excessively between tests, these data suggest that the thrust of efforts to reduce withdrawals might well focus on procedures to increase student contact with text materials rather than to change student behaviors during textbook contact time.

In summary, while it is not entirely clear that smaller units do not help with the problem of student procrastination and student withdrawals, it is also not clear that they do help. If an instructor has a course of fixed duration such that he cannot allow students to make up incomplete grades in a subsequent term, he should recognize that with a constant amount of course material the decision to have small units early in the course commits one to either more units *or* longer units later in the course. Under these circumstances the decision to have more units is also a decision to limit the extent of student self-pacing. On the other hand, if the number of units is held constant and later units are made so that early units can be made shorter, the greatest work requirements of the course will probably occur at a time in the term when students are already at their busiest because of other academic demands. Perhaps this is precisely the time when PSI demands should be lighter. After all, it would seem that our responsibility to our students parallels closely their investment in our course; the more work they have completed, the greater is our obligation to see them through to the conclusion of our course. Clearly this is not a simple problem; we need much more data before we can evaluate the relative trade-offs involved in construction short vs. long units.

THE EFFECTS OF QUANTITY OF AS-SIGNED MATERIAL ON COLLEGE STUDENT ACADEMIC PERFOR-MANCE AND STUDY BEHAVIOR

GEORGE W. O'NEILL
JAMES M. JOHNSTON
WILLIAM M. WALTERS
JEAN A. RASHED

THE GOAL OF THE RESEARCH PROGRAM at Georgia State University may be most usefully seen in three stages. The first is to empirically define those independent variables in the college student's academic environment which affect his academic performance. Second, the exact nature of the relationship between those variables and academic performance must be fully described in carefully designed studies. It is only then that the third stage of actually designing optimal teaching techniques for each instructional situation may be initiated.

We are clearly still at the first two stages. Previous studies examining the effects of grade labels and the effects of minimum performance criteria defining course grades (Johnston and O'Neill, 1973) have already shown the considerable influence of these variables on various aspects of student academic performance.

Another variable which we have suspected of affecting performance is the quantity of assigned material in a unit of course material which is assigned and tested. Data from pilot studies concerning quantity of subject matter have strongly suggested that there are a number of ways in which this variable affects different aspects of college students' academic performance.

In the paradigm used in this study, quantity of assigned material was defined as the number of pages of text per unit of course material. This definition simply means the amount of material which the students were assigned, studied, and were tested on. The paradigm used to generate baseline performance was the same as that described in Johnston, O'Neill, Walters & Rasheed (1974).

College students routinely enrolled in a junior-level course in abnormal psychology in two different quarters were each exposed to a different sequence of variations in the number of textbook pages in seven units of course material (not counting the first unit). There were three unit sizes; the large unit was ninety pages, the medium unit was sixty pages, and the small unit was thirty pages. Each student in group one (N = 9) used a MLSLMSM sequence. Each student in group two (N = 21) used an SMSMLML sequence. Because each student progressed through the units at his own pace, this permitted the possibility of within subject, between subject, within group, and between group levels of analysis examining the effects of unit size and the effects of any sequence of sizes. All variables other than the size of the units were held constant, including the number of fill-in items in each unit (one-hundred) and the degree of familiarity with the items on each attempt within a unit. The student's familiarity with the items was controlled by arranging the items so that after the first attempt on a unit, the students saw 50 percent new items and 50 percent items that had already been encountered in earlier attempts on that unit. On the first attempt, of course, the students saw 100 percent new items.

The dependent variables included 1) the quality of performance (percent correct) on the first attempt of each unit, 2) the quality of performance on the final attempt of each unit, 3) the number of days between the completion of one unit and the first attempt on the next unit, 4) the number of days between the first and subsequent attempt within each unit, and 5) the total number of attempts required on each unit to meet the ninety percent correct criterion. Study behaviors measured in the manner described in Johnston, et al. (1974) were also dependent variables in this experiment.

RESULTS

The influence of the quantity of unit material on these dependent variables is observed in the data shown by the following figures.

The upper portion of Figure 21-1 is a plot of the number of pages in the different units. The lower graph shows the mean percent correct on the first attempt on each unit for all students in condition I. It shows a consistent inverse relationship to the

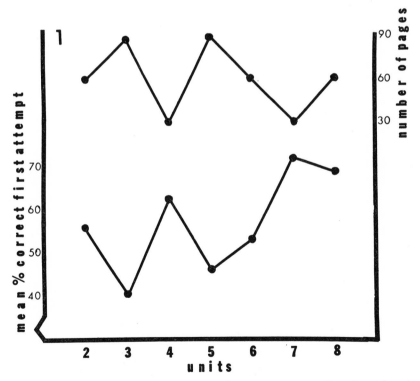

Figure 21-1. Mean percent correct on first attempt as a function of unit size for group 1.

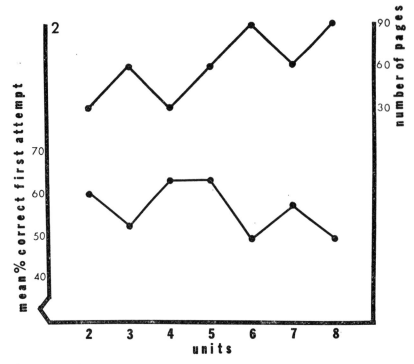

Figure 21-2. Mean percent correct on first attempt as a function of unit size for group 2.

size of the units. That is, the larger the unit, the poorer the performance on the first attempt.

The group data for students exposed to SMSMLML sequence is presented in Figure 21-2 and shows the consistency of this effect on the quality of the first attempts. If the unit size data were inverted, it would (with the exception of unit five) nearly be congruent with the performance data.

Figure 21-3 shows the mean performance on the final attempt on each unit for both groups compared to the different unit sizes. There are no marked or consistent variations in the final performance related to unit sizes. This is because the minimum performance criterion of 90 percent across all units produces a high degree of control over the performance seen in the final attempt (Johnston & O'Neill, 1973). Our earlier research strongly

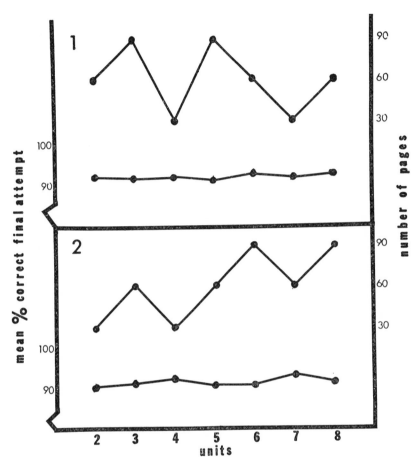

Figure 21-3. Mean percent correct on final attempt as a function of unit size.

suggests that this would also have been the case had the minimum criterion been 75 percent or 60 percent. That is, the performance would have likely attained those criteria by very narrow margin and shown little variation related to unit size.

Figure 21-4 shows a strong and consistent direct relationship between the mean number of days between the final attempt on one unit and the first attempt on the next and the variations of unit size. Thus, as unit size increases, the latency between units increases. Latency is the appropriate term here since the students were free to come in and perform again on a unit or to start a new

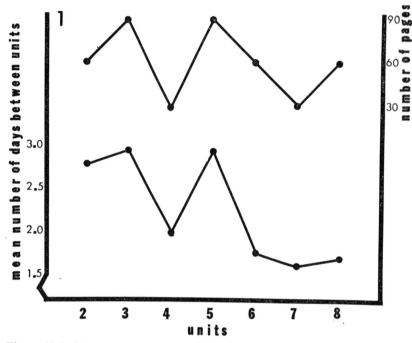

Figure 21-4. Mean number of days between units as a function of unit size for group 1.

unit whenever they liked. It should be noted that, because of the variety of things beyond as well as within the academic environment which can influence attendance, the variability here is slightly greater than is the case with the other measures.

The same data for students in group two is presented in Figure 21-5 again show the same effect of the unit size. The only exception appears in unit two and may be due to a slight warm-up effect which is frequently observed.

Figure 21-6 shows the mean number of days between attempts depicted for each attempt *within* a unit. Of course, as the number of attempts increases from one to four or five, there are fewer students taking that many attempts to attain the final criterion. Here, the first try on each unit is the latency for the first attempt which was just seen in the two previous figures. What should be noted here is mean latency for the second, third, fourth, or fifth

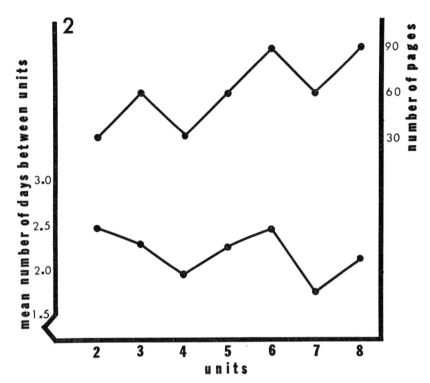

Figure 21-5. Mean number of days between units as a function of unit size for group 2.

attempts as the data allows. It may be clearly observed that there is no influence of unit size on these within unit latencies. Generally, the latencies beyond the first attempt on each unit average quite near to the minimum possible latency of one day.

The same general effect may be seen in this within unit latency data for group two (see Figure 21-7), although there is a slight effect due to unit size on the second attempt on each unit.

Figure 21-8 shows the mean total number of attempts per unit for group one needed to attain the ninety percent criterion. Clear influence of unit size on the mean total number of attempts may be seen. The larger the unit, the more total attempts were required to complete the unit.

The same data for students in group two again shows the same

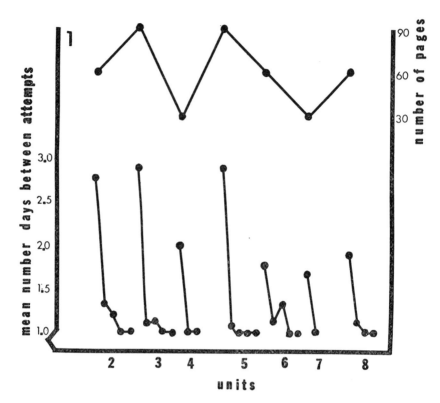

Figure 21-6. Mean number of days between attempts as a function of unit size for group 1.

general effect in spite of many other factors which can affect this data.

This paper will present study data only for group two from the spring quarter experiment because of improvements made in the study reporting system that quarter. The same phenomena were observed for the winter quarter group. Figure 21-10 shows the mean total study time per unit for all students in group two. Again the quantity of material on which students performed clearly affects the reported study time in a predictable manner.

Figure 21-11 shows the mean reported amount of reading the text for the first time as a percentage of the total time. With the exception of unit six, a clear direct relationship may be seen.

The Figure 21-12 graph of the mean percent rereading the

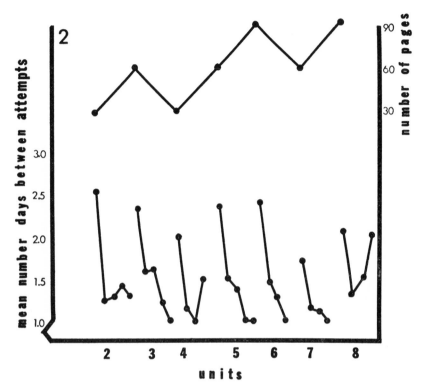

Figure 21-7. Mean number of days between attempts as a function of unit size for group 2.

text shows the expected inverse relationship with unit size. Again note that the figure for unit six is slightly higher than might be expected.

Figure 21-13 shows the reported summarizing as a percentage of total study time across unit sizes. In spite of small actual percentage figures, an inverse relationship can be seen.

Finally, we see in Figure 21-14 the mean percent time spent writing terms, names, and definitions also shows an inverse relationship to unit size. All other reported study behaviors showed no measurable effect of unit size variations.

DISCUSSION

These two experiments have shown that the thirty-, sixty-, and ninety-page variations in unit sizes have had the following effects

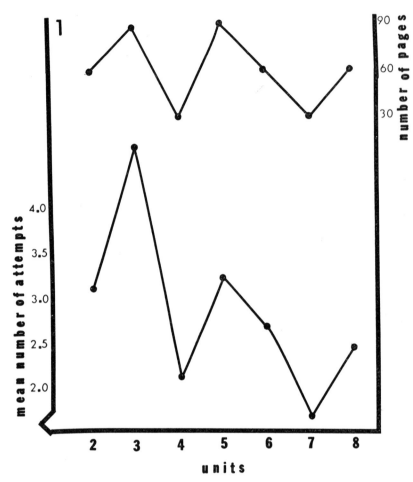

Figure 21-8. Mean number of attempts as a function of unit size for group 1.

on student performance: 1) the larger the unit, the poorer the performance on the first attempt of each unit, 2) the larger the unit, the longer the delay between the end of one unit and the beginning of the next, and 3) the larger the unit, the more total attempts required to attain the ninety percent criterion.

However, no effect of unit size was seen on the quality of performance on the final attempt meeting criterion, and very little effect was seen on the latency between attempts within units.

The observed effects of quantity of material on reported study

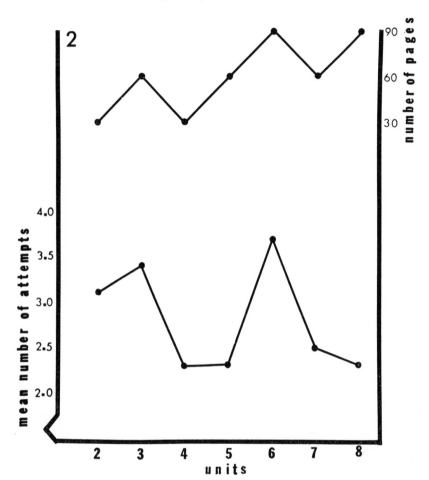

Figure 21-9. Mean number of attempts as a function of unit size for group 2.

behaviors were as follows: 1) the larger the unit, the more time spent studying, 2) the larger the unit, the greater percentage of the total study time spent reading the text for the first time, 3) the larger the unit, the smaller the percentage of total study time spent rereading the text, summarizing and writing terms, names and definitions, and 4) all other study behaviors were not affected by variations in unit size.

The obvious question which must be addressed by this data concerns the optimum unit size for this particular text and course.

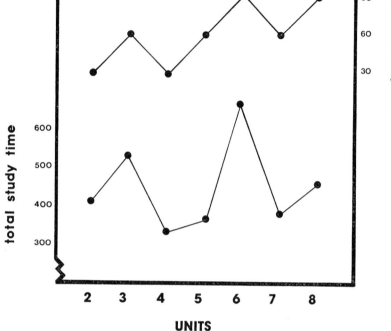

Figure 21-10. Mean total study time as a function of unit size.

That is, if one is concerned with both the quality of performance demonstrated and the quality of effort expended by the students to produce that performance, there is probably one unit size for this course which is maximally efficient in progressing through a body of material. Because there were no effects of quantity of material on the final quality of performance which the students demonstrated, the definition of optimum must be in terms of the number of attempts required to reach the final criterion and the amount of effort or total study time taken to produce criterion level performance. The optimum unit size in this case becomes a matter of efficiency. What unit size will produce the most efficient balance between the number of attempts necessary to meet a high criterion on the total amount of material in the course and the total amount of study required to produce performance?

Although the small units (thirty pages) in this course required

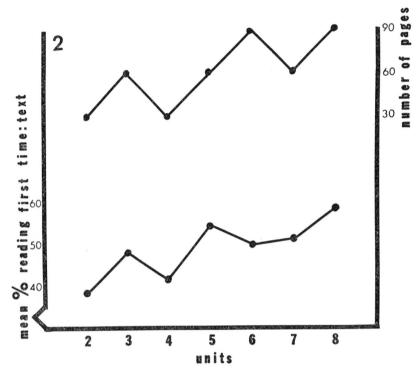

Figure 21-11. Mean percent reading text for the first time as a function of unit size.

fewer attempts and less total study to attain the ninety percent criterion, if the total 420 pages of he textbook covered during the quarter were divided into small units only, the picture might change. For example, fourteen small units of thirty pages in length would be required to cover all the material. If the course were divided into medium or sixty-page units, the total number would be only seven. If only large or ninety-page units were used to cover all the material, there would be only 4.6 units in the course.

If one multiplies the mean number of attempts per unit that group two took on the small units by the fourteen units needed to cover the entire course, the total number of attempts needed to make criterion on all units in the course would be almost thirty-six. The same extrapolation for a course made up of all medium

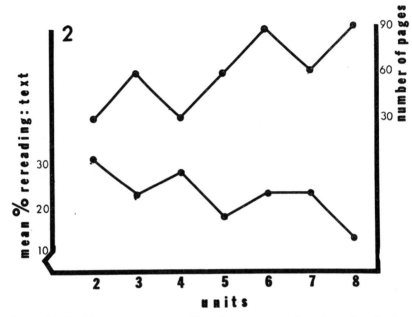

Figure 21-12. Mean percent rereading the text as a function of unit size.

units would necessitate nearly nineteen total attempts. The total number of attempts required for a course constituted of large units would be only fourteen. So the larger the unit, the fewer total attempts would have been taken to produce the same high level of performance, if the students otherwise behaved in the same manner.

The same extrapolations may be made for the total study time per unit for the average student in group two. The data presented has shown that small units took *much* less study time than the large units. For instance, the average student took about six and a half hours on the small units but about nine and three fourths hours on the large units.

If we multiply these average total study times by the number of small or medium or large units needed to cover the entire course, we find that eighty-eight and a half hours would be needed for the small units, about fifty hours for medium units, and only forty-four hours total for a course consisting entirely of large units.

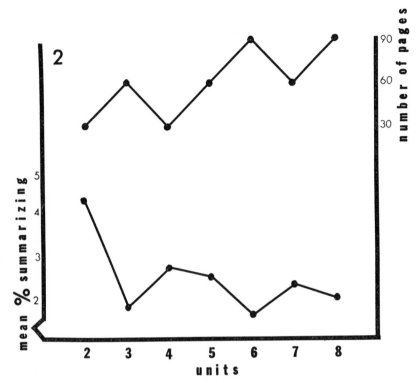

Figure 21-13. Mean percent summarizing as a function of unit size.

(These same calculations have been made for group one with the same pattern of results.)

At first glance, these extrapolations would seem to suggest that if this course were to consist entirely of ninety-page units (as opposed to sixty- or thirty-page units), the students would take fewer total attempts and less total study to meet the 90 percent criterion.

This is not the entire picture, however. It is not necessarily true that the larger the unit the less the effort. At some point in increasing unit size the quantity of material would certainly get sufficiently large that the quality of performance would decrease or that the amount of effort required would begin increasing.

In addition, other considerations affect the choice of unit sizes. The fewer units resulting from large unit sizes would

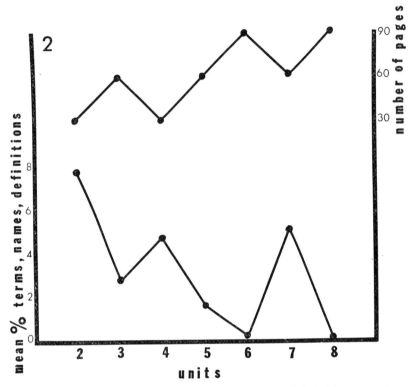

Figure 21-14. Mean percent writing terms, names, and definitions as a function of unit size.

decrease the frequency of measurement, complicating one of the most important variables in college teaching. It is generally well-recognized that frequent measurement is necessary because of its utility in evaluation and as a means of influencing academic performance in a desirable fashion.

Finally, student preferences must be considered. In our experience students can get discouraged by the necessity of a number of attempts on one unit, particularly at poorer performance levels, and tend to take an immediate view of the situation. They might well prefer fewer attempts of higher quality on smaller units even though this meant more work in the long run. However, we have not *formally* determined student preference on this point.

Clearly there are many considerations to take into account in deciding on the size of units in a course. The size of a unit has consistent, powerful, and widespread effects on different performance measures and reported study behaviors, and the quantity of material can be manipulated so as to produce effects which facilitate attainment of the goals of the course. It should further be noted that it is not a variable which can be avoided. If performance is measured over course material, then units have been defined and their size will have some effects on academic responses.

STUDENT PACING

THE FIRST THREE PAPERS in this section concern different aspects of the self-pacing feature which is characteristic of all individualized teaching methods. "An Analysis Of Student Behavior With and Without Rate Limiting Contingencies" displays the various patterns of pacing which can result from these methods. "Study And Test Performance Of College Students On Concurrent Assignment Schedules" and "An Experimental Comparison Of Four Pacing Contingencies" show the influence of different contingencies on the pace at which students study and learn. The fourth paper, "Entry Level Testing And The Pattern Of Behavioral Objectives In A Keller Plan Physics Course," looks at diagnostic entry tests and their potential, while the final paper, "Individualized Systems Of Instruction Are Better . . . For Whom?", examines possible differential effects of these methods on different kinds of students.

READING *22*

AN ANALYSIS OF STUDENT BEHAVIOR WITH AND WITHOUT LIMITING CONTINGENCIES

JAMES R. SUTTERER
ROBERT E. HOLLOWAY

INTRODUCTORY COURSES IN PSYCHOLOGY are generally taken by lower division undergraduate students as either an elective for various majors or as a prerequisite for more advanced coursework in psychology. Both student and discipline demands for psychology courses appear to be increasing nationally. This has aggravated the financial problems of keeping class size to a reasonable number. Since World War II, the typical response to this situation has been the creation of large lecture sections in which the conditions are less than desirable for either teaching or establishing interactive communication between students and teachers. As a consequence of this logistical strategy, the evaluation

James R. Sutterer is an Assistant Professor in the Department of Psychology and Robert E. Holloway is an Associate in Development with the Center for Instructional Development, Syracuse University. The authors would like to express their appreciation to a number of individuals who have rendered various forms of assistance during this continuing project: to Dr. Robert Diamond who has provided encouragement as well as financial support, to Dr. Edward Kelly who provided generous time and assistance concerning the statistical analyses which appear in this report, and to a number of undergraduate students who helped with the course and the collection of these data.

of student performance is typically reduced to two or three objective tests rather than being a continuous process. This procedure reduces the chances of success as well as the opportunity to provide constructive feedback which could aid in the modification of academically relevant behaviors. The role of the student for the balance of the semester is of a passive nature. The passive nature of the system produces a general disillusionment and alienation with which most of us are all too familiar. The rigidity of this system restricts students who are able and eager to proceed at a faster pace as well as those who need slower pacing, have difficulty pacing themselves, or wish to branch into interests outside the basic core.

If one maintains that the traditional large lecture technique results in an efficient and high level of performance, then the absolute number of students does not appear to be a relevant consideration. However, as Wilson and Tosti (1972) indicate: "There is convincing evidence now that in conventional group-paced instruction, changes in class size influence learning only when the class has fifteen or less students; learning effectiveness in a class with more than twenty students is not influenced much if the number is raised to thirty or to three hundred (page 35)." The challenge is to retain the advantages of the active nature of small group instruction within the constraints of the economic imperative of large course enrollment.

In response to this situation several faculty members of the Department of Psychology at Syracuse University have undertaken a program of development in conjunction with the University's Center for Instructional Development.

A personalized system of instruction developed by Dr. Fred Keller of Western Michigan University served as a basic model which provided many of the objectives which it was hoped would be accomplished. During the Spring semester of 1971 the first attempt was made at using Keller's Personalized System of Instruction.

The use of contingency-managed instruction in combination with self-pacing is a relatively wide spread innovation. This design allows for a greater degree of personalization through proctoring. Early findings indicate the design is equal or superior to traditional instruction (McMichael & Corey, 1969; Corey, McMichael and Tremont, 1970). However, more work on specifics of the design and the prior question of the operant level remain to be more completely explored. Thus, the first attempt was particularly interesting because of its simplified structure: the only explicit requirements of the course consisted of the completion of a specified number of units by the end of the semester. The course was free of most external time restraints imposed by the instructor on the students' behavior. By studying the behavior of students in such an unrestrained course it was hoped useful information would be gained regarding the optimal use of contingencies in future courses. The focus of this paper will be a description of the course, an analysis of student behavior, and a comparison of these data with those gathered in a subsequent semester.

Method
Spring, 1971

Content of the Course

The entire course consisted of twenty-five units of material which had to be mastered in succession before the final examination could be taken. Individual units were from ten to forty textual pages in length. A total of 534 pages were covered which constitutes approximately 78 percent of Kendler's (1968) *Basic Psychology*. It was later discovered in discussion with other instructors that this amount of material is considerably more than is typically covered with a large class lecture method.

Study outlines were provided in a unit workbook by Corey and McMichael (1970) which is keyed in Kendler's textbook. The workbook gave the page assignments in the textbook and supplied from two to five pages of questions for each unit. The workbook stressed the material upon which the unit tests were based.

Large lectures were scheduled, but not required, for three fifty-minute classes on Monday, Wednesday and Friday.

Testing

Unit tests which were given by student proctors consisted of five or ten questions in multiple-choice, short answer, or fill-in-the-blank formats. A perfect score was required on each test. If a student did not succeed in making a perfect score, an alternative form was taken at a later date. In addition, the proctor explained to the student what he missed on the test and suggested readings in preparing for retaking the examination. There was no minimum or maximum number of unit tests that had to be completed each week.

Proctors

Assistance on unit tests could be obtained from proctors at scheduled times each week. This schedule included both day and evening hours and totaled twenty-six hours. The fifteen proctors were advanced undergraduates who were qualified to help explain the material in the study guides and to administer and grade the unit tests. Their main responsibility was to help the students with difficult material. Most of the proctors were students who had completed the undergraduate introductory course and had expressed an interest in obtaining experience by working with his system. Each proctor also earned three hours of academic credit.

Grading

Since each student had to complete each unit with a perfect score the grade for the unit tests at the end of the semester was determined by the number of units which were completed. The scale was as follows:

A———————————	25 units
B———————————	24 and 23 units
C———————————	22 and 21 units
D———————————	20 units
F———————————	19 or less

This was an extremely narrow scale but was designed to increase the probability that a student would try for an A in the course. That such a procedure will produce the desired effect is suggested by the work of Lloyd (1971) and Johnston and O'Neill (1973).

RESULTS

Since this was a first experience with this type of instruction, the primary question concerned the individual differences in behavior regarding the manner in which the course work was completed. The strategy employed for examining the behavior of the students was in the form of cumulative records of test-taking behavior. In order to classify student records into categories, four people independently distributed cumulative records of 111 students into five groups at the end of the semester. In the distribution of the records among the five groups, all four raters agreed upon the same classification for seventy-eight records, and three of the four raters agreed on all records but three. Thus, the high degree of consistency suggested that the five categories adequately described the different patterns of behavior. The five groups are as follows:

Group 1: Late Group

A number of students (n = 27) completed the course in a manner which can be described as a "fixed-interval" pattern of behavior. After a number of weeks had passed during which time an insignificant amount of work had been completed, these students started working at a high rate until the course work was completed during the last two weeks of the semester. Cumulative records from three students in this group are presented in Figure 22-1.

In a sense this pattern of behavior is self-defeating since it

INTRODUCTORY PSYCHOLOGY

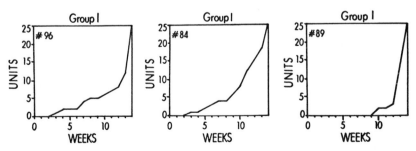

Figure 22-1. Three individual cumulative records of students in Group 1: the late group.

produces a situation for the student which is similar to the more traditional system in which large amounts of work come at specified times during the course. In addition, such a pattern of behavior adds to the difficulties of giving and evaluating large numbers of tests during the late portion of the course by the instructor and proctors.

Group 2: High Rate Group

A number of students (n = 12) completed relatively more units during the first two to three weeks of the course and continued until they had completed the entire course in a matter of weeks. Cumulative records from three students in this group are presented in Figure 22-2. As the figure illustrates, the behavior of these students is very similar to behavior generated by a fixed-ratio schedule. This pattern has been reported by others (Edwards and Powers, 1973; Lloyd and Knutzen, 1969) and is typically associated with a higher probability of obtaining an A in the course.

Group 3: Steady-Rate

The majority of students (n = 36) completed two to three units per week which allowed them to complete the course during the last two weeks of the semester. The only deviation from this pattern for a small number of students was a pause around Spring vacation with the typical pattern consisting of a cessation of activity for a one or two week period either before or after the vaca-

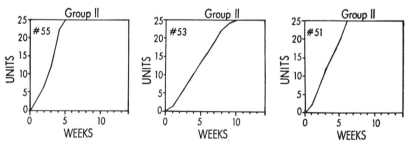

Figure 22-2. Three individual cumulative records of students in Group 2: the high rate group.

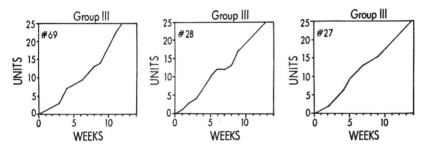

Figure 22-3. Three individual cumulative records of students in Group 3: the steady rate group.

tion period. Cumulative records from three students in this group are presented in Figure 22-3.

Group 4: Inconsistent Moderate Rate

This group (n = 24) behaved very much like students in Group 3, except that there was more frequent pausing, and longer pauses when they were taken. In other words, their behavior was slightly moore inconsistent than Group 3 although, in general, a moderate rate of behavior would be a good overall characterization of their behavior. Cumulative records from three students in this group are presented in Figure 22-4. As the figure illustrates, these three students displayed more pauses and longer pauses than those in Group 3.

Group 5: Miscellaneous

This was a rather small group of students (n = 12) composed of students who: dropped the course, make a C or less, or took an

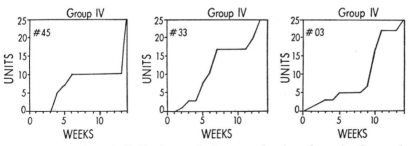

Figure 22-4. Three individual cumulative records of students in Group 4: the inconsistent moderate rate group.

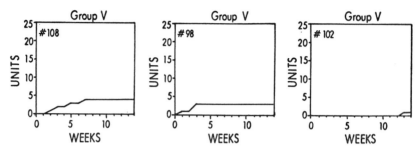

Figure 22-5. Three individual cumulative records of students in Group 5: the miscellaneous group.

incomplete for the semester. The heterogeneity in this group is quite large, but they all have in common the fact that in one way or another they failed to complete the course requirements. The only exception is that several students who took an incomplete for the course subsequently finished the course during the following year. Cumulative records from three students in the group are presented in Figure 22-5. The average performance for all five groups is presented in Figure 22-6. Thus, it would appear that by the method of visually classifying cumulative records that five

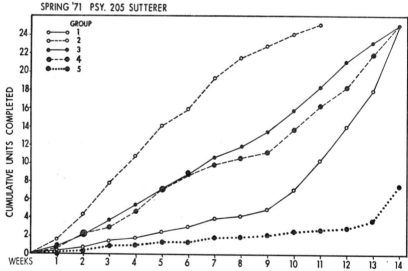

Figure 22-6. The average amount of work done per week for the five groups.

fairly distinct groups have emerged. In terms of their overall average performance only two groups, 3 and 4, did not appear to be substantially different. The common characteristic is that these two groups took tests at a fairly regular pace over the semester with group 4 being only slightly less regular in this regard.

As an independent check on our visual classification system, we compared the groups on a variety of measures calculated from the individual cumulative records which we believed should reflect these differences. Failure to find substantial differences with this type of data would have indicated that the groups were not, in fact, very different. The results are presented in Table 22-I. The data provided from this procedure confirm our visual classification of the cumulative records based on group averages. For example, for Group 2, the high rate group, the longest pause averaged less than one week, while Group 1, the late group, averaged over four weeks. The differences between groups 3 and 4 appear in these data in five measures: amount of work completed by the end of the fourth week, longest ratio (units completed in the same week), longest pause in weeks, total number of weeks during which no work was completed, and the number of pauses. While the average cumulative performance for these two groups did not differ a great deal, qualitative aspects of the individual cumulative records of these five measures confirmed our contention that these students should be considered as two relatively distinct groups.

Another interesting aspect of these data concerns the amount of work completed by the end of the fourth week in the course. At the low end of the scale are the miscellaneous group (average = .91 units completed) and the late group (average = 1.66 units completed). By the end of the fourth week, the high rate group had already completed an average of 10.58 units, 42 percent of the total units required. Between these two extremes were groups 3 and 4 with averages of 5.36 and 4.62 units completed, respectively. These data would suggest that individual differences in behavior appear very early and perhaps continue throughout the course. Inspection of the cumulative records suggested that not only are there distinct behavorial patterns, but that these patterns manifest themselves very early and continue through the course.

TABLE 22-I

Number	Group 1 27	Group 2 12	Group 3 36	Group 4 24	Group 5 12
Amount of work completed by the end of the 4th week	1.66	10.58 units	5.36 units	4.62 units	.91 units
Longest ratio (units completed the same week)	9.74 units	5.0 units	4.52 units	6.33 units	4.41 units
Weeks to complete the course	13.66 weeks	8.92 weeks	13.30 weeks	13.58 weeks	......
Longest pause (weeks)	4.40	.33	1.08	2.95	9.66
Total number of weeks during which no work was completed	6.66	.33	1.69	4.75	11.66
Number of pauses (weeks with no work)	2.59	.33	1.50	2.50	2.08

As an initial attempt to examine this finding, a correlation was calculated between the amount of work which a student completed during the first eleven days of the course with the total number of days which were required to complete the course. This correlation was −.79, indicating that those students who started off the course at a high rate completed the course early. The converse held true for the late group. This would corroborate Edwards & Powers' (1973) report that a significant correlation was found between the day an individual started to work and the day he finished (+.56, p = .01). In only a few of the cumulative records were we able to find a student who had started the course with a high rate, taken a long pause, and then completed the remaining portion of units just prior to the termination of the course.

On the basis of these observations a more complete analysis was undertaken. A regression analysis was calculated in which the actual and cumulative amounts of work completed each week were employed to predict the total number of days to complete the course. The results are presented in Table 22-II and indicate that the performance during the early weeks is a good predictor of when the course will be completed. By the end of the fourth week of the course the correlation between

TABLE 22-II

Week	Mean number of units completed per week (N = 101)	Correlation between work completed each week and total number of days	Multiple correlation	Variance accounted for
1	.65	−.55	.55	30.2%
2	1.24	−.63	.69	48.2%
3	1.52	−.67	.79	62.2%
4	1.45	−.61	.82	66.7%
5	1.90	−.37	.82	67.1%
6	1.44	−.29	.82	68.0%
7	1.59	−.28	.83	69.4%
8	.94	−.27	.84	69.8%
	SB			
9	1.11	−.06	.84	69.8%
10	2.23	+.15	.84	69.9%
11	2.49	+.19	.84	70.6%
12	2.53	+.25	.84	70.9%
13	2.71	+.47	.84	71.1%
14	3.23	+.51	.84	71.4%

the amount of work completion and the total number of days was .82 and accounted for 67 percent of the variance in date of completion of the course. The addition of the subsequent weeks added little to the ability to predict the completion date.

As mentioned previously the spring vacation period which occurred between the eighth and ninth weeks of the course appears to be one stimulus event which initiates a pause in the test-taking behavior of some students. Figure 22-7 presents the individual cumulative records of eight students which are representative of this observation. In all eight cases there appears to be a relationship between the initiation of a pause and the occurrence of spring vacation.

The number beside each cumulative record indicates the group from which the students came. In the top panel are cumulative records from students who took no tests during the two to four week period prior to spring vacation. The two records from Group 4 indicate that students both emitted a fairly high work rate during the first five weeks of the course and had completed approximately 55 percent of the required work at that point. The pause in work-rate was terminated the first or second week following the holiday at which time a high rate was reinstated. For the students from Group 3, who had established a moderate pace, the pause before spring vacation was of shorter duration.

The bottom panel of Figure 22-7 depicts cumulative records from four students who took no tests during the period immediately following the vacation period. In three of the four cases a moderate or high rate of behavior occurred for the first seven weeks of the course, a pause was initiated which was followed by the reinstatement of a high rate during the last three weeks of the course.

METHOD
Fall, 1972

On the basis of our findings during the spring of 1971, we initiated another course with several modifications. Our primary concern focused on devising a strategy to increase the probability that students would initiate work earlier in the semester. This concern can be summarized by the following

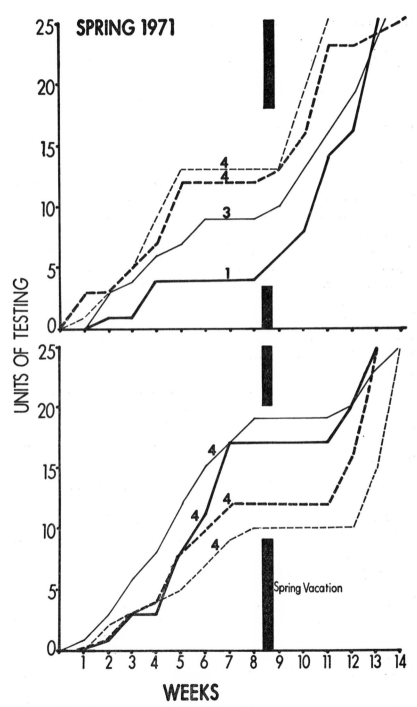

Figure 22-7. The work rate patterns for eight students who paused either before or after spring vacation.

questions: Would the addition of deadlines which required minimum amounts of work by specified intervals in the course produce an early initiation of work? Would the addition of a classroom testing procedure at specified intervals help pace the work-rate early in the semester?

Course Description

The course content of the second offering consisted of a number of items which are commercially available (three modules from *Introduction to general psychology: a self-selection textbook,* 1966, three papers from the General Learning Corp. series in psychology, two chapters from Kendler and Kendler's *Basic Psychology: brief edition,* 1971, and Whaley and Malott's *Elementary Principles of Behavior,* 1971) as well as some material which we had developed through the Center for Instructional Development at Syracuse University (Sutterer, 1972). With the exception of *Elementary Principles of Behavior,* each unit of material was worth twenty points which the student earned upon completion. Seven points of credit was given for each chapter completed in *Elementary Principles of Behavior.* In addition there was a mid-term examination which covered the first five required units of the course worth a maximum of forty points. Thus, the course content consisted of the following point values:

100 points (5 basic required units—20 points each)
 40 points (Mid-term examination)
 80 points (4 optional units—20 points each)
154 points (Elementary Principles of Behavior—7 points per chapter)
374 points Total

Therefore, the course was composed of required units as well as a variety of units from which students could select depending upon interests and curriculum goals. In most cases, the optional material consisted of a branch off of a required unit, so that mastery of a required unit served as a prerequisite for the opportunity to progress into other areas.

Study questions were provided in the Student Manual which provided short answer questions for all units. These directed the student to the more important aspects of the material as well as being a convenient place for taking notes.

Testing and Grading Procedure

A modified version of the Keller system was employed. The initial five units of material were initially tested by the use of forth item multiple choice examinations during a scheduled class period. Each unit was covered in a week to ten days. The date for the class examinations was specified by a calendar in the Student Manual. The criterion on these tests was a score of thirty-two or greater (80%). For students who scored below the criterion score, retesting by proctors was required. The retests usually consisted of three or four short answer questions sampled from the study guide questions and five or six multiple choice questions. Once mastery was demonstrated on these tests the student was given the number of points assigned to that particular unit of material.

The testing of all optional material was done by proctors and consisted of tests similar to the make-up tests for the required units. The following figure illustrates a flow-chart of this type of procedure:

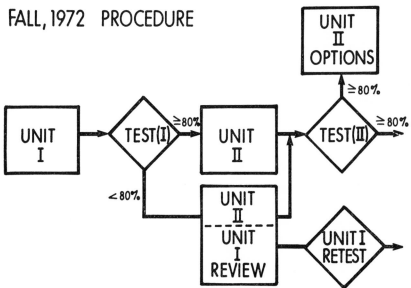

Figure 22-8. A flow chart of the testing procedure employed in the Fall of 1972.

By completing units, a student was able to accumulate points toward a final grade. The introduction of the class testing system was based primarily on three points: First, by using this procedure it helped relieve the proctors of excessively large amounts of evaluation work during the early stages of the course. This had the beneficial advantage of giving the instructor more time to coach the proctors during this time period. Second, by allowing the class to take a test at one particular time it meant that we could concentrate our efforts on a percentage of students who failed to meet the criterion. The students who met the criterion could proceed without additional effort on our part. Third, by establishing set times for examinations during a regularly scheduled class period it was hoped that it would encourage students to initiate work earlier in the semester. In a sense, a student would not have to go "Out-of-his-way" in order to be tested on a unit of material. This last point is based on reports from some students who say that it was difficult to get started because it meant scheduling an examination at some hour other than the class period.

The grading system was:

A = 300 points
B = 250 points
C = 190 points
D = 100 points

Drop = less than 100 points

Deadlines

Two procedures were introduced and fully explained in the Student Manual which were intended to modify the work rate patterns which we had observed earlier. First, with the exception of the chapters in *Elementary Principles of Behavior* (7 points each) a student was advised that he would be unable to take and complete more than one unit per day. This would necessitate that the student plan his schedule for the semester in advance to some degree. Second, and most importantly, four deadline dates were added to the course. The dates and required number as well as the possible number of points are given in Table 22-III.

TABLE 22-III
Deadline Dates and Points Required

Date	Required Points	Possible Points
September 26	20	214
October 17	60	354
October 31	100	374
November 14	140	374

These deadlines represent minimal requirements, and the expectation was that most students would be well ahead of them. The consequence of failing to make these deadlines resulted in an automatic drop from the course. This procedure was, as one might expect, somewhat more than the registrar could comprehend since students typically initiate a drop procedure, not the instructor. This procedure has been modified and presently consists of students being given a failing grade and advised that they drop the course.

Thus, while the earlier data reported had maximal flexibility regarding the limits of work rate in the course, the second offering in the fall of 1972 contained contingencies which were intended to restrict the work-rate within certain boundaries. By not making the tests available for the first five units before a specified date, an upper limit was established. The *deadlines,* on the other hand, established a minimal work-rate for all students. A comparison of the two semesters' explicit contingencies is given in Figure 22-9.

Along with the differences in upper and lower limits of work-rate, the figure also illustrates the fact that the grading scale was different. From the point of view of overall design of the course, the increased grade scale was seen as a desirable change. However, from an experimental point of view, it must be kept in mind that we now have two significant changes between semesters, each of which might possibly contribute to results which we obtained.

RESULTS

The patterns of test taking behavior for individuals who made an A, B, C, D or Drop are presented in Figure 22-10.

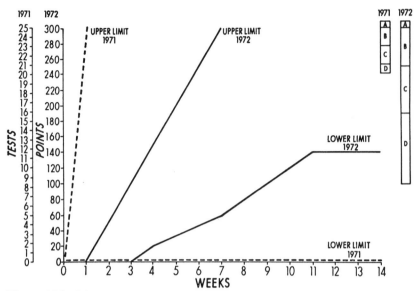

Figure 22-9. The upper and lower limits of work-rate for 1971 and 1972.

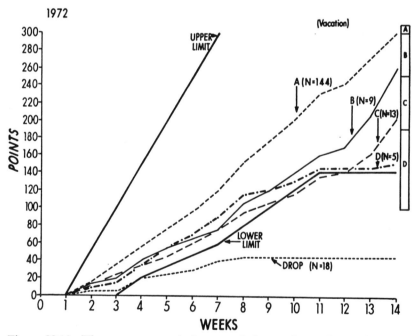

Figure 22-10. The average cumulative records for students who made grades of A, B, C, D, and Drop.

For the 144 students who accumulated three-hundred points in the course, the work rate was fairly steady for the group as a whole, with the only deviation occurring around the Thanksgiving holidays when the rate fell slightly.

For the twenty-seven students who made a B, C, or D in the course, three points are evident: first, the average work rate appears to be consistently just above the number of points required by the four deadline dates. Second, the work rate changes among these three groups only during the last three weeks of the course. The students who ended the course with a grade of D simply stopped working after the last deadline which required 140 points. On the other hand the students who made either B or C in the course continued work during the last three weeks and reached a level just above the minimum number of points required for these grades. Thus, these three groups are practically indistinguishable during the first eleven weeks of the course and only differentiate after the last deadline date. Third, from weeks two through eleven these three groups begin to separate from the group of students who terminated the course with an A. Due to the classroom testing and the deadlines this difference is rather small initially and increases with each successive week. By the eleventh week of the course the average number of points for the B, C, and D groups was 160 or below, while the A group had an average of 230 points.

The students who dropped or were dropped from the course, can be divided into three categories. One group consisted of students for whom we have no record that any work was tried (n = 28). These students probably were never in the course beyond the initial registration period. The second category consisted of students who attempted some work, were unsuccessful, and then dropped (n = 8). The last group (n = 18), which is plotted in Figure 10, on the average completed enough work to make the first deadline (20 points), but then fell below the deadline requirements and was dropped from the course.

In order to examine the relationship between the amount of work completed each week and the number of weeks to complete the entire course a regression analysis was calculated. As with the analysis of the 1971 data, the regression was calculated for only those students who finished the course with an A. The results for both 1971 and 1972 are presented in Table 22-IV. In the 1971 data there were relatively large correlations between the amount of work completed during the early weeks and the time required to complete the course. In the 1972 data the most striking difference from the 1971 sample is the low correlations for the early weeks. This, of course, yielded rather small multiple correlations until week four where the multiple correlation was .51. Thus, the multiple correlations for 1972 did not reach a level comparable to the first week of 1971 until four weeks of the course had passed.

DISCUSSION

As mentioned in the introduction, one of the most unusual dimensions of our 1971 course was the lace of deadlines within the semester. Each student was free to work at his own rate during the semester. The only explicit contingent relationship was between the number of units completed and the final grade. This general procedure is similar to that used by Keller (1968) and McMichael and Corey (1969). Since this was

TABLE 22-IV

Work Rate Versus Time of Course Completion:
A Comparison of 1971 and 1972

Week	Simple correlation		Multiple correlation		Variance accounted for	
	1971	1972	1971	1972	1971	1972
1	—.55	00	.55	00	30	00
2	—.63	—.16	.69	.16	48	2
3	—.67	—.16	.79	.24	62	6
4	—.61	—.44	.82	.51	67	26
5	—.37	—.52	.82	.63	67	39
6	—.29	—.32	.83	.66	68	43
7	—.28	—.48	.84	.71	69	51
8	—.28	—.06	.84	.74	70	55
9	—.06	—.39	.84	.80	70	64
10	.15	.00	.84	.81	70	66
11	.18	.19	.84	.81	71	66
12	.25	.16	.84	.82	71	66
13	.46	.51	.84	.82	71	67
14	.51	.55	.84	.82	71	67

the first time this instructional design had been used, it was considered desirable to collect "baseline" data on how students would perform under these conditions. The results would indicate those behaviors which should be modified or encouraged by additional contingencies. While this design is not unique (Keller, 1968; Lloyd, 1971; Edwards and Powers, 1973) it has not been examined under controlled conditions frequently enough to eliminate the need for replication.

The grouping of the 1971 subjects into five general classifications has given a clear illustration of differences among students. Although the specifics vary, our results are generally similar to those of Edwards and Powers (1973) about which they say:

"Given the diversity of modes of responding under the completely self-paced system used, it would seem premature to characterize student work habits as resembling either a fixed ratio performance (Lloyd and Knutzen, 1969) or a fixed interval performance (Ferster, 1968). Although the contingencies of 30 oral and 10 written exams were specified by the instructor, the time contingencies were not. Under these conditions it would seem reasonable to assume that the self-pacing contingency permits the conditioning history of the student to determine work pace. Since most students in high school and college have been trained in a system in which high sustained rates of working are not reinforced, it is not surprising that this mode of responding does not occur frequently (only 19% of all students displayed a high sustained rate) (Edwards and Powers, 1973, pages 7-8).

We would strongly agree with these conclusions. We did not always observe a fixed ratio pattern of behavior as did Lloyd and Knutzen (1969) whose cumulative records indicate that students worked at the same rate although they started at different times during the semester. In addition, they reported that once work was begun, the students did not stop until they completed all of the work which they could by the semester's end. Cumulative records from both our 1971 and 1972 samples failed to confirm either of these observations. For example, individuals in Group 1, the late group, did not wait until later in the semester to initiate their work, but once work was begun it did not immediately occur at a high rate. For some students there was a gradual increase in the rate over the semester. There are many other instances of variation in the work rate of the students in our samples. In addition, in the 1972 sample, where the work rate was partially limited by our testing procedure and the deadlines, there was still variation in the work rates among students. While there were students who started at a high rate and finished early, there were those who worked only a minimum amount and increased during the last half of the course.

One possible factor which may have been crucial in the production of a high rate in Lloyd and Knutzen's (1969) data was the requirement of an early finish (twelfth week) for those students who wished to complete the necessary activities for an A in the course. Except for the lower limit contingency on work rate in our 1972 study, our courses did not contain explicit contingencies involving payoffs for specified work rates. The differential reinforcement of a high rate could be one important factor in the generation of a high sustained work rate for a number of Lloyd and Knutzen's students.

We also failed to confirm Lloyd and Knutzen's (1969) observation of a high degree of stability of the work rate. For instance, in the 1971 sample, our records indicated that regardless of the rate at which students were working, spring vacation very frequently initiated a pause in behavior which lasted for several weeks either before or after the vacation period. In 1972, the Thanksgiving holidays which occurred even later in the semester had a slight effect on the overall rate for the whole group. Thus, some events can disturb the behavior of students even though they may be working at a fairly steady rate.

The results of a number of studies have found correlations between final grade and the time during the semester at which work was initiated (Lloyd, 1971; Lloyd and Knutzen, 1969). This was not the case for either class in this study. For the 1971 group, ninety-eight of the students earned an A, one a B, four a C, and five an F. There were nine incompletes and twenty-one withdrawals. In the 1972 sample, there were 144 students who earned an A, nine a B, thirteen a C, five a D, and twenty-six were dropped. The group averages indicate that a large number of students must have worked at approximately the same rate during the early weeks of the course, yet they later fell into different grade categories. This would apply especially to the B, C, and D groups which were almost identical during the first eleven weeks of the course, and separated into different grade categories during the last three weeks.

Our data would appear to provide some empirical support for the statement by Wilson and Tosti (1972) when they say,

> . . . The most critical period of the term for the student is the first two weeks. In fact, proctors are often advised that one of their most important responsibilities will be to make sure each student experiences a sense of achievement during that first two week period. The attitude toward the course and the study habits developed during this period are extremely difficult to change later on, and a student's overall achievement in the course depends, perhaps more than anything else, on the way his instruction is managed at the very beginning (page 64).

From our observation of the 1971 sample that performance during the initial stages of the course were related to the time of completion we would make the following two points:

First, the initial four weeks of the course appear to be the most important and should represent the optimal time to introduce contingencies requiring students to initiate their work in the course. In 1972 two procedures were initiated during this time period which were intended to examine this recommendation more fully. The classroom testing procedure seems to be effective for at least getting students to attempt some of the work. Even for students who eventually dropped the course, some degree of effort was evident during the early stages of the course. The establishment of a minimum rate of point accumulation also appears to be partially effective in that these limits specified a work rate for some students. For example, the B, C, and D students worked just above these minimal limits. Without these limits, it is suspected that they would have worked at an even lower rate.

In 1971 the amount of work completed during the first

few weeks of the course was related to the time of completion of the course. The low correlations found for the same variables during the first four to five weeks in 1972 indicates that the initial variability of work rate was considerably reduced. No longer did the initial work rate reflect when a student finished the course. Another observation supportive of this argument was our inability to visually sort the cumulative records into distinct groups as we had for the 1971 sample. Although high rate and "fixed-interval-like" behavioral patterns could be identified, the majority of students fell within these extremes in a variety of patterns.

One could argue, however, that the deadline procedure was not completely successful in that we still had a rather large number of students who attempted some work (n = 26) and later dropped the course. Establishing an initial effort through contingency management, therefore, is not always followed by continued work in the course. Like Edwards and Powers (1973) we were not able to discern any systematic pattern among the students who dropped. In fact, eighteen of the twenty-six had successfully completed some work, yet dropped. If a "success experience" in the initial part of the course is a necessary ingredient, it is not evident in these data. A common assumption concerning this method of instruction is that given an ideal environment consisting of unlimited proctoring hours, individualized instruction, etc. that practically all students would terminate the course with an A. On the basis of our data we would conclude that such an assumption is unwarranted. There appear to be unidentified completing contingencies outside the domain of any specific course which have some control over the outcome.

The second point is that the individual differencs among students are evident during the early stages of the course, continue throughout the course, and probably represent characteristics of their behavior which have resulted in reinforcement in the past. This suggestion has also been made by Edwards and Powers (1973). Thus, the different patterns of behavior which we found in 1971 had little to do with the set of course contingencies, but merely provided a baseline upon which past histories were displayed. The 1971 course represented a unique opportunity to see these individual differences since there was only one explicit contingency in the course: to complete twenty-five units of material by the end of the semester.

A complementary line of inquiry would be an effort to determine what factors lumped under "past history" account for such a diversity of behavior. If it were possible to characterize students who might fall into our late groups, it would then be possible to give special attention to their problems and get their test-taking behavior started early as well as maintaining it throughout the semester. At this point, it has been possible to identify only two significant variables which give some degree of predictive ability. First, spring vacation, or perhaps any vacation period, appears to decrease the output of some students for a period before or after the holiday. It is an unresolved empirical question regarding the temporal location of a holiday period in a course and the behavioral effects which might result. Second, in a course with minimal constraints on work rate, the amount of work completed during the first four weeks gives some indication of how the student will behave during the latter stages of the semester. We are currently searching various sources of information, such as standardized tests, academic performance, personality data, and so on, but have met with little success in determining if and how these students differ along these other dimensions.

That some students have difficulty in pacing themselves is a common finding (Gropper and Kess, 1964; Powers and Edwards, 1971) as is their expressed desire for some external control over their pacing (Lloyd and Knutzen, 1969). The pacing problem frequently creates an unfavorable environment for proctoring toward the end of the semester. In addition, Edwards and Powers (1973) have examined the results of other dependent variables such as attitude toward the course, and the shift toward and away from a major in psychology, and found that students who finish early in the course have a much more positive attitude about the course and more frequently shift to a psychology major. These results would indicate that contingencies which are introduced to maintain a high rate may be an important determinant of the affective experiences of the students as well as a logistical advantage. The simple logistics of making materials available to a large number of rushed students and the multiple test taking and grading within a short period of time make a strong case for contingencies on work-rate aside from any educational considerations. The problem is frequent (Sides and Edwards, 1972) and must be expected if there are no deadlines within the semester to pace student work-rate.

The fact that these problems exist supports arguments for the power of the final grade as a potent stimulus. The use of other rewards is a viable argument as well but first the existing system must be explored to be able to clearly evaluate modification. If only the final grade is examined as it represents mastery of test items, the power of the system is evident. How it may best be used is approached by several studies, most notably that of Malott and Svinicki (1969). The categorization of students into groups by test-taking behavior indicates that we are not dealing with the majority of the student population in this problem.

That the fixed-interval like behavior is predictable as early as the fourth week in the semester and that the potency of the grade is evident gives support to a design in which the grade has some sort of contingent relationship to the work rate as represented by test taking. This, in itself, does not refer to the long-term recall problem though it does make the problem more approachable.

The use of review tests where pacing is regulated is an effort to encourage long-term recall. These modifications may not appear to be directly in line with the original intent of PSI as set forth by Keller (1968). Here the teacher is himself in the position of dictating rates for a minority of the students on the bases of logistics and long-term recall. The logistical problem can conceivably be overcome in other ways such as increasing proctoring hours and the quantity of materials available. The argument for manipulation, such as set forth by Lloyd (1971) must be grounded in the imperatives of maximal learning. This in turn must be defined in this context as both mastery and recall whether one is using cognitive measures or synthesis and application. The use of contingency management simply to smooth out logistical problems is as indefinable as the use of large-group lectures to solve the economics of student-faculty ratios.

The teacher has control of the reward structure and its power can clearly be demonstrated. Futhermore he can, to a considerable degree, define that segment of the population with whom he is dealing when his concern is work-rate. The wide spread concern over establishing an initial high work rate refers directly to, and only to, this group. The burden of proof would appear to be on the teacher and the proof, it would appear, must be set forth in the context of the efficacy of learning.

STUDY AND TEST PERFORMANCE OF COLLEGE STUDENTS ON CONCURRENT ASSIGNMENT SCHEDULES

DANIEL WILLIAM BURT

THE PHENOMENON OF "CRAMMING," or putting off studying until the last few days before a test or deadline, is familiar to every university instructor. Lloyd and Knutzen (1969) reported that even in a contingency management system where the course is broken up into small units, if students are allowed to pace their own studying, many students waited until nearly the end of the term and had only time to complete enough units for a C or B grade. There have been several attempts to overcome low rates of studying early in the term.

Mawhinney, Azaroff, Bostow, and Blumefield (1973) attempted to increase study behavior during the early part of a three-week period by giving academic points contingent upon sixty minutes of early study behavior but found this technique not as effective as daily testing. Lloyd (1971) reviewed three methods utilized to overcome pausing: 1) giving bonus points for work

This investigation is part of a dissertation submitted by the author to Washington State University in partial fulfillment of the requirements for the Ph.D. degree. The author wishes to thank the members of his committee, Tom Brigham, Richard Reinking, James Whipple, Dudley Klopfer and especially his chairman, Kenneth Lloyd for their suggestions and support.

completed early in the term, (2) making the requirements for a D high with less difference between the requirements for a D and an A, and (3) requiring a minimum amount of work to be completed by the end of every two-week period. Only the last of these three procedures was notably effective in reducing early pausing.

Mawhinney, Bostow, Laws, Blumefield, and Hopkins (1971) observed low rates of study behavior in the early period of a three-week interval if students were tested once at the end of three weeks. When tested daily, studying was distributed more evenly over a three-week period. Total study time, however, was greater when students were tested only once every three weeks. The authors did not control for differences in the difficulty of study materials; therefore we do not know whether more difficult study materials resulted in the greater amount of time on the three-week schedule. Neither do we know which testing schedule and subsequent study pattern would produce the best performance on a final examination. Born, Davis, Whelan, and Jackson (1972) reported more total study time for students and higher scores on final examinations when the course was broken into small units with frequent quizzes. However, since Born, *et al.* (1972) compare performance of two different groups of students taught by two sharply contrasting methods of instruction, any number of factors could account for the increased study time and improved test performance.

One method of inducing studying early in a term would be to differentially reinforce high rates of responding. In this differential reinforcement of high rates (DRH) schedule subjects would be reinforced only if their inter-response time (IRT) was shorter than some predetermined interval. Lovitt and Esveldt (1970) stated that they decided not to use a DRH schedule since Ferster and Skinner (1957) had reported difficulties with DHR schedules. Ferster and Skinner (1957), however, attributed most of their difficulty with DRH schedules to apparatus problems. The present study compared the effects of a DRH schedule of reinforcement for study behavior with schedules similar to those traditionally used in undergraduate courses. The dependent variables were the amount and distribution of study behavior and performance on quarterly and final examinations.

METHOD
Subjects

Students in an introductory psychology class were asked to volunteer for an experimental section which would require them to do all of their studying in a study hall. Forty-five students volunteered and twenty-four were selected for the experiment. An equal number of students (eight) with high (3.0 and above on a 0-4.0 scale), medium (2.40-2.99), and low (below 2.40) cumulative grade point averages were chosen for the experiment so that it would be possible to observe how students with different academic histories responded to various assignment schedules.

Materials

Reading material for the course was taken from *Psychology and Life* (eighth edition) by Ruch and Zimardo (1971). Study guides were taken from the *Psychology and Life Unit Mastery System,* a workbook by Minke and Carlson (1972), designed to accompany the *Psychology and Life* text. All questions on four mid-semester examinations and a final examination were taken from the unit quizzes in the *Instructor's Guide* for the *Unit Mastery System* workbook by Minke and Carlson (1972).

None of the students nor any of the undergraduate proctors were told which text or workbook was being used as a source for study materials. Pages of the study materials were cut from the workbook and text, and there were no identifying titles or names on the pages that were used. The text was not being used by any other course during either the semester in which the study was carried out nor in the preceding semester. None of the materials were available for purchase at student book stores.

The fifteen-week semester was divided into one orientation week, four three-week study sessions, and a two-week review session. Study materials were divided into two sets of five units for each three-week session of the semester for a total of forty units. The two sets of materials used concurrently in each session were equated for difficulty as much as possible on three criteria: (1) the length or total number of pages of reading materials, (2) the total number of questions in the workbook section covering the corresponding reading materials, and (3) the total number of terms listed in the workbook section covering the corresponding reading materials. Not all of the terms and questions covering each section were used on the study guides but the total number of questions and terms used for each set of five units within any three-week session was roughly equal. Concurrently used units were always taken from the same chapters or subject matter.

As a further control to separate the differences attributable to the difficulty of study materials from differences associated with assignment schedules, students were divided into two groups and each group had the opposite set of materials assigned to each schedule. The groups were matched for cumulative GPAs; however, due to withdrawals the groups had to be rearranged at the beginning of the second and third sessions.

Setting

The study area was equipped with tables, desks, and chairs to accommodate fifteen students. Adjacent to the study area was a small proctor room with a large window through which proctors could observe all students in the study hall. In the proctor room was a file cabinet with a file for each student. Each student's file consisted of his study materials, notes, and a data sheet. The proctor room, and study hall were locked when not in use and only one graduate student proctor had the keys to these locks. The study hall was open seven days a week for a total of thirty-three hours. One graduate student and eight undergraduates recorded data and served as study hall monitors.

Procedure

During the first week of the semester the twenty-four volunteers met as a group in the study hall. All subjects received a course outline which informed subjects that all of their studying for the course was to be done in the study hall, that they could not remove their study materials from the study hall, and that they must check out their materials from a proctor and return them when finished. Grades for the course were based entirely on total points obtained for answering workbook questions and examinations covering reading materials. Subjects were allowed to attend lectures for the regular section of the course but there were no lectures scheduled for this experimental section. There were no questions from lectures on examinations or points given for attending lectures. No subject ever reported attending a lecture for introductory psychology during the semester. Discussion groups and other optional activities were scheduled if students were interested, but they were not tested over these or given point for attending optional activities. Since the number and weight of examinations and quizzes could change over the semester, the total possible points could (and did) also change. Subjects were told that grades would be determined proportionately, that is, 8/9 of the total points for an A 7/9 for a B, and so forth. Subjects were informed that there would be four one-hour examinations, one every three weeks, and a final examination.

Also on the course outline were initial instructions for the assignment schedules. Subject were told that reading assignments would be scheduled in two ways. Half of the materials (non-paced units) could be studied at the student's own natural pace and could be completed for full credit at any time up to two days prior to a test. For the remaining half of the materials (pace units) credit would be given for any unit if less than four days had elapsed in a given session when no previous pace unit had been completed. Paced units completed after more than four days had elapsed did not earn points. The assignment schedule for the paced units corresponds to a DRH (differential reinforcement of high rates of responding) schedule (Ferster and Skinner, 1957). Dates of completion for both paced and non-paced units were recorded by study hall monitors. The IRT (inter-response time) for the first paced unit was measured from the first day in a session that the study area was open.

During the first session, no points were given for either paced or nonpaced units unless they were completed two days prior to the first examination. The deadline was shortened to one day before the examination for the second session, and for the last two sessions the deadline was the day of the examination. The length of reading assignments varied from four to ten pages, and students were asked to answer about one question from the workbook per page of reading material and received two points per correct answer if the schedule criteria had been met. If a student completed a nonpaced unit after a deadline or waited longer than four days to complete a paced unit, that student received no points for his answers whether correct or not and thus lost, on the average, ten points. Students were required to complete units in succession. Thus, the first paced unit must have been completed before a student was allowed to check out the second paced unit, the first nonpaced unit must have been completed before the second nonpaced unit, and so forth. Completing units included answering questions from the workbooks. On the course outline students were informed that all units must be completed in order to take an examination, however, it appeared that this contingency was too severe and it was dropped. Reasonable excuses, such as illness, were accepted and points were given under extenuating circumstances whereby a student was unable to meet temporal criteria on either the paced or non-paced schedules.

Students were required to study independently but were allowed to smoke and drink coffee or tea. No talking was allowed in the study area except in the proctor room. When a student had finished reading his materials and/or answering his workbook questions he returned his material to the proctor. The proctor would then record the time. Thus, studying behavior in the present experiment was defined as in Mawhinney, *et al.* (1971) and included such things as lighting a cigarette, glancing about the room, and counting pages. If there were workbook questions the proctor would score these by comparing the answers to a key and record the score on the student's data sheet. Generally two points were given for each correct answer to workbook questions. However, when the temporal criterion for the paced and nonpaced schedule mentioned above had not been met, students were told that they were late, and no points were given.

There were procedural changes with each session involving the number and weight of questions on examinations and the assignment of points for answers to questions for the workbooks. Contingencies specific to each session are described below. Each new set of contingencies, including the date of the next examination, were posted on the window of the proctor room and proctors were instructed to request students to review these contingencies prior to checking out their first materials for a given session.

Session 1

During Session 1 students were first given their reading materials. When they had finished reading they checked in their reading materials and checked out the corresponding set of questions from the workbooks to be answered without the aid of the test. Two points were given for each correct answer without the aid of the test. Students were then given an opportunity to correct their answers with the aid of the text. Proctors gave one point for each answer corrected with the aid of the test. Check out and check in times and dates were recorded for the reading materials and workbook questions. Students were allowed only one opportunity to correct their answers with the aid of the text. This system of giving points for answers to workbook questions applied to both paced and non-paced units. During Session 1 the only difference between the paced and non-paced assignment schedules were the temporal contingencies mentioned above.

There were thirty-eight questions on the first one-hour examination which covered materials of Session 1. Nineteen questions were from the paced set of materials and nineteen were from the non-paced. Each question on the one-hour examination was worth two points for a total of seventy-six points.

Session 2

It was felt that procedures for the concurrent assignment schedules were sufficiently complex that some students would need more time to adjust to them. Also during Session 1 it became apparent that students were spending excessive amounts of time on each unit. Therefore, Session 2 was a replication of Session 1 except that the total number of pages of reading was less, and units were of more uniform length.

Session 3

Contingencies in traditional college courses resemble fixed interval (FI) schedules in as much as the reinforcement in terms of a test grade comes at the end of a predetermined interval. Mawhinney, *et al.* (1971) report a scalloped pattern in several individual's study performances similar to the scalloping effect observed on FI schedules. Contingencies for the nonpaced materials used in Sessions 1 and 2 were also similar to those of FI schedules except that students were reinforced not only with test points at the end of a fixed interval (three weeks) but also were reinforced for studying on a continuous schedule with points given for correct answers to workbook questions accompanying each nonpaced unit. In Session 3 the contingencies for the non-paced unit were made more similar to an FI schedule by not giving any points for correct answers to workbook questions. To equalize the total amount of points (reinforcement) that could be obtained on the paced and nonpaced units, the same number of questions (twenty-five) were given on the one-hour examina-tion as were used from the workbooks accompanying the study units. For the paced units in Session 3 both workbook questions and examination questions were worth two points each. For nonpaced units workbook questions were not graded but examina-tion questions were worth four points each. Thus, the total possible points for both paced and nonpaced materials in Session 3 was one-hundred. Since the nonpaced units were not graded and students would not have a chance to review their errors, it was decided that workbook questions accompanying both paced and nonpaced materials would be handed out with the readings to be answered open-book during Session 3. A set of new in-structions including the date and weighting of questions for the next one-hour examination were posted on the window of the proctor room at the beginning of Session 3.

Session 4

During Session 3 many students did not answer workbook questions for their nonpaced materials since these were not graded. In Session 4, students were not given workbook questions over nonpaced materials. Further, in Session 4 a different method was used to equate the total possible points. There were twenty-five questions each on the one-hour examination for paced and nonpaced materials, for a total of fifty questions as in Session 3. However, in Session 4 each question on the examination was worth two points whether covering paced or nonpaced materials. There were also twenty-five workbook questions worth two points apiece for the paced materials for a total of fifty points as in Session 3, but the fifty points that normally could be earned on workbook questions over nonpaced materials were given noncontingently during Session 4. Students were told that this fifty points would simply be added to their total. Instructions for Session 4 were posted with the next test date as before.

In the first three sessions students were allowed to review all of their materials, both paced and nonpaced, before the hour examination if they had completed all of their unit assignments. It seemed possible that this reviewing might reduce differences in test performance resulting from the two concurrent assignment schedules. To maximize any possible differences in test performance students were not allowed to review either paced or nonpaced materials in Session 4.

FINAL EXAMINATION. During the last eight days of the semester following the fourth one-hour examination, subjects were allowed to review both paced and nonpaced materials together in preparation for a final examination. To evaluate the effectiveness of this reviewing, subjects were only given access to half of the reading material that would be covered on the final examination. There were ninety-six questions worth two points each on the final. Twenty-four questions for each session were subdivided in the following manner: six questions covered paced materials which were reviewed and six question covered paced materials which were not reviewed; similarly, six questions covered nonpaced materials which were reviewed and six covered nonpaced materials which were not reviewed.

RESULTS

Four of the original twenty-four students withdrew from the course prior to completing the first session. Eighteen subjects took all examinations and completed a majority of the assignments. One of the students did not withdraw but completed only two of the unit assignments and did not take any of the examinations. Another subject did not withdraw but took only one of the examinations and completed only seventeen of forty assignments.

There was a clear difference in the type of assignments which were not completed. Over the entire course for all subjects, twenty-eight of the paced units were not completed and fifty-three of the nonpaced units were not completed. For the eighteen students who took all the examinations, two paced units were not completed and eighteen nonpaced units were not completed. The last unit completed was always a nonpaced unit, thus students always finished their paced units before their nonpaced units. In only three of seventy-two possible occasions did a student check out a nonpaced unit before he had checked out a paced unit for the same session. Thus it appears that the DRH contingencies associated with the paced assignment schedule were effective in inducing earlier starting and completing of assignments.

The eighteen students who took all of the examinations responded very well to the DRH contingency. Six of these eighteen subjects did not have an IRT longer than four days, and they therefore did not lose any points for correct answers to workbook questions over paced materials. The average number of IRTs for paced units that were longer than four days was 1.6 for the eighteen students who took all of the examinations. Only five exceptions had to be made for students who, due to extenuating circumstances such as illness, had more than a four-day IRT on a paced assignment. Since the two subjects who did not take all of the examinations completed few of either, their paced or nonpaced assignments, it is difficult to say how they would have adjusted to the DRH contingency. Of the eighteen units that these two students did complete, however, fourteen were paced units.

Figure 23-1 shows cumulative records of study times for five typical subjects over the course of the semester.

Every subject in Figure 23-1 except Subject 4 shows at least one incidence of an IRT longer than four days on a paced unit as evidenced by the absence of an event mark on the paced curve. Five even marks on the paced curve indicate the student met criteria on all units for that session. Inter-response times for the first paced unit in Session 2 for Subject 1 and the fourth paced unit in Session 4 for Subject 5 were longer than four days but were excused due to extenuating circumstances. As a group eighteen subjects who took all of the examinations were able to meet criterion on the DRH (paced) schedule for 92 percent of their paced units. It is apparent from Figure 23-1 that for the

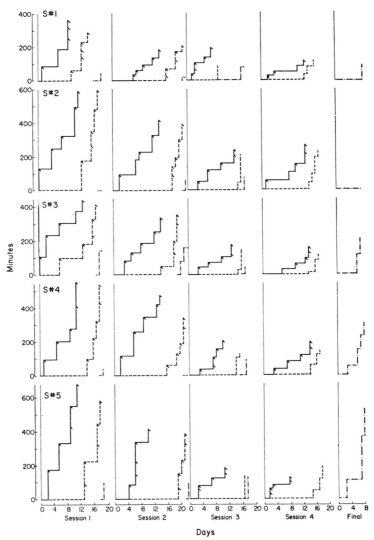

Figure 23-1. Cumulative study time of five typical students on paced assignments (solid lines), nonpaced assignments (dashed lines), and for reviewing of both paced and nonpaced assignments together (dotted-dashed lines) over four approximately three-week sessions and an eight-day period during which students reviewed for a final examination. Event marks on the curves indicate occasions when students received points for answers to workbook questions.

typical subject study behavior under the DRH contingency was distinctly different from study behavior under the contingencies for the nonpaced units across all sessions. For all of the students in Figure 23-1 studying for paced units began earlier and was spread more evenly over the sessions than was studying for nonpaced units.

Of course not all students interacted with the two concurrent schedules in the same way that subjects in Figure 23-1 did. Figure 23-2 shows the somewhat atypical performance of four subjects over the course of the semester.

Data for three subjects with high GPAs, three with medium GPAs, and three with low GPAs were selected for representation in Figures 23-1 and 23-2. Subjects 6 and 7 in Figure 23-2 had low GPAs (1.25 and 1.71, respectively). Subject 6 was one of the two students who did not take all of the examinations. Subject 6 reported he was sick for most of Session 1, but he offered no proof of his illness and did not respond to an offer to make up the work he had missed. Subject 6 did not complete all of the units for any session. Subject 7 did complete all of her paced units for every session, but she did not complete two of her nonpaced units in Session 1 and did not complete a single nonpaced unit in Session 4. It appears that although the study habits which Subject 7 brought to the experiment were poor, the frequency of her study behavior was high enough to be maintained and perhaps strengthened by the DRH contingency of the paced assignments. The study habits which Subject 6 brought to the experiment were so poor that study behavior was not maintained by even the DRH contingency of the paced materials.

Subjects 8 and 9 in Figure 23-2 had high GPAs (3.8 and 4.0, respectively). The study performance for nonpaced assignments for the first two sessions was not much different than performance on the paced assignments for these two subjects. Possibly, these students came to the experiment with what could be considered good study habits. Study behavior under the nonpaced schedule for these two high GPA students changed over the semester and gradually became similar to the nonpaced study behavior of the more typical students shown in Figure 23-1. Study behavior under the DRH contingencies of the paced schedule did not deteriorate.

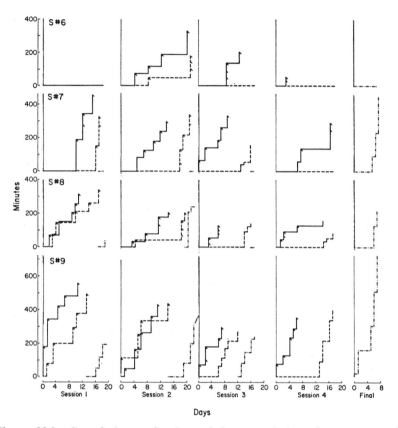

Figure 23-2. Cumulative study time of four atypical students on paced assignments (solid lines), nonpaced assignments (dashed lines), and for reviewing of both paced and nonpaced assignments together (dotted-dashed lines) over four approximately three-week sessions and an eight-day period during which students reviewed for a final examination. Event marks on the curves indicated occasions when students received points for answers to workbook questions.

It appears as if there was more study behavior early in the three-week period of Mawhinney, *et al.* (1971) than occurred early in the three-week session of the present investigation. Mawhinney, *et al.* compared study performance on their three-week testing schedule to performance of animals on fixed interval (FI) schedules of reinforcement. If the nonpaced schedules used in the present study do in fact have an FI component, then perhaps the low rate of responding early in the three-week session is attributable to a local interaction effect resulting form the concurrent design of the present investigation. Catania (1966) describes similar phenomena when FI schedules are programmed concurrently with ratio schedules. Such a local interaction could also account for the change in nonpaced performance for Subjects 8 and 9 in the last two sessions of the experiment.

Figures 23-1 and 23-2 show students did not accumulate equal amounts of study time for all sessions and possibly not equal amounts of time for both schedules over all sessions. To determine whether these apparent differences were in fact significant, an analysis of variance of the total study time for eighteen subjects across all four sessions was carried out. Differences in total study time between sessions ($p = 0.01$) were more significant than differences between schedules ($p = 0.05$). This is probably due to the fact that workbook questions for Sessions 1 and 2 were answered without the aid of the text. Mean study time was greater for the paced scredule in all sessions. A Newman-Keuls comparison of schedule means showed that only the difference between the total time for paced and nonpaced assignments in Session 4 was significant ($P = 0.01$). Thus although students spent slightly more time studying on the paced schedule, especially in Session 4, the greatest difference in study time can be attributed to the differences between procedures for the first two sessions and the last two sessions. Naturally, it would be of interest to know whether the differences reflected in mean total study time are also reflected in scores on the one-hour examinations and the final examination.

The analysis of variance of percentage of errors on the one-hour examinations revealed a significant sessions effect, a nonsignificant schedules effect, and a nonsignificant schedules by sessions interaction. Mean number of errors on the one-hour examinations was greater for the last two sessions than for the first two sessions, and Newman-Keuls comparisons of the difference between the mean number of errors for Sessions 3 and 2, 3 and 1, and 4 and 2 were significant ($p = 0.01$). Thus, subjects not only spent less total time studying during the last two sessions, but they made a significantly greater percentage of errors on the one-hour examinations for those sessions as well.

It does not appear that the reviewing done by students prior to the one-hour examinations obscured possible differences in test scores over paced and nonpaced assignments. Students were not allowed to review for the examination in Session 4. The difference between mean errors over paced and nonpaced materials covered by the examination in Session 4 was not significant as determined by a Newman-Keuls comparison. Thus, reviewing for the one-hour examinations did not differentially affect paced and nonpaced assignments.

An analysis of variance was also done for errors on the final examination. A highly significant reviewing effect but nonsignificant schedules effect and schedules by reviewing interaction is consistent with the performance on one-hour examinations. Since the reviewing by schedule interaction was not significant, reviewing dose not appear to have reduced any differences between errors on the final examination covering paced or nonpaced assignments. It does not appear, therefore, that study behavior which occurred under the paced contingencies resulted in better examination performance than study behavior under the nonpaced contingencies.

Interestingly enough, although the mean number of errors was always less for assignments for which subjects were allowed to review, a Newman-Keuls comparison between the mean number of errors for reviewed and not reviewed assignments yielded a significant difference only for Session 1 assignments ($p = 0.01$). It appears that reviewing for the final was primarily beneficial only for assignments studied during the earliest three-week period of the course. The mean number of errors was generally larger for earlier sessions except for reviewed units from Session 1. Since scores on the one-hour examinations for the first two sessions were higher than for the last two sessions, it appears that the probability of a correct answer decreases with time and also that students may have overcompensated for this in reviewing the units for Session 1.

DISCUSSION

Although the majority of the students did in fact adjust to the DRH schedule, 20 percent (four students) of those who volunteered for the experiment did in fact withdraw from the course. Born (1971) reports from 14 to 25 percent withdrawals from similarly structured courses. At the same university the percentage of withdrawals from three traditional lecture courses ranged from 4.9 to 5.8 percent. The purpose of the present experiment was not to demonstrate an ideal instruction program but to observe the effects of DRH contingencies on study behavior and examination performance. Restrictions imposed upon subjects due to the necessary experimental controls could understandably lead to a large number of withdrawals. Student withdrawals from the course described in this present investigation, while high, did not appear to be exceptional for similarly programmed courses which did not use a DRH schedule.

Study performance on the nonpaced schedule used in the present study appears to be representative of "cramming." Traditionally cramming is considered to be less desirable than the early and more regular study performance that occurred on the paced assignment schedule. Results form the present investigation give only modest support to this traditional viewpoint. Cramming in the present study resulted in slightly less total study time and did not result in significantly poorer scores on either the one-hour or final examinations. The primary disadvantage of cramming appeared to be that some students ran out of time and did not complete all of their unit assignments. This agrees with the findings of Lloyd and Knutzen (1969) with student-paced assignments. In the present study, however, only a few of the subjects failed to complete many of their unit assignments. Further, these subjects generally had low cumulative GPAs and presumably poor study skills. The performance of these subjects on questions from the examinations over units which they had completed may not have been significantly better than performance on questions over units which they had not completed. Perhaps if the number of unit assignments was increased, a greater difference between examination performance on paced and nonpaced assignments would be observed.

The most significant difference in terms of examination performances observed in the present investigation was between the first two sessions and the last two sessions on the one-hour examinations. The major procedural difference between the first and last two sessions was the way the workbook questions were used. That is, workbook questions served as quiz questions for Sessions 1 and 2. In Sessions 3 and 4 the workbook questions could be considered study guides.

The difference between the first and last two sessions on the one-hour examinations is consistent with the findings of Born *et al.* (1972), McMichael and Corey (1969), and Sheppard and MacDermot (1970) who all found examination performance by students in programmed courses who were frequently quizzed superior to the examination performance of students in courses where no quizzes were given over reading assignments. Performance across sessions on the final examination is inconsistent with the findings of the above authors. However, it appears as if a possible recency effect may have been the predominant influence on final examination scores, since overall scores were higher for more recently studied material.

Possibly the most important result of the present study was that ninety percent of the subjects adjusted readily to the DRH contigencies of the paced assignment schedule. In terms of producing earlier starting and spreading study behavior more evenly over the three-week session, the DRH contingencies were clearly more effective than the more traditional contingencies associated with the nonpaced schedule. It is also likely that the DRH contingency would be more effective than giving bonus points for early studying, since Lloyd (1971) and Mawhinney, *et al.* (1973) reported little success with that method of reinforcing early study behavior. The multiple-ratio schedule of Lovitt and Esveldt (1970) was effective in increasing rates of responding, but it was used in the context of a daily assignment schedule. Therefore, we do not know if the multiple-ratio schedule would reduce delays early in a session. The most successful method for reducing delays and maintaining high rates of academic behavior early in a session has been to utilize frequent (often daily) testing (Lloyd, 1971; Mawhinney, *et al.*, 1971; Born, *et al.*, 1972). The main difference between the frequent testing contingencies of past studies and the DRH contingency of the present study is the determination of the interval between tests. Previous studies have generally set fixed intervals between tests (i.e. one day, one week) or due dates for assignments. In the present study assignments were not always due for all subjects on the same day. Subjects were allowed to vary their rates of responding on the paced schedule as long as the rate did not fall below one unit every four days. It is difficult to say whether the DRH contingencies investigated in the present study maintain early studying more than the frequent testing or use of short fixed intervals for due dates as in previous studies. However, the DRH contingencies certainly do not appear to be less effective than these methods.

Perhaps the ease with which students in the present study adjusted to the DRH contingencies can be attributed to the fact that subjects were given complete instructions concerning the DRH contingencies. Some recent studies suggest that acquisition of new behaviors with human subjects is more rapid with instructions and reinforcement than with either condition alone (Vogler, Masters, & Morrill, 1971) ; Herman & Tramontana, 1971). Data from the present study suggest that for students who have been given appropriate instructions, DRH contingencies can be effectively used to reduce delays in responding. Perhaps, then, Lovitt and Esveldt (1970) were premature in rejecting the DRH schedule for use with human subjects.

The results of the present investigation suggest that a better method of teaching a college course would involve frequent quizzing and that if this quizzing were done on a DRH schedule, regular studying would be maintained and students would be more likely to complete all of the course requirements.

AN EXPERIMENTAL COMPARISON
OF FOUR PACING CONTINGENCIES

George Semb
Dan Conyers
Robert Spencer
Juan Jose Sanchez Sosa

KELLER (1968) HAS IDENTIFIED student self-pacing as one of the five major features of personalized instruction. According to Keller, the go-at-your-own-pace feature permits a student to move through a course at a speed commensurate with his ability and other demands upon his time. Very few studies in the field of personalized instruction, however, have allowed students to progress at their own rate such that they have an infinite amount of time to complete the course (Lloyd & Knutzen, 1969; Myers, 1970). Most courses have relied on some form of instructor pacing, or a combination of student pacing and instructor pacing. For example, Malott and Svinicki (1969) allowed students to work as fast or as slow as they wanted as long as they finished the course before the last day of the semester (Doomsday). Failure to complete the course

This research was supported in part by grants from the General Research Fund (3317-5038 and 3316-5038), Office of Research Administration, University of Kansas, and in part by the University of Kansas Computation Center. Reprints may be obtained from George Semb, Department of Human Development, University of Kansas, Lawrence, Kansas, 66044.

by Doomsday resulted in an F in the course. Semb, Hopkins, and Hursh (1973) and Semb (1973) used the concept of a minimum rate contingency to maintain student progress. If the student's rate of progress fell below the minimum rate of quiz mastery set by the instructor, the student was forced to withdraw from the course. In a recent experimental analysis of self-pacing, Miller, Weaver, and Semb (1973) demonstrated that instructor-set target dates backed up by a course withdrawal contingency (complete the assignment by the target date or withdraw from the course) produced higher rates of quiz-taking than no target dates and contingency.

Pacing is an important part of personalized instruction in terms of classroom logistics. Ideally, instructors would probably prefer to maintain a relatively small, constant ratio of students to proctors throughout a course and to avoid large numbers of students piling up at the end of the term. If very many students put off the majority of their quiz-taking until the end of the term, serious problems could arise. One solution would be to schedule several proctors during the latter part of the term, but it would be difficult to predict just how many. An alternate solution is to impose contingencies on students to maintain relatively consistent rates of progress through the course. The present experiment was designed to investigate four different pacing contingencies. The dependent variables included course withdrawals, student distributions of quiz-taking, examination performance, and student evaluations.

METHOD

Subjects, Setting and Course Personnel

Students enrolled in an introductory child development course served as subjects. During enrollment students were randomly assigned to groups of forty-two students each. Each of the four groups in the present study met for 150 minutes a week during three fifty-minute class periods (Monday, Tuesday, and Wednesday evenings). The semester lasted for fourteen weeks (forty-two class days, excluding the first two days which were used for proctor training, student orientation, and administration of a pretest); however, students were not required to come to class everyday.

One graduate teaching assistant, an undergraduate teaching assistant and six student proctors managed each group. Each proctor was responsible for seven students. Proctors had completed the course during the previous semester with a grade of A and received course credit for their work. Students reported to class (a small lecture room) to take quizzes and exams, to receive feedback on their performance and to interact with course personnel. A course outline distributed during enrollment explained the teaching procedures in detail.

Procedure

The course was divided into four major content areas (parts), and each part was further subdivided into four units. A unit consisted of a thirty-page reading assignment[1] and twenty short-answer, essay study questions. The study questions were designed to emphasize major points in the course readings.

To progress through the course, students had to master sixteen unit quizzes and take four hour exams and a final. The unit quizzes corresponded to the unit assignments and the mastery criterion was defined as 100 percent correct. Students could take as many different forms of a unit quiz as necessary to reach the mastery criterion. Unit quizzes consisted of eight items randomly selected from the student's set of twenty study questions.

When the students completed a unit quiz, he or she took it to his proctor who graded it immediately. The proctor grades each item as either correct, partially correct or incorrect by determining how closely the student's answer matched responses provided in the instructor's answer manual. The student could try to justify or explain answers which the proctor marked as partially correct. If the student's oral explanation satisfied the proctor, the item was graded as correct. To progress to

---

[1] Course materials included *Readings in Developmental Psychology Today* (Cramer, 1970), *Elementary Principles of Behavior* (Whaley & Malott, 1971) and *Human Development Lecture Notes and Study Guide* (Semb, 1973).

the next unit, the student had to meet the 100 percent correct mastery criterion; otherwise, he was required to take an alternative form of the quiz.

The pretest and hour exams contained two types of items—study question items taken directly from the student's study questions and nonstudy question items, items which the students were not given in advance. Nonstudy question items generally required the student to integrate major concepts, ideas, or procedures. The instructor and three graduate assistants wrote twenty-four nonstudy items for each of the four parts of the course. Each nonstudy item was checked by each of the four individuals to insure that it did not match any of the study question items. If consensus was not reached, the item was eliminated or revised until the four writers agreed that it was a "novel" (nonstudy) item.

The pretest and four hour exams were arranged as part of a multiple baseline testing procedure (Miller & Weaver, 1972; Semb, 1973). Tables 24-I and 24-II outline the source and number of study and nonstudy items for each test. To understand the tables, *read down each column* to determine how many items were selected from each content part of the course. The pretest consisted of twenty-four items, sixteen randomly selected study questions (four from each part) and eight nonstudy items (two from each part). Students were required to take the pretest on the first day of class, but their performance on it did not contribute to their grade in the course.

TABLE 24-I

Multiple Baseline Testing Procedure: Source and Number of
Pretest and Hour Exam Study Question Items

Conditions	Pre-Training	Post-Training			
Exams	Pretest	Hour 1	Hour 2	Hour 3	Hour 4
Source of Items					
Part 1	4	14	2	2	2
Part 2	4	2	14	2	2
Part 3	4	2	2	14	2
Part 4	4	2	2	2	14
Total Study Question Items per Test	16	20	20	20	20

TABLE 24-II

Multiple Baseline Testing Procedure: Source and Number of
Pretest and Hour Exam Non-study Question Items

Conditions	Pre-Training	Post-Training			
Exams	Pretest	Hour 1	Hour 2	Hour 3	Hour 4
Source of Items					
Part 1	2	2	1	1	1
Part 2	2	1	2	1	1
Part 3	2	1	1	2	1
Part 4	2	1	1	1	2
Total Non-Study Items per Test	8	5	5	5	5

The hour exams occurred at the end of each part and consisted of twenty-five short-answer, essay items. Twenty items were taken directly from the overall pool of study questions and five were selected from the pool of nonstudy items. Furthermore, each hour exam covered all four parts of the course as part of the multiple baseline testing procedure. Fourteen study question items and two nonstudy items were randomly selected[2] from the part of the course students had just finished studying. The remaining nine items were selected from the three parts of the course which had not been explicitly trained for that particular hour exam. Two study question items and one non-study item were randomly selected from each of the three remaining parts of the course.

Hour exams were graded outside of class by one of the teaching assistants. Each answer was scored as either correct, partially correct, or incorrect with points of 2, 1, and 0, respectively, for each question. To earn an A, students had to score twenty-four points on the Part 1 Hour Exam, twenty-eight on the Part 2 Hour Exam, thirty-two on Part 3 and thirty-six on Part 4. The number of points required for an A increased

---

[2] Items on the hour exams were randomly generated by a computer program which also printed the exams. The program was written to insure that items would be selected from all four units in the part the student had just completed studying. No more than four study question items could be selected from any one unit. Likewise, no more than one non-study item could be selected from the first two units of the part. Similar precautions were taken in generating the pre-training and post-training items.

during each successive part because the percentage of post-training or retention items increased (see Tables 24-I and 24-II). Students received points for correct answers to pre-training items as well as post-training items. Points needed for a B on each of the hour exams can be derived by subtracting six points from the number of points needed for an A.

The final exam was available after a student had completed all unit quizzes and hour exams. The final consisted of sixty-four multiple-choice items. Four items were sampled from each of the sixteen units which made up the course. Two of the items were based on the student's study questions (recall items) and two required the student to integrate major aspects of the course (probe items). Probe items which appeared on the final, however, were not the same as the nonstudy items which appeared on hour examinations. The instructor and three graduate assistants determined by consensus whether each item should be categorized as recall or probe.

The staff constructed sixty-four recall and sixty-four probe items. The final used in the present study consisted of two randomly selected probe items and two randomly selected recall items from each of the sixteen units in the course. Two different forms of the final were prepared by rearranging the order of the multiple choice alternatives, and the order of questions on the exam. Students were informed that there were several different forms of the final. The final was available on Thursday evenings throughout the semester, and on the last day of classes. Students were encouraged to take the final as soon as they completed the Part 4 Hour Exam. Answers were recorded on IBM answer sheets and machine graded.

Each item on the final was worth 1.5 points and contributed to the student's final grade in the course. Points earned on the final were added to hour exam points and pacing points (to be described later) to determine the student's course grade. For course grades of A, B, and C, students needed 248, 212, and 184 points, respectively. Students who failed to earn enough points for an A were allowed to re-take the final during exam week at the end of the semester.

Finally, students were asked to complete a course evaluation at the end of each of the four parts of the course. The evaluation form consisted of twenty-four items covering course readings, course procedures, grading fairness, the student's teaching assistant, the student's proctor and student satisfaction. Each item was rated on a five-point scale. Students were encouraged to complete the evaluation form at the end of each part; however, it was not part of the formal course requirement.

Experimental Design

All students were informed on the first day of class that they would receive a Progress Chart with course days listed on the abscissa and tests shown on the ordinate. Second, they were told that a line would be drawn from the lower left corner of the chart to the upper right corner; this was referred to as a minimum rate line. This line represented a "reasonable" rate of progress throughout the course—roughly, a quiz or hour exam every two class days. An enlarged section of a Progress Chart is illustrated in Figure 24-1.

The four groups were exposed to different pacing contingencies as shown in Table 24-III. Students in Group 1 (No Contingency) were informed that they would receive four points for every unit quiz they mastered and that these points would be added to hour exam and final exam points to determine their course grade. Further, they were told that the minimum rate line was merely a suggested rate of progress, and that nothing would

TABLE 24-III

Pacing Contingencies for the Four Groups

Group	Unit Quiz Points	Hour Exam Points	Extra Points	Rate Contingency
1—No Contingency	4	0	0	None
2—Point Loss	4	0	0	Lose 25 points for each day below minimum rate line
3—Point Gain	3	4	0	Earn points only if above rate line when event occurs
4—Extra Point	4	0	1	Earn extra point only if above rate line when event occurs

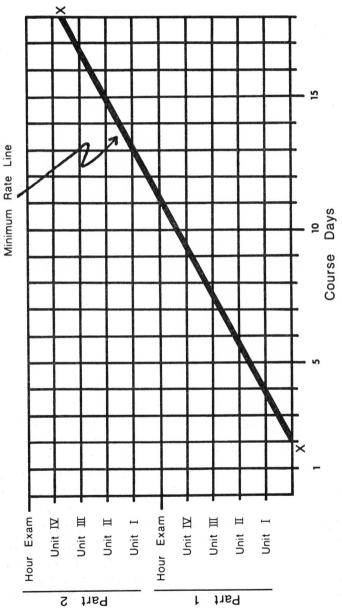

Figure 24-1. An enlarged section of a Progress Chart. Unit quizzes and hour exams are plotted on the ordinate, course days on the abscissa, and a minimum rate line runs diagonally from the lower left corner to the upper right corner.

happen if they stayed above the line or fell below it. That is, students in Group 1 earned four points per unit quiz mastered regardless of whether they were above the line or below it.

Students in Group 2 (Point Loss) also earned four points for every quiz they mastered. However, in addition, they were informed that they would *lose* twenty-five points for every day they were below the minimum rate line. Group 2 was instructed that any points lost would be deducted from the points they earned in other course activities (mastering unit quizzes, hour exams and the final).

Students in Group 3 (Point Gain) earned points for staying above the minimum rate line. They received three points for every unit quiz they mastered and four points for every hour exam they took, as long as they were above the minimum rate line when either event occurred. The rather strange point schedule can be explained as follows. Students in Groups 1 and 2 earned points for mastering unit quizzes, regardless of whether they were above or below the line. The total number of points possible per part (four quizzes *x* four points per quiz) was sixteen. To make Group 3 comparable with Groups 1 and 2 in terms of total points possible per part, the students in Group 3 could earn three points for the hour exam, as long as they were above the minimum rate line when the event occurred.

Students in Group 4 (Extra Point), similar to students in Groups 1 and 2, received four points for every unit quiz they mastered, regardless of whether they were above or below the line. However, they earned one extra point for every unit quiz mastered and hour exam taken, as long as they were above the line when the event occurred. Thus, they were similar to Groups 1 and 2 in that they earned points for unit quizzes mastered, but different in that they could earn one extra point for being above the line. It should be pointed out that students in Group 4 could potentially earn five extra points per part (twenty more points overall) than students in the three other groups.

Students in all four groups were told that if they failed to complete the course by the last class of the semester, they would receive an Incomplete and be able to finish the course at a later time with no penalty. Students in Group 2 (Point Loss), however, were told that all points lost would be carried forward; thus, for all practical purposes, the Incomplete option did not exist for Group 2. Similarly, students in Group 3 (Point Gain) were warned that they would not be able to earn unit quiz and hour exam pacing points if they elected to take an Incomplete. Students in all four groups were given the option of withdrawing from the course at any point during the semester for whatever reason with no penalty. University policy stipulated that students who withdrew from a course after the fourth week of the semester had to be graded as Passing or Failing at the time of Withdrawal. The present course adopted a simple policy—any student who withdrew received a grade of Withdraw Passing.

To review the point system in the present course, students could earn points for performance on the four hour exams (approximately 45% of the course grade), the final exam (approximately 30%) and by the various pacing contingencies outlined for each of the four groups (approximately 25%).

Reliability Measures

To establish a measure of grader reliability, a second grader randomly selected at least five different hour exams from each part for each group. The second grader covered the marks left by the first grader, then independently scored each item. If both graders assigned point values of 0-0, 1-1, or 2-2, it was defined as an agreement. If there was any discrepancy between point values, it was defined as a disagreement. A total of 103 hour exams (2575 items) were checked for all groups combined. There were 2371 agreements and 204 disagreements. Reliability, calculated by dividing the number of agreements by the number of agreements plus disagreements, was .922.

RESULTS

Course Withdrawals and Incompletes

The number and percent of course withdrawals and incompletes are listed in Table 24-IV. Ten students (23.8%)

TABLE 24-IV

Course Withdrawals and Incompletes

Group	Incompletes	Withdrawals	Total	Percent
1—No Contingency	5	5	10	23.8
2—Point Loss	0	1	1	2.4
3—Point Gain	0	3	3	7.1
4—Extra Point	1	3	4	9.5

in Group 1 (No Contingency) failed to complete the course. Five withdrew and five elected to take Incompletes. Only one student (2.4%) from Group 2 (Point Loss) withdrew from the course as compared with three (7.1%) in Group 3 (Point Gain). Four students (9.5%) in Group 4 (Extra Point) failed to complete the course (three withdrew and one elected to take an Incomplete).

Distribution of Student Test-Making Behavior

The percentage of quizzes and hour exams taken by each group during each successive eight days of the course are plotted in Figure 24-2. The percentages were computed by dividing the number of quizzes and hour exams taken during each eight day period by the total number of tests (including retakes) completed during the semester. The data are based only upon students who completed the course. Students in Group 2, 3, and 4 took approximately 20 percent of their tests during each fifth of the course, except during the last fifth when the percentage decreased slightly. This indicates that the average student in Groups 2, 3, and 4 did not put off his quiz-taking until the end of the semester; in fact, the opposite appears to have occurred. That is, the contingencies used in Groups 2, 3, and 4 appear to have promoted relatively consistent rates of test-taking during the course with a slight decrease toward the end of the semester. Students in Group 1 (No Contingency), however, exhibited a different pattern of test-taking behavior. During the first twenty-four days of the course, test-taking progressed at a relatively slow rate, but increased dramatically, especially during the last eight days of the course when they completed 30.1 percent of all quizzes and hour exams. It should be pointed out, however, that these data do not reflect actual

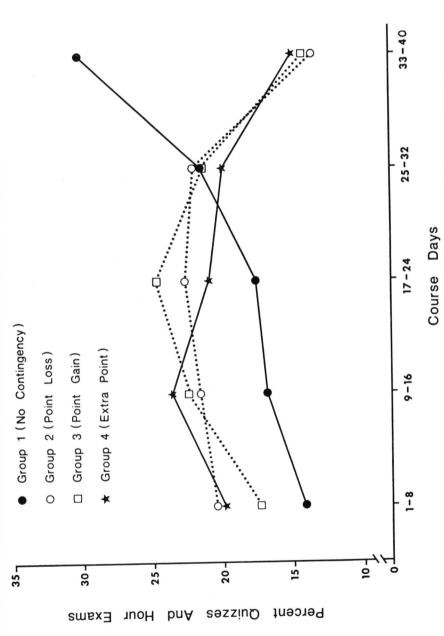

Figure 24-2. The percentage of quizzes and hour exams during successive eight days of the course. The four groups are represented by different symbols as shown in the figure.

demand upon proctor time at the end of the semester. Of the five students who elected Incompletes, four completed a total of sixteen quizzes during the last eight days in an attempt to finish the course before the last day of classes. Had these data been included, the percent of tests taken during the last eight days would have been 31.9 percent.

Performance on Hour Examinations

Sample results (Group 1—Noncontingency) generated by the multiple baseline testing procedure are presented in Figure 24-3. Mean percentage correct for both study and nonstudy items is plotted for the pretest and each of the four hour exams. Items from each of the four course parts are represented by separate plots on the ordinate. The pretest and four hour exams are shown on the abscissa. Percentages correct on both types of items were first computed for each individual student by summing the total number of points earned on each test and then dividing by the total number of points possible. The mean percentages shown in Figure 24-3 refer to the arithmetic mean across individuals.

Percentage correct on both types of items was low during pretraining conditions for each part. Increases in percent correct were functionally related to the introduction of the instructional package for that part. For example, percent correct on Part 3 items was low during the Pretest and on Hour Exams 1 and 2. On Hour Exam 3, however, performance on both study and nonstudy items for Part 3 increased markedly over their pre-training level. At the same time, performance on Part 4 items (ones which had not yet been trained) remained low. During all of the post-training conditions, Group 1 performed consistently better on study question items than they did on nonstudy items. Furthermore, these differences remained relatively stable on subsequent Hour Exams throughout the semester, a finding identical to that reported by Semb (1973).

The results from the multiple baseline testing procedure were nearly identical for the remaining three groups (not shown). In every case, the results illustrated that the training package produced increases in percent correct on both types of items

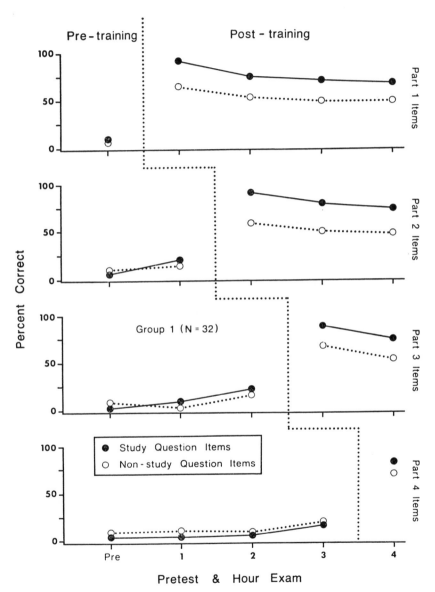

Figure 24-3. Mean percent correct on study question items (closed circles) and nonstudy items (open circles) on the pretest and four hour exams for Group 1. The four course parts are plotted vertically on separate ordinates and the five tests are shown on the abscissa.

over pre-training levels. These data do not, however, allow one to make comparisons between the experimental conditions. To compare the effects produced by each manipulation, *percentage gains* over pretest levels were calculated. Percentage gains were derived by subtracting each student's pretest performance from his Hour Exam performance on the part which had just previously been trained. Mean percentage gains (plotted in Figure 24-4 for all four groups) were derived by summing individual student gains and dividing by N. For example, Group 1 (Figure 23-3) averaged 7.4 percent correct on Part 2 study question items on the Pretest. After Part 2 materials had been trained, percent correct on Part 3 study question

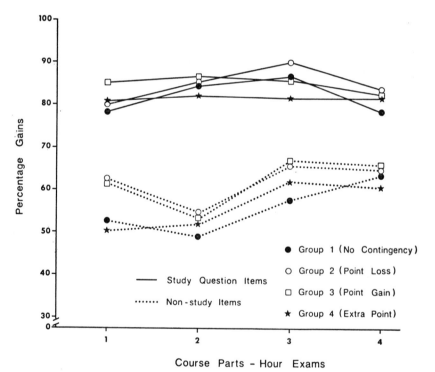

Course Parts - Hour Exams

Figure 24-4. Mean percentage gains over pretest levels for each of the four parts of the course as measured on the hour exams. Study question items are represented by solid lines and nonstudy items by dashed lines. The four groups are represented by different symbols as shown in the figure.

items increased to 91.7 percent correct. The difference between 91.7 percent and 7.4 percent represents the mean gain in performance realized as a function of training Part 2 materials. Percentage gains among course parts (a within-subject comparison) were not significant for study question items (F = .53, df = 3,429, NS), nor were they significant for nonstudy items (F = 1.84, df = 3,429, NS). More importantly, difference between the four pacing conditions were not significant for either study question items (F = .72, df = 3,143, NS) or nonstudy items (F = 2.17, df = 3,143, NS), although there was a slight tendency for Group 1 to score lower on probe items. In short, there were no significant differences either between groups or within groups across the four parts of the course.

Performance on the Final Examination

Performance on the final examination was analyzed for each of the four parts of the course. Mean percentages correct for recall items were derived by summing the number of students who answered each of the eight recall items correctly from each part and dividing by the total number of possible correct answers. The same procedure was used to calculate mean percentages correct for probe items. Mean percentages correct on both recall and probe items for each of the four groups are presented in Figure 24-5. Over all four parts of the course, Group 1 (No Contingency) averaged 84.1 percent correct on recall items and 72.1 percent on probe items. Group 2 (Point Loss) averaged 79.7 percent on recall items and 68.2 percent on probe items. Group 3 (Point Gain) scored 79.0 percent and 67.9 percent, respectively, and Group 4 (Extra Point) averaged 79.7 percent and 66.4 percent. Differences between groups across the four parts of the course were not statistically significant on either recall items (F = 2.62, df = 3,252, NS) or probe items (F = 2.24, df = 3,252, NS). Visual inspection of Figure 23-5, however, appears to indicate that Group 1 (No Contingency) scored slightly higher on the first three parts of the final, but these differences were not statistically significant. Overall, Group 1 averaged 4 to 5 percent better on both recall and probe items.

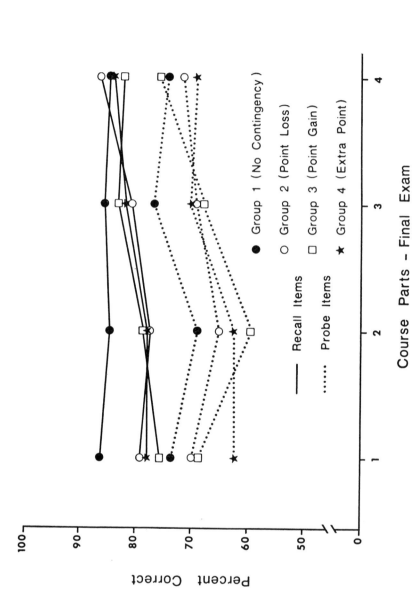

Figure 24-5. Mean percent correct on recall and probe items for each of the four parts of the course as measured on the final examination. Recall items are represented by solid lines and probe items by dashed lines. The four groups are represented by different symbols as shown in the figure.

Course Evaluations

Over 90 percent of the students in each group completed each of the four course evaluations. Mean ratings, derived by summing the individual ratings and dividing by the number of ratings (no responses not included), are presented for the four groups in Figure 24-6. A rating of 5.0 represents the highest possible, positive response. These data do not include ratings from students who withdrew from the course or elected to take Incompletes. Students in Group 1 (No Contingency) tended to rate the course higher initially (Part 1), but there appear to be no appreciable differences between or within groups for the remaining three parts of the course.

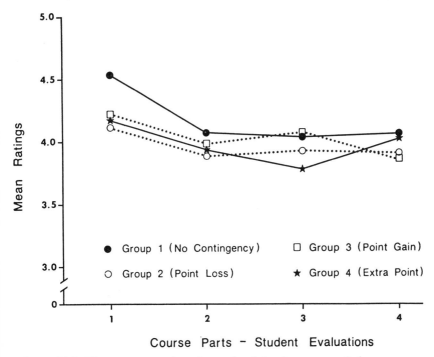

Course Parts – Student Evaluations

Figure 24-6. Mean course ratings for each of the four parts of the course as measured by student evaluations. A score of 5.0 indicates the highest possible, positive rating. The four groups are represented by different symbols as shown in the figure.

DISCUSSION

Several investigators (Born, Gledhill, & Davis, 1972; Born & Whelan, 1973; Keller, 1968) have reported relatively high rates of student withdrawals from personalized instruction courses in comparison with lecture courses. The results of the present experiment suggest that when no pacing contingencies are placed on student progress, a large percentage (23.8%) of students do not complete the course. The use of pacing contingencies in the same course, however, appears to have produced lower percentages of noncompletion. Lloyd and Knutzen (1969) reported that students in their study maintained relatively steady rates of progress once they began work in the course. Students in the present experiment (with the exception of Group 1) were motivated to begin the course promptly either to avoid a point-loss contingency (Group 2) or to earn points (Groups 3 and 4). Perhaps all that is required is to motivate students to begin the course promptly, but the remains for experimental analysis.

Students in Groups 2, 3, and 4 distributed their quiz-taking about equally throughout the semester with a slight decrease during the last fifth of the course. Students in Group 1 (No Contingency), however, put off over 50 percent of their quizzes and hour exams until the last sixteen days of the forty-day term. Given the way in which most universities operate, this is probably more a function of the student's past history with deadlines (term's end) than it is a product of scheduling quizzes according to other demands upon his time (Keller, 1968). In terms of classroom logistics, relatively steady rates of progress enabled the staff to manage students efficiently and effectively. There were seldom large numbers of students waiting to take quizzes or to have them graded in the three contingency groups. However, there was a notable strain upon all of the staff in Group 1 near the end of the semester. It should be pointed out that requiring students to maintain a minimum rate of progress *did not* affect students who wanted to move quickly through the course. None of the pacing contingencies used in the present study had any apparent affect on students who worked rapidly, but perhaps they provided extra encouragement for slow students to keep going.

Performance on the hour exams and final presents somewhat of a paradox. Students in Group 1 (No Contingency) tended to score lower on nonstudy items on the hour exams, but higher on both recall and probe items on the final than any of the other three groups. None of these differences, however, were statistically significant. The lack of any statistical differences indicates that the pacing contingencies (or lack of them) used in the present study did not produce any appreciable differences in student examination performance. Give that many instructors evaluate the effectiveness of their procedures on the basis of such measures, the present results suggest that any of the pacing procedures described might be effective as far as student achievement is concerned.

The multiple baseline testing procedure (Miller & Weaver, 1972; Semb, 1973) used in the present study deserves special comment. Although it may appear complex, it is a relatively easy way for an instructor to insure that his teaching procedures are functionally related to changes in student academic performance. The use of a comprehensive course examination, administered several times throughout the term, allows the instructor to measure student performance on material that has recently been trained as well as on material that has previously been trained (retention) and on material that has not been trained (pre-training or baseline items). Furthermore, by calculating percentage gains over pre-test or baseline levels, it is possible to compare the effects of different teaching procedures, either within groups (Semb, 1973) or between groups (the present study).

Results from the student evaluations also indicated that there were no appreciable differences between groups on measures of student satisfaction, although Group 1 (No Contingency) initially rated the course more positively than the other three groups. These results suggest that student ratings were not differentially affected by the four pacing contingencies investigated. The measures of student evaluations used in the present study, however, provide a nice model for assessing changes in ratings as a function of different treatments over short portions of material (content areas or parts). It is impressive that over ninety percent of the students in each group completed evaluations over each part of the course. More research is needed to investigate the utility of such a student evaluation procedure.

Finally, with respect to the three pacing contingencies investigated in the present experiment, it was much easier for the staff to apply points for staying above the progress line (Groups 3 and 4) than it was for them to deduct points for being below it (Group 2). In many cases, the staff yielded and restored lost points (Group 2), especially when it was the student's first exposure to the point-loss contingency. It is our recommendation to instructors who use a minimum progress contingency to award points for staying above the minimum rate, rather than remove points for being below it. Given the small and insignificant differences between Groups 2, 3, and 4 in terms of course withdrawals, distribution or test-taking, and examination performance, it seems much more reasonable to use a positive, as opposed to a negative, approach.

ENTRY LEVEL TESTING AND THE PATTERN OF BEHAVIORAL OBJEC-TIVES IN A KELLER PLAN PHYSICS COURSE

DAVID BOWEN
WILLIAM FAISSLER

IN THE PROCESS OF CONDUCTING a Keller Plan or PSI course in elementary Physics, data was collected bearing on three questions of interest to science teachers, particularly those using PSI:

1) Do mathematics entry skills influence a student's subsequent performance in a science or math course?
2) If so, can students with critical deficiencies be identified by entry level testing and then remediated?
3) Does mastery of memorization and comprehensive objectives, typically requiring that a student state and paraphrase the basic physical laws and the definitions of terms appearing in them influence the ability to master application and analysis objectives, exemplified by the traditional physics exam questions requiring analysis of given situations?

Method

The procedures described in Keller (1968) were followed closely in designing this course. The course was conducted with seventy randomly selected freshmen engineering students, chosen by taking the last two from every group of twelve in an alphabetical list. The remaining students were given an independent traditional lecture-recitation course by two other instructors.

A mathematics diagnostic entry exam was developed which was administered to all students in the PSI course on the first class day. The correlation of these results with the first-quarter final exam results bears on questions one and two as stated above.

The over-all objective for an analytic physics course is that the student apply the basic physical laws to solve problems. Final exams in a traditional lecture-recitation course, for example, typically consist entirely of problems. The objectives used here required in addition that the students be able to verbally and mathematically state each law and define the terms in it. The intent was to completely specify the sequence of steps necessary to reach the desired end of application and analysis. These "define" and "state" abilities were tested on each unit mastery exam and on the final exam for the second quarter of the three-quarter sequence. For the first and third quarters, there was a common final with the lecture-recitation students, and the other instructors did not want such questions put to their students. The correlation from the second quarter final exam of the student performances on "define" and "state" questions with those for problem solving bears on the third question described above.

The comparison of the performances of students in the traditional and PSI versions on the common finals is not the central concern of this paper, but since the comparison may be of general interest, we report that the PSI students did a little better than average the first quarter and a little worse the third quarter, but in both cases the spread of points within each group was much larger than the small differences between the groups. Such results for the first trial of a PSI course in physics have been reported before by Phillipas and Sommerfeldt (1972) who said that perhaps their inexperience with PSI caused this result. This is also certainly a cause in this study, but it should be pointed out that PSI is progressive. That is, by setting explicit performance standards and measuring student performance against them, instructors using PSI can see precisely where amplification and revision are necessary. Improvement from this type of analysis would be expected, apart from any general gain in experience such as that mentioned by Phillipas and Sommerfeldt.

The diagnostic entry exam consisted of fifty multiple choice questions dealing primarily with arithmetic, algebra, graphs and trigonometry.[1] The main emphasis of the trigonometry questions is on the right triangle, which is used heavily for analysis. Since, as is usual, all mathematics was to be reviewed during the course, it was felt that a multiple choice exam requiring only recognition of the correct answer would be sufficient. We designed the exam so that a student with a high score would have demonstrated familiarity with all graphical and mathematical skills to be used in the course, with the exception of calculus which was taken concurrently.

RESULTS AND DISCUSSION

In taking the exam, students recorded their answers on mark-sense cards which were then analyzed to give each student an over-all score and a score in each of the several areas. The first figure shows the over-all results from the diagnostic exam versus the final exam results from the first quarter. The data show that no student scored significantly higher on the final than he did on the diagnostic, but that the reverse was possible. These results may be interpreted as showing that mathematical skills are prerequisite to high performance in an analytical physics course, but do not in themselves guarantee success ("mathematics is necessary but not sufficient for physics"). The correlation between the two scores is 0.38 for fifty-nine students, significant to the ½ percent level.

It is of course possible that an indirect explanation is correct, such as "a good student in high school physics is likely to do well in high school math (and hence on the diagnostic exam) and also in university physics." It would certainly take more detailed results to rule out such a possibility, but the data do not seem to support such a simple correlation hypothesis. The data points do not form anything approximating a straight line; rather, one half of the graph is populated while the other is empty. The variables are not linearly correlated.

---

[1] Copies of the exam are available upon request. A selection of course materials is also available.

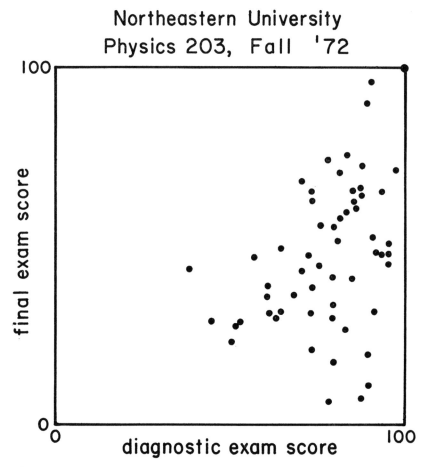

Figure 25-1. Student performance on entry-level diagnostic mathematics exam versus performance on final examination for physics course (r = .38).

The data indicate that entry level testing can be valuable in identifying students who will have trouble in such a course. The next question is whether or not remedial programs can be devised to correct each student deficiencies. It was arranged for programmed remedial materials to be available to deficient students on a voluntary basis, but only one student used them, and he only partially. Most students, despite dire warnings, excused their performance with something like, "I really knew the answers; I'm just rusty from the summer." A demonstration that remediation results in better physics performance would of course establish the hypothesis that math skills are prerequisite.

Students who achieved high diagnostic exam results but low physics scores are presumably evidence of deficiencies in some other area, or of deficiencies in the materials for or operation of the course.

The experience with students' performance on different types

Final Exam
Northeastern University
Physics 204, Winter '73

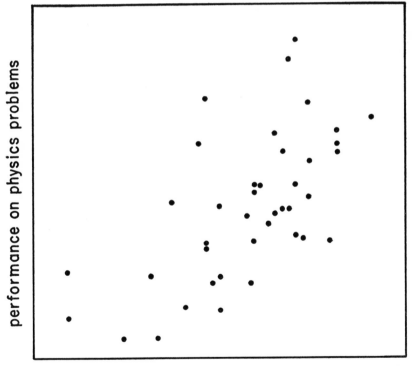

performance on memorization and comprehension

Figure 25-2. Student performance on memorization and comprehension questions (see text for explanation) versus problem-solving performance, both for final examination for physics course $(r = .62)$.

of objectives led us to believe that memorization and comprehension skills are indeed prerequisites for application, analysis, and synthesis skills; that is, that students will not be able to apply principles if they cannot state the principles and define the quantities appearing in them. This idea was tested with the final exam for the second quarter of the sequence. As well as being asked to solve typical problems, the students were asked to define terms appearing in the basic physical laws. The second figure exhibits the performance on "define" and "state" objectives versus performance on the problems and shows that the two are roughly proportional. The correlation is 0.62 for thirty-seven students, significant at the $\frac{1}{10}$ percent level. In a traditional physics course, the basic definitions are usually treated as "obvious" or "intuitive" and are often not made explicit. The effective emphasis on the basic laws is their application, not on the statement or comprehension of them. In contrast, these data suggest that the ability to write a clear, explicit definition of quantities such as velocity and kinetic energy and the ability to state and paraphrase the basic laws, are nontrivial prerequisites for the ability to solve problems.

As before, these data are suggestive of the conclusion, but do not constitute proof. Further research is needed.

INDIVIDUALIZED SYSTEMS OF INSTRUCTION ARE BETTER.... FOR WHOM?

W. SCOTT WOOD
RUTH G. WYLIE

> It appears that any new instructional technique that proves good for the educational "have nots" proves even better for the "haves."
>
> Arthur Jensen, 1973

THERE HAVE BEEN NUMEROUS STUDIES citing the advantages of college instructional systems patterned after Keller's "Personalized System of Instruction" (PSI) both in terms of student performance and attitude. However, these reports frequently describe relatively large numbers of students who withdraw. For example, the results of a *Personalized System of Instruction Newsletter* questionnaire indicated that drop out rate was the second most frequently cited problem in PSI classes, with student procrastination as number one (June, 1972). Born and his colleagues have attempted to shed some light on the nature of this somewhat contradictory finding by analyzing some characteristics of this student population (Born & Whalen, 1973). The present investigation extends these efforts, based upon a statistical analysis of college aptitude and performance differences among freshmen in a large (600 per semester) individualized Introductory Psychology course.

In the fall of 1972, the Department of Psychology at Drake University offered an individualized Introductory Psychology course in its undergraduate curriculum. The program incorporated Keller's (1968) suggestions for course design in higher education; self-pacing, student proctors, minimal formal lectures, and emphasis on the text as the primary information source, and the requirement of a high degree of unit mastery.

After a relatively successful semester in which both students and faculty reacted favorably to the program (Wood, Hause, & Myerson, 1973), a few changes were introduced into the program for the spring of 1973 semester and were evaluated (Hause, 1973). The program described herein includes those revisions.

The textbook, Individual Learning System's *Introductory Psychology,* contained twelve units. It was supplemented by optional enrichment lectures, movies, and unit reviews. Students came to a learning center (Wilson & Tosti, 1973) for tutoring, test taking, and remediation when necessary. The learning center, open approximately thirty-six hours a week, was located in the basement of a campus dormitory. At least one graduate student and four proctors were present at all times in the center. The proctors were undergraduate students who were receiving two hours of graded academic credit for their assistance.

The grading system was based on the accumulation of points for various course activities and the performance on the final exam. Points could be earned from unit exams, lecture attendance, and for passing unit exams at a reasonable rate throughout the semester.

Each unit had three forms, consisting of twenty four-item multiple choice questions. A passing score was considered 85 percent, and the students were given the opportunity to take a unit exam three times. These exams could be taken any time the learning center was open. Approximately 72 percent of the available points could be earned on the unit exams. Progress points could be earned for maintaining a rate equivalent to passing a unit approximately every six school days. Points so earned amounted to approximately 12 percent of the possible points, and were awarded four times during the semester. In addition, students received points for lecture attendance, including enrichment topics, films, or unit reviews, up to a total of 15 percent of the possible points available during the semester. The remaining 1 percent of the potential points was earned by passing a quiz over the handout describing the course. This quiz had to be accomplished prior to taking any unit exams.

Points earned in these activities determined a pre-final grade according to the following scale:

$$85-100\% = A$$
$$78-\ 84\% = B$$
$$71-\ 77\% = C$$
$$64-\ 70\% = D$$
$$0-\ 63\% = F$$

The final examination was offered twice during the semester, once approximately six weeks before the end of the semester and again at the end of the semester. Any student could elect to take the early final; however, if he did so, his course grade was determined at that time. Subsequent lecture attendance or unit examinations would not increase that grade. The exam itself consisted of one-hundred multiple choice questions over the text material. A student's performance on the final exam determined his course grade on the following scale:

$$85-100\% = \text{raise pre-final grade one letter}$$
$$64-\ 84\% = \text{maintain pre-final grade}$$
$$0-\ 63\% = \text{lower pre-final grade one letter}$$

During the 1973 spring semester, a rather disconcerting fact came to the instructor's attention. A graduate student, while conducting research on student attitudes towards the learning center's location in a dormitory, had discovered a relationship between grade point average and amount of earned progress points. The data is indicated in Figure 26-1 and displays an almost perfect positive correlation.

Since these progress points had been included as positive incentives for maintaining a reasonable study and exam rate, the fact that the students who presumably could use them the most were not acquiring them was discouraging. It was decided to pursue more seriously the question of who is doing well and who is doing badly in individualized courses of this type.

The first effort was to compare grade point averages (GPA)

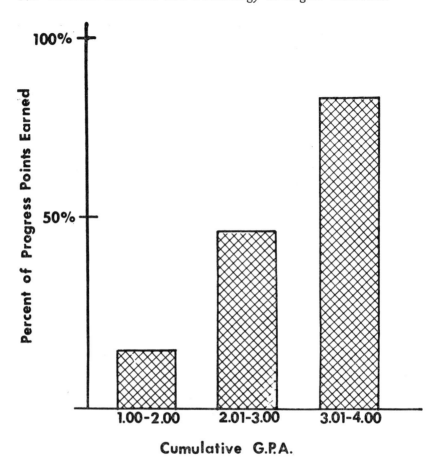

Cumulative G.P.A.

Figure 26-1. Average number of earned progress points per cumulative G.P.A. (L.A. Males, fall 1972, n = 147).

and scores on a standard college aptitude test, the American College Testing (ACT) composite score, of those who earned different grades in Introductory Psychology in the spring of 1973 at Drake University. Secondly, the predictive relationship of ACT scores to final exam performance was assessed.

Methods

Subjects

The population for this study was restricted to freshmen for several reasons: First, the large majority of students in the Introductory Psychology course were freshmen. Second, as displayed in Figure 26-2, the distributions of scores for freshmen and upper-classmen were quite similar. The higher number of F/NC grades for freshmen only points to the importance of analyzing this group separately. (At Drake University, F grades for freshmen are recorded as No Credit or NC, and are not calculated in their GPA.) Finally, ACT scores were difficult to obtain for nonfreshmen because Drake has only recently been requiring them for admittance.

Procedure

Comparing ACT and GPA with final grades: Freshmen subjects were grouped according to their final grade classification in

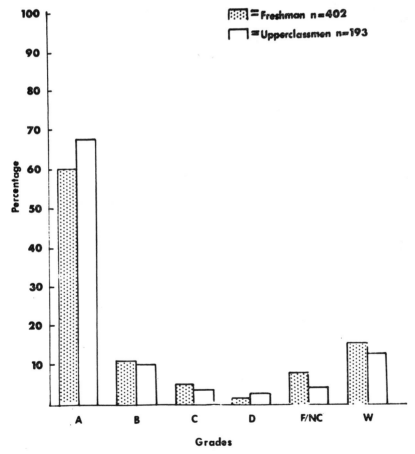

Figure 26-2. Grade distribution of freshman vs. upperclassman Introductory Psychology, Spring 1973.

Introductory Psychology, spring semester, 1973. Groups C, D, and NC included all freshmen receiving those respective grades in Introductory Psychology and for whom ACT scores were available. Because of the large and unequal numbers involved in groups A1 (early final), A2 (regular final), B, and W (withdraw), a random sample of thirty students was drawn from each of these groups. A total of 166 students were used in seven groups. ACT composite scores were collected for each subject. Additionally, the grade point average attained during the fall semester preceding enrollment in Introductory Psychology was recorded for each subject.[1]

In order to avoid the assumptions that the scores were drawn from a normally distributed population or that the scores were drawn from populations of the same variance, a nonparametric test was used to evaluate differences in central tendencies between the groups.

Comparing ACT composite scores with final exam performance: The relationships between the ACT scores and performance on the final exams were separately assessed for students who took the early final and students who took the final at the end of the semester. For the first assessment, those who took the early final, the sample was the same group of students who received an early A (group A1) in the preceding analysis. Since all but two students in the course who took the early final did receive an A, the same sample was thought to be sufficiently representative. However, for those who took the regular final, a layered random sample of thirty students was selected, with fifteen drawn from freshmen with ACT scores above 23.3 (the mean of Drake's freshmen population) and fifteen below.

RESULTS

Comparing ACT and GPA with Final Grades

The average scores for each group in terms of ACT composite score, equivalent ACT percentile rank, and GPA are summarized in Table 26-I.

---

[1] The authors would like to express their appreciation to Ms. Anne Connolly for her assistance in data collection.

TABLE 26-I

Central Tendency of Grade Groups

Group		Central Tendency Measure	
	Mean ACT	Equivalent Percentile Ranking of Mean ACT	Mean GPA (4.0 Scale)
A1	24.87	61%	2.88
A2	22.73	45%	2.63
B	20.63	31%	2.51
C	17.28	9%	2.20
D	19.13	18%	2.19
F/NC	18.60	18%	1.82
W	18.57	18%	2.15

The Mann-Whitney U test showed a highly significant directional difference between ACT composite scores for group A1 and group NC. ACT scores for group A1 were also significantly higher than group A2. Group A2 scored significantly higher than group B, and, in turn, group B average significantly higher ACT scores than group C.

No significant difference was found between group C and group D, between group D and group NC, or between group NC and group W. Table II gives z scores and their level of significance for group comparisons tested with Mann-Whitney U.

The mean ACT composite scores as reported in the class profile for the freshman class at Drake University during school year 1972–73 was 23.3 with a standard deviation of 4.6. The mean ACT score for group A1 fell above that point ($\overline{X} = 24.87$) while

TABLE 26-II

Art Score and GPA Comparisons Based on Grade Groups

Comparison Groups	Measure	
	ACT	GPA
A1–A2	1.84*	1.56
A2–B	2.23*	.68
B–C	2.46**	1.40
C–D	U = 59.5	U = 74
D–F/NC	U = 73	U = 47.5
F/NC–W	.15	2.24*

Note.—Entries indicate z computed when samples were large enough to approximate a normal distribution. In other cases, U values are shown.
* p < .05.
** p < .01.

group A2's mean fell below $(\overline{X} = 18.60$ and 18.57, respectively).
Grade point averages were not definitive in distinguishing
differences between most grade groups, but one significant result
was found. In contrast to the data based upon ACT composite
scores, group W's average GPA was significantly higher than the
F/NC group. The lack of significant differences among the grade
groups when comparing GPA's in probably attributable to the fact
that these GPA's were based upon a single semester performance.
The average grade of a first semester freshman is unlikely to
demonstrate his college aptitude nearly as well as a GPA based
upon more course performances across a longer period of time.
Interestingly, however, the W group had obtained a significantly
higher GPA in the previous semester than had the F/NC group,
a difference which was not revealed in the ACT comparison
between the same groups. It suggests that one difference between
the low grade group and W students may be in their sensitivity
to the importance of the GPA. A student who withdraws rather
than remains in a course where he has a good chance of receiving
a low grade at least protects his GPA, even if he forfeits whatever
knowledge might be obtained by remaining.

Comparing ACT Composite Scores with Final Exam Performance

Spearman rank-order correlation coefficients were computed
between ACT composite scores and the percent correct on the
final exam within each group. The coefficients for the early
final and regular final were .34 and .59, respectively. Both of these
were significant ($p < .05$ and $p < 0.05$ respectively).

This finding is comparable to Morris and Kimbrell's (1972)
data demonstrating a high positive correlation between Scholastic
Aptitude Test scores and final exam performance in an Introductory Psychology course taught by the PSI method.

DISCUSSION

The preceding results further substantiate earlier observations
by other researchers concerning the relationships between standard
academic aptitude and performance measures and performance in
individualized courses. Specifically, it appears that it is the less

apt student who profits least, rather than most, from these courses. This conclusion can be reached both on an analysis of those who withdraw from such courses and who it is that performs "best," with respect to rate of course completion, final examination scores, and overall course grades; good students (according to traditional measures) get A's and complete the courses quickly, average students get A's by hanging in there, studying, and taking tests in a noncompetitive atmosphere, but many of the poorer students either fail or withdraw.

There are at least two clear implications of these observations. The first is rather obvious. One can not honestly compare student performances in our courses with those from lecture-type classes unless the "drop out" population is considered, since apparently more poor students withdraw from individualized courses than they do from other courses. For example, the percent of students who withdrew from Drake's individualized Introductory Psychology course was 16.0 percent in the fall of 1972 and 12.0 percent in the spring of 1973. These compare to a withdrawal rate of only 1.5 percent in a previous semester of Introductory Psychology as a strictly lecture-quiz course (spring 1970). Other researchers have disclosed similar high withdrawal rates in their individualized courses as well (Born & Whalen, 1973; Morris & Kimbrell, 1972). In the past, some researchers have considered these facts in presenting their comparisons, and others have not.

More important, at least in terms of educational improvement, is the implication concerning the design of courses in the future. This paper has avoided referring to all the classes involved in this approach as PSI courses, since some feel that the term "PSI" should be used to describe only those courses which contain all of Keller and his colleagues' design parameters. Nonetheless, these courses are more similar than dissimilar, and are radically different from the conventional lecture classes along several common dimensions. To the best of my knowledge, however, the observation herein concerning withdrawal rates is a typical finding among many of these courses, true PSI or revisionist version. It seems these observations concerning college aptitude measures will apply across most of these courses as well. For example, Born and Whelan (1973) based their conclusions on a state university population which was largely nonresidential. However, the same general observations about student performance are found to be true for freshmen living on-campus at Drake University, a relatively small, private, Midwestern university.

The problem is simply that our courses may be failing to teach some members of a certain student population, since these students are withdrawing in even larger numbers from our courses than from conventional lecture courses. Rate contingencies, "doomsday" contingencies, and unlimited course completion times do not seem to be effective in reducing the withdrawal problem, although they do have demonstrable effects on the procrastination problem (Hess, 1971). No one would fail to describe these results as clear improvements, but the problem of how to deal with the less academically apt student is not yet resolved by our efforts. At Drake, we are most effective with the middle of the academic ability distribution, while letting the high end pass quickly through our course and, frankly, not doing much for the low end.

It is now apparent, however, that it is possible to predict low performers and the potential drop outs with conventional aptitude measures. Some preventative remediation will be initiated by pre-course grouping of potential low scorers and drop outs into experimental and control groups for the purpose of evaluating some forced tutoring as a possible aid, and it would seem that others are initiating efforts to deal with the same problem in other universities as well. In any case, it seems that if problem students can now be predicted with some certainty, our technology ought to be up to the task of providing a solution in the near future.

STUDY TACTICS

ALL OF THE MANY FACTORS which influence how the student learns in a course do not affect academic performance directly, but affect the propensity of the student to study the material. It is really the quantity and quality of a variety of distinct study behaviors which directly produce effects on learning.

This selection of papers comprised a symposium concerned with the kinds of study tactics students use to learn course material. The series of papers describes the development and validation of a major research tool which can produce detailed information about how students study under different conditions and how they can be taught to study more efficiently and effectively.

THE MEASUREMENT AND ANALYSIS OF COLLEGE STUDENT STUDY BEHAVIOR: TACTICS FOR RESEARCH

JAMES M. JOHNSTON
GEORGE W. O'NEILL
WILLIAM M. WALTERS
JEAN A. RASHEED

As HAS BEEN POINTED OUT BEFORE (Johnston, Roberts, O'Neill, 1972), the study tactics engaged in by college students probably constitute the single most important variable which influences academic performance. However, the amount and quality of empirical research concerning student study behavior is disproportionately miniscule to this importance. Most counseling and instruction concerning study tactics centers around teaching self-control and auxiliary skills (such as note-taking) which are useful in getting the student in a position to study, but little evidence at all exists about the actual study behaviors which constitute that amorphous class of responses we call studying. It seems unlikely that all of these different responses are equally effective and efficient in their effects on academic performance. Could this possibility be one of the reasons contributing to the fact that two students can study for equal periods of time and produce widely varying performances or exhibit the same quality of performance as a result of extremely different amounts of study? A great many such intriguing questions face us in our research effort to thoroughly investigate college student study behavior.

Such a program faces difficulties, however. One of the reasons for the paucity of empirical research in this area probably stems from the fact that in most institutions of higher education, student study behavior both within and across students occurs at the choice of the individual student in a wide variety of physical settings at all hours of the day and night. In addition, not all of what we commonly refer to as study is objectively observable. Many study behaviors are silent, as opposed to oral or written, and may practically be considered to be unobservable private events. In other words, observation and measurement present considerable problems.

Two general methodological approaches to this problem are available. First, it is possible in some circumstances to bring the behavior of interest into a controlled or laboratory setting. This has the advantage of providing the opportunity for obtaining objective measures of *some* of the many individual study behaviors. However, this tactic has some critical disadvantages. Access to course material outside the laboratory setting must be controlled and this control must be demonstrated. Forcing students to study in such an artificial setting at restricted times for limited periods may disturb the natural characteristics of study behavior under more normal conditions, and thus present problems of generalization of research findings to non-laboratory conditions. For example, the rules of the group study room probably prohibit any oral study behaviors or much variation in body position and probably discourage breaks, etc. because of the check-in, check-out system. These difficulties are not beyond amelioration, but some other problems seem to be. Without disturbing the student, it is difficult to measure very much more than the total time the student spends in the study room in a position to study. Whether the student is daydreaming or studying and exactly what actual study behaviors are being used when and in what proportions are not measurable by an outside observer.

These seem to be crucial, even fatal, limitations for this laboratory approach. The alternative tactic is not without its difficulties, however. This second approach involves the use of a self-measurement and reporting sytem. Here the students themselves observe and record their own study behaviors as they occur under normal conditions. In this case, there seems to be much less risk of seriously disturbing the normal patterns of study than with the creation of an artificial study environment. In addition, with the students recording their own study behaviors, it becomes *possible* to measure behaviors not otherwise observable. In other words, there is no a priori limit on which study behaviors can be measured. All of these features mean that there is a less serious problem of generalizing research results to new settings.

The obvious complication with this general tactic concerns the development of an appropriate measuring instrument and the demonstration of its validity. The question is, can undergraduate students be successfully taught to observe and record their own study behaviors as instructed so that valid measures of studying result? The difficulty of demonstrating this validity lies in the fact that no useful criterion measures of truth seem to be available in this case; that is, there are few ways to objectively measure the details of study behavior to which the subjective measures can be compared as a test of their validity.

Fortunately, this is not a new or unusual problem in the history of science, and methodological tactics are available to address it. The practice is called affirming the consequent and is thoroughly described by Sidman (1960). Logicians among you may recognize this as a logical fallacy. Sidman describes it as follows:

> We begin with the statement: "If A is true, B is true." We then perform an experiment and find that B is indeed true. From this, we conclude that A is also true. Our conclusion may be wrong, however, since we did not state that the truth of A was a necessary prerequisite for the truth of B. A might be false, even though B does not turn out to be true. The truth of B does not logically permit any inference concerning A.

However, he goes on to point out:

> The logician cannot be gainsaid in this matter, but there is a problem. Few students in the elementary logic course have been told that affirming the consequent, despite its logical

fallaciousness is very nearly the life blood of science. There is, in other words, a discrepancy between logical rules and laboratory practice.

The utility of affirming the consequent lies in the fact that the establishment of the truth of B does tell one something about A. It has eliminated one of the conditions which could have demonstrated A to be false. The believability of the truth of A is therefore increased by some unspecified amount, and one can go on to explore other consequences of the truth of A. There are other benefits of this tactic which are related to the fact that it is a form of systematic replication, and it could be described and discussed in much greater detail. There are appropriate cautions which must be exercised as well, and I would again reference Sidman's excellent discussion. It will have to be sufficient here to describe the applications of this methodology to the problem of demonstrating the validity of this reporting system for observing and recording study behavior.

In our case, we are attempting to ascertain whether or not the Study Report Form (SRF) and the system for using it produces valid measures of student study behaviors. If, in the tactic of affirming the consequent, we let "A" represent the assumption that the SRF and its system produces valid measures of study behavior, then we can investigate a number of "B" statements which follow the truth of "A." For instance, we can manipulate course requirements or teaching techniques in such a way that study behavior must unavoidably be influenced, and then we can look at the resulting reported study data to see if it reflects these powerful manipulations. Or we can examine the data from the routine use of the reporting system to see if certain mandatory internal consistencies exist which would be present if the reporting from were being correctly used to report truthful data.

Of course, the successful accumulation of data demonstrating the truth of "B" does not prove that "A," the validity of the reporting system, is true. It merely makes that hypothesis believable. It takes an unspecified number of such successful cases to make the point, and there is no criteria for deciding when the truth of "A," or the validity of the system, has been conclusively demonstrated. A number of factors such as plausibility and negative instances must be taken into account. However, all the while this kind of data is augmenting the generality and overall systematization of this measuring tool and its uses.

The next two papers will show data relevant to the validity of our reporting system in terms of this tactic of affirming the consequent. The fourth paper in this series will describe some basic, typical characteristics of study behavior produced by our behavioral teaching procedures. First it is appropriate to describe the primary details of these teaching methods which apply to the following papers. Finally, this paper will describe in detail the system for measuring student study behavior.

The procedures described here summarize general techniques in use over a number of quarters. Class activities usually consisted of discussions, films, guest lectures, and demonstrations three days a week. No lectures in the traditional sense were given, and no class activities were grade related. The major activity required of the students was Performance Sessions. The students were assigned to a Student-Teacher with whom they worked for the entire quarter. When a student arrived at the Teaching Center at the time he previously signed for on the Student-teacher's posted appointment sheet, the Student-teacher was usually ready with the student's data sheet, his cumulative graph, a pencil, and a watch. When the student announced which text or lecture unit he wished to work on, the Student-teacher shuffled the pool of items in that unit and randomly selected forty of them. Each time a student came in to work on a certain unit, the items worked with were randomly selected from that same unit pool. Thus, on the second and third Performance Sessions of a unit, a student could see new items as well as some of those he might have performed on previously.

The student and his Student-teacher then sat down in a three-sided booth, and after the usual friendly conversation, the student was handed the forty item cards and the Student-teacher quietly noted the starting time on his watch. The student read each item aloud and filled in the blank orally with the correct answer or indicated that he did not know. After emitting either of these two specific alternatives, he turned the card over and read aloud the correct answer. He performed the same operation with all of the remaining items or until ten minutes had expired. After the student was finished, the Student-teacher quickly counted the few missed blanks and gave the cards to the student to review. Then he counted the number of blanks correctly answered (there were sometimes more than one blank per item) and calculated the percentage of reading and answering items correctly.

This done, the Student-teacher and the student spent a variable period of time engaged in dialogue concerning the subject matter. This portion of the Performance Session was characterized by student defense of incorrect answeres, discussion of errors, discussion of book and lecture material, review and suggestion of study techniques, and appropriate praise or curses. There was also discussion of personal and noncourse matters.

Following this period of discusson, the student plotted the percent correct with the Student-teacher watching. His performance was compared to his past efforts and to clearly defined future goals as well as occasionally to the performance of other students. All performance graphs were displayed publicly on bulletin boards and students were free to come by and see their graph at almost any time.

The students could sign for and have Performance Sessions whenever they wished during a fifty-hour week (although no more than one a day). In addition, they could perform on any unit as many times as they needed without penalty to meet the stated 90 percent criterion, although items were always randomly selected from the item pool on each attempt.

A few additional comments are necessary to place these procedures in the proper perspective. They are designed to serve as a vehicle for research and do not necessarily represent in all respects techniques that would be most appropriate for strictly instructional purposes. The class sizes are usually thirty or sometimes sixty students, and this fact plus certain other features allows a greater degree of personal attention to some details than would be feasible or practical in larger, non-research courses. This has seemed to contribute to assisting us in reducing the variability between and within students in their performance as compared to larger courses using a block-time sign-up system.

Over the period of the past two years we have been developing

IMPORTANT!

1. FILL IN DURING OR IMMEDIATELY AFTER STUDY.
2. USE A NEW COLUMN FOR EACH STUDY EPISODE.
3. TIME YOURSELF WITH A CLOCK OR WATCH.
4. OBTAIN TIMES FOR EACH DIFFERENT KIND OF STUDY USED.
5. PUT THE ACTUAL TIME SPENT IN EACH BOX.
6. DO NOT ENTER ZEROS OR CHECKMARKS.
7. DON'T FORGET TO CIRCLE A OR E.
8. INCLUDE ALL EPISODES OF STUDY, EVEN SHORT ONES.
9. BE SUPER—ACCURATE AND THOROUGH.
10. ABOVE ALL, BE HONEST!

STUDY EPISODE – A RELATIVELY UNINTERRUPTED PERIOD OF STUDY SEPARATED FROM OTHER EPISODES BY OTHER ACTIVITIES OF AT LEAST 15 MINUTES DURATION.
LEVEL OF DISTURBANCE – RATE 12345 (LOW TO HIGH) ANY VISUAL, AUDITORY, OR OTHER DISTRACTIONS.
TOTAL TIME OF EPISODE – MARK ACTUAL TIME OF ENTIRE EPISODE TO THE NEAREST MINUTE.
READING FIRST TIME – READING FOR THE FIRST TIME EVER.
REREADING – ANY READING EXCEPT THE FIRST READING.
    WRITTEN AIDS – REREADING ANY OF THE TYPES LISTED.
    LECTURE NOTES – REREADING AFTER CLASS OR TRANSCRIPTION.
MAKING WRITTEN AIDS:
    OUTLINING – CONSTRUCTING FORMAL OR INFORMAL OUTLINES OF ANY PART OF THE MATERIAL.
    UNDERLINING BRACKETS – MARKING ANY PARTS OF THE TEXT, WRITTEN AIDS, LECTURE, OTHER.
    SUMMARIZING – WRITING SUMMARIES OF UNITS, CHAPTERS, PARAGRAPHS, ETC.
    TERMS, NAMES, DEFINITIONS – WRITING TERMS, DEFINITIONS, CONCEPTS, IMPORTANT POINTS, ETC.
    EXAMPLES, APPLICATIONS – WRITING EXAMPLES, APPLICATIONS, USES, ETC.
    TRANSCRIBE LECTURE – COPYING LECTURE NOTES OR TRANSCRIBING TAPED LECTURES.
    QUESTIONS – CONSTRUCTING ANY OF THE LISTED TYPES OF QUESTIONS.
USING AUDIO—VISUAL AIDS
    FILMS, SLIDES, PICTURES – TIME SPENT VIEWING.
    TAPES – TIME SPENT LISTENING.
SELF—QUIZZING – MARK TIME SPENT IN ORAL, SILENT, OR WRITTEN SELF—QUIZZING ON ANY MATERIAL
STUDYING WITH OTHERS
    NUMBER – MARK THE NUMBER STUDIED WITH, NOT INCLUDING YOURSELF.
    DISCUSSION – TALKING ABOUT MATERIAL WITH OTHERS.
    QUIZZING – QUIZZING EACH OTHER ORALLY OR WRITTEN.
    MAKING WRITTEN AIDS – BASED ON GROUP DISCUSSION OR OTHERS' WRITTEN AIDS.
ACTUAL OR ESTIMATED – MARK A OR E IF MOST TIMES ARE ACTUALLY CORRECT OR ESTIMATED.

Figure 27-1. Instruction side of Study Report Form (SRF).

a Study Report Form, part of the evolution of which has already been reported (Johnston, Roberts, O'Neill, 1972). Considerable effort has gone into designing every facet of this instrument as well as its introduction and use, and the increment of change each quarter is progressively less.

The SRF is printed on both sides of 5½ × 8½ heavy weight paper stock. It is folded longitudinally so that the top line on the front side is visible. The back of the SRF includes directions for proper use and definitions of the different types of study behavior. The front side includes a list of the various study behaviors on the left side and eight columns of boxes on the right side with a line for identifying and academic performance information at the top.

This next paragraph will describe the different behaviors which the students observe and record; however, it must be remembered that their introduction to the SRF is much more thorough than time permits here. In the order in which they appear on the SRF, the first item is the number of the study episode. Next is the date on which the study occurred. Next is the total time in minutes of the episode of study, although this is the last item to be filled out. Continuing down the column is reading for the first time the text or any other material. Here, as in almost all other instances, the students record the time (in minutes) spent engaging in each behavior. The next block is rereading of the text, the written aids, the lecture, or any other material. The next block is making any of a variety of written aids, including outlining, underlining or brackets, etc.; summarizing; writing terms, names, and definitions; making examples or applications; transcribing lecture; and creating fill-in, multiple choice, or essay questions. Then comes using audiovisual aids, in the form of films, slides, pictures, tapes, or other media. Next is self-quizzing on the text, written aids, audiovisual materials, or other material. These behaviors are also marked as being oral, silent, or written. The last category is studying with others. The student includes the number studied with and then writes down the time spent discussing, quizzing, or making written aids. At the bottom of the column the stu-

STUDY REPORT FORM-ST ___ STUDENT ___ LATENCY ___ UNIT ___ TRY ___ C ___ IC ___ CC ___ TIME ___

	1	2	3	4	5	6	7	8
EPISODE NUMBER 22								
STUDY EPISODES: DATES 24								
LEVEL OF DISTURBANCE (LOW 1 2 3 4 5 HIGH) 28								
TOTAL TIME OF EPISODE 29								
READING FIRST TIME: TEXT 32								
OTHER ( ) 35								
REREADING: TEXT 38								
WRITTEN AIDS 41								
LECTURE NOTES 44								
OTHER ( ) 47								
MAKING WRITTEN AIDS: OUTLINING 50								
UNDERLINING, BRACKETS 53								
SUMMARIZING 56								
TERMS, NAMES, DEFINITIONS 59								
EXAMPLES, APPLICATIONS 62								
TRANSCRIBE LECTURE 65								
FILL-IN QUESTIONS 68								
MULTIPLE-CHOICE QUESTIONS 71								
ESSAY QUESTIONS 74								
USING AUDIO-VISUAL AIDS: FILMS, SLIDES, PICTURES 14								
TAPES 17								
OTHER ( ) 20								
SELF-QUIZZING: TEXT 23	O:S:W	O:S:W	O:S:W	O:S:W	O:S:W	O:S:W	O:S:W	O:S:W
WRITTEN AIDS 27	O:S:W	O:S:W	O:S:W	O:S:W	O:S:W	O:S:W	O:S:W	O:S:W
AUDIO-VISUAL 31	O:S:W	O:S:W	O:S:W	O:S:W	O:S:W	O:S:W	O:S:W	O:S:W
OTHER ( ) 35	O:S:W	O:S:W	O:S:W	O:S:W	O:S:W	O:S:W	O:S:W	O:S:W
STUDYING WITH OTHERS: NUMBER 39								
DISCUSSING 41								
QUIZZING 44								
MAKING WRITTEN AIDS 47								
ACTUAL OR ESTIMATED: A OR E 50	A/E	A/E	A/E	A/E	A/E	A/E	A/E	A/E

ORAL-O SILENT-S WRITTEN-W

Figure 27-2. Data recording side of Study Report Form (SRF).

dents indicate whether their times were actually recorded with a timepiece or were estimated.

The students record the appropriate responses for each separate episode of studying during or immediately after the episode. They may report any number of episodes using a single column for each. An episode is defined as any period of study separated from other episodes by breaks of more than fifteen minutes. If the break is less than fifteen minutes, the break time is subtracted from the total time of the episode.

This version of the SRF is not exhaustive of all possible study hehaviors, but it is more than adequate for most courses and most students. Since every student comes to a course with his or her own definitions of each of these behaviors, it is important to get them to adhere to only those described on the SRF. This is a central part of the introduction they are given to the form. In practice, almost everything a student does in preparation for testing can be recorded appropriately on the SRF. Actually, the variety of study behaviors exhibited across students is surprisingly limited, and some categories are infrequently used.

The system of which the SRF is the central component is obviously critical to the validity of the data which results. It begins with a forty-five-minute in-class introduction of the SRF to the students. This describes in detail the study project, the system itself, the detailed content of the SRF, and the proper use of the form.

Students complete the SRF as they study and turn it in when they come in for a Performance Session. Thus a number of individual study episodes may be reported in preparation for one attempt to pass a unit of course material. At the conclusion of the Performance Session, the Student-teacher fills in identifying and performance information on the visible top line of the SRF (thus not seeing the study information itself), and the student deposits the SRF into a locked mailbox in the Teaching Center before leaving.

Once a day a graduate assistant not otherwise involved in the course unlocks the mailbox, removes the accumulated SRF's, and proofs them by hand for a variety of specific errors which are easily observable. If errors are discovered on any SRF, the assistant makes the correction if possible and fills out a small correction notice which is immediately attached to the offending student's performance graph. This notice is taken down by the student when he comes in for his next Performance Session and is discussed by him and his Student-teacher to insure that the error is not made again. If the assistant cannot correct the error without more information from the student, the SRF is attached to the graph along with the correction notice so that the student can supply the missing information and redeposit it in the mailbox.

The visually proofed SRF's are sent to the keypunch operator in the Computer Center for transfer to IBM cards. The punched SRF's are returned to the Teaching Center and are filed.

The data cards are then run through an error-check program designed to search each SRF for internal errors too difficult to spot visually. The resulting print-out is examined and data cards with errors are pulled out and corrected by the assistant if possible. If information is missing which is only available from the student, the SRF is retrieved and attached to the performance graph as already described.

All corrected data is put on a computer disk file and is then available for various computer programs which allow us to examine any possible characteristics of interest from individual or group data. These programs are quite complex, and permit this enormous volume of data to be analyzed in any possible manner.

At the end of every quarter, a questionnaire is completed by all students in which they respond to a number of statements concerning their use of the SRF. Some of the statements directly examine how honest they were in observing and reporting the SRF. Even though the students are told not to write their names on the questionnaires, they are actually covertly coded so that each student's paper can be identified. The sole purpose of this is to permit us to identify students who clearly report dishonesty so that we can omit their SRF data from any analyses. Of course, this increases the validity of the total remaining body of data.

It must be clarified that this study reporting system is designed and intended only for research purposes. Although the form could be shortened for any particular course, the details of the system are far too cumbersome and complex for routine use in regular classes. So in this previous instance, it is not necessary that 100 percent of the students in a course be completely honest as long as we have a means of identifying and omitting such invalid data. It is also probably not necessary that each student use the SRF with unswerving accuracy in every detail on every single occasion (although that is a goal toward which it is necessary to work). The minimum degree of validity which is required to provide useful data on questions of interest is probably less than 100 percent and would seem to be related to the specificity of the research question asked.

And there are many such issues to address. This type of system is a tool which allows the educational researcher to use single subject or group designs with study behaviors being either independent or dependent variables. One area with promising potential is the investigation of the effects on academic performance of varying the kinds and amounts of different study behaviors. An equally important approach would entail observation of the effects of different instructional procedures and materials on study behaviors. One of the many goals of such research programs should be to empirically define the most effective and efficient study techniques for different types of subject matters and teaching methods. Finally, one of the most exciting uses of such a tool is not for research, but rather for diagnostic and therapeutic purposes in the individual case of a student with performance problems.

VALIDITY OF THE STUDY
REPORTING SYSTEM-I

WILLIAM M. WALTERS
GEORGE W. O'NEILL
JEAN A. RASHEED
JAMES M. JOHNSTON

ONE KIND OF DATA WHICH CAN lend support to the assumption of the validity of the Study Report Form (SRF) and its associated system comes from routine, nonexperimental use of the SRF. Following the tactics described earlier, if the SRF is being properly used, there are some precise predictions which must follow given the basic design of the SRF. In other words, if the students are being careful in reporting their own study behavior, the format of the SRF should show or not show consistently certain kinds of responses on the part of the student.

This paper will describe some of this data which was collected from three different sections of an undergraduate course in Abnormal Psychology taught during the Spring and Summer quarters of this year. Here data are being used from all students who admitted false reporting on the questionnaire. As usual in this paradigm, no data is presented for Unit I because the SRF is introduced during this time. All teaching and study reporting procedures were the same as those described in the previous paper (Johnston, *et al.*, 1974).

TABLE 28-I

| | Reporting Rereading | | |
	After Reading	Before Reading	%
Spring	276	0	0
Summer	573	0	0

Assuming the validity of the study reporting system, the first prediction was a fairly obvious one. On the SRF there are separate categories for reading the text for the first time and for rereading the text. If the form is being properly filled out, it would be impossible for students to report rereading before they had reported reading for the first time in a previous episode. In other works, you can not reread something unless you have already read it first.

Therefore a count was made of the number of times rereading the text occurred on any unit without any reading first time previously reported on that unit. The number of times that rereading was properly reported on any unit after reading first time had already been reported on that unit was also tabulated. This is not an error that is visually or computer checked, and students receive no feedback on it. The first table shows the resulting frequencies for Spring and Summer quarters. In a total of nearly 850 instances in which rereading the text was reported as a study tactic, it was never reported to have occurred before reading on that unit was reported.

A similar prediction from the assumption of a high degree of validity of the study reporting system is that students would report making written aids before reporting rereading written aids or self-quizzing on written aids on the same unit. In other words, this prediction is not as unequivocal as the previous one because students will reread or self-quiz on the written aids of other students. Although this may be an effective and valuable study tactic, it probably is relatively infrequent in occurrence. Table 28-II shows the data from Spring and Summer quarters. This prediction is also supported by the evidence although not as clearly as in the first table.

A third prediction which follows from the assumed validity of the system concerns the type of test items that students some-

TABLE 28-II

	Rereading: Written Aids			Self-Quizzing: Written Aids		
	After Reported Written Aids	Without Reported Written Aids	%	After Reported Written Aids	Without Reported Written Aids	%
Spring	100	11	9.9	69	5	6.8
Summer	118	31	20.8	131	17	11.5

times create as part of their study. It may be recalled that the SRF has a place under making written aids for indicating the time spent making up fill-in items, multiple-choice items, and essay items. As described earlier, the only item that students are tested on in the course are fill-in items. Because of this fact, it is extremely likely that students would report constructing fill-in items much more frequently than other types. This prediction is tempered by the fact that the students may have histories of writing other types of items in studying for other courses and that the contingencies in our courses may not always overcome this influence. The number of reported instances of constructing each of the item types is shown in Table 28-III. The data shows that in two quarters no type other than fill-in was reported by the students.

If the study reporting system is producing accurate and honest data from the students, there are a number of categories which should rarely if ever be used. It is possible to make this prediction because the teaching method described previously is extremely unlikely to produce certain kinds of study which might be more frequently observed in other courses.

For example, lectures in the traditional sense are not given in these courses. Although we often talk in front of the class, there are no grading contingencies based on what is said. Thus, it is very unlikely that students would report rereading lecture

TABLE 28-III

	Fill-in	%	Multiple Choice	%	Essay	%
Spring	17	100	0	0	0	0
Summer	35	100	0	0	0	0

TABLE 28-IV

Study Behavior	Quarter	Total Possible	Actual Observed	%
Rereading Lecture	Spring	968	0	0
	Summer	1044	3	0.3
Transcribing Lecture	Spring	968	0	0
	Summer	1044	1	0.1

notes as a study behavior if the system is producing valid information. An identical prediction may be made about the category of transcribing lecture notes. Table 28-IV shows the total possible number of study episodes in which rereading lecture and transcribing lecture could have been reported, the actual number of instances in which they were so reported, and the resulting percentages. The percent figures in the right-hand column are 0, one tenth of one percent, and three tenths of one percent.

In a similar manner, we may expect that using films, slides, and pictures and using "other" audio-visual aids will be rarely reported. No such aids are available for this course, and they are unlikely to be created by the student. Thus their use should not be reported if the system is producing valid information. Table 28-V shows data for both of these categories for Spring and Summer quarters. Again, we see that the prediction is strongly supported by the data.

Finally, there are similar predictions which may be made concerning the self-quizzing category, quizzing oneself on audio-visual aids or on "other" material. As before, no audio-visual

TABLE 28-V

Study Behavior	Quarter	Total Possible	Actual Observed	%
Using Audio-Visual: Films	Spring	968	0	0
	Summer	1233	2	0.2
Using Audio-Visual: Other	Spring	968	0	0
	Summer	1233	0	0

aids are available, and the remaining categories are sufficiently exhaustive so as to preclude the frequent use of the "other" category. These predictions are also borne out by the data shown in Table 28-VI. The reporting of these categories is quite rare.

An entirely different source of data regarding the validity of the system is derived from unusual patterns of academic performance which are occasionally observed in students and which should usually show corresponding variations in study if the reporting system is doing its job.

One of these patterns infrequently seen we call a reversal. This occurs when, on a particular attempt on a unit, a student's performance drops below the level of a previous performance already demonstrated on the same unit. This lower performance attempt is then followed by a performance increase on the next attempt on that unit. Such a pattern is unusual and is often due to a lack of needed study for the lower attempt. If study is a major influence in producing such performance, then a valid measuring system should show related changes in study. In this case the only clear expectation is that the total time of the study for that performance would co-vary appropriately. However, this prediction is not unequivocal. There are other variables which can influence academic performance on any particular attempt, such as health. It is also clear that the study already accumulated and the familiarity with the items both resulting from previous attempts have a cumulative effect on performance within a unit. Furthermore, different study episodes may consist of different study behaviors of varying effectiveness.

TABLE 28-VI

Study Behavior	Quarter	Total Possible	Actual Observed	%
Self-Quizzing: Audio-Visual	Spring	968	0	0
	Summer	1233	5	0.4
Self-Quizzing: Other	Spring	968	0	0
	Summer	1233	3	0.2

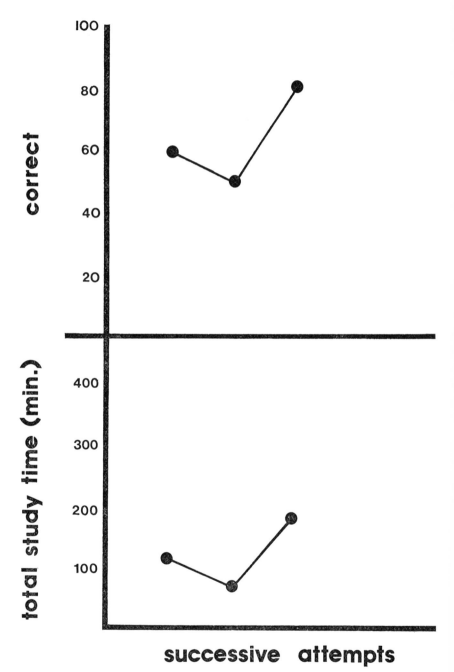

Figure 28-1. Corresponding reversal between correct performance and total study time for one student.

In spite of the potential influence of these other variables, we examined a number of such reversals for corresponding reversals in the total time studied. The upper portion of Figure 28-1 shows the performance of a student on three successive attempts within a unit in terms of percent correct. The lower graph shows the total time in minutes the student reported studying for each of those three attempts. The expected relationship may clearly be observed. Figure 28-2 shows a similar

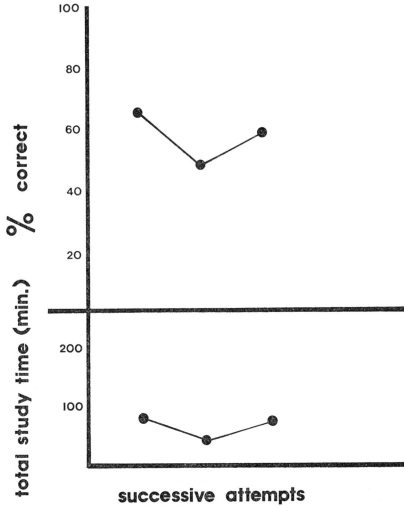

Figure 28-2. Corresponding reversal between correct performance and total study time for one student.

reversal from a different student on a different unit of material. Again, there is a corresponding reversal in the amount of study. Figure 28-3 shows four successive attempts and the related study for still another student. Although the actual range of study time varies from one student to another, as one would expect,

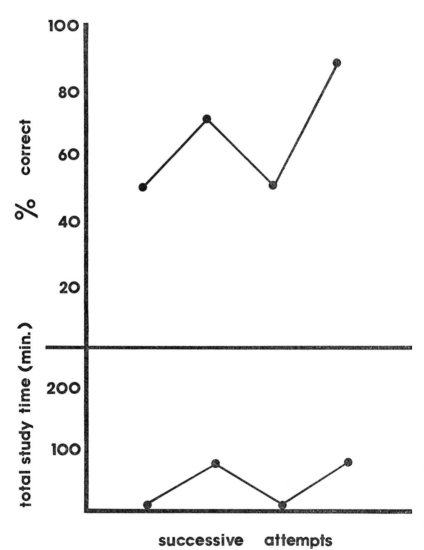

successive   attempts

Figure 28-3. Corresponding reversal between correct performance and total study time for one student.

the same direct relationship may be observed. The consistency of this prediction is not flawless. Figure 28-4 shows two such reversals on different units for the same student. The second example is expected, but the first shows a decrease in study for the low performance attempt but no increase in reported study for the following attempt of increased performance. This is similar to the failure of study to reflect the increase in performance on the fourth attempt on a unit, although the relationship is as expected for the other two changes in performance

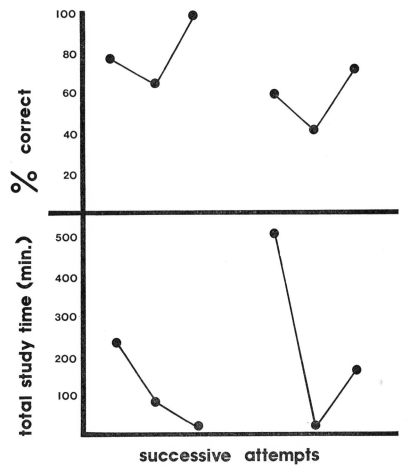

Figure 28-4. Corresponding reversals between correct performance and total study time for one student.

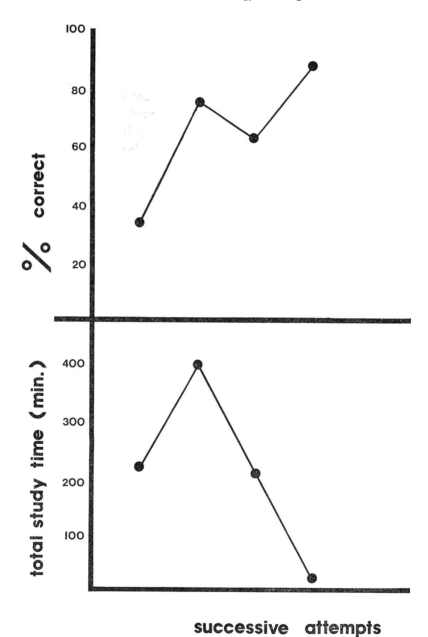

Figure 28-5. Corresponding reversals between correct performance and total study time for one student.

(see Figure 28-5). Finally, we looked at a different pattern of performance to discover if predictable amounts of study would be observed. The upper portion of Figure 28-6 shows typical performance from a student on all attempts on units two through eight. However, the fact that this student attained units three

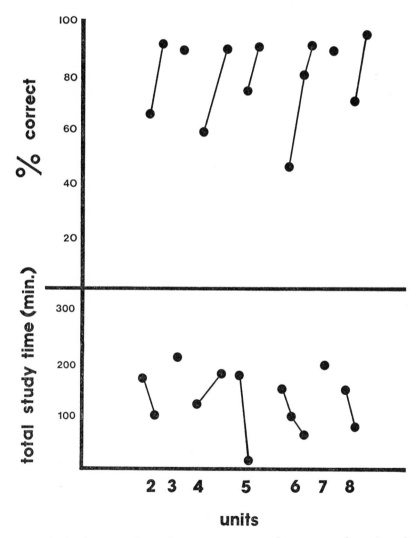

Figure 28-6. Correspondence between correct performance and total study time for one student.

and seven with only one attempt stands out from the two or three attempts required on other units. An examination of the total study times shows, as predicted, that both units three and seven have higher study times than any of the remaining units.

None of this data *proves* that the SRF and its system can or does routinely produce valid measures of student study behaviors. However, this kind of data does strongly support such a contention. The quantity, consistency, plausibility, and other characteristics of the data stand in contrast to the absense of conflicting evidence and clearly suggest a useful level of validity of this measurement system for its intended purposes.

VALIDITY OF THE STUDY REPORTING SYSTEM-II

GEORGE W. O'NEILL
WILLIAM M. WALTERS
JEAN A. RASHEED
JAMES M. JOHNSTON

A DIFFERENT SOURCE OF EMPIRICAL EVIDENCE regarding the validity of the study reporting system results from major experimental manipulations in critical variables which must unavoidably influence study behaviors.

One such variable is the quantity of subject matter which is assigned and tested. Substantial variations in the amount of this material must unequivocally cause appropriate variations in certain study behaviors, such as time spent reading for the first time, if the study reporting system is producing valid information.

This kind of data was collected as an auxiliary project to a series of experiments concerning the quantity of material or the size of a unit of subject matter. The procedural details of these studies and the resulting performance data are described in O'Neill, Johnston, Walters, and Rasheed (1974). Only the minimum details necessary to understand the paradigm will be presented here.

Data from two separate but nearly identical experiments will be presented. A total of twenty-six undergraduate students from two different quarters served as subjects. They were students who completed a junior-level course in Abnormal Psychology taught in the manner previously described in Johnston, O'Neill, Walters, & Rasheed (1974).

The independent variable was the amount of material assigned and tested, measured by the number of textbook pages in a unit. Three different size units were used in a single subject design. The small unit was approximately thirty pages in length, the medium-sized unit sixty pages long, and the large unit included about ninety pages of text. The sequence of unit size through which the students progressed in the Winter quarter was MLSLMSM. The Spring quarter sequence was SMSMLML. These particular sequences were carefully chosen from other possibilities to show all magnitudes of change in both direc-

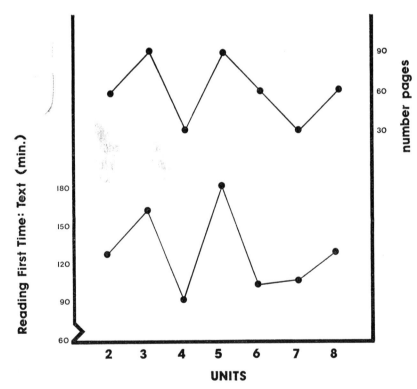

Figure 29-1. Mean time spent reading the text for the first time as a function of unit size in Winter quarter.

tions as well as to maintain the continuity of subject matter within the units. All variables other than unit size were held constant during the quarters. The number of items was controlled by presenting the student with half new and half previously seen items on each attempt on a unit after the first attempt with all new items.

There were two clear predictions from the assumption of the validity of the study report form. First, the time spent reading the text for the first time should covary strictly with unit size. Second, the total time of study for each unit would also be expected to show fairly consistent variations related to unit size, but there are obviously other variables which can influence total time of study. No clear predictions can be made for other study behaviors because we do not know how they might be influenced by variations in unit size.

The resulting influences on study behaviors may be seen in

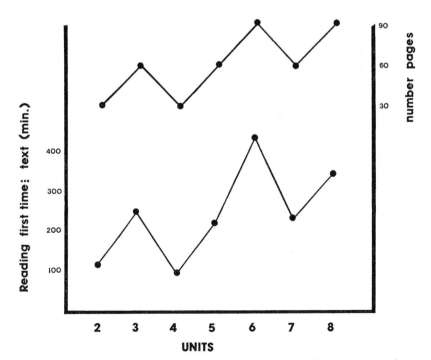

Figure 29-2. Mean time spent reading the text for the first time as a function of unit size in Spring quarter.

the following figures.   The lower portion of the first figure shows the reported mean total minutes of reading first time for all students in the Winter quarter for the sequence of different sized units.   The upper portion of the figure shows the unit sizes plotted by the number of textbook pages. You can see that the reported mean times correlate fairly closely with the unit sizes.   The same group data for Spring quarter is shown in Figure 29-2.   The correlation here between reading time and unit sizes is nearly perfect, probably due to improvements made in the study reporting system.   Figure 29-3 shows the reported

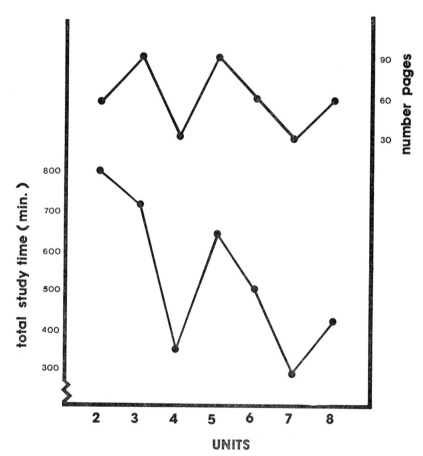

Figure 29-3.   Mean total study time as a function of unit size in Winter quarter.

total study time for all Winter quarter students. It must be understood that other variables are probably influencing total time. For instance, study times are usually slightly higher early in the quarter and slightly lower late in the quarter. Nevertheless, the same general pattern of correspondence between total study times and unit sizes may be clearly noted here. In Figure 29-4 the spring quarter students again show the predicted pattern.

This group data clearly shows the patterns of study time which would be predicted from the assumption of the validity of the study reporting system. The data for individualized students also show the same effects with great consistency. However, there are exceptional patterns of study which sometime show up, and Figure 29-5 shows one such example. Only four of the six possible changes in direction of the total amount of reported study from one unit size to the next are in the appro-

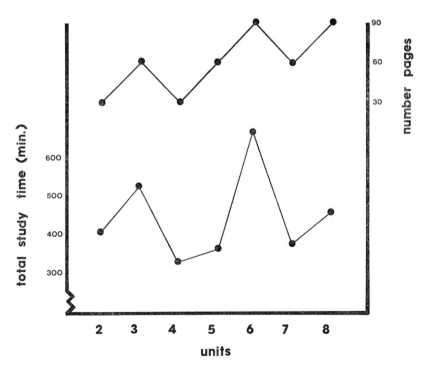

Figure 29-4. Mean total study time as a function of unit size in Spring quarter.

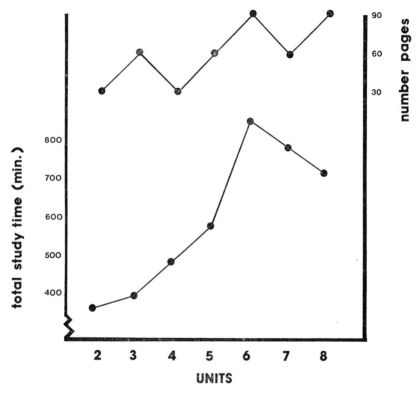

Figure 29-5. Total study time as a function of unit size for individual student.

priate direction. More unusual is the fact that for this individual student study time apparently starts off low early in the
quarter and gradually increases during the quarter. This is the
opposite of the pattern of study times usually seen. The individual student in Figure 29-6 showed four out of the six changes
in reading first time in the predicted direction as he worked
through the different unit sizes. However, the two occasions
where he showed a decrease rather than an increase were late
in the quarter, and the decreases were relatively slight. It has
typically been found that a student's study gets more efficient
as the quarter progresses, so this pattern is somewhat more un-
derstandable, except that even these slight deviations should not
be seen in the category of reading the text for the first time.

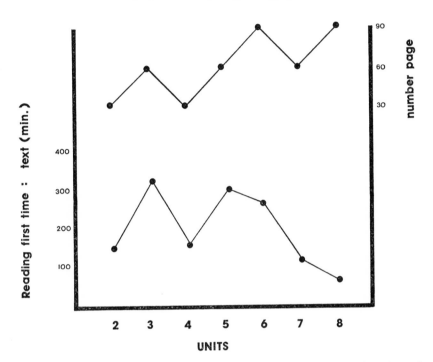

Figure 29-6. Time spent reading the text for the first time as a function of unit size for an individual student.

However, the two individuals in the next two figures show more typical patterns of times. The typical total study times or times spent reading for the first time are in the predicted direction and at about the predicted magnitude. The Figure 29-7 graph of total time shows the expected study varying as unit sizes change during the quarter. The graph presented in Figure 29-8 shows reading the text for the first time across unit sizes for another individual student. As should be the case with this particular study tactic, it covaries almost precisely with the number of pages in a unit. These two students show patterns which are more representative of the pattern shown by all the students in the group. Using the Spring quarter students, there are one-hundred and fourteen changes in total study time for all individuals. Of this total, eighteen were either in the un-predicted direction or did not change. This means that 84

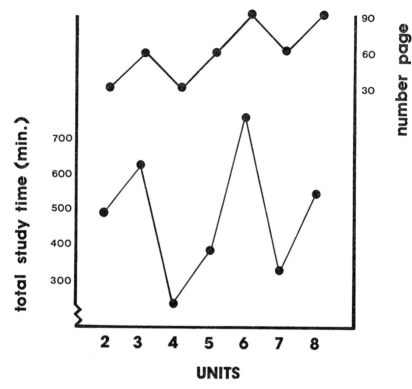

Figure 29-7. Total study time as a function of unit size for an individual student.

percent of the total possible changes were in the predicted direction. For reading the text for the first time, thirteen out of the one-hundred and fourteen changes were either in the unpredicted direction or did not change. This means that 89 percent were in the predicted direction.

As has been pointed out previously, neither the data presented here nor that presented by Walters, O'Neill, Rasheed, and Johnston (1974) in itself prove a useful level of validity for the Study Report Form and its system. However, these data reported must clearly be accepted as having strongly supported such a contention. This research program is now continuing to collect evidence concerning the validity as a part of other

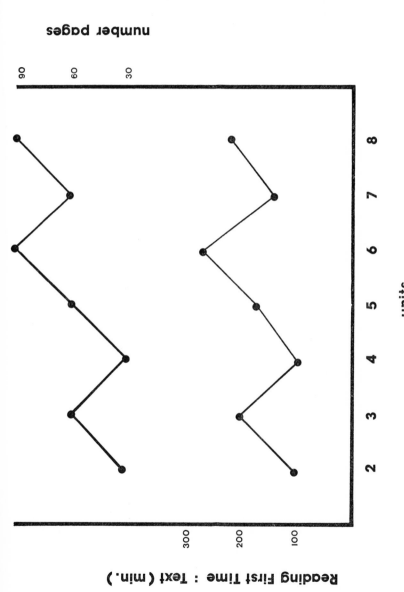

Figure 29-8. Time spent reading the text for the first time as a function of unit size for an individual student.

experiments and through manipulations directly related to the Study Report Form. It is also continuing to make refinements in the reporting system itself. However, it seems that the existing evidence is sufficient to permit the collection of data regarding basic study phenomena.

A DESCRIPTION OF TYPICAL STUDY BEHAVIORS IN A BEHAVIORALLY TAUGHT COURSE

Jean A. Rasheed
George W. O'Neill
William M. Walters
James M. Johnston

In the process of developing and beginning validation of this study reporting system, and as a part of experiments on different independent variables in the academic environment, the study behavior of a large number of students has been measured and observed over a number of quarters. Working primarily with the adnormal psychology course, we have already acquired both formal and informal data concerning the study tactics generated by our own instructional paradigm and the course textbook.

This paper describes some of the more basic characteristics of these study tactics using data from a routine nonexperimental section taught this past summer quarter. First we will look at some average group data. The first Figure shows two measures of the mean percent correct performance produced by the entire class using the procedures described earlier. The lower graph shows group performance averaged over all attempts on the units to attain the 90 percent criterion. Because the early attempts show lower levels of performance, the average of all attempts on

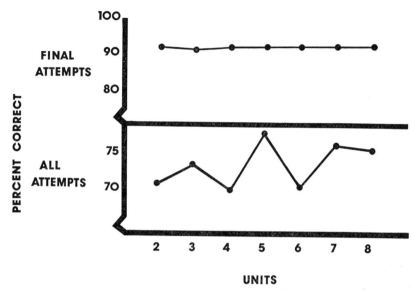

Figure 30-1. Mean correct performance on the final attempt and for all attempts across units.

each unit is always less than 90 percent. No data from Unit One are included on this or any other figures.

The upper graph shows the mean percent correct for all students on their final attempt on each unit; that is, the attempt on which the criterion was met. There is less variability in these data, and the average is predictably higher than the average of all attempts. In both graphs, the average group performance is quite stable across units, with no unit of subject matter producing markedly higher or lower performance than others. There is typically fairly little variability between students in performance data, not shoul very much be expected if the instructional procedures have a powerful effect, and if major variables are well controlled. However, by looking at study behavior a wider range of variability becomes apparent, although this variability is well hidden in group data, which can misrepresent different patterns of study between individuals.

Figure 30-2 and the following figures showing individual study data illustrate such misrepresentation. Figure 30-2 shows the mean performance and study data of all students in the course. The figure is made up of a series of graphs coordinated along the

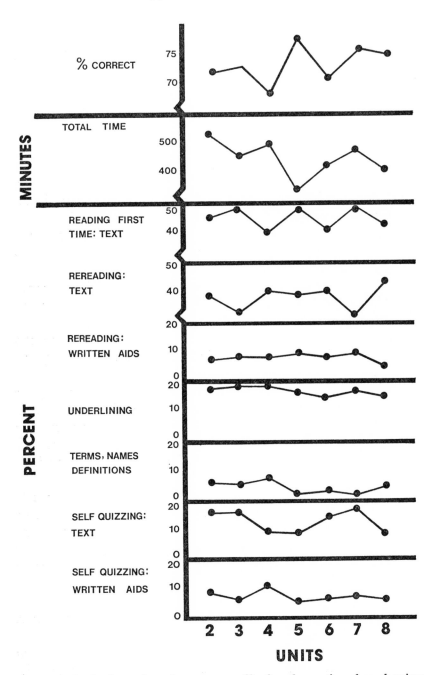

Figure 30-2. Study and performance profile for the entire class showing average data for all attempts on each unit.

abscissa showing group performance data at the top and associated study data underneath for each of units two through eight. Only data for some of the more frequently used study behaviors are shown in order to simplify the figure. Walters, O'Neill, Rasheed, and Johnston (1974) showed in this particular course, such behaviors as using audio-visual aids are rarely reported and are consequently not included.

The graph at the top of the figure is the same mean group performance data for all attempts across units shown in the first figure. The graph underneath the top one shows the mean total time in minutes for the group across each of the same units. Total study time apparently declined slightly across units during the quarter, although most units required an average of between four hundred and five hundred minutes total study (roughly seven to eight hours per unit).

All of the remaining graphs show the use of different study behaviors expressed as a percentage of the total time. It is important to keep in mind in all of the following slides that the component percentages will not necessarily add up to exactly 100 percent, since certain study behaviors (such as reading and underlining) can be emitted concurrently.

In order moving down the column of graphs are reading the text for the first time, rereading the text, rereading written aids, making written aids such as underlining and brackets, making written aids such as term, names and definitions, quizzing oneself on the text, and quizzing oneself on the written aids which were created.

Approximately 40 to 50 percent of the total time was usually expended on reading the text assignment for the first time, while thirty to forty percent of the total time was devoted to rereading the text as a study tactic. The other sudy behaviors graphed below show lower percentages of use varying around 5 to 20 percent of the total time.

The minimal variability between units in these group data masks the greater degree of variability which is characteristic of individual students, particularly with respect to the different study tactics various students use and the relative proportions of use within different students. In examining study behavior data, it becomes necessary first to separate categories of students based on the quality of performance. Thus, using standards such as the number of attempts taken to reach the ninety percent criteria and the quality of the first attempt on each unit, we can define groups of high and low students and, with less certainty, medium students. (Because of the skewed distribution of performance in this type of course, the medium students tend to be quite similar to the high students in both performance and study characteristics.) We can then look at group data or at representative individuals from these groups.

Figure 30-3 shows the performance and study data of a student who showed typically good performance. He took two to three attempts per unit with the first attempt usually being around 75 percent correct.

The total time studied per unit on the first attempt ranged between three-hundred to five-hundred minutes, with time expended on subsequent units dropping sharply to around one-hundred minutes. The percent of the total time spent reading the text for the first time was around 50 percent on the first attempt, dropping to approximately zero on susequent attempts. In other words, the student read the entire unit before his first performance on a unit. The next graph down the column shows that he used rereading as a study tactic only on three occasions.

Continuing down the column, underlining was used at almost exactly the same times and in the same percentages as was reading the text for the first time, illustrating a fairly typical pattern.

The next graph shows that this student began the quarter by not quizzing himself at all on the written aids which he had created (underlining and fill-in questions). However, on all units after the first two, self-quizzing on these two types of written aids constituted a major study tactic for second or third attempts within units.

Finally, on a few occasions, this student studied with other students using quizzing as a tactic.

Figure 30-4 shows the same data for another representative "good" student. His performance data indicate that he usually took only two attempts per unit, but his first attempts were a bit lower than those of the previous student. Total times on

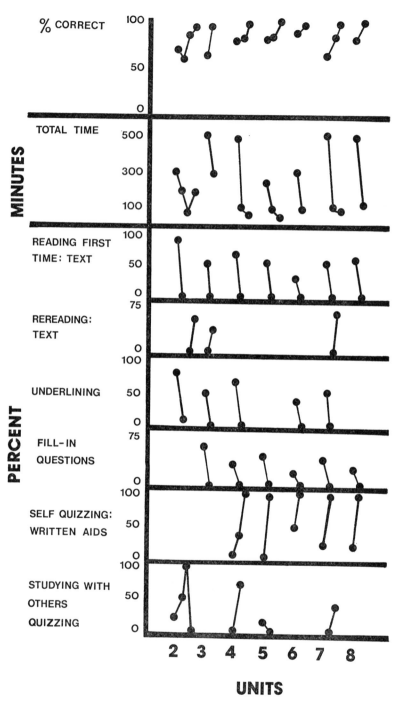

Figure 30-3. Individual study and performance profile showing all attempts for a representative good student.

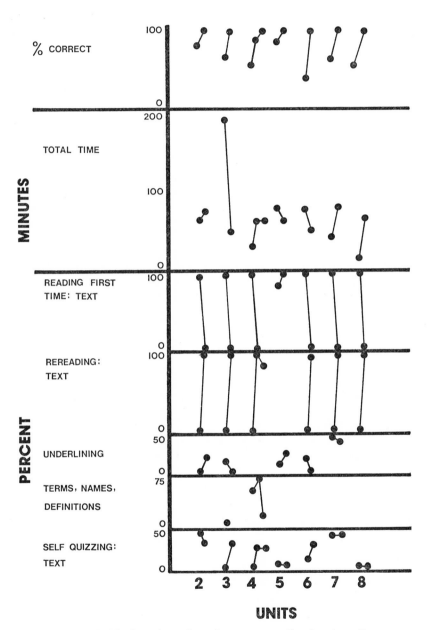

Figure 30-4. Individual study and performance profile showing all attempts for a representative good student.

first attempts were (with the exception of Unit Two) quite stable near seventy-five minutes—dramatically shorter than the total times of the first student. Also different for this student is the fact that on half of the units there was an increase in study time on the second attempt. This increase is consonant with the fact that his first attempts were lower than those of the first student, and that he produced a big jump in performance in order to make criterion on the second attempt. The first student, in contrast, often took three attempts.

Continuing down the column of graphs, reading first time data and rereading data show the same patterns as observed on previous figures; that is, all the reading of the text occurred on the first attempt (except on Unit Four) and rereading was used only on subsequent attempts.

Written aids were not a major study tactic with this student, although he fairly regularly reported that he quizzed himself on the text. Such patterns are consistent with his high level of rereading the text and low level of making any written aids on which he could quiz himself.

Figure 30-5 shows a student who produced what can be generally characterized as "poor" performance. Examination of the percent correct performance graph at the top of the figure indicates that he took three to four attempts per unit, with small increments in performance on each attempt and low quality of performance on the early attempts on each unit.

Total study times were around three-hundred minutes on first attempts but were variable on subsequent attempts. Reading the text for the first time was typical in pattern, and underlining (next to the bottom) shows highly correlated patterns. Rereading the text was fairly variable in occurrence, sharing percentage points with rereading written aids (underlining and occasional terms, names, and definitions).

Figures 30-3, 30-4, and 30-5 showing study tactics and performance for three individual students give a picture of typical basic study behaviors generated by these teaching methods. However, they are overly full of data, and make specific comparisons somewhat difficult. Pulling out parts of this individual data to examine in more detail may be instructive. For the purposes of

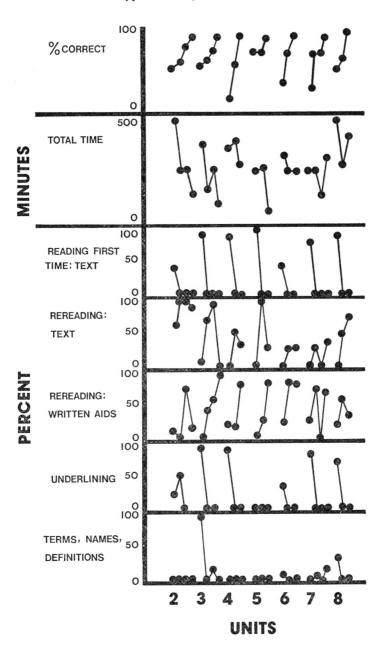

Figure 30-5. Individual study and performance profile showing all attempts for a representative poor student.

analysis, the data of the first and third students just seen will be used. The first might be generally characterized as a "good" student and the second as a "poor" student.

The next two graphs will show the percent correct performance for all attempts across units and the total study time which produced that performance. However, here the total study time have been plotted cumulatively in order to show more clearly the total quantity for study time which accumulated within each unit. Also note a change in the scale of the percent correct graph.

Study on the fifth and sixth units for this good student stands out because there was relatively less of it compared to other units. However, the total study time cumulated throughout attempts on most units was more than six-hundred minutes.

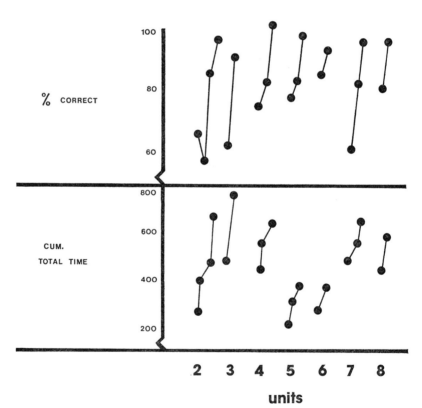

Figure 30-6. Correct performance and total study time for the good student.

Compare this data with that of the poor student shown here in Figure 30-7. (Again note a different scale for percent correct.) The amount of study for the first attemepts is about the same. However, because of the greater number of attempts required to meet criterion, this student finally accumulated more total study time within most units by the time he attained the 90 percent criterion. That is, he seemed to be using much less efficient study tactics to get to the same final level of performance as that of the good student.

It is useful to examine further details of the study of these two students to determine a possible explanation for this inefficiency in the study tactics used. Figure 30-8 shows the same performance and total time data for the good student, except that the ordinate scales are different and total time is once again plotted noncumulatively. These are repeated in order to relate to them his reading first time and rereading data. Around 50 percent of the total time was spent reading the text on first attempts,

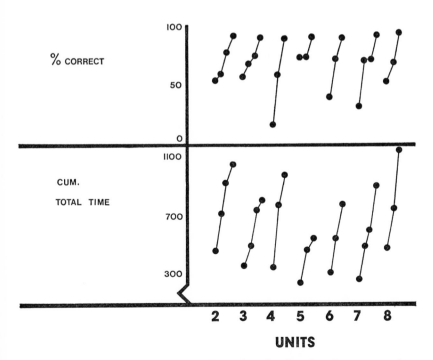

Figure 30-7. Correct performance and total study time for the poor student.

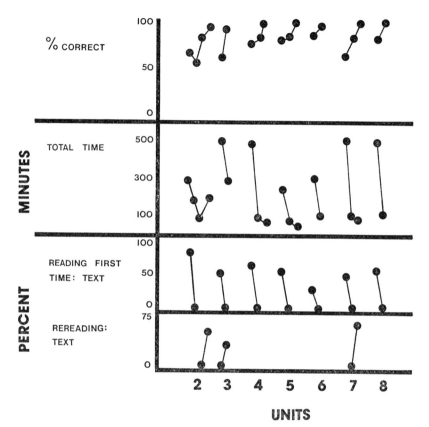

Figure 30-8. Performance and study data for the good student.

and rereading was used as a study tactic in only three attempts.

Figure 30-9 shows the same categories for the poor student. Although is percent reading first times were usually higher, his rereading percentages were much higher. Rereading was much more frequently used, suggesting that one of the contributions to the poorer performance and lowered efficiency of this student could be the extensive reliance on reading and particularly on rereading as study tactics.

It is important to look in detail at some of the remaining study behaviors shown by these two students. Figure 30-10 shows data from the good student for two categories of making written aids—underlining and writing fill-in questions, and for rereading written

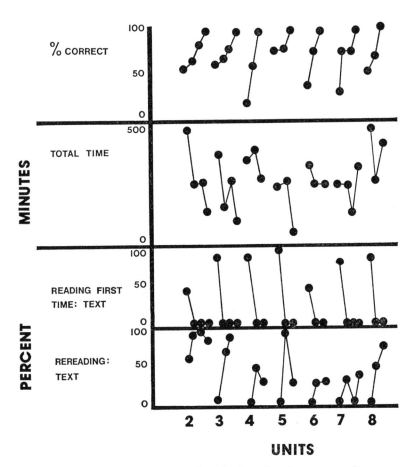

Figure 30-9. Performance and study data for the poor student.

aids and self-quizzing on written aids. After reading the text, this student spent much of his time on the first attempts making up his own fill-in questions in addition to underlining while he read. Notably, he spent no time at all rereading these written aids; instead, after Unit Three, he spent a good bit of time quizzing himself on the written aids.

Figure 30-11 shows the poor student's data for most of the same categories. He also underlined or marked in his book as he read for the first attempts, as well as writing down terms, names, or definitions on a few occasions. He spent a great deal of time,

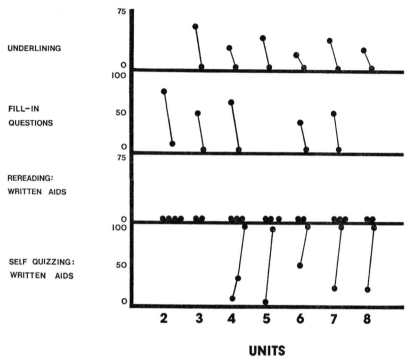

UNITS

Figure 30-10. Study data for the good student.

however, rereading his written aids and no time at all quizzing on written aids.

These data again suggest that rereading may be a relatively weak study tactic, and that self-quizzing may be a relatively strong one. This observation is only a casual one which data over a period of time have suggested. Proposing at this stage that these observations are anything more than tentative hypotheses would be inappropriate.

Efficiency in study behavior, that is, the least effort for the most performance, is a real concern in this area. Instructional methods exist which can produce a narrow and consistently high level of performance within a wide range of students. The only difference between students, then, is in how much effort it takes to get to that level. Study tactics are a class of variables which are potentially available to the teacher and the student to manipulate in order to minimize the effort required to produce good

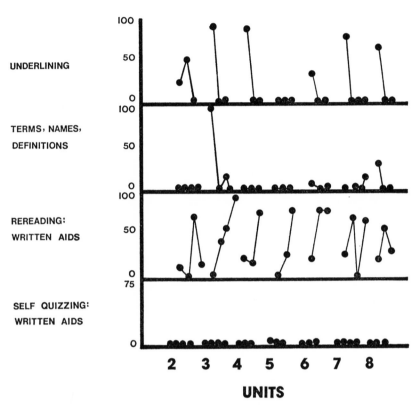

UNDERLINING

TERMS, NAMES, DEFINITIONS

REREADING: WRITTEN AIDS

SELF QUIZZING: WRITTEN AIDS

UNITS

Figure 30-11. Study data for the poor student.

performance, in the same way that other variables such as test frequency, unit size, or performance criteria may be manipulated.

The purpose of this paper has been to show the kind of data which this study reporting system produces and one of the means by which they can be analyzed, as well as to describe some basic study tactics which are produced by these teaching methods.

The study of studying is an investigation of one of the major variables in the academic environment which has too long been neglected. The empirical approach taken here to address this variable has required a great deal of developmental groundwork to reach this stage, and additional preliminary work remains. However, this program is increasingly close to being in a position to launch a major, long-term investigation in college student study behavior.

SOME GENERAL PROPOSALS

THIS FINAL SELECTION OF PAPERS is primarily constituted of non-data position statements having broad generality. The first paper, "Behavioral Instruction In College Classrooms: A Review Of Methodological Procedures," is a discussion of research considerations which should be of concern to future investigators. The second paper, "The Findley Procedure: A Method For Examining Choice-Making Behavior In Academic Settings," describes a method for determining student preferences by letting students actually choose a method (or other feature) and live with that choice for a while. The next paper presents a means of actually applying accountability notions to teaching efficiency and effectiveness. The next paper discusses the definition of teaching itself and presents a proposal for changing the orientation of traditional definitions. The final paper takes this definition and other corollaries of this approach to instruction and proposes a reorganization of the entire structure of our institutions of higher education.

BEHAVIORAL INSTRUCTION IN COLLEGE CLASSROOMS: A REVIEW OF METHODOLOGICAL PROCEDURES[1]

JOHN S. WODARSKI, PH.D.
DAVID BUCKHOLDT, PH.D.

F EW EDUCATORS WOULD DISPUTE THE FACT that it behooves us to design better methods for teaching on the college level. One new method which appears to have some logical appeal as well as empirical support is the personalized instruction method suggested by Johnston and Pennypacker (1971), Keller (1966, 1968), and Malott and Svinicki (1969). The essential common elements of the personalized instruction method, with variations, are as follows:

1. Course content is divided into sub-units.
2. Students move from one unit to another only when they demonstrate mastery of a preceding unit.
3. Students progress through the units at their own rate.
4. Lectures and demonstration are used primarily as vehicles for motivation rather than as sources of information.
5. Student proctors are used to provide repeated testing,

[1] Preparation of this manuscript was facilitated through funding from U.S.P.H.S. research grant MH18813, awarded by the National Institute of Mental Health, Center for Studies of Crime and Delinquency.

immediate scoring and feedback, personalized tutoring, and interpersonal support.

6. Student learning goals are defined in terms of behavioral objectives.

Since different investigators use different combinations of the procedures mentioned above and a pat technology does not exist, it may be inaccurate to use the term "personalized instruction" to refer to the general area. Therefore, a more generic label, such as behavioral instruction, which can inculde a variety of specific operations such as personalized instruction, precision teaching, and so forth with the common denominator being an empirical approach to teaching may be a more appropriate term and will be used throughout the manuscript. Numerous claims have been made that this method of teaching is more effective than other methods, particularly as compared to the standard lecture methods (Alba and Pennypacker, 1972; Born, Gledhill and Davis, 1972b; Cooper and Greiner, 1971; Keller, 1966, 1968; McMichael and Corey, 1969; Morris and Kimbrell, 1972; Sheppard and Mac-Dermot, 1970).

The purpose of this paper is twofold; first to examine some general methodological problems with studies in behavioral instruction, particularly problems related to the lack of control of biasing factors which make the interpretation of experimental results ambiguous; and second, to suggest several methodological precautions which will help to make future studies of behavioral instruction more reliable and thus more conclusive. A review of twenty articles provides the basis for this crituque.

Since the review will be critical at times, the authors feel a need to explain their motivation for writing this article. Both authors are involved in the design and evaluation of intervention programs based on operant principles. They both believe that regorous research and development in various areas of behavior analysis will establish reliable procedures for the remediation of many social and educational problems, such as inadequate reading and math skills among children, anti-social behavior exhibited by deviant children, potential dropouts capable of college level performance, and so forth. However, the authors are alarmed at the zeal of some of their colleagues. Zeal, in this case, is not meant as a synonym for enthusiasm, but rather as a tendency to make scientific statements about behavioral instruction which go well beyond the available evidence. Certainly a productive scienctist is committed and enthusiastic but he is also continually suspicious. He cannot afford to become overly dedicated to a set of hypotheses or procedures for he is likely to be misled into finding the expected when other factors may actually be operating. To avoid this possibility, the good scientist constantly searches for alternative explanations of his data. As rival hypotheses emerge, additional experiments are conducted to control for them. If the original hypotheses are retained in the process, the scientist has taken an important step in convincing himself and others that he is correct.

This paper will examine the evidence and the claims about the data from a number of studies on behavioral instruction programs. It will provide no new data and the review will not evaluate each study individually unless a particular point is pertinent to the items being reviewed. Instead, the authors will identify potential biases in many of the studies and in the process suggest possible alternative explanations of the data. The paper is written with the hope that future studies on behavioral instruction will be better designed and thus will provide more reliable and more conclusive evidence on the effects of this new teaching method. Specific items discussed are the importance of adequate controls, experimenter bias, identification of effective components of behavioral instruction, choice of dependent variables, and generalization effects.

The Importance of a Control Group

The traditional experimental designs in behavior analysis research are the reversal, the multiple baseline single subject designs, and the variations of these two designs (Baer, Wolf, and Risley, 1968; Bijou, Peterson, Harris, Allen and Johnston, 1969; Leitenberg, 1973). These designs use subjects as their own controls rather than comparing them with another control group(s). As Baer (1971) notes, these designs are appropriate for functional studies in which the investigator is studying or demonstrating the relationship between one behavior and another, or an environmental contingency, but they generally will not suffice when an investigator is asking comparative questions of group behavior rather than analytical questions of individual behavior. For Baer the questions which traditional experimental control groups are to answer are actuarial questions, not analyticones. They do not ask how behavior works, they ask only if the procedures employed in the experimental group will solve the referred problem at a higher probability than chance.

The optimal strategy for developing an effective program for behavioral instruction may be to isolate, functionally analyze, revise, and improve each component of the program until the important elements can be integrated to form a total program through the use of reversal and multiple baseline designs. With a few exceptions (Miller & Weaver, 1972), however, investigators in the field have not chosen this strategy. Instead, they generally have begun with an experimental program which they then compare with one or more control groups which receive some form of traditional instruction, e.g. lectures, exams covering large portions of the text, and so forth. Some studies report positive results of the experimental group with no mention of a control group (Collier & Smith, 1971; Keller, 1966, 1968; Malott and Svinicki, 1969; Myers, 1970).

The best control procedure for forming experimental and control groups is to randomly assign students to one condition or the other. Random assignment provides the best protection against rival hypotheses that can be postulated to account for the data (Campbell, 1967, Campbell, 1969, Campbell & Stanley, 1967). Born and his associates (1972b) used random assignment plus GPA's in assigning students to various groups. These procedures protected against rival hypotheses that could be postulated to account for the findings. Hence, a basic requisite for any study is the provision of adequate control through random assignment.

If random assignment is not possible, as is often the case in natural settings, there are statistical (analysis of covariance) and other control procedures which can be used to adjust for initial group differences. Sheppard and MacDermot (1970) placed students whose last names started with the letters from *A* through

O in the experimental group and the others in the control group. Unless there is some reason to believe that students whose last names come at the front of the alphabet differ from students whose last names come at the end, such an assignment strategy is probably an acceptable compromise to random assignment. It is certainly better than comparing an experimental group to a comparison group from another geometric area (Keller, 1968), a comparison group from another year (Farmer, Lachter, Blaustein, and Cole, 1972; Sullivan, 1972), or a self-selected control group from the same population (Alba & Pennypacker, 1972; Cooper & Greiner, 1971; McMichael & Corey, 1969; Morris & Kimbrell, 1972; Stalling, 1971; Whitehurst, 1972). Likewise, indicating that groups which are not randomly composed are not significantly different on initial measures such as an inventory of multiple choice items designed to measure knowledge of psychology, grade point average, and so forth, does not control for different maturation rates of different groups which can confound the results of the study (Campbell, 1969).

When random assignment is not practical, it is imperative that pre- as well as post-test data are obtained. The experimental treatment can then be evaluated through an analysis of change scores between T_1 and T_2, with adjustments made for initial group differences at T. Most of the studies in this area (Born, et al. 1972b; Farmer, et al., 1972; McMichael and Corey, 1969) have used post-test measurement only. Without some guarantee that the experimental control groups started at the same level of psychological knowledge at T_1, several rival hypotheses are plausible to account for post-test differences at T_2, especially since many of these studies are characterized by nonrandom assignment of subjects. For example, the experimental groups may have had more students with an interest in psychology or brighter students who had a special interest in creative or different teaching methods. The control group may have had more males than females or more athletes who wanted to meet only minimum requirements. Several researchers have hidden the nature of the experimental treatment from enrolling students (Alba & Pennypacker, 1972; Cooper & Greiner, 1971; Farmer, *et al.* 1972; McMichael & Corey, 1969; Sheppard & MacDermot, 1970, Whitehurst, 1972) but, without random assignment, this is no substitute for testing initial differences before the experimental intervention. Thus, it would seem that the basic experimental design that is required in order to test the efficacy of utilizing behavioral modification technology in the classroom would be a design where students are pre-tested at T_1 and then post-tested at T_2 and randomly assigned to experimental and control groups. However, in some instances because of financial considerations, time, administrative concerns, manpower, and other factors pre-test data may not be available. In these instances the investigator must assume that random assignment controlled for initial differences.

There are three final points with respect to control groups. First, even when groups are compared at T_1 and statistical control procedures such as covariance are used to correct for initial differences, the researcher needs to carefully consider the covariates to insure that he is controlling for important variables, i.e. variables that have some conceptual association with the dependent measures. Variables such as pre-test scores on a psychology exam, sex, year in school, and interest in psychology may be important to control in an evaluation of a psychology course using behavioral instruction. Verbal and math scores on SAT or overall grade point average may not be as relevant for control purposes (Born, *et al.* 1972b; Morris & Kimbrell, 1972; Stalling, 1971). The covariant should be equating all the groups at T_1 on a scale that measures or is directly related to the performance criteria being used in the investigation. Consequently, it would seem that for psychology courses the appropriate covariant would be an inventory that assessed knowledge of psychology.

Second, control groups do not necessarily provide needed controls merely because they are labelled as control groups. They serve their purpose best when they provide subjects as similar to the experimental subjects as possible and when they experience the same conditions as the experimental treatment except, of course, for the experimental condition. In most studies on behavioral instruction where a control or control groups are used it is not clearly specified what the procedures are controlling for. For example, in many instances behavioral instruction is composed of student proctors, special projects, daily evaluation, testing and feedback, reinforcement contingencies, increased time spent studying, increased interaction among students and the professor, different grading procedures (assignments are repeated until they reach acceptability) and so forth. In order to get a clear specification of what variables account for the largest percentage of variance in the students' academic behavior each one of these factors would have to be controlled. Farmer and his associates (1972) provide a good example of how to utilize control groups to evaluate whether different amounts of peer proctoring had an effect on final exam performance. Each of the five groups in the study were exposed to either the 0 percent, 25 percent, 50 percent, 75 percent, or 100 percent proctoring condition. This procedure enabled Farmer and his associates to specify how each condition affected final exam performance.

Finally, one potent issue to be resolved is whether adequate controls are provided through traditional experimental procedures, i.e. where certain groups of individuals are only exposed to certain experimental and control procedures, or where subjects serve as their own controls in reversal or multiple baseline designs. This issue is best evaluated in terms of the questions the investigators are asking, resources available for the study, and the desired amount of protection against uncontrolled factors which may systematically bias the data.

Reversal and multiple baseline designs have a number of advantages. They are easy to implement, that is, they are inexpensive in terms of money, energy required to implement them, administrative execution, and so forth. They provide the necessary data to analyze which person's behaviors have changed in comparison to group designs where such changes are difficult to assess. Through the use of repeated measures of dependent and independent variables behavior modification designs enable the investigator to monitor change daily. Moreover, since these designs employ repeated measures of the dependent variable they provide a more accurate estimate of experimental effects than procedures. However, if several variables are being investigated these designs generally produce confounding effects among experimental treatments. Moreover, if a few cases are used which are not randomly picked from the target population a worthwhile procedure may be abandoned after a few unsuccessful trials because of a treatment subject interaction; or if a large number of experiments are conducted and only the successful ones are reported a procedure that is effective only with students who have certain characteristics may be promoted for all. Computer programs are now available which alleviate one of the biggest criticisms leveled against reversal designs; that is, the nonutilization of statistical procedures to assess results (Gentile, Roden, and Klein, 1972; Gottam, 1973; Leitenberg, 1973; Poor, 1973).

Since academice behaviors are the primary concern in a behavioral instruction study, a reversal design may be inappropriate because many times the behaviors in the second baseline period will not return to the level of the first baseline rate; that is, performance behaviors once acquired may be brought under the control of a stimulus different from the experimental one, such as self-contingencies, natural environmental contingencies, and so forth. In multiple baseline designs the behavioral changes can generalize to other behaviors prior to the implementation of modification procedures for these behaviors (Gottman, 1973; Hartman & Atkinson, 1973; Deitenberg, 1973). This problem can be alleviated through the specification of behaviors in such a manner that they are independent.

The use of the reversal design in college settings may also pose some ethical questions. Since various learning behaviors are brought under stimulus control the investigators have the ethical responsibility to program the students' environment after the experiment to insure that the beneficial behaviors are brought under the control of the natural contingencies of a college environment through some type of fading procedures (Baring & Stover, 1971; Hartman & Atikinson, 1973).

In comparison, traditional designs have the following characteristics. They do not produce confounding effects and there are established statistical procedures for the evaluation. They are, however difficult to implement, the criteria of random assignment is hard to meet, if random assignment is not used students' changes may be alleviated due to unequal variances and regression factors, and so forth.

Consequently, the issue of which design to utilize must be

resolved in terms of the question being asked and the data needed to answer it sufficiently. In many instances an incorporation of positive features from both behavior modification designs and traditional experimental procedures may lead to a strong investigation.

Experimenter Bias

When human observation or interpretation is involved in experimental or evaluative research, biasing factors can affect the dependent variables unless adequate methodological procedures are used. Rosenthal and others have documented the importance of what they called expectation effects, experimenter effects, data analysis contamination, and so forth on the results of experiments (Goldstein, 1962; Rosenthal & Rosnow, 1969; Shapiro, 1971). More recent studies have shown that the behavior of a human observer or rater can vary, depending on whether the observer is aware of the experimental hypotheses, knows that the behavior is being simultaneously used by others to assess reliability, and so forth (Johnson and Bolstad, 1973; Jones, 1973; O'Leary and Kent, 1973; Romanczyk, Kent, Diament, and O'Leary, 1973; Skindurd, 1973).

The contaminating effects of experimenter bias could enter research studies on behavioral instruction in several ways. The first, and probably the most important, bias could come in the teaching of the control classes. The control class may be less stimulating than usual. The researcher may unintentionally communicate his hypothesis that control students will not perform as well as experimental students. Control classes may receive fewer cues about future exam questions and/or less encouragement to study hard and earn high marks. In one study the experimenter conducted both the experimental and the control classes (Sheppard and MacDermot, 1970). There is no way to estimate how much if any bias resulted from this practice, but unless such potential bias is controlled or measured, there will always be some suspicion that the expectations or enthusiasm factors were operating in favor of the experimental group. A second way in which bias can enter occurs during student evaluation. If subjective or essay questions are used and the graders can distinguish experimental from control subjects, the risk of bias from graders who have a commitment to the experimental hypothesis is considerable. Even in more objective examinations, there is contamination risk if the graders can distinguish control from experimental subjects. Due to inadequate reporting the reviewers could not determine, except in two cases (Alba and Pennypacker, 1972; Born, *et al.* 1972b), whether tests were graded by people who had knowledge of the subject coming from the experimental or control group. In our own research, we have occasionally discovered considerable unreliability in even the transfer of objective scores from coding forms to summary data sheets, and the unreliability generally has favored the experimental group. Likewise, examinations for evaluation were prepared by investigators who knew the purposes of the study (Born, *et al.* 1972b and Stalling, 1971). Examinations were given by instructors or proctors who had some commitment to the experimental hypotheses (Johnston and Pennypacker, 1971; McMichael and Corey, 1969; Stalling, 1971). It is difficult to assess the actual effects of such factors.

Investigators in the drug research field have discovered that the contaminating effects of the experimenter, observer, and subject expectation can be so significant that blind, and even double-blind, precautions are needed. In the simple-blind experiment, the subjects either do not know they are participating in an experiment or they do not know whether they are in the experimental or control treatment groups. In the double-blind situation, the observers, raters, testers and other data takers do not know the nature of the hypotheses and/or do not know which subjects are in the experimental or control groups.

Such precautions may be difficult, if not impossible, for research on behavioral instruction at the college level. However, researchers might protect themselves from potential bias in several ways. First, they could conceal the group identity of subjects when tests are graded or other ratings are made and provide adequate reliability procedures to insure consistent collection of data. For example, Born and his associates (1972b) disguised the identity of the students' examination questions and had three investigators independently rate the questions; the students were then assigned the average of the three ratings. Likewise, Alba and Pennypacker (1972) used a blind disinterested party to grade examination performance. Second, researchers might gather some independent comparisons of the two teaching methods on dimensions such as teacher enthusiasm, encouragement, support, and classroom climate. Third, they could interview students from both groups to discover if they perceived that different expectations were held for the different experimental or control groups and to determine how they reacted to these behavioral cues if they perceived them. Fourth, an investigator may wisely consider the possibility of several experimental and several control groups with several instructors in each condition who are enthusiastic about their teaching methods. Such a procedure may allow some control for expectation effects as well as give estimates of both treatment and teacher effects. Finally, independent examination construction and administration could protect against rival hypotheses that could be postulated to account for the data.

Thus, although expectation biases are generally not intentional, they often introduce extraneous factors into experiments. In the future, we need to carefully control for these unwanted effects if our data is to be reliable. We do not want to follow in the footsteps of Verplanck (Azrin, Holz, Ulrich, and Goldiamond, 1961).

Identification of Effective Components of Behavioral Instruction

If we assume for the moment that the available studies on behavioral instruction were well designed and analyzed correctly, and if we also assume that these studies support the hypothesis of a significant difference between behavioral instruction and other modes of instruction, we still would not know which components of behavioral instruction contribute to its success and which do not. Does the method require student proctors, frequent quizzes, continuous monitoring and feedback, special contingencies such as the Doom's Day contingency (Malott and Svinicki, 1969), special grading practices, some combination of these elements or all of them? Some critics may argue that the superior effects of behavioral instruction are attributable to an increase in student tutoring behavior. Since there is some evidence of the positive effects for students who tutor one another (Ettres, 1967; Fraser, Beaman and Kelem, 1972; Gartner, Kohler and Riessman, 1971), it may be that tutoring is responsible for the success of behavioral instruction. Others may argue that the important component is the more frequent quizzing and feedback in behavioral instruction than in traditional instruction and additional time required for the behavioral instruction. Born and his associates (1972a) found that students do spend more time studying in behavioral instruction classes as compared to regular classes. Only one study minimally controlled for the factor of time on task (Morris and Kimbrell, 1972). Likewise, overt responding, feedback, and more frequent questioning may influence student performance (Tobias, 1973). The timing of questions and feedback may also be important. Rothkopf (1968), for example, reports that questions imbedded every few pages in prose material improves reading performance over no questions, questions presented only before reading, or questions presented only after reading. Moreover, Dustin (1971) provides data that suggests that students grads improve with increased frequency of testing. Still others may claim that the contingency is important, that is, a student must complete a prior unit before moving on to another unit and his grade is determined by how many units he completes in a maximum amount of time.

A serious, long-term evaluation of behavioral instruction must consider the contribution of each component of the model. It may be that some elements are essential to the success of the program while others are not so important or may even contribute nothing. Investigators should clearly identify the important elements of their model and then investigate which elements are essential to the success of the model (Greenspoon and Simkins, 1968; Siegal and Siegal, 1967). A good example of this sort of component analysis can be found in the analytic study which replicated the effects of the "Good Behavior Game" (Barrish, Saunders and Wolf, 1969) and experimentally analyzed the component parts to determine which elements contributed to the success of the game (Medland and Stachnik, 1972).

Dependent Variables

Dependent measures vary from study to study. Some investigators have used objective written questions such as multiple choice, true-false, and fill-in-the-blanks while others have used essay questions and/or personal interviews. The use of a variety of measures has resulted in some interesting findings. For example, students experiencing behavioral instruction do better on examinations containing essay and fill-in-the-blank questions than students experiencing lecture-type courses (Born, *et al.* 1972b). However, such a diversity of measures leads to a problem of comparability between studies. A more important problem, however, is the apparent assumption that behavioral instruction will lead to gains on multiple dependent measures, regardless of the specific response modes that the students practice during instruction. For example, students who practice on frequent multiple choice tests during the semester may do better on a post-multiple choice test than a control group but they may do no better on an essay examination. On the other hand, students who are tested through frequent personal interviews may do better than their controls on post-test interviews but may do no better on fill-in-the-blank questions. There are really two issues here. The first concerns the problem of whether an instructional procedure will show significant gains over a control procedure on multiple different response modes or whether the gains will be limited to the response or testing mode used during instruction. The second issue is whether the superiority of the experimental group is due to the fact that they actually learned more in the course or that they had more practice with the response mode during instruction. For example, if experimental subjects take multiple-choice tests frequently during a semester while the control subjects do not, post-test difference on multiple-choice tests may be due to actual treatment differences or to more frequent testing and more familiarity with multiple-choice tests in the experimental group. To control for this potential bias, control subjects should take the same number and same kind of tests that are required of the experimental subjects. An investigator may also want to gather some dependent measures which are unrelated to the response or testing mode of either group during instruction. Thus, it would seem that an adequate conceptualization of what dimensions should be evaluated and what measures would provide the necessary data are called for. Certainly, final exam responses in all modes are relevant dependent variables. Likewise, proctor, interview, and studying behaviors may be relevant to the hypothesis being tested. Reliability procedures for all dependent as well as independent variables, such as utilization of videotapes and independent observers' ratings of the performance of experimental and control subjects' interview behaviors should be developed.

Finally, methodological procedures of different grading systems for experimental and control groups and among investigations confound the comparisons that could be made among studies (Born, *et al.* 1972b; McMichael and Corey, 1969; Sheppard and MacDermot, 1970; Whitehurst, 1972). For example, in the study conducted by Born and his associates (1972b), in addition to the various elements of behavioral instruction, one experimental condition included a special project, e.g. doing a small experiment, reading and writing a report on material related to the course, and so forth, so the student could earn extra points for his final grade. It is obvious that these additional projects confound the variable of behavioral instruction.

Generalization

Questions of generalization concern problems about the extension of conclusions to other situations or circumstances. Researchers want to know if the relationships they discover in one setting apply generally to many settings or whether they are limited to some special set of situational variables. With the exception of Myers (1970), who used behavioral instruction in a statistics course, and Keller (1968) who reports the use of behavioral instruction for a physics course, the majority of behavioral instruction studies have been carried out on psychology students, particularly undergraduate students enrolled in introductory psychology. Consequently, we know very little about how appropriate or effective behavioral instruction would be with other types of students, other courses of instruction, or other instructors.

The generalization question which is probably of most immediate concern is the question of possible interaction between behavioral instruction and student ability and the aptitude-treatment interaction question (Cronback and Snow, 1969). In reading research investigators have discovered that children with more visual sequencing skills do better on look-say reading instruction while children with poorer visual sequencing skills do better with phonetic instruction (Della-Piana and Ando, 1973). The same sort of ability-treatment interaction may hold for behavioral instruction. Low ability students or students with less self-discipline (whatever that is), may do better on behavioral instruction while high ability students may learn more in courses which are less structured and give them license to explore new areas and to read more widely.

Discussion

The studies reviewed for this paper support the general hypothesis that behavioral instruction is an effective strategy for college training. However, the majority of the studies contained one or more of the following methodological pitfalls which make their interpretation ambiguous.

1. An adequate control group is not provided in most of the studies. Without random selection of experimental and control subjects or pre-measure, which can be statistically equated or covaried, the audience cannot be sure that the two groups were equal at the beginning of the experiment.

2. In general no attempt is made to isolate the effects of each of the several components of the behavior instructional model. Since several of the components have individually shown significant effects in other research, the andience does not know if the effects of the behavioral instruction are due simply to one or two components or depend on the combination or interaction of the several components. It is essential to isolate the effect, i.e. com-

ponents, in order to make the technology more powerful and delete those factors which would add to the cost of implementing the procedures in college classrooms.

3. Does the success of behavioral instruction depend on a course content with specific, concrete goals or would literature courses or other courses with similar definable objectives also benefit from this technology? The available research does not shed much light on this question.

4. Is there an aptitude-treatment interaction or do some students do better with this instructional technology than others? Some investigators have begun to isolate student characteristics, e.g. poor academic skills (Born, *et al.* 1972b; Born and Whelan, 1973; Sheppard and MacDermot, 1970) and other factors in a student's environment, such as part-time work, which might interact with the effectiveness of behavioral instruction.

5. Experimental or evaluative research in behavioral instruction needs to be replicated. Since social science research generally allows contamination by numerous biasing factors, replication by independent investigators is essential (Campbell, 1969). The reporting of experimental procedures and controls will, in many cases, have to provide more detail before replication is possible.

6. Ethical considerations in conducting experiments are minimal. However, the authors believed certain issues mentioned here are relevant for review by the field, such as the arbitrary assignment of subjects to experimental and control conditions, not programming for generalization effects, not informing the subjects that they are in an experiment, and so forth.

The intent of this paper has not been to play the game of who can discover rival hypotheses, nor to suggest that behavioral instruction is not an effective instructional practice. Nor has the intent been to suggest that researchers in this area are less competent than others. Instead, the goal was to encourage more extensive and better controlled investigations in an area which the authors feel holds great promise. In effect, we are recommending that current studies be viewed as pilot studies which provide incentive and experience for more rigorous analysis and evaluation. Miller and Weaver (1972) gave the same advice when they concluded their paper with this sentence: "Let us remember what happened to the programmed instruction movement as it floundered on the shoals of faith unaccompanied by hard nosed experimental evaluations."

THE FINDLEY PROCEDURE: A METHOD FOR EXAMINING CHOICE-MAKING BEHAVIOR IN ACADEMIC SETTINGS

KATHLEEN A. LOCKHART
JESS SEXTON
CAROLYN LEA

THAT THERE IS A NEED FOR controlled, careful studies of complex human behavior is undeniable. Indeed, Findley, in his 1962 monograph, "An experimental outline for building and exploring multi-operant behavior repertoires," suggests that while there have been many careful analyses of specific operants, data concerning larger samples of behavior (which he terms multi-operant responses) have been restricted primarily to casual observations in natural settings.

Yet current research in education has produced a wealth of data concerning the management of behavior in an effort to maximize academic performance: control of disruptive classroom behavior, motivational factors in education, token systems, etc.— all of which certainly involve complex multi-operant responses.

One area that has received little attention, however, is that of choice-making behavior and its effects on school performance. The importance of this area in education is apparent. Not only should the student perform well but he should also be sufficiently favorably disposed toward the conditions under which he performed well that he will choose to work under them again if he is given the opportunity. Undoubtably, many students are turned off, not to the course material they must learn, but rather to the manner in which it is presented and the conditions under which they must learn it. Thus, information about the individual student's preference for different academic conditions and his performance in each would certainly be of benefit both to the student and to those involved in the educational process. It would allow for the development of the most efficient *and* reinforcing (for teacher as well as student) educational program.

To accomplish this objective first a reliable method must be established for determining preference and for studying its effects on performance. Probably the most frequently used procedure is to ask the student (at the *end* of a course) what he thought about it and what changes he would make. Although these data are useful, they are also limited. It has frequently been observed that responses to these questions are not always valid for a variety of reasons. Even when answers are honest, they may not always accurately reflect on-going behavior. A behavioral approach therefore seems warranted.

Simple concurrent schedules of reinforcement have been used in animal research to assess preference (Ferster and Skinner, 1957; Findley, 1958). Although these methods typically generate substantial switching behavior with a higher frequency of responding under one condition than the other, the schedules themselves provide for no control over the switching responses or order of presentation of conditions. Indeed, they do not require that the organism even experience both (or all) conditions. If there is not exposure to all conditions, one cannot directly infer that the organism prefers the condition in which he worked to the other condition.

Findley has managed to solve these problems of control with several modifications of the basic concurrent schedule (1962). His procedure calls for a mini-max design: typically the organism is permitted to choose a given condition sequentially for a maximum number of reinforcements, after which he must work in the alternate condition for a minimum number of reinforcements. After the completion of this number, the subject is again permitted to choose either condition. Thus the direction and the timing of the switching response in this procedure assume significance. If the organism consistently stays in condition A for the maximum number of reinforcements, it may be assumed that a preference exist for that condition, particularly if it switches out of condition B after the minimum number of reinforcements. A forced switch, then, indicates preferenct for the condition from which the subject is switched, whereas a voluntary switch indicates preference for the chosen condition. This forced-choice format likewise provides for subjects' exposure to all conditions.

In addition, because the organism must remain in a given condition until it obtains at least one reinforcement, and may not ever switch before the completion of any component, data analysis for each condition is simplified—there is no confounding of stimulus conditions within a given component. Findley refers to this state of affairs as a non-reversible option: once chosen, it must be completed.

In summary then, the experimenter may set a minimum completion requirement, a maximum completion requirement, or both for switching. He may also make the options reversible or non-reversible, and, theoretically at least, combine any number of simple behaviors into a complex series of chains and options. In this method the subject serves as his own control, thus allowing the experimenter to evaluate the effects of his manipulation on each individual organism. Finally, the experimenter can measure at least three factors: the degree of preference for a given condition, the quality of performance under a given condition, and the interaction of preference and performance.

The present study represents an attempt to apply Findley's preference procedure to a current problem in education, that of test item type. Do students prefer fill-in-the-blank items or multiple-choice items? Which item type generates better performance? To reiterate, the authors considered it important not only to reveal the differential effects of the manipulation on performance but also to assess students' preference for it. An allied issue is that of the effects of preference on performance: does a student come to prefer a condition simply because he does well in it, or must a student like a given condition to do well?

METHOD

Subjects

This study used as subjects fifteen undergraduates enrolled in a basic psychology course concerning the experimental analysis of behavior. The textbook for the course was the programmed text, *The Analysis of Behavior* by Holland and Skinner (1961). The basic instructional method used was that described in detail by Johnston and Pennypacker (1971).

Procedure

Tests for students in this course were administered by student managers who had previously demonstrated their understanding of course-related material and the principles of behavior management. These managers received course credit for working with their students.

Tests were administered during performance sessions scheduled by appointment between manager and students. Each student worked with the same manager throughout the quarter. These sessions, usually twenty to thirty minutes in length, occurred in small experimental rooms furnished with a table and two chairs.

The testing materials were based on materials presented in *The Analysis of Behavior*. The text was divided into eight units and a deck of eighty item cards was generated for each unit. Half of these cards were fill-in blank items, the other half multiple-choice items. The fill-in items were taken directily from the text, eliminating only cue words. Then multiple-choice questions were constructed to match each of the fill-in questions as closely as possible for content and style. Thus forty different items were covered by the tests.

During the performance session the manager presented the cards to the student who read each card aloud, answered the question, read aloud the correct answer on the reverse side of the card, and placed the card in the appropriate stack of correctly or incorrectly answered items.

The choice manipulation was introduced as follows: the subject was permitted to choose either condition (multiple-choice or fill-in items) after each ten items in a forty-item unit. He was permitted to choose the same condition a maximum of two times consecutively before he was forced into the alternate condition for a minimum of one sub-unit. The limitations imposed on the selection of conditions was continuous across units. For example, if a student performed under one condition in the last two ten-item sets of a performance session, he was required to switch at the beginning of the next. To insure adequate exposure of subjects to the conditions, no choice was permitted in the first session: conditions were presented in a predetermined alternating order, half of the subjects starting the first session under the multiple-choice, half under the fill-in condition.

At the end of the session the student's rates and percentages of correct and incorrect responses for each ten-card sub-unit were calculated, and he was informed whether he had met criteria for passing the unit (95% accuracy). A student was permitted to attempt the next unit only after he had passed the previous one. All students who completed all units were awarded "A" regardless of the number of attempts they required to master each unit.

RESULTS

To determine if a situation preference was evident, the percentage of free-choice situations in which subjects selected multiple-choice and fill-in-the-blank questions was computed. A paired-difference t-test was performed to compare the percentage of free choices for multiple-choice questions. The mean of the differences between multiple-choice and fill-in-the-blank choice percentages was 36.85 percent. The percentage of choices for multiple-choice questions was found to be significantly greater than the percentage of choices for fill-in-the-blank questions ($t = 4.84$, p $< .01$).

Given all of the free-choice situations, the percentage distribution over the two question types for the initial question type (first state) and the question type selected (second state) data show that the first state situations were almost equally distributed between the two question types. In the second state of a free-choice option more than two-thirds of these situations ended with multiple-choice or fill-in condition switched into the multiple-choice condition if that option were open.

Two analyses of variance were performed on performance data across free and forced options, and arross multiple-choice and fill-in-the-blank question type. One analysis was done on the frequency of errors within trials, across the four conditions. The second analysis considered a rate measure (rate correct minus rate incorrect) across the four conditions. The analysis of the rate measure found question type to be significant ($F = 3.67$, df $\frac{1}{14}$, $p < .1$). The rate on multiple-choice questions ($\overline{X} = 4.01$) was significantly higher than the rate on fill-in-the-blank questions ($\overline{X} = 3.67$). No other factors were found to be significant.

DISCUSSION

The results of this experiment demonstrate a conclusive preference for multiple-choice questions over fill-in-the-blank questions. This perference is possibly due to the presence of cues in the format of the question. In a multiple-choice question the answer is included in the question; whereas, in a fill-in-the-blank question the student must produce the answer. As easily as this preference is explained, it is also confounded by the format of the text which was used: *The Analysis of Behavior* is a pro-grammed text using a fill-in-the-blank format. A less dramatic preference would have been expected due to the text's format.

The distinct trend toward higher performance rates in multi-ple-choice across free and forced options was not coupled with a similar trend in the frequency of error, which indicated that students performed equally well under the criterion across condi-tions, but the rate under the preferred condition was higher in both forced-and free-option situations. Although rate as a measure of response has been cited as a universal and sensitive measure (Pennypacker, Koenig, and Seaver, 1973) in that all behavior occurs with respect to both time and number, the fact that rates in the multiple-choice condition were higher than in the fill-in condition may be attributable simply to the fact that the student was not required to construct his own answer for the multiple-choice questions. This explanation is supported by the fact that there were no differences in accuracy between the two conditions.

Although the results of this experiment are in and of themselves interesting, there is a more important point at issue: just what is the relationship between preference and performance? Does a student necessarily do higher quality work in a preferred condition than in a nonpreferred condition? Apparently from these data the answer must be no, at least not always. Still, the issue of choice is a critical one. It is the opinion of these authors that the role of instructor includes, among other things, the responsibility of exciting students to the subject matter being taught. Given that students may be able to learn quite well under extremely aversive conditions, what is the end result? Students can always elect the option of not returning to school or of never taking another course taught in that manner. And what is the purpose of using a less-preferred method so long as the preferred method accomplishes the task? Skinner (*The Technology of Teaching*, 1968) has made the point well that education traditionally has employed aversive contingencies, and that the process involved was one of avoidance—of failing grades, humiliation, etc. It would seem that with the technology available to determine preference, it may be possible to employ more positive contingencies through allowing students to choose the conditions under which they shall work. In the traditional lock-step, required-course type of education prevalent today, the Findley procedure allows students at least some leeway in choosing the type of learning environment they prefer, as well as providing researchers a useful tool for assessing the effects of preference on performance.

ACCOUTABILITY: COST EFFICIENCY AND EFFECTIVENESS MEASURES IN BEHAVIORAL COLLEGE TEACHING

JESS W. SEXTON
CHARLES MERBITZ
H. S. PENNYPACKER

THE HALLMARK OF ALL BEHAVIORAL PROCEDURES is the relatively frequent and direct measurement of performance. Investigators have long stressed the necessity of sensitive measurement for the evaluation of key independent and procedural variables. These measurement criteria, familiar to all experimental analysts, also permit integration of the vast quantities of performance data that result from any behavioral teaching procedure into statements of effectiveness and efficiency that more than meet the needs of today's administrators.

This extension is rather immediate and straightforward. Given that performance is measured on an individual basis and that this measurement occurs frequently over time, it is a simple matter to describe the amount or rate of behavior change that takes place over time. Such a change measure is a measure of the effect of the given teaching procedure on the behavior of the individual. In order to compare effects across individuals, courses, etc. it is necessary to employ a standard measure of change per unit of time, since different amounts of time will inevitably arise. A change-per-unit-of-time measure reflects the efficiency of the procedure. Two procedures may bring about the same amount of change (effect), but the one that does it faster is the more efficient. By attaching to these measures estimates of the cost of various procedures, we can assess them with regard to cost efficiency and cost effectiveness. Before considering the application of such extensions, however, it is first essential that we have a proper unit of behavioral measurement upon which to base our analysis. As in all the work conducted at the University of Florida, basically summarized in Johnston and Pennypacker (1971) and in Heaton (1971), rate or frequency is this basic dependent variable.

Undoubtably, the identification and use of frequency of response as a basic scientific datum is a major factor behind the successful development of the experimental analysis of behavior and its subsequent applied technologies. Frequency is the measure of choice for two basic reasons: its superior sensitivity as a descriptive measure of behavior and its obvious utility as a predictive index of future behavior. B.F. Skinner is, of course, responsible for the early use of frequency as a dependent variable (1938, 1950, 1953, 1957) and has presented data and convincing arguments favoring its use over other dependent measures. For example, he noted in 1953 that frequency, in addition to being an orderly datum, is also a continuous account of many basic behavioral processes. To the extent that all behavior occurs in time and in discrete and countable units, frequency is also a natural, but more importantly, a universal datum for a science of behavior. Moreover, since learning is the focus of our concern, our ultimate interest is with the future behavior of the organism (Skinner, 1953). Predicting future behavior is a matter of determining its probability of occurrence. The best predictor of the probability of occurrence of a given response, to date, is its frequency of occurrence in the past.

The change in behavior over time is of paramount interest in behavioral education. This fact is underscored by the emphasis placed on the frequent or continuous recording of student performance found in most behavioral teaching situations. To the extent that learning, however defined, is generally inferred from observations of changes in the frequency of behavior, the focus on behavior change is easily understood. However, until recently, a measure of the change in behavior frequencies over time has been lacking. Fortunately, a measure of this nature was developed by O.R. Lindsley in 1969 and was subsequently extended by Pennypacker in 1972. The unit, celebration, is defined by the general form: movements/unit of time/unit of time. It is, of course, the first derivative of frequency with respect to time. To the extent that celeration describes changes in the universal behavior unit (frequency) over time, it then, is a universal measure of behavior change.

Historically, progress in every branch of science and the develpment of its applied technologies has generally been preceded by the generation and acceptance, by investigators, of a common set of tools, techniques, and language with which to record, describe, and otherwise deal with the phenomena of interest in that area. This, of course, allows for the broad and meaningful dissemination of information which can be readily understood and acted upon by all interested parties. Similarly, the identification of frequency of response, the extensive use of the Skinner box and cumulative recorder, and the widespread agreement upon and acceptance of the basic methodological tactics and strategies in the experimental analysis of basic behavioral processes has led to, what today, is a highly sophisticated and precise experimental science of behavior.

Although much progress has been made in applied behavior analysis, an equivalent level of sophistication and precision has not uniformly been reached. In the area of measurement, however, a significant step in the direction of remedying this problem has been taken with the introduction of the Standard Behavior Chart by O.R. Lindsley in 1968.

It should be noted that the abscissa of the chart is days while the ordinate is frequency. It should be similarly noted that the frequencies are scaled in ratio or logarithmic fashion. Although an in-depth justification of the ratio (log) scale will not be offered here, to the extent that a scale of this type is not in widespread use in psychology and education as it is in the natural sciences and engineering, several of its advantageous characteristics will be pointed out.

The ratio scale affords us a much greater range of frequency values, (1,000 per minutes) than does an interval scale of the same length and local sensitivity. Thus, to the extent that the ratio scale accomodates more than what is likely to be the entire range of human behavior frequencies of educational interest, it undoubtably exceeds the criteria for a standard and universal measuring tool to be used in education.

Another property of the ratio scale which is of paramount importance in the measurement of behavior and behavior change in general, is as follows: equal distances represent equal ratios. This principle assumes added importance when applied to educational measurement. If we chart the frequency of both correct and incorrect performance on a given academic task for a given day, the distance separating these two points on the chart is a measure of the accuracy of performance. Furthermore, due to the equal ratio nature of the frequency scale, the distance on the chart representing a given measure of accuracy is independent of the particular absolute frequencies of the accuracy pair. This means that the comparison of performances of vastly different frequencies can be undertaken with respect to this measure of their accuracy. So, by virtue of charting the frequencies of correct and incorrect academic performance, we now have an additional measure of performance made available to us without any additional expenditure of time or effort on our part. It should be added that the accuracy ratio can readily be expressed as either a multiple or a percentage.

The measure of behavior change, celeration, may be represented by fitting a straight line to a given series of daily behavior frequencies. The slope of this celeration line is proportional to the ratio or percentage of behavior change taking place over a given period of time. It should be also noted that celerations are usually expressed as ratios or multiples of frequency. (e.g. times 3 movements/minute/week, divide 3 movements/minute/ week, etc.). This is the case in so far as the most convenient time unit for assessing behavior change in one week.

An important feature of the celeration measure is that like the accuracy measure, it is independent of frequency. Consequently, just as equal distances between frequencies on a given day represent the same degree of accuracy, equal proportions of change in the frequencies of two different behaviors will share the same celeration values and will be represented by parallel celeration lines. Here, again, it is possible to directly assess and compare rates of changes in behaviors occurring as vastly different frequencies.

Two final measures derived from the Standard Behavior Chart are the Effectiveness Index (E) and the Momentary Accuracy Multiplier (MAM). The E index is a combination of two accuracy measures, taken usually at the beginning and end of a curriculum unit. As such, it represents the ratio of change in accuracy which occurred in the presence of that unit. E is defined as the ratio of the accuracy of the ending performance to the accuracy of the beginning performance. The resulting index is independent of either accuracy score, just as accuracy is independent of frequency. E yields our measure of effectiveness, defined in terms of accuracy change.

In order to assess changes in accuracy over time, a measure analagous to the celeration measure is required. In our laboratory, the time unit of interest has been the minute, rather than the day or week. Consequently, by extracting the nth root of E, where n is the number of minutes taken to produce the accuracy change represented by E, we derive a measure of the rate at which accuracy is changing each minute. This value, which we have designated the Monentary Accuracy Multiplier (MAM) is our basic measure of efficiency since, for a given degree of accuracy change or effect, the smaller the amount of time required to obtain it, the greater must have been the efficiency and hence the larger will be the MAM.

Let us now examine the results of applying this measurement system within the context of a rather complex program of general education for freshmen at the University of Florida.

The data presented here are intended only as an illustration of our measurement system and how the resulting measures may be used in determining both the efficiency and effectiveness of a given set of instructional procedures. To that extent, they are not offered as evaluative of the particular procedures in effect in our program. That analysis is conducted continuously and is far too complex and extensive to describe in this paper.

The teaching procedures of interest here were of generally the same form as those in the individualized instructional model described by Johnston and Pennypacker in 1971, with several variations. Students performed in a specially built teaching laboratory. Student managers were used along with self-paced unit tests and unit perfection criteria procedures. Basically, the variations included the absence of any absolute frequency criteria. In most cases, the criterion for passing a unit test was the accuracy of performance on that unit. In the interest of simplification, these accuracy criteria were expressed as percentages. However, it should be emphasized that all educational decisions by the students, managers, or advisors were made with respect to the charted frequency of the student's daily academic performance.

Up to 184 students in any given quarter of the academic year were each enrolled in from one to four individualized program courses. In the quarter from which data are presented, there were thirteen course sections with a total program section enrollment of 367 students. The subject areas covered included freshman level social science, physical science, and logic. Grades were controlled by instructors who took the students' laboratory performance into consideration in their determination.

Table 33-I presents a simple summary, section by section, of the mean number of performance minutes required for each of the possible letter grade measures of student's achievement. Examination of Table 33-I reveals that some areas (e.g. Social Studies) required far greater expenditure of time for high grades than did others and that within areas, there was considerable variation among sections.

If one considers grade outcome as a measure of the effect of a course upon a student's behavior, it is easy to calculate the average cost within the program required to generate a given grade and thus arrives at a traditional type of cost effectiveness ratio. Applying such a procedure to the present data indicates that an "A" was slightly "cheaper" than a "B," on the average, but this reversal from expectation is accounted for by a single social science section; in most other cases, a decreasing relation between time an grade earned was obtained.

Since our primary interest, however, is in direct measures of

TABLE 33-I
Mean Performance Minutes for Each Grade by Course Sections

Course	Code	A	B	C	D	E	Other	Total N
Logic								
CLC 11X	211	200.50	157.40	0.00	0.00	0.00	738.00	17
CLC 12Y	212	227.90	69.20	261.40	122.00	0.00	69.06	30
CLC 12Y	222	249.30	237.40	0.00	0.00	0.00	29.00	17
CLC 12Y	232	231.60	173.60	0.00	0.00	0.00	5.00	39
CLC 12Y	242	313.10	236.40	0.00	0.00	0.00	0.00	16
CLC 12Y	252	220.80	145.00	0.00	0.00	0.00	78.70	13
Physical Science								
CPS 11Y	311	191.30	105.00	0.00	0.00	0.00	274.00	40
CPS 12Y	312	222.00	0.00	98.00	294.00	0.00	0.00	34
CPS 12Y	322	138.60	44.00	98.30	0.00	87.50	0.00	42
Social Science								
CSS 11X	411	668.60	462.80	299.00	99.00	50.00	0.00	42
CSS 11X	412	0.00	302.50	0.00	0.00	0.00	23.75	27
CSS 12Y	421	690.00	752.00	459.30	0.00	0.00	0.00	26
CSS 12Y	422	0.00	0.00	271.00	0.00	0.00	267.00	24
Total/N		240.45	206.56	1143.38	39.61	10.58	114.90	367

student behavior and behavior change, let us proceed to consider the measured effectiveness of the various courses in improving the academic behavior of the students served.

In addition to instructors salaries and other expenses incurred in traditional college teaching, the program described here cost 37,500 dollars for each quarter of operation. By dividing the total number of student performance minutes into this cost figure we arrive at a measure of the cost per minute. In as much as the 367 students enrolled in the thirteen sections logged a grand total of 117,377 minutes in performance, the total cost per minute was calculated to be twenty-six cents.

Table 33-II is a summary, section by section, of our various effectiveness, efficiency, and cost efficiency measures derived from the charted changes in student academic behavior.

When we raise the MAM (change in accuracy per minute) to the power of the appropriate number of minutes we arrive at a measure of total effect. With respect to a particular course section, if we raise our total effect measure to the power of the reciprocal of the appropriate number of students included in that course section we derive the total effect per student. These values are found in the appropriate column of Table 33-II. They reflect the average percentage change in accuracy achieved by a student in that course section. As can be seen from the table, these percent accuracy change values range from 22 percent in one social science section to 204 percent in one logic section. One measure of efficiency we have found useful is the time to double accuracy. These values for the various sections are also found in Table 33-II. As might be expected, the relationship between effect and efficiency is such that in those sections producing the largest percent accuracy change the time to double accuracy will be the smallest. For example, in CPS 12Y-312, we find that the percentage change in accuracy (effect) is 204 percent. Consequently, the smallest amount of time of additional performance, ninety-nine minutes, would produce a doubling of accuracy at a cost of $25.74 per student. Conversely, in the course sections producing the smallest percent change in accuracy the cost to double accuracy is the highest. Examination of Table 33-II indicates that the physical science sections produced the most

TABLE 33-II

Effectiveness and Efficiency Measures for Each Course Section

Course	Code	MAM	Total Effect Per Student	% Increase in Accuracy per Student	Time to Double Accuracy**	Cost to Double Accuracy	Total Minutes	N
CLC 11X	211	1.001	1.45	45	693	$180.18	6,337	17
CLC 12Y	212	1.000	.....	.....	.....	.....	9,204	30*
CLC 12Y	222	1.001	1.45	45	693	$180.18	6,409	17
CLC 12Y	232	1.001	1.45	45	693	$180.18	14,510	39
CLC 12Y	242	1.002	2.12	112	346	$ 89.96	6,044	16
CLC 12Y	252	1.000	.....	.....	.....	.....	5,889	13*
CPS 11X	311	1.005	2.53	153	138	$ 35.88	7,437	40
CPS 12Y	312	1.007	3.04	204	99	$ 25.74	5,422	34
CPS 12Y	322	1.004	1.85	85	173	$ 44.98	6,515	42
CSS 11X	411	1.002	2.51	151	346	$ 89.96	19,407	42
CSS 11X	412	1.001	1.22	22	693	$180.18	5,272	26
CSS 12Y	421	1.002	2.29	129	346	$ 89.96	11,226	27
CSS 12Y	422	1.002	1.51	51	346	$ 89.96	5,002	24

* Since the MAM = 1.000 for these sections, there was no measurable increase in accuracy.
** Time to double accuracy is in minutes.

effect per student, with social sciences producing the next highest effect, and logic the smallest effect. However, it should be noted that there is wide variability between sections of each course with respect to their effectiveness and efficiency.

Table 33-III presents an analysis of the effectiveness of each curriculum unit of a particular course (CSS 11X-411). The range of percent increase in accuracy over curriculum units is from 1.0 percent to 446.0 percent. Obviously, some units were both more effective and efficient than others. If one chose to, he could determine both time and cost to double measures for each particular curriculum unit.

In summary, we feel that the measures presented here go a a long way toward producing a highly sophisticated system of educational accountability. The implications of these measures are far reaching. It is highly probable that they could serve as a basis for course evaluation, in as much as direct comparisons between courses can be undertaken in terms of their effectiveness, efficiency, and cost. It is possible that this system can be used as a basis for determining promotions, salary raises, and other rewards for teaching staff. Another possible extension of these techniques might be to the area of counseling of individual students to the extent that we can project the time and cost that will be involved in taking the student from a given performance to a prestated goal. In conclusion, we must state our belief that

TABLE 33-III

Effectiveness of Units in One Course (CSS 11X-411)

Unit	MAM	Total Effect	% Increase in Accuracy	Minutes
1	1.006	1.01	1.0	127
2	1.021	1.96	96.0	1,363
3	1.019	1.46	46.0	858
4	1.026	5.46	446.0	2,779
5	1.030	3.89	289.0	1,932
6	1.028	3.05	205.0	1,700
7	1.027	3.21	221.0	1,842
8	1.030	2.62	162.0	1,369
9	1.032	3.50	250.0	1,672
10	1.035	4.00	300.0	1,694
11	1.033	3.29	229.0	1,544
12	1.027	2.29	129.0	1,311
13	1.035	2.70	170.0	1,216

only by starting with the individual students performance has a data based evaluation system been developed for up-through-channels accountability that is faithful to the needs of the ultimate beneficiaries of any program or set of procedures—the students.

"... TO BEAT BACK THE FRONTIERS OF IGNORANCE"

James M. Johnston

How do you define teaching? Addressing that question to my colleagues, students, and acquaintances over a period of time has produced, perhaps not unexpectedly, a considerable variety of responses. (The title of this paper is one of my favorites.) Equally predictably, the dictionary offers little assistance with its offerings which include "to cause to know a subject," "to direct as an instructor," and "to impart the knowledge of." The most noticeable characteristic which denotative as well as personal working definitions seem to reliably share is the depiction of teaching as the activities of one individual called a teacher in relation to another individual called a student. In fact, this feature seems to extend beyond mere definitions to the more practical level of the classroom where it generally seems that whatever is done by a teacher to or for students is commonly accepted as teaching. It is almost as if the label "teacher" denotes whatever such a person does with respect to students as teaching. The circle becomes complete whenever we define a teacher as one who teaches. Of course, we might all insist that we know better intellectually, but our daily words and actions would probably be a more representative and meaningful source of a definition.

This attitude can be observed at all levels of education, and its effects are subtle but pervasive. An important aspect of this kind of definition is that the behavior of only one of the two parties involved is mentioned. It is the teacher's activities which define teaching, and the definition is usually considered to be independent of the effects of the teacher upon the academic performance of students. For instance, we often characterize a lecture or a teacher-led group discussion as teaching without considering or measuring whether or not it influenced the students in educationally desirable ways. As a matter of fact, we tend to consider a particular procedure as teaching in all applications without acknowleding that its effects on students can vary. We call a certain activity teaching for 100 percent of a class even when we have evidence that only 75 percent were beneficially influenced by it. In other words, in practice we too often view as teaching whatever a person called a teacher does in educational settings without considering whether or not or how the teacher's behaviors influence those of the student.

Another effect of such an orientation is that it encourages us to look for new teaching methods predominantly in terms of the activities of the teacher. Listen to the discussions about methods (new or old) in faculty lounges, methods courses, workshops, and so forth and you will hear mostly about the things the teacher can *do* rather than the ways in which student performance might be improved which do not directly or actively involve teachers. As a matter of fact, the single variable which seems to affect the quality of a student's performance more than any other does not directly involve a teacher. This is the usually solitary studying which most students engage in (at least occasionally) and which is never described as a teaching variable. Not surprisingly, we know with certainty very little at all about this category of student behaviors. In part, because it is not considered a teaching variable, it is very infrequently the result of well-designed empirical research. The books which are available to instruct the wayward pupil in these skills (dangerously assuming that those performing adequately have and are exercising such skills), are mostly a hodgepodge of aged truisms and untested common sense.

Neither should it be surprising that such an orientation does not encourage us to measure with any frequency or real precision the response of the student to the teaching methods, which in turn prevents many potential uses of such vital information. As a result of this paucity of measurement, the evaluation of teaching methods is made from a theoretical rather than an empirical perspective. A particular approach is judged in terms of its adherence to or congruence with theories (of personality or education) rather than in terms of actual measures of the effects of the techniques on students' academic activities. Thus, old methods never die in battle with young better ones; they simply fade into neglect as the newer fads blossom in popularity (although not necessarily in greater success for the student).

One of the ways in which we protect such a definition is by our explanations of the many occasions in which a teacher's activities do not apparently affect the student. In such cases we talk about a student's poor motivation, lack of study skills, low intelligence, or lack of attentiveness or attendance. The facility with which we postulate such "causes" of failure serves to maintain our conviction that we're teaching but they're not learning. The mere existence of the phrase "ineffective teaching" demonstrates this viewpoint by implying that if the teacher did it, it was teaching, even though desirable results were not seen in the student. One of the confusions resulting from this "teacher-oriented" definition is in distinguishing between excellent and poor teaching. Those in positions of judgment as well as teachers themselves tend again to talk about the quality of teaching in terms of the things the teacher does in relation to certain abstract values and hypothetical constructs embodied in some theory. The discussion of "really good teaching" usually shows a notable lack of consideration of the student's academic performance which resulted. The good college teacher is usually one who has a personality that is well-liked by both students and superiors, who has a good reputation as a teacher among students (which probably means that he or she is entertaining in class), or who does things in the classroom which are a bit different from other teachers (but not too different). Likewise when we talk about a "poor" teacher, we do not discuss how his or her students are doing, rather we mean the teacher's activities as compared to traditional methods or to personal and theoretical values.

All of these problems are perhaps most easily seen in college-level teaching. The college teacher is usually hired not on the basis of his teaching skills (because, in addition to reasons already mentioned, we do not seem to be able to define them), but for his experience as a student in some area of subject matter, his productivity and skills as a researcher, and his personality. He or she most likely has never had any formal training as a college teacher. The emphasis is on what to teach, not on how to teach it. Once on the job, the teacher will be promoted or fired for reasons rarely related to the quality of his teaching. The lecture is still the most used "teaching" technique, inspite of suggestions that it is an extremely poor way to disseminate information and that it probably beneficially affects the academic performance of very few students. For the multitudes who do not seem to be inspired, the professor will explain with "well, most of them aren't really motivated for an A," or "a lot of students just don't have it," or "if they would come to more of my lectures, they would do better." Related to the lecture's popularity among teachers, the biggest changes over the years in college teaching techniques have been audio-visual means of presenting material to groups of students. And most professors seem to be still measuring and grading student performance on the basis of two or three group tests (most frequently multiple choice in large classes or essay in smaller sections) over a ten to fifteen week period. Finally, most discussion of a college teacher's quality concerns the requirements of his job other than teaching. It is only in recent years that the students have increasingly been asked to express their opinions about their teacher's methods. Fortunately, few propose that these opinions define good or bad teaching any better than the opinions of teachers and administrators.

It would seem that there are many practical implications of how we approach a definition of teaching. Salvation from the solipsistic bias described in this conceptualization was initially offered by the development of a program of scientific analysis of the variables of which all human behavior is a function. The past decade has seen this research extended to all aspects of the field of education. The conduct of methodologically sound empirical investigations into academic behaviors exhibited by students (elementary, secondary, and college) and the factors in the educational environment to which they are functionally related has led to the accumulation of a sizable body of evidence about the nature of these variables and their affect on student's academic work. The existence of this growing literature now forces a new perspective toward our definition of teaching.

By being able to specify the variables which can be demonstrated to affect student academic performance in educationally desirable way, we may now call teaching the arrangement of environmental conditions which expedite such performance (Skinner, 1968). The most valuable feature of this viewpoint is that teaching is no longer defined by teacher acitivities but only by student academic performance. With this definition whatever a teacher does to or for a student is called teaching only if as a result directly measurable and academically appropriate changes occur in the student's repetoire.

This approach results in a number of important though potentially disconcerting corollaries. For instance, it places both traditional and new teaching techniques in the unforgivingly critical light of empirical data by providing the unequivocal yardstick of student progress with which to evaluate instructional methods. It is likely that some of our most cherished methods (like the centuries-old college lecture) may not (at least for all students) deserve the title of teaching because they do not produce appropriate changes in student performance. How many of today's instructional procedures would meet this stringent criterion? This definition means that new techniques can no longer be evaluated on the basis of their consonance with popular educational or developmental theories. The test of their utility must be their impact on the student behaviors which are the teacher's targets. How often do we use new products, curricula, or methods because they are personally appealing or professionally popular without also seeking direct measurement of their effects on our students?

Of course, not only are a teacher's efforts worthy of definition as teaching only when successful student performance results, but *any* procedures which have these effects on student academic behaviors may also earn that appellation, whether or not they involve the teacher. In other words, a wide variety of classroom and nonclassroom activities are eligible to be categorized as teaching, including even the methods we use to measure changes in student performance. If, for example, it were shown that the assignment and administration of classroom tests have desirable effects on academic performance, then such assessment techniques should rightfully be considered teaching procedures. There is data being produced at the college level that suggests that this may well be the case—that the traditional separation of teaching and testing is misleading and wasteful because testing is an effective teaching technique. Thus this view of teaching encourages us to look beyond the direct activities of the teacher himself to the other features of the academic setting in a search for ways to improve student learning.

This kind of definition also makes such phrases as "ineffective" or "poor" teaching contradictory and meaningless. Methods which do not produce desirable changes in academic performance are simply not described as teaching, thereby preventing their innocent perpetuation and consequently encouraging the instructor to turn to other arrangements of the educational environment. The task of evaluating faculty and finding the good teacher is also simplified by the availability of an unambiguous standard. Accountability at any level of education can only be meaningful and practical when the teacher's job can be stated in terms which are directly measureable, as are changes in student academic performance.

It should be clear by now that this definition tends to impose greater responsibilities than before on us as teachers. By placing such importance on student academic performance, it unavoidably emphasizes the precise and frequent measurement of that performance. The reliability and validity of assessment techniques becomes crucial in the accurate specification of the extent to which teacher's efforts may be called teaching. Inaccurate evaluation may result in ignorance of valuable instructional methods or continuation of less effective or ineffective practices. Direct measurement must also be a continuous and individual process in all areas of instruction so that procedures can be immediately and sensitively responsive to their effects on students.

Finally, it is easy to see that this mandate fits more closely certain realities of which most teachers are already aware—that what constitutes successful teaching for one individual may be woefully inadequate for another. The use of a group statistic to characterize the influence of a technique masks the unique reactions of each individual to a uniform method and implies that it is equal in effect upon all students. This kind of definition requires individualization in our measurement of student performance and consequently in our description of procedures as teaching.

Our definition of teaching is clearly central to many of our everyday practices. The definition of teaching in terms of student rather than teacher behaviors seems to propose practical changes of considerable significance.

In Skinner's 1968 article on high school teaching he wrote of the difference between training and teaching:

The traditional distinction comes down to this: when we know what we are doing, we are training; when we do not know what we are doing, we are teaching (p. 708).

It would seem that this kind of "student-oriented" definition of teaching and the perspective it offers can facilitate our progress toward removing that distinction.

READING 35

ACADEMIC TRADITION AND INSTRUCTIONAL TECHNOLOGY

LAWRENCE E. FRALEY
ERNEST A. VARGAS

Introduction

LEARNING IS CHANGE IN BEHAVIOR and can be prescribed, produced, and guaranteed like any other product. It is now
possible to specify the desired performances of learners and arrange the circumstances of learning such that those performances
will be developed and exhibited by the learners. The behavioral
products, explicitly delineated in advance, can and should be
guaranteed. There is no theoretical reason why schools should
produce ill-formed and inadequate behavioral products while
we expect manufacturers of physical products to produce near
perfect items. It is only that our physical sciences are older, and
the technologies which they support have evolved over a sufficiently long time to shape high performance expectations. The
corresponding behavioral sciences are new and their technologies
only now emerging. We are not yet accustomed to exploiting
them fully.

The ancient mysticism surrounding "wisdom" and "knowledge" has tenuous remnants in the present society. Educators re-
sort to them to explain what they are trying to do. It is not
popular to speak of controlling and producing behavior as a

product. Yet educators do entertain behavioral goals for their students. However indirect they may insist the link between teaching and behavioral outcomes to be, they nevertheless nourish some desire that the learners will ultimately manifest behavioral evidence of their educational experiences. This is not surprising because there is no other kind of evidence for learning. Educators would be far more prepared for their task if they recognized that they are in the behavior changing business.

With the national commitment to mass education and the increasing demand that it be met with higher standards, there is an increasing concern with how to produce new behavior in learners rather than simply "teach at them," hoping that desirable effects may result. Today's learners live in a society so complicated that they must be highly skilled and sophisticated just to act responsibly. The repertoires of many people are taxed by the complexity of acquiring necessary information, casting an intelligent ballot, utilizing the transportation systems, or being an effective part of today's communication networks.

To meet these challenges, today's instruction must become equally technological and sophisticated. Traditional instructional arrangements, though often viewed with nostalgia, cannot do the job of providing mass training to high skill levels. This is because traditional arrangements were not evolved to control a sufficient number of the critical variables affecting learning.

The Traditional Academic Ecosystem

It might seem that education would be willing or even eager to adopt the changes needed to meet these challenges, but such change is subdued by strong tendencies to preserve reward struc-tures embedded in methods that have to be altered.

It has been assumed in academic settings throughout history that the essence of instruction is in its content, and therefore the content expert has assumed authority there. Most of the or-ganizational and structural patterns in educational institutions have been built on the assumption that content expertise is the critical dimension of instruction. Originally, knowledge was equated with power, and to a large extent it still is. Those who have knowledge in any content area are presumed to have extraordinary qualities such as wise judgment in areas far removed from their expertise. No one questions that an expert in a particular field can teach in that field even though teaching skills are of a far different sort. For example, the geologist may possess many concepts about slip faults, and he may be able to cite numerous contexts in which desirable consequences would accrue from the exercise of the repertoire. But how to teach about rocks is not a geology problem; nor is how to teach about quadratic equations a mathematics problem; rather, they are instructional problems, and they will not be solved by either geologists or mathematicians. Problems in how to instruct are going to be solved only by instructional engineers.

The assumed transfer of skills from those of a discipline to those of teaching underlies the academic practice of having experts in one field pass judgment on the curriculum requests of those from another. A long series of progressively unjustified assumptions continues to put the academic content expert in control of complex technological and administrative systems of instruction.

There is an unfortunate trend in higher education, through a mix of ignorance and design, to avoid the objectivity of the newer behavioral and instructional technologies by obscuring the nature of the instruction process in a shroud of mystic elusiveness. Academicians propagate many ideas of that type: The goal of instruction is to impart truth and wisdom; instruction is a meeting of the minds; the essence of instruction is in the power of the living word; or, the path of knowledge is only through the warm personal tutorial contact. By defining instruction in terms which defy translation to objective operational processes, the academic content expert can mitigate the organization of criteria by which he might become excluded from his position of control.

Academicians invoke the false issue of academic freedom in support of retention of the current arrangements for teaching. However, teaching is a technical process and has nothing directly to do with academic freedom. That concept is legitimately applied only to the determination of what to teach and to the search for new knowledge where various rights and interests must be protected under the rubric of Academic Freedom. But the current use of the emotional appeal of that concept to bolster class-room arrangements which are nothing more than inadequate instructional techniques is an evasive defense of rewards intrinsic to those modes. Those who argue that it is their right to pursue traditional teaching techniques under the guarantees of academic freedom invalidly transfer a concept related to the scope and type of knowledge to the technical nuances of teaching that knowledge.

The error of permitting the rewards to shift from successful attainment of objectives to methods of working toward them has been allowed to drift to extremes in education because of the historical delays in developing better techniques. If a steady evolution of the technology of teaching had been forcing frequent changes in methods, sclerosis of method would not have occurred. Unfortunately, it is only in very recent times that substantial alternatives have become practical. In the meantime, the poor results were not improvable for want of technologies not yet developed and came to be accepted as adequate. The rewards for educators, which could not derive readily from results that poor and ill defined, rather easily slipped from the province of results to that of the fixated methodology.

Teachers come under the control of such contingencies as unregulated working hours, student deference born out of fear of their subjective whims, and work assessment schemes lacking an objective measure of productivity. In addition, teachers are reinforced by the status of knowledge and by the control of instruction. In the privacy of the classroom, good humor, learner satisfaction, and other social dynamics, all valid concomitant attributes, unfortunately replace learning as criteria for instructional success. Pseudo-objective techniques are employed to suggest that learning was being carefully produced and measured, for example, distributing grades according to the normal curve. Both the public and students have permitted educators to arrange contingencies for themselves such that student performances can be ranked and grades "A" through "F," awarded by making use of the normal variation in test scores regardless of whether learning occurs. The implications of the fact that this could be done as easily on the first day of class as on the last day have not been sufficiently appreciated and explored. Although the classroom represented nothing more than a set of current teaching techniques, the concept of classroom autonomy was introduced, not because those techniques were good enough to preserve, but because the concomitant rewards had become reinforcing enough to protect.

As a result of these developments, the academicians find themselves with the responsibility for teaching, but without the capability to do it. Confronted with increasingly higher levels of expectation for results, today's teachers are frustrated, especially in higher education. Even while pressed to produce more and better learning, they exist in an institutional reward structure that pays much better for research and publication than for good teaching.

The education administrators have tended to remain attached to the tratditional reward structures and, in general, have not effectively attacked the problem of institutional change for better instruction. For example, administrators have seldom reorganized the instructional missions of their institutions to better accommodate full system approaches, but they have frequently entertained an assortment of diverse "innovative" schemes which share only the property of noninterference in academic reward patterns. It is not difficult to find amateurs experimenting wastefully with new technologies about which they know very little, while enjoying the substantial subsidy of their administration simply because they represent an innovative image. And, at the same time, because of their ignorance about instruction, they fail to challenge the assumption that their efforts can succeed without changing the structural arrangements which protect academic rewards and foster old technologies that ignore to many critical variables.

The careful preservation of traditional organization arrangements in academic settings has resulted in the proliferation of academic departments, each composed of similar collections of role types, all related to content and not to the process of instruction. Each new department is like the existing ones, so large schools teach no more effectively than do small ones.

Presently in academia, the proposition that learners in huge college lecture courses be taught sufficiently well that all would perform at the level traditionally reserved for the "best" students is treated evasively. It is argued that most students are innately incapable of such learning, or that the necessary teaching techniques do not exist, or that the recent surge of high grades, suddenly appearing throughout academia as if some new renaissance were upon us, actually demonstrates that the proposition is already being accommodated in practice. What few standards existed are being abandoned in efforts to further obscure the increasingly evident fact that content experts in the various disciplines do not know how to teach but may appear to succeed only because a few of their students already know how to learn. There is, however, a rapidly growing field known as Instructional Technology, based on a science of human behavior, and dedicated to the proposition that how to teach and learn can be taught, and given sufficient behavioral expertise, learning can be produced as a prescribed product.

The Necessary Organizational Structures for Instruction

The Carnegie Commission, which recently completed a major study of higher education, concluded that instruction was a complex process requiring the inputs of a diverse spectrum of expertise. The Commission found that most institutions are lacking in many of these types and proposed that more of them be trained and involved in the instructional process.

The Commission refers to the wave of technology sweeping education as the "fourth revolution." Despite wide enthusiasm for it, and Federal money behind it, educators have little awareness of what is implied when new technological processes are introduced into organizational structures as tradition-bound as education.

Modern instructional technology is being superimposed on, or forced within existing organizational arrangements which were evolved to accommodate other philosophies and modes of instruction. The new technologies cannot be successfully used until we reorient our organization structures, roles, and responsibilities away from patterns and reward structures that assume the essence of instruction to be in its content.

Instructional experts—the scientists and technologists whose discipline is the instructional process—find themselves subordinated to instructionally inept content experts. Education administrators act to continue this inappropriate relationship. Most of these administrators come from the ranks of content experts and have their positions not because they understand the technology of education but because they are good politicians.

However, instruction is the process of changing the behavior of others, and behavioral technology is the means by which this is done. But instruction demands more than new combinations of methods, hardware, facilities, and energies. New technologies must also have the appropriate organizational arrangements which serve as the matrix for other system elements. Instruction is a process, and the new organizational structure needed to accommodate our instructional missions must reflect the process itself.

A complex process is accommodated by a system. Current popularity of the "system approach" in educational jargon stems from an increasing awareness that instruction is a more complex process than traditionally presumed. A system is a set of things or principles so related as to form a unity in which a change in one part will affect others. The system concept includes processes as well as things and covers any regular orderly methodology, including the logic by which order is specified. The system approach to problem solving requires a perspective in which there is substantial attention not just to the elements or parts, but to their integration. An instructional system organizes the total resources for instruction and delineates the functions to insure operational integrity.

The instruction process initially involves the design of specific instructional systems with their materials and facilities. Following this design comes instructional production, the physical creation of all that has been specified. This is followed by the interaction of the target populations of learners with the instructional systems, during which the learners engage in the learning experiences. And finally, there is the extensive collection of data on all aspects of the systems' performances, their analysis and evaluation, and the recycling of the instruction.

Although these steps are not new, the models of instruction being developed today making use of these steps, are new. It should no longer be acceptable to batch-process students in large groups without regard to the complexities of their individual differences. No longer is it acceptable to succeed with only a small percentage of the students, those who get the "A's," while sweeping instructional failures under the rug of lower grades.

There must be worthwhile behavioral objectives at all cognitive, affective, and psychomotor levels. Test items must be addressed directly to those objectives, weighted according to their relative importance, and tested in proportion to those weights. Performance levels must be specified for each objective and all learners must attain them, so that learner progress is contingent on learner attainment of the objectives. The individualized, modularized curriculum must be employed so that each learner can have a custom-tailored prescription. There must be a humanization of instruction through a technological consideration of the uniqueness of the individual.

The existing organizational structures in education will not support such rigorous and precise models of instruction, because traditional structures do not permit sufficient control over the many variables affecting instructional accomplishments. New structural arrangements are demanded which provide the expertise for this control.

The new organizational structure needed to provide for this kind of instruction features divisions based on the major instructional functions. Figure 35-1 presents a logical possibility. First there is the Curriculum and Design Division which delineates the curriculum, and designs instructional systems. This division features instructional system technologists whose expertise is to specify how skills and concepts are to be taught. This critical role brings together elements from several areas of specialization including the psychological skills for assessing the learning characteristics of students, and the skills of system analysis, human factors engineering, and instructional materials design. In this division critical skills in how to teach are combined with content expertise in what to teach.

The Production Division is staffed by persons whose expertise is to physically create whatever has been designed. It includes instructional illustrators, narrators, photographers, TV producers, document production specialists, and others expert in producing and acquiring finished and raw materials.

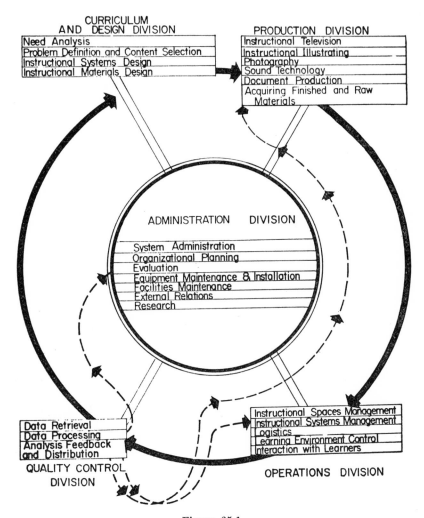

CURRICULUM
AND DESIGN DIVISION

Need Analysis
Problem Definition and Content Selection
Instructional Systems Design
Instructional Materials Design

PRODUCTION DIVISION

Instructional Television
Instructional Illustrating
Photography
Sound Technology
Document Production
Acquiring Finished and Raw
Materials

ADMINISTRATION DIVISION

System Administration
Organizational Planning
Evaluation
Equipment Maintenance & Installation
Facilities Maintenance
External Relations
Research

Data Retrieval
Data Processing
Analysis Feedback
and Distribution

QUALITY CONTROL
DIVISION

Instructional Spaces Management
Instructional Systems Management
Logistics
Learning Environment Control
Interaction with Learners

OPERATIONS DIVISION

Figure 35-1.

The Instructional Operations Division deals directly with the learners. The division is staffed by facilities management personnel and by the content knowledgeable personnel associated with specific instructional programs. These individuals interact with the learners to provide tutoring, counseling, or other live instruction, or evaluate student work and provide modeling behavior for the learners.

The Quality Control Division develops the feedback information flow by which the instruction is recycled. This division analyzes performance data on all aspects of the instructional operation and organizes the results. It then distributes those findings to the most appropriate part of the organization for direct correction of performance deficiencies. This division includes instructional researchers, computer specialists, data processors and analysts.

The organization is administered by a division responsible for maintaining a strong integrity in the total operation. This division includes administrators, system theorists, and instructional technologists. The organization is directed by an instruction technologist who is expert in the process of instruction, not by an expert in some other subject matter.

This new organizational structure represents a technological capability to deal effectively in any content area and with any target population of learners. Regardless of the content or the type of learners, the instruction must adhere to the same basic process; it must be designed, produced, operated, and correctively recycled. The proposed organization provides the flexible capability to follow those steps for any instructional program. The organization provides the expertise needed to produce and operate complete systems which include all necessary instructional arrangements.

These organizations are designed to grow by the accretion of diverse expertise applicable to the instruction process. Academic departments tend to grow only by the addition of more content expertise, which contributes little improvement to that process. The new structures would readily accommodate diverse roles and skills as soon as their potential positive contributions to the instruction process were established.

The instruction process represents a behavioral engineering operation, and the complexity of human beings requires the fullest application of the behavioral sciences. These organizations are structured to better provide for that. The content expertise that is now accorded the overwhelming role and responsibility for instruction is only a part of the total process, having some application in curriculum design and instructional operations. But the primary responsibility in instruction is how, exactly, to insure that each learner shall attain the specified performance criteria.

In a modern technological society it is difficult to comprehend that education is not technologically organized for its mission. People who would view with ridicule an industrial or political organization as inappropriately constructed as a university, tend to accept without question the poor performances emanating from educational institutions. This is primarily because the behavioral sciences have emerged only recently and the public is not cognizant of the newer standards which can now be applied. If the behavioral technology of today had been available during the historical origins of our educational institutions, those institutions would be organized in a substantially different fashion, because the basic assumptions about what is required to change behavior are very different from those from which traditional organizational arrangements were derived. There is little point in generating further discussion about the nuances of behavioral technology for application in higher education if we neglect the organizational structure which will make them feasible. The proposed reorganization for institutions of higher education supports applications of the science of human behavior through a technology of instruction.

The new organizations must replace the academic departments as the locus of the instructional missions of institutions, and their directors should report directly to superintendents or, in higher education, to the Academic Vice President of the institutions.

Benefits to Academic Departments and Institutions

The essence of the academic department is not a function of those responsibilities which would transfer to the Instructional Systems Organization. First, the academic department would neither cease to exist nor be relegated to a less significant mission, and second, the "department" would be freed of severe resource drains which have traditionally caused great stress. It could shape its destiny along directions compatible with its more valid purposes.

The department is a locus of content expertise in a specific area of knowledge. It promotes the necessary and useful dialogue among those aided by the sharing of knowledge in its field. The academic department is the coordinative center of research in its content area. Further, it is the department which is best able to provide the advanced student in its field with professional models and with liaison with the outside professional establishment. The department can specify what skills qualify an individual as a specialist in that area and be involved in certifying which individuals have such skills. These are all significant and needed functions.

Unfortunately, the academic departments have traditionally had their pursuit of these endeavors contaminated by the concurrent responsibility for teaching, in many instances, vast numbers of students especially at the undergraduate level. The low priority given the teaching function is reflected in the fact that academic departments have always demanded subject matter competence at the expense of teaching competence. There have been few academic departments in all of higher education that required even the slightest formal training in the skills of instruction.

As a consequence of this reluctance to compromise the more significant aspects of their missions, the academic departments have done a relatively poorer job of instruction as the numbers of students have increased and as the technology of instruction has evolved to levels of sophistication well beyond their reach. Today the departments are facing a difficult dilemma, because the imbalance in priorities is too great and much attention is focusing on their instructional failures.

Across the nation, within institutions of higher learning, a belated wave of remedial action is beginning to stir. Departments see no alternative but to accept their instructional obligations, so they are beginning to experiment amateurishly and expensively with new instructional approaches. New faculty members are now being added to some departments on the basis of their degrees in instructional technology rather than their strength in the content area. But even though this is all that the department can do under current organizational structures, it is usually not realized that such efforts are ill-conceived, because the departments lack the resources to develop instructional systems of the type required to do the job, and their occasional "new man" is ineffective when isolated within that departmental setting.

What is needed is an organizational alternative to get the departments out of this bind before the current proliferation of costly, small semi-systems debilitates the universities any further.

The responsibility for instruction should transfer from the departments to Instructional Systems Organizations, beginning with the undergraduate courses which attract large numbers of students. The departments would assign their content experts to duty with the Instructional Systems Organization for as long as the instructional development projects might require them. Those content experts would retain their departmental affiliation at all times and would temporarily join the instructional organization as team members there to contribute their content expertise. They would be trained by the instructional systems organization to fill those positions. This arrangement also provides the departments with an appropriate assignment for those personnel who are strongly teaching-oriented at the undergraduate level. Those who desire to continue working personally with students may thus continue to do so in the Instructional Operations Division. Here again departmental affiliation would be retained by those individuals in the form of a professional association within the university.

Departmental teaching responsibilities should be viewed as initiating scholars of their content area into a professional niche. Thus, departments could concentrate primarily on graduate level instruction, which is validly more of an apprentice-type arrangement, wherein each student is a "hand-crafted" product of the department. The departments would be free to commit their growth resources into the more significant facets of their mission that have long been starved by the demands of routine instruction. If academic departments in universities are to be construed to have a mission significantly different than content area departments in high schools, then these changes in organizational structure should occur without further delay.

The newly proposed reorganization of instruction also has implications for mitigating external controls over universities. Boards of Regents across the nation are composed mainly of political appointees or elected officials who usually are not expert in education in general, or instruction in particular. Nevertheless, these bodies are charged with the responsibility of guiding the affairs of the nation's public institutions of higher learning. The regents tend to respond by seeking tighter controls over the institutions as they become sensitized to rising costs, public demands for greater accountability, and student demands for improved instruction. They believe that this is necessary because the institutions appear too slow in solving these problems and because boards reflect a certain amount of the general public resentment of what might be called the "academic luxuries." Boards are demanding increased teaching loads for all faculty members.

Unfortunately, however, most Boards of Regents lack the technical expertise to deal effectively with the vast problems facing the institutions. They are quite incapable, in most instances, of formulating sound, radical proposals of the scope needed to make the substantial changes required. Thus, the Boards of Regents are left with only the capability of continuing to try to squeeze more results out of the old models even though it is the breakdown of those models that is causing many of the difficulties.

The existing models of university instruction, featuring the autonomous teacher and the classroom system, offer no lasting protection against such pressures. The more significant functions of the universities and their academic departments are eroded, because the old system allows for the shifting of departmental resources back and forth between teaching research, writing, and public service functions. These new pressures simply force a shift toward the teaching dimension while permitting lip service to any consequently neglected aspect such as research or public service.

The restructuring of the institutions placing instruction missions within Instructional Systems Organizations would get the academic departments and their more valid and significant functions out of the line of this fire. The target would shift to an organizational model actually designed to invite and accommodate the kind of critical scrutiny under which the older models are suffering.

The Emergence and Investiture of Instructional Technology and Behavioral Engineering

The historical tradition that today results in subordinating instruction process experts to content experts is an outmoded relic of the past, stemming from a time when there was no science of human behavior and no technology of instruction. But today these fields do exist, and it is time to apply the rational principle that the responsibility for a task should rest with those most competent to perform it. It is time to cease arranging instructional roles and responsibilities according to the absurd proposition that a geologist's expert knowledge about rocks provides him with a concomitant expertise in the psychology of human behavior and the technology for changing it. The content expert must take his place as a team member, one of a dozen or more top level experts who feed their inputs into the instructional process, and the organizations which subsume this total process must be headed by instructional experts.

The new arrangements proposed here call for certain changes in the training of instructional technologists. The complex and difficult task of teaching demands much sophistication in the basic behavioral sciences and system theory. Behavioral psychology is the physics of instruction and more emphasis on such fundamentals is needed in training programs in instruction.

The field of instruction technology must change from its heavy emphasis on the design and production of specific instructional materials and turn more toward the tasks of instructional system design and development. It must turn from excessive concern with better teaching aids to the broader perspectives of behavioral engineering. Instructional technology must subsume the concept of teaching and all of the instructional aspects of what is now lumped together under the rubric of Education.

It is time for a critical analysis of the traditional curriculum in education featuring assorted departments competing to be useful to classroom teachers. The classroom model of instruction, with its autonomous teacher-generalists, is dead because the complexity of the instructional process implies demands beyond its capabilities. The corpse of that model will linger among us for many years, a monument to an incredible underestimation of the instructional task.

Whatever the contribution to instruction that might come from such traditional sources as educational psychology, curriculum and instruction, education administration, and similar fields, those contributions, if of any value, must be construed to be a part of the relevant technology of the instruction process. Instructional technology with its system approach integrates the instructional process, and only within that framework is there a logical place for any input to that process.

All across the nation, education administrators are openly and loudly reaffirming that the final voice on all matters of instruction must rest with the academic content experts charged with responsibility for the instruction. That premise has been deemed inviolate, accepted by all, and repeated like the pledge of allegiance. But that premise is also illogical.

So is the notion that the content experts can be quickly trained to perform as instruction experts. Millions of dollars are being wasted to try to transform traditional faculty members into instructional developers. This money is being sacrificed to the entrenched sacrosanctity of the academicians. The notion that a few workshops and inservice training programs can create a behavioral engineer or an instructional designer is simply another manifestation of the ignorance which prevails within education relative to the behavioral sciences. A person who is not a competent instructional technologist has no business with responsibility for instruction.

It is time for a new academic tradition to begin—a tradition based on more valid premises about human behavior and on new organizational structures more suited to pursuing the implications of those premises—a new tradition rewarded not by academic privilege, but by the degree of learning that occurs.

That new tradition will embody the essence of humanization and will accommodate the uniqueness of the individual. Only through technology can that be done. The simplistic and shallow emotionalism that today passes for attention to human needs and effective goals will give way to more powerful and useful techniques by which individuals control their own behavior and emotions, and ultimately their own destinies as well.

REFERENCES

Alba, E., and Pennypacker, H. S.: A multiple change score comparison of traditional and behavioral college teaching procedures. *J Appl Behav Anal, 5:* 121–124, 1972.

Armor, D. J., and Couch, A. S.: *An Introduction to Computerized Social Data Analysis: Data Text Primer.* New York, Free Press, 1970.

Azrin, N. H., Holz, W., Ulrich, R., and Goldiamond, I.: The control of the content of conversation through reinforcement. *J Exp Anal Behav, 4:* 25–30, 1961. Reprinted in *J of Appl Behav Anal, 6:* 186–192, 1973.

Baer, D. M.: Behavior modification: you shouldn't. In Ramp, Eugene A., and Hopkins, Bill I. (Eds.) : *A New Direction for Education: Behavior Analysis.* Lawrence, University of Kansas Support and Development Center for Follow Through, Department of Human Development, 1971.

Baer, D. M., Wolf, M. M., and Risley, T. R.: Some current dimensions of applied behavior analysis. *J Appl Behav Anal, 1:* 91–97, 1968.

Barrish, H. H., Saunders, M., and Wolf, M. M.: Good behavior game: effects of individual contingencies for group consequences on disruptive behavior in a classroom. *J Appl Behav Anal, 2:* 119–124, 1969.

Biehler, R. F.: *Psychology Applied to Teaching.* New York, Houghton Mifflin, 1971.

Biehler, R. F.: *Psychology Applied to Teaching, Selected Readings.* New York, Houghton Mifflin, 1972.

Biehler, R. F.: *1972 Supplement for Instructors, Psychology Applied to Teaching.* New York, Houghton Mifflin, 1972.

Biehler, R. F., and Littlejohn, M.: *1973 Supplement for Instructors, Psychology Applied to Teaching.* New York, Houghton Mifflin, 1973.

Bijou, S. W., Peterson, R. F., Harris, F. R., Allen, K. E., and Johnston, M. S.: Methodology for experimental studies of younger children in natural settings. *The Psychol Rec, 19:* 177–210, 1969.

Bitgood, S. C., and Kuch, D. O.: A contingency managed graduated point system in an introductory psychology course. Report to the Council on Teaching, University of Iowa, 1971.

Block, J. H., (Ed.) : *Mastery Learning: Theory and Practice.* New York, Holt, Rinehart and Winston, 1971.

Blough, D. S.: The shape of some wavelength generalization gradients. *J Exp Anal Behav, 4:* 31–40, 1961.

Born, D. G.: *Instructor Manual for Development of a Personalized Instruction Course.* 1971. Available from College Book Store, 200 University Street, Salt Lake City, Utah 84112, 6.25.

Born, D. G.: *Proctor Manual for Development of a Personalized Instruction Course.* 1971.

Born, D. G.: Student withdrawals in personalized instruction courses and in lecture courses. Paper presented at the Rocky Mountain Psychological Association, Denver, May, 1971.

498   *Behavior Research and Technology in Higher Education*

Born, D. G., Davis, M., Whelan, P., and Jackson, D.: College student study behavior in a personalized instruction course and in a lecture course. In Semb, George (ed.) with Donald R. Green, Robert P. Hawkins, Jack Michael, Ellery L. Phillips, James A. Sherman, Howard Sloane, and Don R. Thomas: *Behavior analysis and education,* 1972a.

Born, D. G., and Davis, M. L.: Amount and distribution of study in a PSI course and in a lecture course. Submitted to the *J Appl Behav Anal,* 1973.

Born, D. G., Gledhill, S. M., and Davis, M. L.: Examination performance in lecture-discussion and personalized instruction courses. *J Appl Behav Anal, 5:* 33–43, 1972b.

Born, D. G., and Herbert, E. W.: A further study of Keller's personalized system of instruction. *J Exp Educ, 40:* 6–11, 1971.

Born, D. G., and Whelan, P.: Some descriptive characteristics of student performance in PSI and lecture courses. *The Psychol Rec, 23:* 145–152, 1973.

Born, D. G., and Zlutnick, S.: Personalized instruction, or what to do when they put a number on the back of your sport coat, issue you a bullhorn, and schedule your class in the football stadium. *Educ Tech,* September: 30–34, 1972.

Bostow, D. E., and Blumenfeld, G. J.: The effect of two test-retest procedures on the classroom performance of undergraduate college students. In Semb, George (Ed.) with Donald R. Green, Robert P. Hawkins, Jack Michael, Ellery L. Phillips, James A. Sherman, Howard Sloane, and Don R. Thomas: *Behav Anal Educ,* 1972.

Brown, D. A.: A new approach to teaching German. *Bull Assoc Dept of For Lang, 3:* 10–13, 1971.

Browning, R. M., and Stover, D. O.: *Behavior Modification in Child Treatment: An Experimental and Clinical Approach.* New York, Aldine-Atherton, 1971.

Bushell, D. J.: Textbooks and programs: antithesis or synthesis. *Nat Soc Prog Inst J, 4:* 3–5, 1965.

Campbell, D. T.: From description to experimentation: interpreting trends as quasi-experiments. In Harris, Chester W. (Ed.): *Problems in Measuring Change,* 1967.

Campbell, D. T.: Reforms as experiments. *Am Psychol, 409:* 429, 1969.

Campbell, D. T., and Stanley, J. C.: *Experimental and Quasi-Experimental Design for Research.* Chicago, Rand-McNally, 1967.

Catania, C. A.: Concurrent operants. In Honig, W. K.: *Operant Behavior: Areas of Research and Application.* New York, Meredith, 1966.

Collier, K. L., and Smith, R. V.: A behavior-based laboratory course in educational psychology. *Educ Tech,* 24–28, 1971.

Cooper, J. L., and Greiner, J. M.: Contingency management in an introductory psychology course produces better retention. *The Psychol Rec, 21:* 391–400, 1971.

Corey, J. R., and McMichael, J. S.: *Unit Workbook for Kendler's Basic Psychology: 2nd edition.* New York, Appleton-Century-Crofts, 1970.

Corey, J. R., McMichael, J. S., and Tremont, P. J.: Long-term effects on personalized instruction in an introductory psychology course. Paper presented at the 41st Annual Meeting of the Eastern Psychological Association, Atlantic City, New Jersey, 1970.

Cramer, P.: (Ed.) *Readings in Developmental Psychology Today.* Del Mar, California: CRM Books, 1970.

Cronbach, L. J., and Snow, R. E.: Individual differences in learning ability as a function of instructional variables. Final report, U. S. Office of Education Contract #OEC4-6-061269-1217, Stanford University.

Della-Piana, G. M., and Ando, G. T.: Reading research. In Travers, Robert M. W. (Ed.) : *2nd Handbook of Research on Teaching.* Chicago, Rand-McNally, 1973.

Dressler, A. J.: (Ed.) *Proceedings of the Keller Method Workshop Conference.* 1972. Available from Space Science Center, Rice University, Houston, Texas 77001, 1.35.

Dustin, D. S.: Some effects of exam frequency. *The Psychol Rec, 21:* 409–414, 1971.

Edwards, K. A., and Powers, R. B.: Self-pacing in a personalized system of instruction: work patterns and course completion. Paper presented at the Association for Educational Communications and Technology National Convention, Las Vegas, Nevada, April 8-13, 1973.

Etters, E.: Tutorial assistance in college courses. *J Educ Res, 60:* 406–407, 1967.

Farmer, J., Lachter, A. D., Blaustein, J. J., and Cole, B. K.: The role of proctoring in personalized instruction. *J Appl Behav Anal, 5:* 401–404, 1972.

Ferster, C. B.: Individualized instruction in a large introductory psychology college course. *Psychol Rec, 18:* 521–532, 1968.

Ferster, C. B. and Perrott, M. C.: *Behavior Principles.* New York, Appleton-Century-Crofts, 1968.

Ferster, C. B., and Skinner, B. F.: *Schedules of Reinforcement.* New York, Appleton-Century-Crofts, 1957.

Findley, J. D.: Preference and switching under concurrent scheduling. *J Exp Anal Behav, 1:* 123–144, 1958.

Findley, J. D.: An experimental outline for building and exploring multi-operant behavior repertoires. *J Exp Anal Behav, 5:* 113–166, 1962.

Fraser, S. C., Beaman, A. L., and Kelem, R. T.: Two heads are better than one: modification of college performance by peer monitoring. Paper presented at Western Psychological Association Convention, Portland, Oregon, 1972.

Fry, W., Kelleher, R. T., and Cook, L.: A mathematical index of performance on fixed-interval schedules of reinforcement. *J Exp Anal Behav, 3:* 193–199, 1960.

Gallup, H. F.: Personalized instruction in introductory psychology. Paper presented at the meetings of the Midwestern Psychological Association, Chicago, May, 1969.

Gallup, H.: Problems in the implementation of a course in personalized instruction. Unpublished paper presented at the meetings of the American Psychological Association, Washington, D.C., 1971.

Gartner, A., Kohler, M., and Riessman, F.: *Children Teach Youth.* New York, Harper and Row, 1971.

Gentile, J. R., Roden, A. H., and Klein, R. D.: An analysis-of-variance model for the intrasubject replication design. *J Appl Behav Anal, 5:* 193–198, 1972.

Goldstein, A. P.: *Therapist-patient Expectancies in Psychotherapy.* New York, Permagon Press, 1962.

Gottman, J. M.: N-of-one and N-of-two research in psychotherapy. *Psychol Bull,* volume 80, 2: 93–105, 1973.

Green, B. A., Jr.: Physics teaching by the Keller plan at MIT. *Am J Phy, 39:* 764–775, 1971.

Greenspoon, J., and Simkins, L.: A measurement approach to psychotherapy. *The Psychol Rec, 18:* 409–423, 1968.

Gropper, G. L., and Kress, G. C.: Individual differences in learning from self-paced programmed instruction. *Am Instit Res,* 1964.

Hammer, M., and Henderson, C. O.: Beat the "loaf-cram" cycle with computer tests. *Coll Manag,* October: 25–27, 1972a.

Hammer, M., and Henderson, C. O.: Improving large enrollment instruction with computer generated, repeatable tests. *Proceedings of the 1972 Conf Comp in Undergrad Curr.* Southern Regional Education Board, Atlanta. 209–216, 1972b.

Hammer, M., and Henderson, C. O.: A program for improving large enrollment instruction. Winner of Western Electric Fund 1972–73 Award for Educational Innovation in Higher Education for Business, *AACSB Bulletin,* October: 1973.

Hammer. M., Henderson, C. O., and Johnson, L.: Some promising techniques for improving large enrollment instruction. *AACSB Bulletin* October: 18–30, 1972.

Hartman, D. P., and Atkinson, C.: Having your cake and eating it too: a note on some apparent contradictions between therapeutic achievements and design requirements in N = 1 studies. *Behav Ther, 4:* 589–591, 1973.

Hause, J. M.: A comparison of two variables affecting student performance in an individualized introductory psychology course. Unpublished thesis, Drake University, 1973.

Heaton, K. L.: Effects of time-out following errors in precision teaching performance sessions. Unpublished Masters thesis, University of Florida, 1971.

Herman, S. H., and Tramontana, J.: Instruction and group versus individual reinforcement in modifying disruptive group behavior. *J Appl Behav Anal, 4:* 113–119, 1971.

Hess, J. H.: Keller plan and instruction: implementation problems. Paper presented at the Keller Plan Conference, Massachusetts Institute of Technology, 1971.

Holland, J. G., and Skinner, B. F.: *The Analysis of Behavior.* New York, McGraw-Hill, 1961.

Hoberock, L. L., Koen, B. V., Roth, C. H., and Wagner, G. R.: Theory of PSI evaluated for engineering education. *IEEE Transac Educ,* Volume E-15, *1:* 25–29, February, 1972.

Johnson, S. M., and Bolstad, O. D.: Methodological issues in naturalistic observation: some problems and solutions for field research. In Hamerlynck, Leo A., Handy, Lee C., and Mash, Eric J. (Eds.): *Behavior Change, Methodology, Concepts and Practices.* Champaign, Illinois: Research Press, 1973.

Johnston, J. M., and O'Neill, G. W.: The analysis of performance criteria defining course grades as a determinant of college student academic performance. *J Appl Behav Anal, 6:* 261–268, 1973.

Johnston, J. A., O'Neill, G. W., Walters, W. A., and Rasheed, J. A.: The measurement and analysis of college student study behavior: tactics for research. In Johnston, James M. (Ed.): *Behav Res Tech High Educ.* Springfield, Thomas, 1974.

Johnston, J. M., and Pennypacker, H. S.: A behavioral approach to college teaching. *Am Psychol, 26,* (3) : 219–244, 1971.

Johnston, J. M., Roberts, M. D., and O'Neill, G. W.: The measurement and analysis of college student study behavior. In Semb, George (Ed.) : *Behavior Analysis and Education.* Lawrence, The University of Kansas, 1972.

Jones, R. R.: Behavioral observation and frequency data: problems in scoring, analysis, and interpretation. In Hamerlynck, Leo A., Handy, Lee C., and Mash, Eric J. (Eds.) : *Behavior Change, Methodology, Concepts and Practices.* Champaign, Research Press, 1973.

Keller, F. S.: A personal course in psychology. In Ulrich, Roger, Stachnik, Thomas, and Mabry, John (Eds.) : *Control of Human Behavior.* Glenview, Scott, Foresman, 1966.

Keller, F. S.: Good-bye teacher. . . . *J Appl Behav Anal, 1:* 79–89, 1968.

Keller, F. S.: A programmed system of instruction. *Educ Tech, 2:* number 1, 1969.

Kendler, H. H.: *Basic Psychology,* 2nd ed. New York, Appleton-Century-Crofts, 1968.

Kendler, H. H., and Kendler, T.: *Basic Psychology: brief edition.* New York, Appleton-Century-Crofts, 1971.

Koen, B. V.: Self-paced instruction in engineering: a case study. Presented at the American Society for Engineering Education Annual Meeting,

Ohio State University, Columbus, Ohio, June 22–25, 1970. Modified version in *IEEE Trans Educ*, E-*14*: 13–20, 1971.

Koen, B. V.: Determining unit structure in a PSI course. Presented at the American Society for Engineering Education Annual Meeting, Texas Technical University, Lubbock, Texas, June 19–22, 1972.

Kraft, J. M.: The Dartmouth College experiment. *Bull Assoc Dept For Lang, 4:* 18–21, 1972.

Leitenberg, H.: The use of single-case methodology in psychotherapy research. *J Abnor Psychol* volume 82, *1:* 87–101, 1973.

Lindsley, O. R.: Sample standard behavior chart. *J Appl Behav Anal, 1:* 1, 1968.

Lindsley, O. R.: Personal communication. 1969.

Lloyd, K. E.: Contingency management in university courses. *Educ Tech, 11:* 18–23, 1971.

Lloyd, K. E., Garlington, W. K., Lowry, D., Burgess, H., Euler, H. A., and Knowlton, W. R.: A note on some reinforcing properties of university lectures. *J Appl Behav Anal, 5:* 151–155, 1972.

Lloyd, K. E., and Knutzen, N. J.: A self-paced programmed undergraduate course in the experimental analysis of behavior. *J Appl Behav Anal, 2:* 125–133, 1970.

Lovitt, T. C., and Esveldt, K. A.: The relative effects on math performance of single- *versus* multiple-ratio schedules: a case study. *J Appl Behav Anal, 3:* 261–270, 1970.

Lowy, L., Bloksberg, L. M., and Walberg, H. J.: *Integrative Learning and Teaching in Schools of Social Work.* New York, Asssociation Press, 1971.

Malott, R. W.: Student centered education project. Paper presented at the second annual Behavior Analysis in Education Conference, Lawrence, Kansas, May, 1971.

Malott, R. W., and Svinicki, John G.: Contingency management in an introductory psychology course for one thousand students. *Psychol Rec, 19:* 545–556, 1969.

Matson, M. B.: *Field Experience in Undergraduate Programs in Social Welfare.* New York, Council on Social Work Education, 1967.

Mawhinney, V. T., Bostow, D. E., Laws, D. R., Blumenfeld, G. J., and Hopkins, B. L.: A comparison of students studying-behavior produced by daily, weekly, and three-week testing schedules. *J Appl Behav Anal, 4:* 257–264, 1971.

McMichael, J. S., and Corey, J. R.: Contingency management in an introductory psychology course produces better learning. *J Appl Behav Anal, 2:* 79–83, 1969.

Medland, M. B., and Stachnik, T. J.: Good behavior game: application and systematic analysis. *J Appl Behav Anal, 5:* 45–51, 1972.

Miller, A., and Gimpl, M. P.: Operant verbal self-control of studying. *Psychol Rep, 30:* 495–498, 1972.

Miller, L. K.: *Principles of Everyday Behavior Analysis.* Monterey, Brooks/Cole, 1974.

Miller, L. K., and Weaver, F. H.: A multiple baseline achievement test. In Semb, George (Ed.) with Donald R. Green, Robert P. Hawkins, Jack Michael, Ellery L. Phillips, James A. Sherman, Howard Sloane, and Don R. Thomas. *Behavior Analysis and Education.* Lawrence, The University of Kansas Support and Development Center for Follow-Through, Department of Human Development, 1972.

Miller, L. K., and Weaver, F. H.: The use of generalization programming to teach behavioral concepts to undergraduates. In Johnston, James M. (Ed.) : *Behavior Research and Technology in Higher Education.* Springfield, Thomas, 1974.

Miller, L. K., Weaver, F. H., and Semb, G.: A procedure for maintaining student progress in a personalized university course. *J Appl Behav Anal,* 7: 1974, in press.

Minke, K. A., and Carlson, J. G.: *Psychology and Life Unit Mastery System: Instructor's Guide.* Glenview, Scott, Foresman and Company, 1972.

Morris, C. J., and Kimbrell, G. McA.: Performance and attitudinal effects of the Keller method in an introductory psychology course. *The Psychol Rec, 22:* 523–530, 1972.

Myers, W. A.: Operant learning principles applied to teaching introductory statistics. *J Appl Behav Anal, 3:* 191–197, 1970.

Naylor, H. H.: *Volunteers Today—Finding, Training, and Working with Them.* New York, Association Press, 1967.

Nelson, T. F., and Scott, D. W.: Personalized instruction in educational psychology. *Mich Acad, 4:* 293–302, 1972.

Ohlin, L. E.: Urban community development. In Kramer, R., and Specht, H. (Eds.) : *Readings in Community Organization Practice.* Englewood Cliffs, Prentice-Hall, 1969.

O'Leary, K. D., and Kent, R.: Reversibility: the strength or weakness of behavior modification. In Hamerlynck, Leo A., Handy, Lee C., and Mash, Eric J. (Eds.) : *Behavior Change, Methodology, Concepts and Practices.* Champaign, Research Press, 1973.

O'Neill, G. W., Walters, W. M., Rasheed, J. A., and Johnston, J. M.: Validity of the study reporting system-II. In Johnston, James M. (Ed.) : *Behavior Research in Technology in Higher Education.* Springfield, Thomas, 1974.

Pennypacker, H. S., Koenig, C., and Lindsley, O. R.: *Handbook of the Standard Behavior Chart.* Kansas City, Precision Media, 1972.

Pennypacker, H. S., Koenig, C. H., and Seaver, W. H.: Cost efficiency and effectiveness in the early detection and improvement of learning abilities. Proceedings of the Fifth International Conference on Behavior Modification, Banff, Alberta, Canada, 1973.

Phillipas, M. A., and Sommerfeldt, R. W.: Keller vs lecture method in general physics instruction. *Am J Phys, 40:* 1300–1306, 1972.

Poor, D. S.: Analysis of variance for repeated measures designs: two approaches. *Psycho Bull, 80* (3) : 204–209, 1973.

Powers, R. B., and Edwards, K. A.: Personalized introductory psychology at Utah State University; a progress report, 1970–1971. Paper presented at the meeting of the Utah Academy of Science, Arts, and Letters, Logan, Utah, September, 1971.

Powers, R. B., and Edwards, K. A.: Some characteristics of student performance in a self-paced introductory psychology course. Unpublished manuscript, Utah State University, 1972.

Rasheed, J. A., O'Neill, G. W., Walters, W. M., and Johnston, J. A.: A description of typical study behaviors in a behaviorally taught course. In Johnston, James M. (Ed.) : *Behavior Research and Technology in Higher Education.* Springfield, Thomas, 1974.

Romanczyk, R. G., Kent, R., Diament, C., and O'Leary, K. D.: Measuring the reliability of observational data: a reactive process. *J Appl Behav Anal, 6:* 175–184, 1973.

Rosenthal, R.: *Experimenter Effects in Behavioral Research.* New York, Appleton-Century-Crofts, 1966.

Rosenthal, R., and Rosnow, R. L. (Eds.) : *Artifact in Behavioral Research.* New York, Academic Press, 1969.

Roth, C. H.: Continuing effectiveness of personalized self-paced instruction in digital systems engineering. Presented at the American Society for Engineering Education Annual Meeting, Texas Tech University, Lubbock, Texas, June 19–22, 1972.

Rothkopf, E. Z.: Two scientific approaches to the management of instruction. In Gagne, and Gephart (Eds.) : *Learning Research and School Subjects.* Itasca, F. E. Peacock, 1968.

Roueche, J. E., and Pitman, J. C.: *A Modest Proposal: Students Can Learn.* San Francisco, Jossey-Bass, 1972.

Ruch, F. L., and Zimbardo, P. G.: *Psychology and Life,* 8th ed. Glenview, Scott, Foresman, 1971.

Sapp, G. L., Edwards, B. C., and Thomas, J. D. Reinforcement principles in an introductory educational psychology course. *J Educ Res, 66:* 72–75. 1972.

Sather, G. A.: Evaluation of self-paced learning for sophomore engineering students. Presented at the American Society for Engineering Education Annual Conference, Texas Tech University, Lubbock, Texas, June 19–22, 1972.

Schuster, R. H., and Rachlin, H.: Indifference between punishment and free shock: evidence for the negative law of effect. *J Exper Anal Behav, 11:* 777–786, 1968.

Semb, G.: *Human Development Lecture Notes and Study Guide.* Lawrence, Department of Human Development, University of Kansas, 1973.

Semb, G.: The effects of mastery criteria and assignment length on college student test performance. *J Appl Behav Anal, 7:* 1974, in press.

Semb, G., Hopkins, B. L., and Hursh, D. E.: The effects of study questions and grades on student test performance in a college course. *J Appl Behav Anal, 6:* 631–642, 1973.

Shapiro, A. K.: Placebo effects in medicine, psychotherapy, and psychoanalysis. In Bergin, Allen E., and Garfield, Sol L. (Eds.): *Handbook of Psychotherapy and Behavior Change: An Empirical Analysis.* New York, John Wiley, 1971.

Sheppard, W. C., and MacDermot, H. G.: Design and evaluation of a programmed course in introductory psychology. *J Appl Behav Anal, 3:* 5–11, 1970.

Sherman, J. G.: Application of reinforcement principles to a college course. Paper presented at American Educational Research Association, New York, February 17, 1967.

Sherman, J. G.: A permutation on an innovation. Paper presented at American Psychological Association, September 6, 1971.

Sherman, J. G.: PSI: some notable failures. Paper presented at Keller Method Workshop Conference, Rice University, Houston, Texas, March 18, 1972.

Sherman, J. G.: *PSI Newsletter,* Psychology Department, Georgetown University, Washington. D.C.

Sherman, J. G., *Personalized System of Instruction Newsletter.* Georgetown University, Washington, D.C. Issue #5: June, 1972.

Sides, E., and Edwards, K. A.: Testing in a personalized system of instruction. Paper presented at the Meeting of the Rocky Mountain Psychological Association, Albuquerque, New Mexico, May 10–12, 1972.

Sidman, M.: *Tactics of Scientific Research.* New York, Basic Books, 1960.

Siegel, L., and Siegal, L. C.: A multivariate paradigm for educational research. *Psychol Bull, 68* (5): 306–326, 1967.

Siegel, S.: *Nonparametric Statistics: For The Behavioral Sciences.* New York, McGraw-Hill, 1956.

Skindrud, K.: Field evaluation of observer bias under overt and covert monitoring. In Hamerlynck, Leo A., Handy, Lee C., and Mash, Eric J. (Eds.): *Behavior Change, Methodology, Concepts and Practices.* Champaign, Research press, 1973.

Skinner, B. F.: *Behavior of Organisms.* New York, Appleton-Century-Crofts, 1938.

Skinner, B. F.: Are theories of learning necessary? *Psycholog Rev, 57:* 193–216, 1950.

Skinner, B. F.: *Science and Human Behavior.* New York, Macmillan, 1953.

Skinner, B. F.: Some contributions of an experimental analysis to behavior as a whole. *Am Psychol, 8:* 69–79, 1953.

Skinner, B. F.: The experimental analysis of behavior. *Am Sci, 45:* 343–371, 1957.

Skinner, B. F.: *The Technology of Teaching.* New York, Appleton-Century-Crofts, 1968.

Stalling, R. B.: A one-proctor programmed course procedure for introductory psychology. *The Psychol Rec, 21:* 501–505, 1971.

Sullivan, A. N.: A structural individualized approach to the teaching of introductory psychology. In Davis, Ira K., and Hartly, James (Eds.) : *Contributions to an Educational Technology.* London, Butterworths, 1972.

Sutterer, J. F.: *Student Manual for Foundations of Human Behavior.* Syracuse, New York, Syracuse University, 1972.

Swirsky, R.: Application of the proctorial method of self-paced instruction to an extension course in electrical fundamentals. Presented at the American Society of Engineering Education Annual Meeting, U.S. Naval Academy, Annapolis, Maryland, June 21–24, 1971.

Tobias, S.: Review of the response mode tissue. *Rev Educ Res, 143:* 193–204, 1973.

Vernon, J. (Ed.) : *Introduction to General Psychology: a Self-selection Textbook.* Dubuque, W. C. Brown, 1966.

Vogler, R. E., Masters, W. M., and Morrill, G. S.: Extinction of cooperative behavior as a function of acquisition by shaping instruction. *J Gen Psychol, 119:* 233–240, 1971.

Walters, W. M., O' Neill, G. W., Rasheed, J. A., and Johnston, J. A.: Validity of the study reporting system—I. In Johnston, James M. (Ed.) : *Behavior Research and Technology in Higher Education.* Springfield, Thomas, 1974.

Warren, R. L.: A community model. In Kramer, R., and Specht, H. (Eds.) : *Readings in Community Organization Practice.* Englewood Cliffs, Prentice-Hall, 1969.

Weaver, F. H., and Miller, L. K.: The effects of frequent quizzes plus make-up requirement on university students' quiz performance. Paper presented at American Psychological Association Convention, Montreal, Canada, August, 1973.

Whaley, D. L., and Malcott, R. W.: *Elementary Principles of Behavior.* New York, Appleton-Century-Crofts, 1971.

Whitehurst, G. J.: Academic responses and attitudes engendered by a programmed course in child development. *J Appl Behav Anal, 5:*283–291, 1972.

Wilson, S. R., and Tosti, D. T.: *Learning is Getting Easier.* San Rafael, California; Individual Learning Systems, Incorporated, 1972.

Winer, B. J.: *Statistical Principles in Experimental Design.* New York, McGraw-Hill, 1962.

Witters, D. R., and Kent, G. W.: Teaching without lecturing: evidence in the case for individualized instruction. *Psycholog Rec, 22:* 169–175, 1972.

Wood, W. S., Hause, J. M., and Myerson, A.: A dormitory learning center at Drake University. Paper presented at the National Society for Performance and Instruction Annual Conference. San Francisco, April, 1973.

SUBJECT INDEX

A

Abnormal behavior, 48
Abstraction, 45
Accountability, XV, 6, 23, 472
  (*See also* Cost analysis)
Achievement, student, 22–26, 44, 71, 105,
  115, 126, 135, 182, 283–99, 325, 367,
  373, 468
Achievement test, 26, 106, 107, 126, 135,
  139, 140
ACT, 378–82
Adjusting point system, in contingency
  managed instruction, 203
Affirming the consequent, 389–91
Aggressive behavior, 41
Alienation, 304
Analytical reasoning, 76
Animal behavior, 48, 49, 55, 72, 166, 223
ANOVA, 191
Anti-social behavior, 440
Aptitude test, 25
Architecture course, 7
Assignment, xiv, xv, 16, 218, 221, 222,
  225–99, 301, 305, 330–47, 350, 411,
  412, 445
Audio module, 16
Audio tape, 21, 22, 28, 105, 112, 113,
  175, (*See also* Tape)
Audiotutorial instruction, ix
Aversive control, 49–51, 53, 222, 223,
  269, 462
Avoidance, 170, 222, 462

B

Baseline, 9–12, 14, 27, 38, 46, 49–53, 112,
  174, 176–78, 230–34, 253, 254, 262,
  284, 323, 326, 351, 352, 360, 367,
  441, 442, 445, 446
Behavior,
  abnormal, 48
  aggressive, 41
  animal, 48, 49, 55, 72, 166, 223

anti-social, 440
choice-making, xv
community service, 6–14
conceptual, 45
fixed-interval schedule, 307, 308, 323,
  326, 328, 336
frequency, 464-68
instructor's, 219, 480
multiple-ratio schedule, 346
operant, 38, 40, 440, 456
political, 47
proctor's, xiv, 143, 160, 168–82
research, 55
respondent, 38
sex-role specific, 35, 40, 41
student, xiv, 6, 51, 151, 155, 157, 166,
  181, 182, 186, 200, 202, 207, 222,
  225, 227–36, 269–82, 301,
  303–29, 358–60, 445, 446, 450,
  456–63, 468, 470, 477, 480
superstitious, 39
switching, 457, 458, 460
target, 44, 45
verbal, 39, 41, 55, 72, 157, 171, 227,
  228, 251, 255, 267, 370, 393–95
"weak," 41
Behavior control, 39, 235, 236
  aversive, 49–51, 53, 222, 223, 269, 462
  institutional, 37
Behavior modification, 64, 74, 76, 160,
  162, 273, 304, 323
Behavioral analysis, 45, 46, 139, 141,
  146, 169, 194, 305, 440, 441, 445, 459,
  464, 465
  of women's roles, xiii, 3, 34–43
Behavioral concept, xiii, xv, 3, 44–57,
  170
Behavioral instruction, xv, 437, 439–55
Behavioral language, 35–41, 51, 55, 170,
  194, 465
Behavioral psychology, ix
Behavioral science course, 481
Behaviorism, 40, 42

507

AUTHOR INDEX

513